THE ADMIRAL

THE · GIFT

THE
OF · THE
STATES
OFFICERS ·
· OF · THE
SQUADRON
COMMAND
MODORE
DEWEY

OF
PEOPLE
UNITED
TO · THE
AND · MEN
ASIATIC
UNDER · THE
OF · COM
GEORGE

The Dewey Medal, awarded by Congress to all American sailors in the Battle of Manila Bay, May 1, 1898.

THE
ADMIRAL

by LAURIN HALL HEALY
and LUIS KUTNER

CHICAGO · ZIFF-DAVIS PUBLISHING COMPANY · NEW YORK

TO THE MEN

OF THE

UNITED STATES NAVY

CONTENTS

ACKNOWLEDGMENTS

The authors wish to express their gratitude to the many friends whose wholehearted assistance and counsel has helped so much in the preparation of this biography of Admiral George Dewey.

To George Goodwin Dewey, son of the Admiral, we are indebted for his close co-operation and his wealth of personal reminiscenses of his father, as well as for lending us innumerable unpublished letters, documents, pictures, diaries, and personal records.

To the Honorable Josephus Daniels, World War I Secretary of the Navy and former U.S. Ambassador to Mexico, a great editor and a close friend of Admiral Dewey, gratitude is expressed for his many suggestions.

To Miss Elizabeth Ellicott Poe of Washington, D. C., confidante of Mrs. Mildred Dewey and a close friend of the Admiral, the authors owe much for her material concerning Dewey's personal life in his later years.

Dr. L. Hubbard Shattuck and Mrs. John A. Barclay of the Chicago Historical Society, a mint of Deweyana, gave generously of their time and counsel in providing much pertinent information. Dr. P. M. Hamer, Director of Reference Service of the National Archives in Washington, and Miss Mary Fawcett of his staff, made possible the access to many valuable historical documents.

Mr. David C. Tyler of Evanston, Illinois, once a coachman for the Admiral, gave us many illuminating recollections of sidelights on Dewey's career.

We are especially grateful to Patricia K. Healy, who outlined and annotated a vast amount of historical material. To Mrs. Andrew Will Radescich, Jr. and Charles C. Swank, as well as to many others, the authors are deeply obligated.

LAURIN HALL HEALY
Lieutenant (jg) USNR
LUIS KUTNER

FOREWORD

*T*his book is both a complete life of Admiral George Dewey and a comprehensive history of the Navy, to which he made so large a contribution. Besides being a great mariner and fighter, Dewey was a great naval diplomat who will live in history as The Naval Statesman of America. In season and out of season Admiral Dewey advocated a Navy second to none. His supreme passion, aside from winning victories over the enemy in every engagement in which he fought, was to see the Navy of the United States strong enough and big enough to meet and defeat any possible antagonist. Long experience and technical knowledge guided his statesmanship.

In the long years of his service as president of the General Board, Admiral Dewey demonstrated his knowledge of international law, diplomacy, and history, thereby not only demonstrating his versatility and high ability, but also helping to win preliminary battles of diplomacy for his country. He and his associates, notably Admiral Charles J. Badger, laid broad and deep the foundations of naval strength.

When I became Secretary of the Navy in 1913, one of my first visits was paid to Admiral Dewey. I had been stirred, along with all patriotic Americans, by his glorious achievement at Manila Bay. I sought his counsel often after that, and it was always given with frankness and enlightenment. When President Woodrow Wilson became convinced in 1915 that the American Navy ought to be the most adequate Navy in the world, I naturally turned to Admiral Dewey and the General Board for a policy of construction. This became the Three Year Program, embracing the largest naval building program ever undertaken by any nation not actually at war. Those plans made the American Navy the strongest in the world. Admiral Dewey did not live to see the full execution of his cherished hopes nor the shortsighted scrapping of warships after the Washington Naval Conference of 1922. But he died in the full knowledge that his country had come to rely upon his judgment as a naval statesman and followed where he led.

As this biography discloses, Admiral Dewey was not afraid of criticism. He spoke out fearlessly for what he believed to be right, regardless of popular pressure. *The Admiral* does not gloss over any of these facts. It analyzes them impartially and in that way makes an important contribution to the knowledge of the times. From the legacy of Admiral Dewey's personality and professional integrity and leadership emerges brilliantly the vital lesson to America, the lesson taught by Alfred Thayer Mahan and expounded so resolutely by George Dewey that the United States must be strong upon the seas.

To maintain her greatness, as George Dewey so manfully urged, America must possess an effective, powerful fleet. To that goal we must all devote our energies and our united purpose.

JOSEPHUS DANIELS

PREFACE

$\mathcal{I}$t is interesting to note that in the midst of a war where America's sea power has emerged as a dominating factor, a book should appear which sheds much new light on America's original coming-of-age at sea. Back as far as 1812 Americans were convinced that they were the equals of any peoples of any nation anywhere. Other nations, it must be admitted, did not always agree with our conception of ourselves. We were looked upon as upstarts, cocky and given to much empty bragging. It was not until 1898, when we brought one of the proudest navies on the seas to its knees, that we actually took our place as a first-class nation in the councils of the great powers. The Spanish fleet was routed at Santiago, but the real hero of the Spanish-American War was made in the Bay of Manila where a comparatively minor naval action took place.

That is not to say that Admiral George Dewey was not a hero in his own right. The bold measures which he took in the face of seemingly overwhelming odds stamped him as a man fit to command a fleet, a man of iron will and supreme confidence in the fighting ability of his fellow Americans as compared with that of the enemy. Subsequent decisions following the capture of Manila proved, too, that George Dewey was statesman as well as fighter; his correspondence with the defeated Admiral Montojo, both before and after the latter's capitulation, still is looked upon as possessing exactly the proper tone, the fitting sternness, yet withal the naval courtesy which each officer of our Navy today might well study to good purpose.

The Admiral is an excellently told story of George Dewey and the years through which he lived. The authors have reached out into contemporary history and drawn around their central character details of politics, economics, morals, and public thought that add significance to each incident in Dewey's life and career. Before allowing the future Admiral to be born in Vermont, for instance, the authors first set the stage by giving the reader a good understanding of what the people of New England and other sections of the country were thinking and doing at the time, of how the shorthanded American Navy was literally struggling for its existence, and thereby they make it much easier to understand the thoughts and the desires coursing through young Dewey's mind and heart during his formative years before entering the United States Naval Academy as a midshipman from Montpelier. It is thus throughout the book. Current events of the time are sketched on the broad canvas portraying the Admiral's career.

There is much concerning Dewey in Navy Department files. This material has been drawn on time and time again for articles and books on the hero of Manila Bay until literally its arms are out at the elbows. The authors of *The Admiral* were fortunate in having the complete collaboration of Admiral Dewey's son, including access to family papers and correspondence heretofore unavailable to historians. Much of the material concerning Dewey's action and subsequent procedure at Manila, for instance, has been drawn from George Goodwin Dewey's recollection of his father's own accounts. In addition the journals and private letters of several relatives and family friends were made available, together with journals of Dewey's staff officers.

Chapters of this book detailing the triumphant return of the nation's greatest hero to New York Harbor, his tours of American cities, and finally the enthusiastic attempts of his admirers to have him nominated for the Presidency are searching and completely frank in detail. It is to the credit of the Dewey family that the authors were allowed to bare facts never before published in connection with this grand old man of the sea. Few national heroes have been so widely misunderstood as Dewey was; few have had to adjust themselves to universal acclaim overnight as Dewey did; it is no wonder that the Admiral should have made a few mistakes in what today we would call his public relations in trying to adjust himself to the halo that grateful countrymen insisted he wear.

This book about an officer trained under Farragut is a welcome addition to the library of naval lore which is growing at such a fast pace under the impetus of America's seven-ocean fleet and current naval actions.

LELAND P. LOVETTE
Captain, U. S. Navy

INTRODUCTION

$\mathcal{M}$y relationship to the Admiral of the Navy, George Dewey, has given me the privilege of knowing the naval officers of the late nineteenth and early twentieth centuries. Like my father, they were all fine gentlemen, unselfish and courageous. The traditions they learned at Annapolis made them ready to stake their lives for their country.

In reading the manuscript for this work, I have relived all my associations with my father and with his associates. I know that he would be pleased with this presentation of his career and of the story of the Navy, which was his life. I have read many biographies of him, but none have approached the thoroughness and accuracy contained in *The Admiral*.

My contemporaries and I can remember vividly the momentous day of May 1, 1898, when my father and his squadron destroyed a Spanish fleet at Manila Bay without the loss of a single American life. In consenting to help with the preparation of this book and in approving its publication, it is my hope that the generation of Americans fighting World War II will know better the great legacy which my father and his generation gave our country.

I am glad this book does not deify my father. That would be the last thing he would desire. Instead it is pleasing to see that every phase of his career has been thoroughly covered, and it intensifies my pride to realize that nothing need be hidden, for nothing in his life impaired his greatness.

Reading this book has made my memories of Father even deeper than they were before—memories of his friendships and associations with such men as Badger, Clark, Rodman, Evans, Fiske, Sampson, Schley, Lamberton, Brumby, Caldwell, Sargent, Butler, Wood, and Dion Williams, to mention only a few of those who helped create the great tradition of the Navy.

I am happy that young people today will have an opportunity to understand better and to appreciate that heritage and the unconquerable spirit of the American Navy, which has endured from the time of John Paul Jones through the eras of Farragut and Dewey down to the Navy of Admirals King, Nimitz, and Halsey. *The Admiral* catches that spirit and shows how it was intensified by my father's skill and bravery in building a greater naval service for the safety of our nation.

GEORGE GOODWIN DEWEY

Chicago
April, 1944

PROLOGUE

𝒥t was December 7. In the streets of San Francisco hourglass-figured ladies of Nob Hill stepped to the ground from their phaetons. Shoeshine boys sang "Oh Susannah" and "Daisy, Daisy" as they polished the boots of dandies on the board sidewalks of Market Street. The cable cars toiled up the steep hills. Down on the Barbary Coast bearded prospectors told wild tales of newly discovered Yukon gold over their nickel beers. San Francisco was a world of gilt and splendor. Its opera, theaters, and hotels were rich from the money of men made wealthy by gold rushes and new land. The menace of Japanese labor in California troubled no one. William McKinley was in the White House and Republican prosperity dimmed memories of the depression of 1893.

America on that December day of 1897 was a nation of forty-five states. Between the Mississippi and the reaches of the Sacramento was a land of plains and mountains, of pioneer towns, lonely ranches, and the endless range.

There was hint of neither destiny nor infamy as the boilers of the Pacific mail steamer *Gaelic* worked up steam for the passage to Japan. Yet destiny selected that day, long before another December 7 which would stand for infamy, to launch new forces leading to the cataclysms of two world wars. In Washington the fifty-fifth Congress of the United States convened to hear President McKinley's message, which promised that America would give a fair trial to the Spanish pledges of reform in Cuba. In Madrid Señor Sagasta, new head of the Spanish government, praised the speech and said "the imminent dangers are past." Compromise and conciliation were in the air.

But in New York William Randolph Hearst's papers printed stories about two more emissaries to the Cuban revolutionists who were hanged in cold blood. In Berlin the German Reichstag debated Germany's first big naval bill, and in faraway Kiaochow, China, two thousand of the

1

Kaiser's marines, with a pair of machine guns, dispersed swarms of Chinese foot soldiers and demanded a long-term lease of the bay.

The United States Senate was debating whether to annex Hawaii, and it seemed the ratification treaty would not pass, although there were men in the land who warned that the Japanese were already looking covetously at Pearl Harbor.

In America free land was at an end, and the nation looked for more distant fields.

Queen Victoria, after sixty years upon the throne of Great Britain, had celebrated her Diamond Jubilee that June. The navies of the world sent their best ships to Spithead for a review that spring, and Kaiser Wilhelm II was "chagrined" because the German men-of-war made a poor showing. "I greatly regret that I cannot give you a better ship," he telegraphed his brother, Prince Henry, vice admiral of the fleet, "but I will never rest until I have raised my navy to the same standard as that of my army."

America was awakening to the coming naval race. Her new fleet—almost every fighting ship was less than twelve years old—was ready for a new century and for new fights for the undeveloped markets of the world.

The passengers waiting on the San Francisco dock to board the *Gaelic* were scarcely aware of the currents in their lives. They little noticed a short, gray-haired man striding with long, military steps toward the gangplank of the steamer.

A gray mustache covered his long upper lip, and he walked with energy and purposefulness. His bright yellow shoes were the height of fashion in Washington, and his expensive, well-tailored suit and gray traveling cap denoted a man of authority and means. Behind him two younger men, towering above his five-feet-seven-inches, walked in step. When the elder saluted a group of young ladies on the dock, the younger men followed suit, smiled, and looked as if they would like to pause, but their senior hurried on toward a wagon piled high with trunks and boxes. It was a large amount of luggage for three men starting a transpacific trip, but the length of the voyage and the uncertainty of its outcome demanded readiness for anything. In the van were clothes for many climates and crates of books, which, if anyone could have seen them, would have revealed much. There were histories of the Philippine Islands, of China and Japan; charts of the South Seas rolled up in long, cardboard cylinders; the works of Captain Alfred Thayer Mahan on naval strategy and Lafcadio Hearn's *Glimpses of Unfamiliar Japan* and *Out of the East*.

The trio walked up the gangplank. Few knew who they were. There was little reason to know. The gray-haired man was George Dewey, a commodore in the United States Navy. But if his name and appearance

2

held little public interest, in his own heart lay a feeling of destiny. Since the Civil War, when he had fought under Admiral David Glasgow Farragut, he had believed himself a marked man. Thirty-five years before, when the old frigate *Mississippi* had sunk in flames near New Orleans, Dewey, then a young lieutenant, had leaped from her burning decks unharmed. The experience convinced him that he was different. Shells would never destroy him. Somewhere, sometime, fame awaited him.

But the long years had intervened without opportunity to prove that destiny to himself or to the world. What is a naval career in peacetime? he had often wondered. Little more than tedious years at sea, dull bureau assignments in Washington, and the niceties of polite society. Now, almost sixty years old, he remained a commodore, while some of his Annapolis juniors flew the flag of rear admiral. Two years of duty in the waters of the Orient lay ahead. In two years he would be retired from the active list. What would those years bring? War with Spain, perhaps? And if so, would there be death or glory in the Philippines? To Americans at large, as Mr. Dooley said, the Philippines might have been canned goods, but to Dewey they were untested fields for immortality.

Americans looked to Cuba as the scene of glory in a war with Spain. The admirals in Washington had cornered that theater, and Dewey must seek elsewhere. Inspired by the zeal of Theodore Roosevelt and the faith of Senator Redfield Proctor of Vermont, whose influence gave him his last remaining chance, Dewey turned to the Orient. Only a few weeks before Secretary of the Navy John D. Long had begrudgingly awarded him a commission as commander-in-chief of the Asiatic squadron. But the appointment had not carried promotion. No officer of his rank had been in command in the Pacific since 1854, when Matthew Calbraith Perry opened Japan to the Western World. The coincidence seemed significant to Dewey, who had served on the frigate *Mississippi,* one of the ships that had sailed in Perry's squadron to Yeddo Bay near Tokyo.

Flanked by his flag lieutenant, T. M. Brumby, and his flag secretary, Ensign H. H. Caldwell, the Commodore leaned over the *Gaelic's* rail and gazed at the hills of San Francisco. He might have preferred other aides, but all his tentative invitations had received embarrassed refusal. An old commodore's flagship, eight thousand miles from a possible scene of war, was no place for active young men. Dewey felt a special affection, therefore, for the two who had gambled much to go with him.

A few naval officers from the Mare Island Navy Yard were there to bid the Commodore farewell. Stiffly, they wished him good luck. Then, thinking perhaps to cheer him up, one of them remarked, "You are fortunate that you do not have to leave a wife behind on this trip, sir."

The old man jerked his head toward the officer, pulled a gold watch from his vest pocket, opened its case and displayed a tiny photograph inside. Engraved on the case beneath the picture were the words, "My Susie."

"My wife goes with me always," the Commodore answered quietly. "Whom God hath joined together, Death cannot put asunder." He replaced his watch and walked sadly to his cabin. Susie Goodwin Dewey had been dead for twenty-seven years, but it was her loss which had sent him searching for comfort at sea. Years lost to the land, but rich in what they taught him about the waterways of the world and the powers of its navies. Grief is given to men of greatness to steel them for their trial, he felt. And Dewey, who was Navy through and through, and strove above all to conform, knew that his trial would surely come. He saw a triangle whose bases were Perry and Farragut. Would its apex become a short Vermonter who, God willing, might triumph over the Dons of Spain?

The beat of Pacific combers on the *Gaelic*'s bow during the sixteen-day passage to Japan was the beat of drums he had awaited for almost sixty years. Most of the crossing he spent studying the charts of Oriental waters and the books of Hearn and Mahan. During that trip he reminisced about his own life in distant Vermont. Victoria had just been crowned the girl queen of England in 1837, when he was born, and now she was an old woman, secure in her fame, while he was either at the threshold—or at the end. In Dewey's mind was the familiar story of America and its Navy. Heroes lived anew in his thoughts: John Paul Jones, Truxton, Preble, Decatur, Hull, Perry, and Farragut. The historical pattern of the past, to which he hoped to add his own brave part, lived with him as the *Gaelic* pounded through the seas. And as he studied he fashioned his dreams.

THE SHIPS STARTING

*A*T MANILA BAY in 1898 America, like a mighty river, flowed into the oceans of world power. Insularity was dead, although many did not realize it, for that battle linked the United States with Asia in bonds of ownership and responsibility. From that day onward, for good or ill, the United States could no longer remain aloof from world war or rivalry.

Like a river, her Navy flowed down the bed of history from the day of the eighty-ton privateers of the Revolution, with their six-pounder guns, to that of the ten-thousand-ton battleships, with their half-ton thirteen-inch shells, which fought the Spanish War. From there, it grew in size and power till the 1940's, when it became the dominant force upon the seven seas.

In the little skiffs of 1775 the Navy had its birth. Its men founded the tradition that made George Dewey the kind of naval officer he was, the tradition which lives in the seamen and captains of today.

In the history of the American Navy lies the drama of the nation, for its needs were the nation's needs; its stagnant spells were the winters of the nation's growth; and its fate was the fate of the land.

First there was Jeremiah O'Brien of Machias, Maine. When the Minute Men fought the Redcoats at Lexington on April 17, 1775, O'Brien and his townsfolk were stirred by the valor of their commonwealth. The next month, with Revolution a reality, the British sent the armed schooner *Margharetta* into Machiasport to obtain pine trees for more British masts. With pitchforks and axes Jeremiah O'Brien and his neighbors seized a merchant sloop, the *Unity,* and with it captured the British vessel.

Six years before the war the men of Newport, Rhode Island, had burned the British customs sloop *Liberty*. In 1772 Abraham Whipple had destroyed the *Gaspe* in Narragansett Bay, and in 1773 Bostonians had jettisoned English tea into Boston Harbor. But O'Brien and his friends were the first naval victors of the American Revolution. They lit the spark which started privateering on the New England coast. Before the war was over, Congress had issued letters of marque to 1,697 merchant ships that sailed as privateers.* But hundreds more privateersmen were operating under the jurisdiction of the thirteen states.

Those privateers were little boats of only one hundred tons, carrying iron deck guns that threw a six-pound ball of lead a few hundred feet. As the war progressed the ships grew bigger. The *Boston* was of four hundred tons, and some ships went up to six hundred and carried nine-pounder guns. Swivel guns mounted in sockets along the ships' rails augmented these heavy broadsides, and some of the biggest vessels had "coehorns," large caliber guns like modern mortars, which were placed in the vessels' crow's nests for close-in work.†

The privateer captains were hardy, picturesque, and bold. One was Samuel Tucker of Marblehead, whose exploits in the Mediterranean against the pirate Corsairs of Algiers spread his fame throughout the world. Even the British were impressed by his accomplishments. He was offered a commission to serve "His Gracious Majesty," but Tucker was an American.

"Hang His Gracious Majesty," he snorted. "Do you think I am the sort of man to fight against my country?"‡

The naval warfare of the Revolution was waged by American privateers until the French fleet became the decisive factor in persuading King George III to give up his western colonies. The destruction of commerce was almost the sole aspect of the war at sea. Congress, which could not feed Washington's armies, had no funds for capital ships, and continental vessels had to pay for themselves.§

Under the leadership of John Adams, Congress, on October 13, 1775, resolved to fit out two vessels for intercepting British cargo ships. So far as legislation was concerned, this was the birth of the American fleet.¶

In December Congress slacked its sheets to sail with the wind. A construction program, providing for five thirty-two-gun men-of-war, five

*Dudley W. Knox, *A History of the United States Navy* (New York: G. P. Putnam's Sons 1936).
†*Ibid.*
‡Charles Morris, *Heroes of the Navy in America* (Philadelphia: J. B. Lippincott Co., 1919).
§Samuel Eliot Morison and Henry Steele Commager, *The Growth of the American Republic*. (New York: Oxford University Press, 1930).
¶Knox, *op. cit.*

twenty-eight-gun ships, three twenty-four's, all frigates, and twenty other vessels, was approved.

Yet in 1777 the United States fleet consisted of only thirty-four ships in commission, and by 1782 there were only seven on the sea. It was French seapower which won the battle of Yorktown and which assured America's independence.

So began America's "pendulum" tradition of naval building: to be unprepared when there is war, to build furiously, and, when the peace treaty is signed, to scrap the fleet. That was the policy George Dewey saw and mourned after Appomattox, and the one he helped to change after the fall of Manila. It was the policy his successors in the Navy Department saw fulfilled disastrously at the Washington Naval Conference in 1922.

United States privateers, by capturing merchant vessels, were more valuable in winning the Revolution than they were in the slight attrition accomplished against the Royal Navy. By boosting marine insurance rates, the fast privateers so wearied Britain that she preferred peace to fighting for her colonies.

Supplying arms and munitions for the men of Valley Forge was another contribution of the nascent fleet. In this manner, skippers like Esek Hopkins, Nicholas Biddle, Abraham Whipple, and Samuel Nicholas provided great aid to the colonial cause. Under the command of Captain Hopkins, a fleet seized Nassau in the Bahamas and spent a fortnight in the harbor loading munitions aboard its ships. The *Wasp,* the *Hornet,* and the *Cabot,* namesake sailing ships of twentieth-century aircraft carriers, sailed with that fleet and thereby added to the naval tradition sanctified today.

John Paul Jones was a lieutenant on the Nassau raid. Twenty-nine years old at the time, he had been at sea since the age of twelve, and though a Scot by birth he became an American at heart. Jones, whose contribution to American naval tradition remains unparalleled, had landed in Virginia while on a cruise and had settled there.

In 1775 he offered his services to the new nation, convoying cargo ships for the defense of New York, sailing in the Nassau raid, and on a free-lance commerce raiding cruise helped the cause and proved he was a sailor of rare ability. In November, 1777, Congress made him a captain and dispatched him to France to announce the defeat of Burgoyne at Saratoga. That news was of great advantage to Benjamin Franklin, who was in Paris seeking to persuade the French to aid America in the war.

Jones, with Franklin's help, obtained a rotted French ship of forty-two guns. He named her the *Bon Homme Richard* in tribute to Benjamin Franklin's *Poor Richard's Almanac,* and with two frigates and a brig sailed around England. The little fleet seized many prizes before it reached Flamborough Head in the North Sea. There, Jones and his fleet of three French-commanded boats spent two days sinking a fleet of English merchantmen.

On the evening of September 23, 1779, two haughty English men-of-war appeared—the *Serapis,* with fifty guns, and the *Countess of Scarborough*— which were guarding a convoy of merchantmen. John Paul signaled his ships, the *Alliance,* the *Pallas,* and the *Vengeance,* to form line and attack. Jones headed stright for the *Serapis,* a bigger, faster ship, with eight more guns than the stodgy *Bon Homme Richard.* Ignoring the odds, Jones sailed into range and a devastating, brutal fight began. The *Serapis'* broadside wreaked havoc on the *Richard.* Guns of the old vessel burst in the firing. Water-line hits started leaks, and fires raged throughout the bloodied ship. The struggle went on for three and one half hours.

To keep his ship afloat, Jones came to close quarters and managed to lash the *Richard* to the *Serapis.* Bow to stern the giants fought. In the tops the Americans excelled, and the British masts were emptied of their men. But on the *Bon Homme's* decks the British guns spread death.

Through the melee John Paul Jones roared like a madman. His twenty-eight nine-pounders had been silenced, and only three of the other guns remained to fight the fire from the *Serapis'* still intact cannon.

The *Bon Homme's* master-at-arms, seeing his ship filling with water, released English prisoners from the hold. Racing for the deck to fight the *Richard's* crew, they were met by Jones with a brace of pistols in his hands. Lieutenant Dale shouted, "To the pumps," and the prisoners went below and worked to save their lives and keep the sieve of a ship afloat.

A frightened gunner on the *Richard,* who could stand carnage no longer, shouted surrender to the English. Jones, a pistol in his hand, smashed the coward's head.

Captain Pearson of the *Serapis* echoed the words, "Have you struck?"

Then, on the *Richard's* blood-strewn deck, with the full moon dimmed by fires blazing all over his ship, John Paul Jones roared:

"No, I have not yet begun to fight."

The battle went on in redoubled fury. The *Alliance* finally joined the fray, but her shells hit the *Richard* more often than the *Serapis.* Jones, firing guns himself when their crews were killed, refused to give up. Captain Pearson, with his mainmast shattering to the deck, and his magazines exploding from hand grenades, finally lowered his flag. The *Richard* was in far worse condition, however, and Jones, the indomitable conqueror, moved the remnants of his crew to the British *Serapis,* where he watched the victorious *Bon Homme Richard* sink into the sea.*

Jones was a Scotsman but he became the inspiration and founder of the American Navy. In 1777, when he took command of the *Ranger*,† he wrote: "That flag and I are twins, born in the same hour from the womb of destiny. We cannot be parted in life or death. So long as we can float, we shall float together. If we must sink we shall go down as one."

Oft-quoted as they are, John Paul Jones' comments on what a naval officer should be have probably had more influence on naval tradition than any book of sermons ever printed:

It is no means enough that an officer of the Navy should be a capable mariner. He should be as well a gentleman of liberal education, refined manners, punctilious courtesy, and the nicest sense of personal honor. When a Commander has, by tact, patience, justice, and firmness, each exercised in its proper turn, produced such an impression upon those under his orders in a ship of war, he has only to await the appearance of his enemy's topsails upon the horizon. When this moment does come, he may be sure of victory over an equal or somewhat superior force, or honorable defeat by one greatly superior. No such achievements are possible to an unhappy ship with a sullen crew.‡

On Lake Champlain in 1776, Benedict Arnold had been feverishly building a navy to stop the British on their way from Canada. His was a motley fleet, built by Dutch settlers and amateur carpenters. It was an orange-crate task force of four galleys with ten guns each, eight three-gun flat-bottoms, a schooner, and one sloop.§ On October 10, 1776, the British opened a two-day fight. Outnumbered, outgunned, and outmanned, the tyro Americans fought the British seamen valiantly but to no avail. On the second night Arnold and his tired crews beached what boats were left, burned them, and escaped through the woods. It was a costly venture in

*After the Revolution Jones served in the Russian Navy but soon resigned because of intrigues against him. He retired to Paris in 1790 and died there on July 19, 1792, at the age of forty-five. For a century his body lay forgotten in a cemetery in Paris. Finally, in 1905, General Horace Porter, United States Ambassador to France, rediscovered the grave, and Jones' body was returned to the United States and reinterred at the Naval Academy, Annapolis.

†Jones' commission to command the ship was dated June 14, 1777, the same date on which Congress made the stars and stripes the official national flag.

‡Captain Leland P. Lovette, in his splendid work, *Naval Customs, Traditions and Usage*, points out that this letter was not actually written by Jones but was compiled from various letters and possibly rewritten and polished by Augustus C. Buell in his work, *Paul Jones, Founder of the American Navy*. While not condoning Buell's "literary sharpness," Lovette says that it represents the "essence of the brave, dashing officer's code. For there are a variety of influences that have shaped our naval tradition, yet none have been of greater importance than the life and writings of the founder of the American Navy."

§The sloop was the first *Enterprise*. The second *Enterprise* served in the War of 1812, winning the appellation *Lucky Enterprise* for its successes against British ships.

9

men and toil, but the expendability of Arnold's men paid dividends. Ice came before the damaged English ships which were to carry Burgoyne's men south could be repaired. By the next summer the colonists were ready at Bennington and Saratoga.

Defeats piled up for the Continental Navy. Privateering paid well in cash and psychological attrition, but the ships grew waterlogged and old. When the war was over, Congress closed its books and abolished the infant fleet.

After 1783 America began to dissolve into a land of many states. The Continental Congress, with no emergency to compel adhesion, flickered weakly. But for the energy of such men as Washington, Jefferson, and Hamilton, dissolution might have ensued. The nation's Navy was non-existent.* But the separate states maintained their trade. Sea commerce in Yankee bottoms grew apace, and, in a world of piracy and nationalism, trouble was bound to come. The adoption of the Constitution did not bring a reversal of naval policy. Until 1794 the United States was a country with no fleet to protect its maritime trade.†

The privateer captains of the Revolution had done their bit nobly and well. Yet, because their ships represented the captains' entire wealth, the skippers were slow to follow the necessary policy of any war—expendability. And because the captains had often been more willing to run instead of fight, the Navy lost prestige.

In 1793 American ships, striving for their share of the world, found themselves at a great disadvantage. With their country scorned by European powers, Americans were prey to privateers on all the seas. For years the Barbary pirates in the Mediterranean had seized American ships. Tribute had been paid, and still the seizures continued. Privateersmen in English, French, and Spanish ships laughed at congressional protests and seized more American shipping.

Finally, in 1794, Congress became aroused. A bill was passed authorizing the construction of six frigates to halt the depredations. Work was begun, and immediately the Algerian piracy ceased. Work on the ships was stopped. Matters became worse. Frenchmen, in the midst of Revolution, launched bold raids against American shipping even along the Atlantic seaboard.

Then Congress awoke and completed the three most advanced frigates— *Constellation, United States,* and *Constitution*—in 1798. Designed by Joshua Humphreys, a Philadelphia Quaker, the vessels embodied prin-

*This entire period bears a striking resemblance to the Harding era in American foreign policy.
†The frigate *Alliance,* the last ship remaining from the Revolution, was sold in 1785.

ciples of naval construction that are still followed by the United States fleet. If the Navy of the United States had fewer ships than had other major powers, Humphrey's ships were more formidable, with greater speed and heavier guns. This principle still holds today. American battleships and American planes fire more and bigger shells, are better armored, and, even if less maneuverable than their enemies', can give them large odds in battle and emerge victorious.

Ships of the *Constitution* class were 175 feet long, with a mainmast 180 feet high. Most frigates of the time carried thirty-two eighteen-pounder guns. The *Constitution* had thirty twenty-four-pound cannon on its gun-deck, with twenty-two twelve-pound guns on the quarter-deck and fore-castle.

With only these three frigates and a flotilla of cutters and armed merchant ships, President John Adams decided mighty France must be taught a lesson. In 1798 he told commanders of American ships that they were "hereby authorized, instructed, and directed to subdue, seize, and take any armed vessels of the French Republic."*

Thus began a war of isolated actions and privateering that produced more heroes for United States naval traditions and trained more commanders for coming wars with Tripoli and Britain.

At the start of the war Congress took a logical, though belated, step. It removed the administration of the Navy from an uninterested War Department and created the Navy Department with Benjamin Stoddert as the first Secretary of the Navy.

Commodore John Barry, "the Irish champion of Delaware," was in command of the *United States*. Captain Samuel Nicholson skippered the *Constitution,* and Thomas Truxton, known as "our blessed privateer," commanded the *Constellation*.

For nearly three years of undeclared war American ships fought spasmodically against the French. By the end of the war the United States fleet consisted of fifty-four warships—thirty frigates and ships of the line and twenty-four cutters and privateers. To fight these the French had a mighty battle fleet of more than two hundred warships and nearly one thousand privateers.

Thomas Truxton, who took the French frigate *Insurgente* after a bloody fight, was one whose story became part of naval history.†

"I have been shattered in my rigging and sails, and my foretopmast rendered from wounds, useless; you may depend the enemy is not less so,"

*Edgar Stanton Maclay, *A History of the United States Navy from 1775 to 1901* (New York: D. Appleton & Co., 1901).

†February 9, 1799, off the Island of Nevis.

Truxton wrote after the battle. The score: French killed and wounded, seventy; Americans, three.

So successful was the Navy in the undeclared war against France that Congress decided not to scrap all fifty-four ships of the fleet this time. It decided to have a permanent Navy, and fourteen ships were retained.

During the French "war" America's export trade had risen above $200,000,000 annually, American ships were rich prizes, and the Tripolitan pirates resumed their depredations. They had forced the United States to pay $525,000 in ransom in 1795 as well as a new thirty-six-gun frigate, and more than $20,000 worth of naval stores.

In 1799 the Dey of Algiers had forced an American, Captain William Bainbridge, to raise the Algerian flag at his helm and carry hundreds of slaves, cattle, and $1,000,000 worth of presents to the Sultan of Turkey. Bainbridge protested, but his ship was under the Dey's guns, and threats were made that American ships would be seized again if Bainbridge did not go. Bainbridge complied.

So do the roots of appeasement run deep in history. The Dey, the Pashas of Tripoli, Morocco, and Tunis raised their ransom demands, asking more tribute. Finally Congress realized appeasement would avail nothing, and war against the pirates of North Africa was begun.

Commodore Edward Preble had assumed command of the *Constitution* and of United States forces in the Mediterranean. With Captain Bainbridge, who had captured a Moroccan ship which had just seized a Salem brig, Preble sailed into the port of Tangier and frightened the Sultan into capitulation.

Later, Bainbridge, as captain of the *Philadelphia,* chased a pirate off the coast of Tripoli. An uncharted reef interposed itself and the *Philadelphia* went aground. A fleet of Tripolitan gunboats refloated the *Philadelphia* and anchored it in the harbor of Tangier.

Stephen Decatur was a young skipper on the *Enterprise* at the time. The *Philadelphia* in Corsair hands threatened to upset the American balance of power in Tripoli. The ship had to be destroyed, and Decatur was picked to do the job.

On the night of February 7, 1804, Decatur and eighty-four Americans boldly sailed the ketch *Intrepid* into the bay of Tangier. With a Sicilian pilot, they hailed the Corsairs aboard the *Philadelphia,* said they were blockade-runners, and tied up under the mighty frigate's side.

It was too late when a sharp-eyed Tripolitan saw the Americans in the ketch. With a whoop Decatur's men stormed over the side, swinging cutlasses and scattering the Corsairs. The Americans fired the *Philadelphia,* jumped back into the *Intrepid,* and were out of range of the fort's guns when the *Philadelphia* blew up.

Lord Nelson called the feat "the most bold and daring act of the age." It made Decatur a name to live eternally in heroic annals, and added luster to the great tradition of his Navy.

Preble was the guiding spirit of the Tripolitan wars. When he gave up command the campaign died down. A half-hearted war continued, and the peace won in 1804 did not settle any important issue. Yet the precepts of Preble carried on. He returned to America the nation's hero and his fame added laurels to the fleet of the young nation. The officers trained under him were the men whose genius for seamanship and gunnery saved the country from disaster in 1812.

Meanwhile war spread over Europe. Napoleon drove his legions across the continent. French and British fleets strove for mastery of the seas. The young American nation was building merchantmen from the pines and spruce of New England. Its ships carried goods for the blockaded nations of Europe and, with the British blockade and the Napoleonic continental system in effect, the fleets of the Union Jack and the Fleur de Lis captured scores of American vessels.

From 1803 to 1807, when Jefferson enacted the embargo on all shipping from American ports, at least 528 ships were captured by the British, and another 389 by the French.

The administration sought to avoid the battlefields of Europe. America withdrew its neck, turtlewise. Congress refused to build any vessels save shore patrol gunboats. All told, 176 of these were built, and when war came with England they proved almost useless.

In 1807 the American frigate *Chesapeake* was overhauled and fired on by the British ship *Leopard,* and four Americans were impressed into the service of the Crown.* Other impressments followed. On June 18, 1812, President Madison formally declared war. America, with no ships of the line, six frigates, and an assortment of smaller boats, went into battle against the Royal Navy with its 124 giant ships of the line, 116 frigates, and some 400 other warships.

The amazing fact was that the United States was not conquered. Frigate skippers and five-hundred-odd privateersmen, who raided commerce on the coast of Britain and sank more than 1,344 English merchant ships, saved the day.

If the Revolution had technically won America its independence, the War of 1812 confirmed it. It was a naval war. England, busy with Napo-

*In 1812 England returned the two survivors of this group and apologized. But the episode had aroused the American people to such an extent that conciliation was impossible.

leon, kept most of her fleet in the east until 1814 and most of her troops in Spain. She sent only enough ships to stop the "mosquito" tactics of Yankee crews.

By and large, the United States fought that war as Germany was to fight a hundred years later. Frigates and privateersmen took the place of U-boats and, because of their speed, fled from English men-of-war just as German submarines escaped Allied fleets in the twentieth century. In both wars the pirate tactics endangered the empire's life line, but in 1814 the United States did not threaten the life of England. Consequently, a compromise peace was possible.

Yet the war at sea created an American Navy. The ships and men of 1812, by their daring and their exploits, created the tradition that was climaxed at Midway and in the Solomons in 1942.

Young George Dewey grew up in Vermont hearing tales of Isaac Hull and Decatur; of "Old Ironsides" Stewart, who lived until after the Civil War, David Porter, Thomas McDonough, and Oliver Hazard Perry. They were heroes who made him love the sea and follow in their wake.

The men of 1812 are among America's best known naval heroes. In their wooden ships and with their iron guns they set a precedent for daring.

First, there was Isaac Hull, heavy-set and bald, who sailed the *Constitution* north from Chesapeake Bay, and declared, "If a fellow wants to fight, Americans will not disappoint him." Off the Jersey coast Hull encountered four British frigates, each a match for the *Constitution,* and a mammoth English ship of the line. As there was no sense in fighting, Hull tried to run away. But a calm set in, and the *Constitution* enacted one of the most dramatic escapes in maritime annals. Boats were put over the sides to tow the great ship to safety. Hull's men pulled like demons, but the British followed suit and closed in. Then Hull dipped into his bag of tricks, carried an anchor far ahead of his ship, and towed *Old Ironsides* ahead with a line. The process was repeated as the *Constitution* "walked" away from the English fleet. But the Englishmen used all their squadron's boats to tow the flagship *Shannon*. It inched nearer the *Constitution*. Then a wind came up, and Hull loaded on sails and picked up his boats at a dead "gallop" as he scudded through the waves. For two days British guns fired but always fell short. Finally, on the third afternoon, storm clouds came, and Hull's next masterpiece was the trick which saved his ship.

Closer to the storm than the Englishmen, Hull sent his men to the tops to reef in every sail. Far behind, the British thought a furious blow was on its way and followed suit. Then with lightning speed, Hull shook

14

out every sail, careened through the waves, and sailed out of the squall to freedom. By the time the British saw his trick he was gone.

It was on August 19, 1812, that Hull sighted the British frigate *Guerriere* off Halifax. Proud and haughty Captain Dacres, believing in the invincibility of his ship, prepared to teach the Yankees a lesson. Dacres' shells whistled through the *Constitution's* rigging. Hull refused to fire until the two ships came closer together.

Then of a sudden he shouted, "Now boys, pour it into them." Shells boomed across the water, slicing off the *Guerriere's* masts. The battle was soon over and Captain Dacres, with nearly eighty casualties, rowed from his flaming wreck to surrender. He was the first Englishman in fourteen years to be beaten on the sea.

Oliver Wendell Holmes immortalized that scene in the poem "Old Ironsides":

> "Her decks once red with hero's blood,
> Where knelt the vanquished foe."

Defeating one English ship made little difference in the war, but the effect upon American morale was great. Throughout America riders galloped with the news and the people cheered and sang. Hull was a feted hero, and an aroused America was ready for every wind that blew.

With such a start American frigates went on a rampage across the broad Atlantic. They smashed English ships in five battles. Jacob Jones, whose name has lived in ships of World War II, pitted the *Wasp* against the British *Frolic* and conquered her.

On October 25 Stephen Decatur walked the deck of the *United States* south of the Azores. A mighty British ship, the *Macedonian,* sailed into view and speedily sought to close for a finish fight. But Decatur backed his sails and kept away, while the *United States'* broadsides pounded into the British ship. Her mizzen topmast crumbled, her masts were riddled, and, when the ships closed for the final blow, Decatur maneuvered across her stern to rake. But the *Macedonian* was a mass of wreckage, with 105 men killed or wounded and Decatur forewent the coup de grâce. Only five Americans lost their lives that day.

In seven months three brave English men-of-war surrendered to the underrated Yankee sailors. Upward of five hundred British merchant ships were seized by privateering Baltimore clippers that could outsail anything at sea.

Their successes ended the chance of easy victory for the British. London sent more ships to the west to fight for revenge. Yet even in defeat naval tradition was served, and heroism added inspiration for the coming generations of American seamen and naval officers.

Captain James Lawrence, on the *Chesapeake,* encountered British revenge at the guns of Captain Philip Broke of H.M.S. *Shannon,* off President Roadstead. In fifteen minutes the *Shannon* left the *Chesapeake* a floating hulk. Lawrence, on being taken to his cabin in a dying condition, uttered the immortal words: "Don't give up the ship." On Lake Erie Commodore Oliver Hazard Perry emblazoned the phrase on a flag when he smashed the British fleet on September 10, 1813, adding new words of his own: "We have met the enemy and they are ours—two ships, two brigs, one sloop, and one schooner."

And so it went. Tradition and folklore grew as the ships sailed. Captain David Porter swept the Pacific clean of British whalers. Porter's cruise on the *Essex* is one of the most cherished traditions of the United States Navy. The first American warship to sail the blue Pacific, the *Essex* won a name as a wanderer before she sank under the guns of the British ship *Phoebe* near Valparaiso, Chile.

Aboard the *Essex* was John Downes, the first of four American naval officers to bear that name. He was given command of one of Porter's prizes, the *Essex Junior.* In 1819 Downes sailed the *Macedonian* to California, the second time a United States ship had touched our Pacific coast. In 1832 he landed at Quallah Battoo, Sumatra, to avenge the killing of the crew of a Salem clipper. Downes' *Potomac* landed Marines, who stormed three forts, burned the village, and killed 150 natives, among them Chief Po Mahomet, who was responsible for the murder of the Americans. The natives pleaded for peace, promising that no more Americans would be killed. The *Potomac* sailed on around the world, becoming the second American warship to circumnavigate the globe.

The year 1814 was a hard one for the Americans. Blockaded by a mighty British fleet, commerce was at a standstill. New England, most affected, was war weary. The Hartford Convention nearly resulted in a secession move by Connecticut, Massachusetts, and Rhode Island. An English army in Canada was preparing to attack New York.

But the privateers were busy, too. If New England wanted peace, so did Old England. Ships bound for India were seized by fast American raiders on all the seas. Lloyd's rates on marine insurance made shipping almost prohibitive.

When Thomas McDonough stopped the jerry-built British fleet on Lake Champlain, the war was practically over. McDonough's victory was a masterpiece of naval strategy. At anchor, the Americans withstood the fire of the oncoming British. Then, with ships on both sides burning,

16

McDonough dropped a stern anchor, cut his bow line, and swung around to bring his undamaged starboard batteries to bear, and ended the bloody fight.

Old Ironsides was still to gain fresh glory, however. In December, under her fourth commander, Charles Stewart, the mighty ship met the *Cyane* and the *Levant,* with fifty-four guns between them. For four hours Commodore Stewart maneuvered between the ships, smothering both with shells, and finally emerged victorious.

On Christmas Eve puritanical John Quincy Adams and Henry Clay, who attended conferences all day and gambled all night, signed the Treaty of Ghent, and the war was over, a war that elevated heroes of many types for later officers to emulate. "Don't give up the ship," "Pour it into them, boys," "We have met the enemy and they are ours," "I have just begun to fight"—these were the audacious American challenges that became a part of America's naval history.

The end of the war of 1812-1814 brought a surge of commerce to American shipping. Exports rose from $7,000,000 to $53,000,000 in a single year. Imports jumped from $13,000,000 to $113,000,000. This rebirth aroused anew the cupidity of the Algerian pirates. In 1815 Congress declared its fifth war in forty years against the Dey of Tunis and the Pasha of Tripoli. It was again Decatur who commanded the first squadron to quell the uprising.

In America's home waters pirates were also on the loose. In the Caribbean American flotillas carried out spasmodic warfare against the La-Fittes and the privateers of the South American Republics in the era of their revolts against Spanish rule.

By this time the Navy had some ships of the line: the *Independence,* the *Franklin,* and the *Washington,* each with seventy-four guns. The Algerian war was halted in 1816: the pirates succumbed but they were still a threat. For years the American Navy made an annual cruise to the Mediterranean to show its power and intimidate the Corsairs. George Dewey made his first cruise to the Mediterranean in 1858 on the *Wabash* for this purpose.

Expanding trade was nurtured during the ensuing years by the veterans of 1812, who sailed their full-rigged ships around the world, sailing, as through a fog, into the age of steam.

2

VERMONT'S GREEN HILLS

The year 1837 was a quiet one. No wars of magnitude marked it for history, and yet the period was one of invention, changing the way of a world.

America ended at the Mississippi. Michigan had just been admitted to the Union. Martin Van Buren was President and a commercial panic rocked the country. This was the year of Grover Cleveland's birth and of the Patriot "War" in Canada. In March Congress recognized the independence of Texas, and on Christmas Day Zachary Taylor defeated the Seminole Indians at Okeechobee Lake Swamp in Florida.

On July 4 the first railroad in the British Isles was opened, from Liverpool to Birmingham. The Spaniards were fighting over the succession to their throne, and, at opposite ends of the earth, two villages were incorporated: Chicago, Illinois, and Melbourne, Australia.

The decade of the thirties was one of growth and promise. Charles Fourier and Fourierism enjoyed a vogue. There were some who were encouraged by his system of associative enterprise or communal industry that would provide everyone with ample means. Robert Owen at New Harmony, Indiana, had started one of the first "Utopian" experiments, and the Transcendentalists of Brook Farm were pointing the way towards social change. In these years Emerson, Thoreau, Melville, and Whitman dreamed their dreams, and although they exercised little effect upon George Dewey, they did help to set the tone of the times in which he grew.

More important to Dewey, the ten years before and after his birth saw the development of some of the greatest inventions of modern times. The head of the government patent bureau had resigned in 1833, "because he felt that everything of importance had been invented," but applications for patents began to flood into the bureau, and although most of them were not developed until after the Civil War, they enriched the material world in which Dewey would carve his career.

18

In 1829 the first railroad in the United States was constructed between Carbondale and Honesdale, Pennsylvania. In 1834 Cyrus McCormick patented his reaping machine, the machine that was to harvest fields round the world. In 1836 Samuel Colt patented the revolver, and in 1837, the year of Dewey's birth, John Deere developed the steel plow.

Two years later the first practical bicycle rolled through the streets of Dumfries, Scotland; and Charles Goodyear, forgetting that a pan of India rubber was on his kitchen range, learned about vulcanization. Two months before Dewey's birth Samuel Morse gave a practical demonstration of the telegraph, and in 1844 his first real message was flashed from Washington to Baltimore. Elias Howe's sewing machine came in 1846, and five years later France and England were linked by the submarine cable.*

On November 7, 1837, Elijah P. Lovejoy was slain by a mob in Alton, Illinois, and his printing press, which had denounced the cause of slavery in the South, was flung into the Mississippi River. A month later Wendell Phillips, in Boston's Faneuil Hall, assailed the murderers in a speech which ultimately spread the flames of conflict throughout the land. There were more than five hundred abolitionist societies in the North—but Phillips was blackballed by his friends for his sympathies. Five years before South Carolina and John Calhoun had adopted the principle of nullification. The bluff of secession had been called and blocked, but the seeds were in the ground.

The Christmas celebration in the Montpelier home of Dr. Julius Yemans Dewey that Yuletide of 1837 was a simple one. George Dewey was born the next day. He had two older brothers, Charles, eleven, and Edward, eight.

Old Vermont was in the oxcart age. The long winters found farmers and townspeople alike, huddled in their frame houses, with straw packed outside window sills to keep drafts from the dirt cellar-holes. Late springs and early frosts brought short crops and meager returns. In Montpelier dirt streets turned into mud near the fords across the Onion River, a rocky, mountain stream.† The Dewey home, a one-and-a-half-storied shingle house with a steep roof and gingerbread trimmings, was almost opposite the state capitol building. Tall elms shaded the house and kept its parlor dark in accepted nineteenth-century gloom. Whale-oil lamps and wax candles molded by Mrs. Dewey afforded light for reading.

*Cyrus Field's transatlantic cable, laid down in 1866, made communication between America and Europe a matter of seconds instead of weeks.
†The Onion River of Dewey's boyhood is now the Winooski River. It flows westward through Vermont, from near St. Johnsbury to Lake Champlain just north of Burlington.

George grew up learning to chop firewood and care for the horses and hens; he washed in a tub of water warmed on the swinging crane of the kitchen fireplace. Behind the house (fifty steps in summer, thirty on a cold winter night) was the customary outhouse of the period. Beneath the canopied beds the thunder mug reigned supreme; and china wash-bowls, set in small table tops, presented a top coating of ice to break at dawn.

Environment and heredity accustomed young .George to discipline, early rising, and hard work. His father's income as a rural doctor was small and, despite his two older brothers, George was saddled with more and more of the chores as he grew in size and strength.

The ancestry Dewey set store by was not the semi-mythological strain traced after Manila Bay by his eulogists—the strain that started with Thor and Woden, included Hugh Capet and Charlemagne, and by another esoteric bit of genealogy went back to Alexander of Macedon and Constantine the Great. What was important to him was the Puritan spirit that had sent Thomas Dewey to Massachusetts Bay from Sandwich, England, in 1630. George Dewey was the ninth generation of that line. One of Thomas' great-grandsons was the Reverend Jedediah Dewey, a preacher in Bennington, Vermont, who on a September Sunday in 1777 was discussing hell and damnation when the Hessians came to town. Closing his Bible, he led his parishioners out to fight in the battle and later returned to church to resume his sermon.

His son, Captain Elijah Dewey, also fought at Bennington and was at Ticonderoga. A brother of Dewey's great-grandfather, Ensign Simeon Dewey, was also with Ethan Allen when he took Ticonderoga in "the name of the Great Jehovah and the Continental Congress."

Ethan Allen was the hero of nineteenth-century Vermont. His memory stayed as green as the mountains, and his patriotism was a constant spur. George Dewey evinced a type of keen idolatry for him.

In his father Dewey found his greatest influence. Stern and uncompromising in his demands for perfection and progress, the doctor worried about his son and tried to cajole him to make something of himself. In young George's numerous escapades and adventures, the father sometimes must have wondered to what end the Dewey strain was heading.

Born at Berlin, Vermont, eight miles south of Montpelier, on August 22, 1801, Julius Yemans Dewey's earliest memories went back to the days of Jefferson's Presidency. He fought the War of 1812 with his schoolmates, using shingle-frigates in the quarry ponds around the village. He learned his three R's in the village schools and later studied medicine at the University of Vermont at Montpelier, where for three years he taught school to support himself while completing his professional courses. In 1824 he began the practice of medicine, and married, after a two-year engagement, Mary Perrin, his childhood sweetheart of Berlin, who had attended Emma Willard's school in Middlebury, Vermont. In the little white-shingled house across from the statehouse, Julius and Mary began their married life, he to drive a buggy through the muds of spring and the snows of winter to minister to the sick, she to raise a family of four, cook and mend, and die from tuberculosis at the age of forty-four.

Two years after George was born, Mrs. Dewey had her fourth child, whom she named Mary Perrin Dewey. She was George's playmate and the adoring younger sister who helped in all his pranks and projects.

Inculcated with the religious fervor of old New England, Dr. Julius and Mary led a quiet, fruitful life. Grace before every meal and prayers and hymns every Sunday evening were the rule. Dr. Dewey, whose long sideburns and high forehead reminded one of Daniel Webster, led the singing, a hymnal in one hand, his glasses in the other, ready if he should forget the well-known words. The neighbors used to come in for those Sunday vespers and stand in the drafty parlor while Mrs. Dewey thrummed out "Rock of Ages" on the organ. The doctor and his friends were Episcopalians, but Montpelier had no Episcopalian church until after George was born. Under his father's leadership, funds were raised and a frame building erected which became Christ Episcopal Church. It was being built when Mrs. Dewey fell ill; six months later she died, and hers was the first funeral held in the new chapel.*

Four children and a thriving medical practice needed a woman's help. Two years later Dr. Dewey married Mrs. Susan Edson Tarbox, a widow with a daughter, Betsey. A romance developed between Betsey and George's oldest brother, Charles, and they were married in 1848.

There was a curious repetition in life for the Dewey family. Dr. Dewey's second wife died September 11, 1854. In March of the next year he married another widow, Mrs. Susan Elizabeth Griggs Lilley, of Worcester, Massachusetts. Her daughter married the doctor's second son in 1858, and became Mrs. Edward Dewey.

Dr. Dewey, feeling the need of more financial security for his family, in 1850 helped form the National Life Insurance Company with other Montpelier businessmen. First as medical examiner and then as president,

*Adelbert Dewey, in glowing praise of Dewey's mother and her brief but vital influence upon her son, says: "Her spirit still lives to bless mankind. Her contribution to the welfare of humanity, in the son who has earned the right to so warm a place in the affections of the American people, is not a small one: and a people would be ungrateful indeed who did not accord to her, equally with her husband, a place in the pages of history as the mother of such a man as Admiral George Dewey."

he built the new enterprise into a prosperous institution. Charles succeeded his father as president upon the latter's death in 1877, while Edward became vice-president.

Dr. Dewey was surgeon of the First Regiment of the Vermont militia during the Civil War, an honorarium awarded him by Governor Crafts, wartime governor of the state.

Throughout the years of his practice as a doctor and his presidency of the National Life, Dr. Dewey exercised considerable influence in Vermont politics. Respected by his townspeople and influential with the bankers, he became one of Vermont's first citizens. He backed railroad plans, new hotels, schools, and libraries in upper Vermont.

Although half-orphaned at the age of five, George Dewey, with a stepmother coming into the house soon after his mother's death, did not lack maternal care. However, some psychic feeling of loss must have been present, for between father and son there grew an intimacy unusual in its effect.

In his autobiography George Dewey paid tribute to his father: "To my father's influence in my early training I owe, primarily, all that I have accomplished in the world. From him I inherited a vigorous constitution and an active temperament. He was a good deal more than a successful practicing physician. He was one of those natural leaders to whom men turn for unbiased advice. His ideas of right and wrong were very fixed, in keeping with his deep religious scruples."

On Dr. Dewey's knee young George sat by the hour to hear fairy tales, poems, and stories from the Bible that made him into a God-fearing man. By precept and moral lectures, the father sowed the lessons which abided with his son.

Perhaps because his own mother was gone, young George liked one poem of his father's recitations more than any other. It was called "The Poor Little Child of a Tar," and George would call for it again and again. Perhaps the suffering in the poem released a flood of emotion for another's sorrow that made it almost a pleasure to grieve.

According to his sister, the poem aroused alternating emotions of fear, distress, and joy. It was less noted for its literary merit than for turning his eyes to the sea.

> In a little blue garment, all ragged and torn,
> With scarce any shoes to his feet;
> His head all uncovered, a look quite forlorn,
> And a cold, stony step for his seat—

A boy cheerless sat, and as travelers passed,
With a look that might avarice bar,
"Have pity," he cried, "let your bounty be cast
On a poor little child of a tar.

No mother have I and no friends can I claim,
Deserted and cheerless I roam;
My father has fought for his country and fame,
But alas, he may never come home.

By cruelty driven from a neat, rural cot,
Where once in contentment she dwelt,
No friend to protect her, my poor mother's lot
Alas! too severely she felt.

Bowed down by misfortune, Death called her his own,
And snatched her to regions afar;
Deserted and friendless I was then left to roam,
The poor little child of a tar.

Thus plaintive he cried, when a traveler who passed,
Stopped a moment to give him relief;
He stretched forth his hand, and a look on him cast,
A look of wonder and grief.

"What my Willie," he cried, "my poor little boy,
At last I've returned from the war.
Thy sorrows shall cease, nor grief more annoy
The poor little child of a tar."

The legends growing out of George Dewey's youth described him as a harum-scarum lad, a rogue, a daredevil, and a wild young fellow who never gave his teachers a moment's peace. The autobiography of Dewey furthered these impressions.*

"Certainly I was full of animal spirits, and I liked things to happen wherever I was," he wrote. "Probably I had a gift for stirring up the other boys to help me in my enterprises. . . . My memory has kept no account of the number of boyish battles that I was in. . . . One of my favorite deeds of bravado was descending the old statehouse steps blindfolded, with the onlookers wondering whether I would slip on the way and take the rest of the flight head first."

Coasting down the hills on sleds and cake pans was one of the favorite sports of his boyhood. From Seminary Hill to the statehouse a mile-long hill descended; the boys and girls navigated it with whoops and shrieks.

*It is curious how the wording of many passages in the autobiography follows so closely the phrases of eulogistic volumes on Dewey published in 1899.

Behind the state capitol another hill, shorter but steeper, frightened all but the more daring. This was "a favorite spot for the hero of Manila and such of his associates as dared to follow his lead," wrote Adelbert Dewey in 1899.

All the other sports common to boys were followed in Montpelier during the 1840's: marbles, track, tree-climbing, boxing, swimming, ice-skating, and a dozen more.

The convening of the state legislature was a big event in Montpelier. On that day the representatives assembled, stormed the streets, and went into the back rooms for the organizational parleys. Gingerbread and sweet cider were sold on the streets. The boys of Montpelier and nearby towns gathered, too, and with them strength was tested by fists. For Dewey and his friends the honor of Montpelier was at stake, and the boys of town and country would indulge in battles to find out who was best. Dr. Dewey had a busy half hour on some of those days.

Dewey was a good swimmer, he admitted in his autobiography. One contest which established his mettle was an endurance race under water. Another boy having beaten his record, George dove into a pool in the Onion River one summer afternoon to rewin the crown. He stayed underwater so long his companions became panicky and cried for help. Some men nearby dashed to the scene, dove in, and pulled George out, purple in the face and breathing hard, but able to gasp: "Did I break the record?"

When he was ten Dewey turned to the stage. It came as a natural development of his desire for prestige and prowess.

In the barn behind the Dewey house he rigged up a theater, with a buffalo robe for a curtain and the usual pins for admission. George acted as producer, director, stage manager, and matinee idol. One day the ten-year-old heroine was sick with a cold, but true to the tradition that the show must go on, George forced his sister Mary to play the role. She did not know the lines and was petrified at appearing on the stage, but George insisted. Whenever she forgot a line, he pulled out his trusty six-shooter cap pistol and fired a couple of blanks into the hayloft; the confusion of gunsmoke covered up the lapse. The young audience thought the play the best of the season, but the neighbors complained, and the Dewey theater had to be "closed for alterations," some of them possibly to George's posterior.

The same year George was given a book on Hannibal for Christmas. With his father's cows for elephants and a snowpile for the Alps, the Carthaginian wars were fought again. The boys of the neighborhood participated in those battles, but if they had to stay home to do the chores, Mary was drafted as the army of Carthage and struggled behind

George "Hannibal" up the snow-covered hills. One afternoon's campaign put her in bed for a week with a cold, but the casualty scarcely bothered the "general," who directed his unusually fertile talents to other projects.

Guns and explosives fascinated George. When he was twelve Montpelier was celebrating the seventy-fourth Independence Day in the town square. A War of 1812 cannon was installed and primed to administer the final flourish. Montpelier's leading orator had just finished reading the Declaration of Independence, and the selected committee stood by to fire the old eighteen-pounder. George was right up in the thick of excitement waiting for the explosion. When it went off, the gun must have gone with it, for George wound up on his back, his face black with powder.

On another occasion he was showing some friends how his father split maple logs for the fireplace with a charge of powder. This was strictly against regulations, since only Dr. Dewey was allowed to use this method. George bored a hole in a knotty log, inserted some powder and lighted the fuse. Something went wrong. There was a hangfire, and after a minute the boys began to edge up to see what was happening. George, the expert, ordered them back. "First thing you know you'll be killed," he shouted. Instead, he crept close, poked a stick into the hole, and the log blew up in smoke. So did George. His clothes were ablaze. Fortunately, a few feet away stood a sunken barrel used as a watering trough for the cows. George dove into it and came up a minute later drenched but safe.

In his early fights young Dewey demonstrated two characteristics that grew with the years: exceptional personal bravery and an acute sense of justice. Dewey's son, George Goodwin Dewey, said, "Father was always for the underdog. When he saw a horse being mistreated in Washington, he fairly boiled with rage and wanted to whale the unfair owner."

A French-Canadian boy of Montpelier recalled how young Dewey had demanded fair play and even terms whenever anyone molested the French Catholics in the town. Protestant-Catholic tension was common in 1840 and a "Canuck" walking home from school alone was often pounced on by two or three boys. Dewey did not mind a fight but he insisted that attackers come on one at a time. His early hero-worshiping of Ethan Allen and Hannibal made force seem logical as the arbiter of disagreement.

In 1849, at the age of twelve, Dewey studied his Greek verbs and Latin declensions with all the impatience of any boy. At the Montpelier district school he was as adept as any at hiding a thriller behind his big geography or shooting paper wads across the room. In fact, he earned the reputation of being the leader of the boys' underground movement which caused teachers to come and go with appalling regularity.

The newest dominie of the term, an undersized pedagogue of ninety pounds, named Z. K. Pangborn, maintained his authority for the first week, but he had his eye on Dewey, for he "was one of the boldest and brightest of the younger lads, and above all things loved a fight. He was ever looking for trouble, and while there was nothing you could call bad about him, he resented authority and evinced a sturdy determination not to submit to it unless it suited him."

The crisis came after lunch one brilliant day in the winter term. George decided the snow made too good packing to return to school. A messenger from Pangborn found him in the cupola of the old state-house pegging snowballs at the passers-by.

"The teacher says you've got to come back to school, George," the boy called up to him.

"You tell that teacher to go to the devil," was the reply, and an iced snowball chased the lad back to school. Up there in the dome of the great edifice it was easy to denounce authority.

Such rebellion called for action. Dismissing school early, Pangborn set out to quell the uprising. Standing under the dome, dodging snowballs, the teacher ordered the truant to come down.

This time the reply was even hotter.

"Oh, go to hell."

Dewey had deployed his comrades into a smart military ambuscade: some pelted the master from the roof, while the right wing, concealed in the bushes, charged him from the rear, bowled him over, and washed his face in the snow. Mr. Pangborn limped back to the schoolroom after dark, placed a rawhide whip over the door, and hid a few stout sticks of wood under the desk.

The next morning the revolt seemed to have died down. George and his army came into school smiling superciliously. The enemy was beaten, they thought, and they were prepared to enjoy the rest of the term at his expense.

Instead the dominie thundered out, "Dewey, come here." With "a sassy twinkle in his eyes," George sauntered up to the desk. Pangborn unleashed a blistering oration, winding up with an uncompromising demand for complete apology. Dewey laughed and insulted him again.

A second later the rawhide whip cut through the air, and raised welts on Dewey's back. In another moment he was on the floor, a heap of pained schoolboy. The other boys, cowed only briefly, sized up their little schoolmaster, so thin and weak, and seven of them charged him to

26

avenge their fallen leader. Pangborn grabbed a stick of wood, slashed at the first attacker, knocked him down, and ended the insurrection. Judged by modern standards, this was astounding punishment. But that was the day of the spare-the-rod-and-spoil-the-child theory. Pangborn was not the only country schoolmaster who had to use force to keep his pupils in line.

Dewey was taken home by the wrathful teacher, and the two of them argued their cases before Dr. Dewey. At the end a compromise was reached. The old doctor promised that if any more punishment were needed, it would be meted out only at home. Meanwhile, George would be back at school the next day. Then in a private conference with Pangborn Dr. Dewey chastised him severely for his brutalities and secured his promise that in the future order would be maintained by less drastic means.

There was no more serious trouble for Mr. Pangborn that year. Instead, he made a friend and a better student of George. The next year, when the teacher moved to a new school in nearby Johnson, Vermont, George followed him. He saw what Pangborn had to offer—instruction and authority that Dewey could respect, the authority of might and force.

"I shall never cease to be grateful to you," he told Pangborn during the Civil War. "You made a man of me. But for that thrashing you gave me in Montpelier, I should probably ere this have been in state prison."

In his thirteenth spring, while driving home from school at Johnson, Dewey lost his father's buggy. The Onion River was in flood, as it had been for days, but on this particular afternoon it seemed silly to go around by the bridge, and George whipped his horse into a gallop to ford the river. In the middle, the rushing current swept over the floorboards, capsized the vehicle, and dumped the driver into the stream. Hanging on to the reins, he managed to follow his horse to the other bank. The buggy smashed to pieces on the rocks.

It was an expensive rig, and when George's stepmother saw him straggling into the yard, wet and frozen, she decided bed was the best place for him, to protect him from pneumonia and his father's wrath. When Dr. Dewey came home he lectured George sharply, emphasizing that he would never amount to anything. From under the patchwork quilt, his unrepentant son replied:

"You ought to be thankful that I'm alive, and not scold me because I didn't get drowned."

But, although he could answer back with words, fighting was George's real forte. His grades in school and his intellectual interests scarcely promised that he would follow his father's steps. The experience of Mr. Pangborn, who won respect through the use of rawhide, may have influenced

27

Dr. Dewey to complete the education of his son at a military academy.

Then, too, green hills were too confining for George. He dreamed of campaigns against the Indians in the West, of Zachary Taylor and his son-in-law Jefferson Davis on the plains of Buena Vista, of Winfield Scott and the heroes of the Alamo. It would be West Point and a hero's life for him.

George fell in readily with his father's plans, and in the fall of 1852 he entered Norwich University,* on the banks of the Connecticut River. It had been founded in 1818 by Captain Alden Partridge, former superintendent at West Point, as the American, Literary, Scientific and Military Academy. In 1834 Captain Partridge changed the name to Norwich University, but it had remained a military academy. When Dewey entered the school was in the doldrums. An Irish priest was its president, and the academy consisted principally of two brick barracks and a parade ground. Fireplace heat, walls of "brindle" whitewash, slat-bottomed bunks, and rough pine dressers and desks provided all the discomforts necessary to military training.

Dewey remained there two years, distinguishing himself less by his classwork than by his extracurricular activities. One of these took place in the traditional "battle of the torn coats" with the boys of Dartmouth College. One night the Norwich men crossed the Connecticut River and invaded Hanover, New Hampshire. Although outnumbered, with Dewey in their van, they scored a signal victory and returned to study their *Scott's Infantry Tactics* the next morning with only about half as many bashed heads and torn coats as they had left in Hanover.

Another adventure took him into court. As Norwich was a Congregational town, academy commencements had been held for many years in the Congregational Church. But the academy masters (like Dewey) were Episcopalians. In 1854 the fervor of holy war brought the elders of the church to suggest that the school find a quiet meadow for its graduation services. This was done, but the students did not like it.

Reprisals became noticeable. One Sunday morning the congregation found a white horse tied to the altar. Once the deacon was burned in effigy. Another night Dewey and four other academy youths were walking past the church when they heard the singing of hymns. It occurred to one of the cadets that the hymns should stop. So the quintet crept under the stained-glass windows and began to sing lustily negro spirituals and several distinctly unreligious songs. The church meeting was broken up all right, but the boys were haled into court at Woodstock, Vermont.

*In 1899 Norwich University, in the full flush of Dewey's success, raised funds to erect Dewey Hall.

As Woodstock was nearly twenty miles away, it necessitated an overnight trip which George's funds could not stand. After a week of brooding, he screwed up his courage to confess and ask his father for money. The money came back by return mail, but Dewey recalled that the doctor's accompanying letter was "rather tart." "In the start of my educational career away from home I had accomplished more than he had expected," his autobiography stated. "Indeed, I had made such progress that he was convinced that I needed no further education, and my evident knowledge of the ways of the world should make me equal to undertaking the battle of life at once."

But the court trial resulted in a dismissal of the charges. The judge saw the humor of the prank if the townspeople had not. To Dewey this had been just a natural bit of mischief to blow off steam accumulated by hard work, strict discipline, and no relaxation. As a naval officer, he later won a name for tolerance and consideration of enlisted men who had reacted the same way to long months at sea with no amusements.

Like the Woodstock judge, Dr. Dewey relented too. George wanted to go to West Point. But he did not win the Vermont billet to the military academy.

"Competitive examinations were not yet the rule in choosing candidates for either West Point or Annapolis," he wrote later. "Appointments were due entirely to the political favour of representatives in Congress. There was no vacancy for West Point from Vermont. Otherwise I might have gone into Manila Bay on an Army transport instead of on the *Olympia*."

If he could not be an Andrew Jackson or a Winfield Scott, he would be a John Paul Jones. Dr. Dewey used his political influence with Senator Foote of Montpelier. The Senator was already committed to one of Dewey's classmates, George Spaulding of Montpelier, and named Dewey alternate.

Then fate stepped in. Spaulding's mother did not want her boy to be a sailor, and persuaded him to withdraw and enter the ministry instead. The Navy notified George Dewey, aged seventeen, that he had been accepted as a midshipman at Annapolis.

It was the same year that Matthew Calbraith Perry and the steam frigate *Mississippi* were in Tokyo Bay, trading diplomatic tricks with the Japanese and preparing to open up that mysterious land to the Western World.

The hills had flattened out. The world was calling, and George Dewey packed his schoolbooks and his bell-bottom cadet pants with their black velvet seams.

3

IRON ON WATER WILL FLOAT

In the beginning man swam across lakes and ponds with only a fallen log to aid his crossing. Then wiser men hollowed out trees to build canoes and used animal-skin sails.

Sir Francis Drake, Lord Howard, and their enemy Dons drove the armadas of 1588 with wind power. Although improvements were made in sails and rigging, the American Revolutionary War and the War of 1812 were fought in fundamentally the same type of ships.

In Scotland James Watts made an astounding discovery. By heating water above the boiling point, he developed steam pressure that could turn a wheel. That was in 1770. Nothing happened about it for several decades. Finally, however, in the new world, Robert R. Livingston and Robert Fulton made a successful application of Watts' steam engine. They installed it in the *Clermont,* and the first steamboat chugged from Albany to New York in 1807.

Meanwhile experimentation was being conducted to make ships of iron. In the latter part of the eighteenth century an Englishman named Cort invented a process for rolling iron plate. Iron barges were built in 1787 and 1789 for canal traffic in England.* In 1818 the barge *Vulcan* was launched into the Clyde River near Glasgow. In 1824 the British Horsely Company constructed the first true iron steamship, the *Aron Manby,* which made the first oceangoing passage from London to Le Havre.

But iron was viewed with suspicion by the admiralties of the world. Despite the practical use of iron ships in English canal traffic and the developments in the power of guns, navy departments hesitated to armor their ships. It was 1855 before the French demonstrated, in the Crimean War, that ships could be armor-plated to resist shellfire. From then on the development of "ironclads" became more rapid. And yet George

*William Fairbarn, *A Treatise on Iron Shipbuilding* (London: Longmans, Green & Co., 1865).

30

Dewey fought the Battle of Manila Bay with wooden logs fastened outside some of his ships to protect their unarmored hulls from shells.

Steam and iron had no bearing on the War of 1812. But the need for invention to prosecute the conflict, as it has in all wars, accelerated scientific progress. Robert Fulton persuaded the Navy Department to build a steam warship. As a result, the first steamer, the *Fulton,* was begun, although it was not launched until after Fulton's death in 1815, and long after the peace treaty.

The first *Fulton* was an odd craft, built in two hulls with a mammoth paddle wheel between. Coal engines and boilers, in the catamaran hulls beneath the water line, moved clumsy gears to turn the paddle wheel like a mill wheel. Low in the water and with massive wooden sides, the *Fulton* was in many respects the ancestor of the *Monitor* of the Civil War.

Even when the *Fulton* was completed, men failed to realize that it had doomed the sailing ship in war. Captain David Porter, the *Fulton's* first commanding officer, insisted that masts and sails be installed to power the "freak." Until long after the Civil War steamboats were powered by auxiliary sails, for breakdowns were common.

The first *Fulton* did not impress the Navy Department. After a few cruises along the coast, it was turned into a receiving ship at Brooklyn, where it blew up in 1829.

But pioneers made some progress. A second steamer, the *Sea Gull,* was soon built and was called a steam galiot.* It was the first steamship of any Navy to engage in action, when it fought the Caribbean pirates in 1823.

Other developments were beginning to revolutionize naval warfare. From the days of the Spanish Armada in 1588 through the American Revolution, the days of Lord Nelson, and the War of 1812, guns had been loaded from the muzzle, or firing end. On shipboard this caused one grave inconvenience: the guns had to be mounted on rollers so they could be backed inboard while men rammed in gunpowder and cannon balls. This meant that guns could not be based solidly, and accuracy was impaired. Another drawback of the muzzle-loading gun was that it necessitated a smoothbore. Rifling was out of the question, even if it had been conceived. With a smoothbore cannon, balls wobbled in their flight and did not realize their potential concussive power on impact with their objective.

As early as 1742 Benjamin Robbins, an Englishman, wrote a treatise, *New Principles of Gunnery,* urging the rifling of cannon to overcome

*Since the steamer had no sails and was propelled by paddles, it was called a galiot, the name of the oared galleys in the Mediterranean before the time of Christ.

the latter weakness, but it was impossible to accomplish so long as muzzle-loading was the only method used.

During the Revolutionary War guns fired eighteen- or twenty-four-pound projectiles, and by 1815 the navies of the world had some guns that fired forty-two-pound shot.

It was in 1821 that a French artillery officer developed a gun embodying principles still used in modern war. That year Henri Paixhans wrote a document entitled *La Nouvelle Arme*. He urged the abandonment of solid shot for explosive shells. Paixhans constructed a gun on this principle more deadly than any ever known before.

The original Paixhans gun was of 8.6-inch caliber; it was 9.3 feet long and weighed 7,400 pounds. A charge of gunpowder, varying from ten and a half to eighteen pounds, made up its firing charge. Its projectile, used only in mortars until then, was a shell that would explode on contact. The original Paixhans projectile weighed about sixty pounds.* It was quickly adopted by the French Navy and soon proved its worth. Three years later General Paixhans prophesied that his explosive shell would ultimately necessitate the armoring of ships.† In 1841 he drew up plans to armor French men-of-war, but they were rejected.

The Paixhans gun, although no more accurate than earlier ones, was many times as destructive. In the United States the Navy experimented with this weapon and with methods to increase the accuracy of cannon. Flintlocks had been used for generations to fire guns. They were installed in many batteries, even up to 1840. In 1828 the Navy installed percussion locks to fire the guns of the U.S.S. *Vandalia,* with satisfactory results. After 1801 fixed sights on guns began to appear. Until then it had been "by guess and by God," as grimy tars looked over the top of a gun to determine if it were trained on its target. Even with fixed sights, gunners had to estimate the distance of the enemy and decide whether to aim the permanent sights at the skysails, the truck, or the top of the Charley Noble pipe.

In 1836, the year before George Dewey was born, a German, Johann N. Dreyse, invented the Prussian Needle gun, which made practical for the first time the principle of breech loading. Nineteen years later in England,

---

*By way of comparison, modern 16-inch naval rifles throw a projectile weighing about 2,400 pounds, while their powder charge alone weighs around 667 pounds.

†At the same time he advocated that the largest possible caliber of guns be used and that all guns on any one ship be of the same size. It was not until 1906, when the revolutionary British warship *Dreadnought* was constructed, that this principle was followed. The *Dreadnought*, because of its radicalism, made all existing ships virtually obsolete. England's numerical superiority no longer counted. This put Germany and England on an equal footing, since Germany could produce new ships as rapidly as England could. Von Tirpitz was quick to take advantage of this, and Germany rushed into rivalry with England for domination of the seas.

W. G. Armstrong and Sir Joseph Whitworth developed the principles in a gun which has not been radically changed to this day.

The French continued their experiments and in the Crimean War used a primitive type of rifle which proved disastrous to enemy armor. This was a 6.5-inch, cast-iron rifle, which, although a muzzle loader, had a spiraled bore. Studded shells were twisted back to the firing charge. When they came out spinning, they went straighter, faster, and landed with more destructiveness.

Paixhans' prophecy that ships would need armor was ready to come true. In 1856 Henry Bessemer invented his revolutionary process of converting iron into steel. It would be twenty years before steel replaced wood for ships generally, but in 1859 Napoleon III built the first ironclad frigate. Stanislas Dupuy de Lome was its designer, a man whose name ranks with the foremost marine architects of history.

The age of steel was at hand. In 1862 the German Krupp works constructed a cast-steel breech-loading gun. The French and British used this type at the time, but fatal accidents in firing became so commonplace that only the Germans retained the principle.

During the American Civil War about one third of the Union ships were rifled, while the Dahlgren and Rodman smoothbores, built up of forged steel, fought most of the battles at sea.

The period of the 1830's was one of constant experiment in steam and gunnery. The second steamer *Fulton* was built and commanded by Matthew Calbraith Perry, one of America's outstanding naval heroes and a brother of Oliver Hazard Perry who fought his way to fame on Lake Erie in 1813. Armed with Paixhans-type shell guns, the *Fulton* was nothing more than a harbor gun-platform, but its accomplishments in target practice would have impressed anyone save the old captains of the War of 1812, for whom sailing power was the end-all of naval might.

The second *Fulton* was only an experiment. At the time it was completed, four sailing ships were also constructed, and work was underway on thirteen other ships of sail. The *North Carolina*, first of the old-fashioned battleships, carried 102 smoothbores in its three gun decks and was the wonder ship of the world. Two other "line-of-battle" ships were also constructed during the period, the *Delaware* and the *Ohio*.

As time headed toward the climax of the Civil War, the United States Navy slowed its progress. The skippers who had sailed against England grew old. Their midshipmen and lieutenants passed into their thirties without promotion, and enthusiasm and ability declined. Only Matthew Perry exemplified the spirit of progress and foresight. In 1838 he began to agitate anew for more steam boats to bring the Navy to the fore. In

1840, after the election of William H. Harrison and John Tyler, the Navy built a few coal-burning vessels. One of them, the iron-hulled *Princeton*, was designed by Robert F. Stockton, U.S.N., and John Ericcson, a Swede whose genius made perhaps the greatest single contribution to naval development. In 1836 John Stevens invented the screw-propeller principle for driving ships, and the *Princeton* became the first screw-propelled ship in the American Navy. With twelve traditional forty-two-pounders on the gun deck, she was also equipped with a pair of Paixhans guns designed by Stockton and Ericcson. They were gigantic, twelve-inch calibered weapons, more deadly than any installed before. President Tyler and his cabinet inspected the *Princeton* in 1844 and marveled at it and its twelve guns. One of them was fired, for the edification of the statesmen, and exploded, killing the Secretary of State, the Secretary of the Navy, and several Congressmen. Naval progress was postponed.

Another of the revolutionary steam frigates built in the Tyler administration was the *Union*, with paddle wheels which churned on the horizontal.

The third of the ships was the *Mississippi*, rated as a ten-gun steam frigate, with great paddle wheels on either side and a smokestack just aft of amidships that reached almost as high as her three masts. A high overhanging bow and gun ports on the battery deck made the *Mississippi* look like the frigate *Constitution*, except for her black funnel belching smoke into the sky.

The *Mississippi* was a revolutionary and historic ship, identified forever with two great men and two great episodes: Matthew Perry and George Dewey, and the opening of Japan and the conquest of the Mississippi River in the Civil War.

During the 1840's America began to open up vast markets in the Orient. Trade with China boomed, as did commerce with all the world. Between 1846 and 1860 foreign trade more than trebled, from $235,000,000 in the first year to $762,000,000 on the eve of civil conflict. The expansion of Oriental markets was a constant spur to Yankee clippermen and American investors. The prospects in China made the country anxious to find other lucrative fields for commerce. Off the Chinese coast extended a mysterious archipelago inhabited by Orientals who remained a complete enigma to the outside world. To expand American markets the Navy resolved to open this land of Nippon to commercialism. In 1846 Commodore James Biddle tried to open trade relations with shadowy Japan. Three years later Commander James Glynn was dispatched there to secure the release of several American seamen imprisoned by the Mikado. Glynn was firm and successful, and, what was more important, he penetrated the veiled

Japanese psychology in a manner that was to be utilized in the future.

Commodore Matthew Calbraith Perry was selected for the final diplomatic assault upon the inviolability of Japan. In 1853, with an imposing squadron made up of the *Mississippi, Susquehanna, Saratoga,* and *Plymouth,* he sailed into Yeddo (Tokyo) Bay. Perry was greeted with misgiving and reserved cordiality. He carried, in a fancy carved box, a letter to the Mikado from President Millard Fillmore. When a vice-governor came aboard his ship to receive the letter, Perry sent a lieutenant to discuss the situation with him. That impressed the Japanese, who was told that the commander of the fleet was too exalted to parley with anyone below a prince. The next day Perry allowed two commanders to speak with the governor, and after elaborate preparations had been made and special buildings constructed ashore, the commodore deigned to set foot on land. With Marines lined up on both sides of the pavilion, Perry conferred with the Prince of Iwami, and gave him the President's letter to the Emperor. Meanwhile the *Mississippi* made soundings of Tokyo Bay to impress the Nipponese.

Eight months later, in February, 1854, Perry returned with an increased squadron, composed of the *Mississippi, Susquehanna, Powhatan, Vandalia, Southampton,* and *Lexington.* This time the Japanese had four princes on hand to treat with the haughty American personage. After lengthy deliberations the ports of Hakodate and Shamoda were opened to American commerce.

On March 31 the parleys were ended, and the American officers entertained the Japanese commissioners with a gala party aboard the *Powhatan.* Full honors for their rank were extended and gifts were exchanged. The first American luxuries ever imported into Japan, and given by Commodore Perry to the princes of the realm, included revolvers, wine, whisky, plows, perfumery, a telescope, and Irish potatoes. The princes were most impressed by seeing demonstrations of the telegraph and of a railroad system set up on shore. Feudalism and the industrial revolution had come face to face.

In the spring of 1854 the paddle-wheeler *Mississippi* headed home from the historic mission. It was the same spring that George Dewey of Montpelier, Vermont, was accepted as a student at the Naval Academy of the United States.

4

MIDSHIPMAN DEWEY

$\mathcal{T}$he American Navy was becalmed in the 1840's. Men of 1812, grown fat with years, still ran the show. Young men who had entered the service to emulate the gallantries of the Decaturs, Hulls, and Stewarts found a Navy at peace scarcely the place for a career. Young midshipmen grew old in the forecastle, becoming hardened and more coarse with every year as they lived their lives in the company of enlisted crews.

The explosion of the *Princeton's* guns in 1844, killing Secretary of State Abel Upshur and Secretary of the Navy Thomas Gilmer, provided no impetus for progress. In March James K. Polk entered the White House. For the portfolio of the Navy he appointed George Bancroft—later the eminent historian of the United States—an administrator of vision, alert to the progress of science, and aghast at the incompetence present in the service. Like Perry, who instituted cruises to improve the training of new sailors, Bancroft determined to bring modern ideas into the service.

It was no easy task. The *Princeton* explosion had aroused the wrath of Congress, which would do nothing for the fleet, but Bancroft could not be stopped. He borrowed the old Army barracks at Fort Severn in Maryland, cleaned them up, and started a Naval Academy. Compared to West Point, which had operated for decades, the academy at Annapolis was a sorry stepchild. Only three midshipmen entered its opening sessions in October, 1845. Commander Franklin Buchanan was the first superintendent. To him, as to Bancroft, goes much of the glory for establishing an enlightened officer class. As ships put into port, Bancroft transferred midshipmen to old Fort Severn. Many of them had been at sea for years, and to be brought back on land for "training" made them resentful to the point of rebellion. The new midshipmen were, on the whole, little better. As congressional appointees to a little-known institution, they were likely to reflect all the ills of political patronage. Buchanan and Bancroft changed that. The superintendent ruled with an iron hand, enforced tight discipline, and summarily dismissed any wayward cadet. Unpopular as this was with the midshipmen's political sponsors, the dismissals were sustained by Bancroft.

In a few years the attitude toward Annapolis began to change. The growth of steam power, the development of gunnery, and the coming age of science made men aware that officers needed more intellectual training than they could receive at sea.

To Bancroft and Buchanan, the caliber of the new officers who had lived so long in forecastles seemed on the decline. To the men of 1812, fighting and military leadership had seemed the important qualities of a naval officer. To the newer officers, seamanship meant much, for the Navy, untested in war, had almost come to be a merchant fleet with its guns never called into use.

The words of John Paul Jones, lying in a lost grave in Paris during the middle of the nineteenth century, came back with renewed vigor: "It is by no means enough that an officer of the Navy should be a capable mariner." Yet few heeded his words. The academy was founded despite the opposition of Congress and a large portion of the public who regarded armies and navies as potential usurpers of free government, to be born, Athena-like, after war had been declared, and disbanded immediately with the peace.

In September of 1854, the same year that the Crimean War broke out and the month that his first stepmother died, George Dewey, a dark-haired youth of seventeen, left Montpelier with his father on a fateful trip. Dr. Julius Yemans Dewey took his youngest son away from Vermont on the little train down to New York City. There they stopped overnight at the Irving House, on Broadway, opposite the A. T. Stewart department store, which impressed the country boy so much he remembered it sixty years afterward.

The Deweys went to the theater that night to see a comedy. Young George had never seen anything like it, and with his usual lack of inhibition laughed so loudly that his conservative father escorted him abruptly from the theater.

The next day they took a steamer from the Hudson River docks to Perth Amboy. On the sea for the first time in his life, George watched the great paddle wheels churn the waters off New York, saw the black smoke belch from the smokestacks, and felt beneath his feet the exciting motion of the waves upon which he would chart his life. Dewey, with the fuzz just growing on his healthy cheeks, and clad in his tight new shoes and his tight tweed suit, walked up and down the decks, watched the steersman in the pilothouse turn the ship, ran below deck to see the bulky, reciprocating power plant turning ponderously, and stared curiously at the black-faced, sweating coalers who pitched coal into the furnaces.

At Perth Amboy they boarded another steam train for Philadelphia, and rode through that city behind a team of horses before another engine picked them up at the outskirts of Havre de Grace. Luncheon on a ferry across the Susquehanna River was the first of countless meals at sea. Another horse-drawn train took them through the main street of Baltimore, as the conductor blew a horn to scatter pedestrians from the rails. It required twelve hours to go from New York to Annapolis, but every minute of it was a new adventure to the young midshipman entering his government's service.

At Annapolis George took entrance examinations with some sixty other boys. Perhaps his father was pleasantly surprised when his son passed them adequately, for he waited at the old barracks while George took the tests in English grammar, writing, and mathematics.

Then Dr. Dewey started home to his dying wife, with these final words of wisdom for his son: "George, I've done all I can for you. The rest you must do for yourself." There was a note of concern in that advice. Probably Dr. Dewey was thinking of the whipping by Mr. Pangborn in Montpelier and the court appearance in Woodstock. Righteous and conservative as the Admiral was to grow in later years, there was a quality in his youth that must have disturbed his elders. His marks had never been very good in school, and he had come home with more torn clothes and blackened eyes than most boys of his circle.

The advice had its effect, however.

"I have always tried to keep it in mind," Dewey wrote years afterward. When he was commissioned a lieutenant in 1860, third in his class, he took pride in telling his father that he had "done 'the rest' reasonably well."*

The first ironclad ships in the world were withstanding a withering Russian fire with impunity in the Crimean War when George unpacked his clothes in the Fort Severn barracks and began his life as a midshipman, U.S.N. In a room for two he learned to make his own bed, swab the "decks," and polish his buttons with almost religious fervor. Negro charwomen came in to clean, but the midshipmen were responsible for daily inspections to see that not a speck of dust existed.

George was initiated into a new world: hazing, men from the South

*George Dewey, *Autobiography of George Dewey, The Admiral of the Navy* (New York: Charles Scribner's Sons, 1916), pp. 12–14, 39.

who looked with scorn on Vermont "Yankees," boat drills and differential calculus, foreign languages and Navy regulation, that kept him hopping every hour of the day, maddened his youthful desire for fun and frolic, and found him at the end of his plebe year just barely staying in school.

In that first year Dewey went through a period of hazing that caused him to tell his own son, half a century afterward, that Annapolis had just been "hell and discipline." Study and military drill were pounded into him until he often wondered why he had selected a naval life. Greek, Roman, and European history, French, algebra, and geometry filled an endless round of class work from eight in the morning till the evening hours.

"I was very poor in history and geography but excellent in mathematics, which pulled me through," he reported.* There were no organized athletics in Dewey's time except regular military drill and parade sentences around the grounds. Dewey had more than his share of these, for in his first year alone his love of fun brought him a total of 113 demerits. Since two hundred meant dismissal from the Academy, he had to settle down later on to overcome this start. There were no week ends for the cadets. "Stag hops" on Saturday nights were intended to fulfill their craving for social life and amusement, but they hardly satisfied young George.

He suffered most from the indignities of hazing. When he became Admiral of the Navy, he inveighed against the practice and instituted steps to cut it down. Nevertheless, he took it with good grace, and no evidence exists to show that he failed to avail himself of its privileges as an upperclassman.

Dewey, a bit nervous, headed for the chapel one Sunday morning to sing a solo part in the choir. A third classman hailed him as he passed the latter's room and invited him inside for a "drink of lemonade."

Dewey took a big drink of the cool liquid and gasped. It was filled with a strong solution of alum. The upperclassmen expected a burst of profanity, but Dewey's mouth was too dry to say a word. He made a hurried exit.

The story spread. Cadets crowded into the chapel to see the fun. When the choir sang and Dewey's solo came, he stood up, opened his mouth, and in a strong, clear voice sang the hymn.

At noon chow, however, Dewey was a silent man. The alum still robbed him of his voice.

Many days later the hazers learned Dewey had persuaded one of his

*George Dewey, *op. cit.*, p. 19.

classmates in the choir to hide behind a hymnal and supplement Dewey's silent lips with the voice. The entire congregation had been fooled.

In after years the eulogizers of the Admiral cited that tale as proof positive of his ingenuity in a crisis.*

The middies tagged two nicknames on the future admiral—"Lucky" and "Shang."

In 1855 the growing hatred between North and South swelling throughout the land did not escape the Naval Academy, despite faculty efforts to tone it down. One of the great contributions of the Academy has been that it teaches its students to be Americans and not Alabamans or Vermonters. In Dewey's first year, however, concepts of sectional patriotism, engendered in the boys' primary schooling, had not been overcome. Debates on sectional issues frequently resulted in fights in which the belligerent Dewey was a participant.

On one occasion, as Dewey came into the mess, a Southerner across the mess table called him a name, which he described later as one "no man can hear without redress." Rushing around the table, he lashed at the boy with his fists and knocked him to the floor. Separated and taken before the superintendent, genial Captain L. M. Goldsborough, whom Dewey later served as flag lieutenant on the *Kearsarge* after the Civil War, they presented their cases. Dewey repeated the awful word. Captain Goldsborough told him he had done the right thing but gave him ten demerits for vindicating himself at mess, and informed the other midshipman that he had received his just desserts.†

This was a hot-blooded youth, who settled his grievances by primitive, direct methods, not by the approach of the mind. Action was his way of dealing with problems, the way most effective in a world of fighting men. On another occasion Dewey reportedly became committed to a duel with pistols because of an argument with a classmate, although it was halted by the authorities at the Academy.

Of sixty midshipmen who entered with Dewey, thirty-five remained at the end of their first year. Dewey's rating was number 33. This was sailing a little too close to the wind, and the second year he decided to work a little harder and keep away from the superintendent's office. French, German, and Spanish he mastered adequately, and he improved in trigonometry, logic, international law, and physics. History and geography remained his most difficult subjects, but in later years practical experience taught him well. At the end of the second year, when the midshipmen

*Ladies' Home Journal, Oct., 1899.
†George Dewey, op. cit., p. 19.

went home for their first leaves, Dewey had climbed to ninth place out of the thirty remaining members of the class.

He learned to chew tobacco with his classmates and always had a plug handy at his desk. To study navigation and spit resoundingly into the polished brass spittoon in the corner was an accepted evening procedure of the time.

In 1856 Dewey and his twenty-nine classmates gathered on the steps at Annapolis and sang the traditional song of the two-year men, the song of furlough that meant the opening of prison walls, and dancing, romance, and sleeping late in the morning:

> Come all ye gallant middies
> Who are going on furlough;
> We'll sing the song of liberty;
> We're going for to go.
>
> Take your tobacco lively
> And pass the plug around;
> We'll have a jolly time tonight
> Before we're homeward bound.
>
> Our sweethearts waiting for us,
> With eyes brimful of tears,
> Will welcome us back home again,
> For an absence of two years.

In their tight, immaculate midshipmen uniforms, the boys suited action to the word, passed the tobacco plug around, and "chawed" merrily.

George Dewey went home to Montpelier for his thirty-day leave, stopping on the way in New Jersey to pick up his sister Mary who was a student at St. Mary's Hall school. With her and a group of her schoolmates, he boarded the train for New York. Mary was in her Sunday best, sitting primly in the coach next to her uniformed midshipman brother, and behind them were the giggling young ladies of St. Mary's Hall. An incident on the train, concerning a group of young men (rowdies, they were called) who tried to start a conversation with the girls, was magnified years later. The boys apparently were too fresh toward the girls and the others in the car. Finally Dewey stood up in his uniform and offered to thrash the lot of them.*

This was the gallant gentleman defending womanhood. And here again the approach was manual.

For the next two years Midshipman Dewey devoted himself to history

*Adelbert M. Dewey, *The Life and Letters of Admiral Dewey* (New York: The Woolfall Co., 1899), pp. 122–124.

and literature, gunnery, navigation, and naval tactics, learning to become a member of that scientifically trained officer class who would see the Navy through the change from brigs to battleships.

At graduation Dewey had managed to climb to fifth place, in the top third of his class, for only fifteen of the original sixty remained at the finish. He went home for a few days as a full-fledged midshipman instead of an acting one. At that time students at Annapolis were required to take a two-year cruise after their graduation before being granted commissions as officers.

Dewey enjoyed a few short summer days in the old frame house, a few days' more advice from Dr. Julius Dewey, who had by then married a third time, and a few short hours with Mary Silver, the little girl who had kept him from fighting a boyhood rival and who drifted in and out of his life, making scarcely a ripple. The hills were green and the Onion River cool and inviting, but Dewey, almost twenty-one, was too dignified for endurance contests under water. His former schoolmates were policemen and store clerks now, or were practicing law or medicine. Some were in Boston or New York, embarked on city business careers. George Spaulding, who might have gone to Annapolis, was just finishing divinity school, ready to settle into a life of sermons and morning visits to his parishioners in Syracuse.

George Dewey, Spaulding's alter ego in a way, who would fulfill the pastor's middle-aged subconscious desire for adventure, was off to see the world. He was ready to come back with a sword or on a shield. The Civil War was just around the corner. *Uncle Tom's Cabin* was sold in the little stores of Montpelier, but no one knows whether George Dewey read it as he walked the hills that June, for almost the last time in his long life.

The *Wabash*,* flagship of the Mediterranean squadron in 1858, was only three years old, a steam frigate which looked more like the *Constitution* than a steamship, but her four thousand tons made her the pride of the Navy, even if her powerful batteries of broadsides were ranged in portholes along the length of the gun decks. Three towering masts, full-rigged, served as the link between sail and steam. Under steam she had a forced speed of nine knots and a cruising rate of five. With a good wind she could go faster. The Navy of the fifties had no rank above captain. Commanders of squadrons were given the courtesy title of flag officers. White-haired Flag Officer E. F. LaVallette, commander of the squadron, who had fought the battle of Lake Champlain under Thomas Mc-

*Six frigates of the *Wabash* class were built in 1855—the *Wabash, Colorado, Roanoke, Minnesota,* and *Merrimac,* all having forty guns. The *Merrimac,* captured by the South, was the first ship in the New World to be armored with iron plates, and renamed the *Virginia;* she was the ironclad that put the North into a panic because of her early successes.

Donough, still lived in that age. The vibrations of the *Wabash's* two horizontal engines gave him no peace. It was only when she was coasting over the waves quietly under sail that he enjoyed walking the quarter-deck of his command.

The *Wabash* sailed on July 22, 1858, from Hampton Roads for a Mediterranean cruise. In her crew were three young midshipmen, Naval Academy graduates of a month before. One was George Dewey, wide-eyed at being aboard a ship, learning the routine of the deck officer's watch, and gaining firsthand knowledge of the European world, the sea, and ships. Two days out the *Wabash* showed her colors to a Spanish bark, Dewey's first experience with the courtesies of men-of-war at sea. Later in the day the *Wabash* passed the English brig *Fawn*, out of Halifax, and proceeded on the way to Gibraltar, where Dewey saw the famous rock looming on the port hand on August 15.

Since the Tripolitan wars the Navy had dispatched a squadron to the Mediterranean every year, partly to impress the Corsairs, partly to keep step with the European navies which yearly held rendezvous there, and chiefly, to join in the social festivities of courts and ships. A round of formal receptions, balls, and dinners begun when the *Wabash* put in at Gibraltar lasted, almost without letup, for fourteen months, until she headed west again for the Gates of Hercules and the United States.

At Constantinople young Dewey was given his first sight of international intrigue. The Turks were celebrating Mohammed's birthday that October when the *Wabash,* in violation of an international agreement limiting the tonnage of foreign ships which could enter the Bosphorus, reached the port. The British and French had ships there, too, and both countries utilized the occasion to better their position with the Sultan at the expense of Russia. Lord Stratford de Redcliffe, the British Ambassador, was a stern, uncompromising Englishman, proud of his nation's prestige. It irked him that the United States had sent an oversize warship into the Dardanelles. As was his wont, he informed the Sultan Abdul Mejid that the *Wabash* must depart.

Flag Officer LaVallette made plans to leave. The United States had no interest in the connivings of European powers, and he did not wish to become involved. The American Minister, Williams, felt differently, however, and determined not to be outmaneuvered.

Midshipman Dewey was LaVallette's aide at the denouement when the American commander went to the Selemlik mosque to pay his respects to the Sultan. As the pageantry unfolded, the monarch, brilliantly attired in his oriental finery, rode from the palace to the shrine through streets lined with soldiers stiffly at attention while the natives bowed to the ground. Behind him came the red-and-blue clad officers of his staff and the veiled ladies of his seraglio. Returning from the mosque, the Sultan walked up to the two Americans. It was an unheard-of gesture, but, as Dewey related,* the Son of Allah was playing a diplomatic game himself.

Stopping before LaVallette, the Sultan asked the American officer to remain so that he might visit the "beautiful American ship." The *Wabash* stayed, the Sultan came aboard for an official visit amid formal salutes and courtesies and invited the *Wabash* officers to ride in a Turkish vessel up the Bosphorus. The honors were with the Americans, while Lord Stratford wore a red face for days.

From Constantinople the *Wabash* steamed to Beirut, Syria, to more parties and more visits to the world's famed spots. Dewey took a side trip to Jerusalem and saw Gethsemane. At Alexandria the officers left their ship for a brief visit to Cairo, the Sphinx, and the pyramids. Louis Napoleon arrived in Genoa, on the royal yacht *Reine Hortense,* to wed, as the *Wabash* rode at anchor. At Civita Vecchia the man-of-war saluted the Pope's flag, and in Italian harbors she watched the outcome of Napoleon III's war against the Austrians. Always it seemed like the grand tour of the Old World, and Dewey worried somewhat, for he felt he was having almost too good a time to be receiving pay from the people of the United States.

The fashionable court world of Europe that welcomed naval officers of the Mediterranean squadrons made an enormous impression upon the twenty-one-year-old midshipman. Young officers were sought after as partners and escorts for the daughters of ambassadors, nobles, and statesmen in the capitals.

So impressed was Dewey to be part of a world of fashion and so close to royalty after seventeen years of living in northern Vermont and four at the monastic Naval Academy, that he began a photograph album of royalty and bigwigs. Bound in daintily plaqueted yellow wood, the thick volume was filled with pictures of such personages as Louis Napoleon and the Empress Eugenie, Victoria and the young Prince of Wales, Hapsburgs and Hohenzollerns, Bismarck, Cavour, Mazzini, Pope Pius, and a number of princesses.†

A gentlemanly youth, Dewey no doubt did his share of beauing the younger daughters of diplomats to the official functions. But one incident which he recalled indicated that he did not make the social success of his 1858 Mediterranean cruise that he did in 1899. At Constantinople Min-

*George Dewey, *op. cit.,* pp. 26–28.
†The album is now in the possession of the Admiral's son, George Goodwin Dewey.

44

ister Williams had two daughters whom the young officers saw a great deal during the Prophet's birthday celebrations.

Forty years later, when Dewey was at Trieste on the *Olympia,* returning from Manila, the American Consul brought out the autograph book of an American lady, then the Princess Mary di Ligouri. The book was an old one, dating back to mid-century, and before he signed it the white-haired Admiral looked back through its yellowed pages. In the year 1858, he noticed the name of some *Wabash* officers, though his own was not there. Could this be Mary Williams, he wondered, forthwith sending her a note. The next day the old lady came out to the *Olympia* in the Admiral's barge for tea, no end disconcerted because she did not recall the meeting of four decades before, while Dewey, the naval hero, did. Nevertheless, a pleasant chat was held in the Admiral's cabin, a chat about oriental potentates and the dim past.

While in the Mediterranean the *Wabash* officers fraternized with officers of the Royal Navy, through whom Dewey first became aware of the revolution taking place in naval science. He learned of the French ironclads and explosive shells and of their success at Sinope and at Kinburn in the Crimean War. "This, rather than the *Monitor* and *Merrimac* duel, was the first convincing evidence to progressive officers that the future of naval warfare was with the ironclad," he wrote in later years. From the young Royal Navy officers he heard about the British ship *Warrior,* which was on the ways and would become the first modern ship of the British Navy, as the *Monitor* was of the American fleet.

On December 16, 1859, the *Wabash* reached the Brooklyn Navy Yard after a cruise of almost seventeen months. Midshipman Dewey received ninety days of leave and hurried home to Montpelier for Christmas and his birthday. His education was going well but it was not yet complete. Dewey visited the Caribbean and Mexico during the next year, serving first in the *Powhatan,* which had accompanied Commodore Perry to Japan, and then in the *Pawnee.* The latter was commanded by Captain Henry J. Harstene, an eccentric South Carolinian who announced at a banquet in Vera Cruz that if secession came he would take his ship into Charleston harbor and turn her over to the South. Captain Harstene wore a patchwork blouse, made of remnants from all his wife's silk dresses, which gave him a startling appearance on the bridge. On the return voyage, as the *Pawnee* passed Charleston, Captain Harstene rushed out of his cabin, his crazy-quilt jacket blowing in the wind, and ordered Dewey, the officer of the deck, to take in the topgallant sails. Dewey obeyed.

"Now set them again," he ordered. When that was done, Harstene looked on in "a wild, abstracted fashion," and again ordered them taken in "properly." Dewey always felt the eccentric captain planned then and there to sail into Charleston harbor and wait for the Rebellion to begin. But the *Pawnee* kept her course and made a Northern port.

It was January, 1861, when Dewey returned to Annapolis, after more than two years at sea, to take his commissioning examinations. In that time he had put into practice the theories he had learned. His knowledge of gunnery and tactics had been improved at sea, and as he grew aware of the changes taking place in naval tactics and firing, he understood why he had not studied those key subjects harder in the classroom. They had been taught according to the old routine methods of sea warfare.

There had been no discussion at Annapolis of new long-range explosive shells that would end boarding other ships in battle and doom the close work of the days when Marines in the tops could pitch boiling tar onto the heads of the enemy on their decks below. Sea warfare was at the crossroads, ready to take a new turn. The French ironclads had seen to that— and the Paixhans gun, which would some day permit ships to fight more than twenty miles apart without seeing their enemies below the far horizon.

The long cruise had stimulated Dewey's mind. His association with Flag Officer LaVallette and with progressive young Britishers, and even his watches as officer of the deck under mad Captain Harstene, had shown him the practical application of the theories he had studied for tests alone three years before. As a result, Midshipman Dewey walked into the examination rooms, in 1861, and wrote exceedingly well. When the marks were posted, Dewey stood third in his class. Of the two who received higher grades than he, Reed would retire into obscurity as a captain, and Howell would compete against an older George Dewey for the command of the Asiatic squadron in the Spanish War.

At twenty-three George Dewey was commissioned an officer in the United States Navy. He received his lieutenancy in April. Abraham Lincoln had been in the White House only a month, but the Confederate Government was ninety days old, and at 4:30 A.M., on April 12, the Confederate guns fired on Fort Sumter.

5

WITCHES' BREW

*M*idshipman George Dewey was at sea during the last two years of peace. While Abraham Lincoln and Stephen A. Douglas stumped Illinois, Dewey cruised in the Mediterranean, dancing with the daughters of ambassadors at the elaborate balls of the diplomatic set, minimizing the warnings of young British officers that war impended in the United States. The *Wabash* drifted lazily with the Mediterranean squadron in October of 1859, while, three thousand miles away, John Brown and his "army" of thirteen white men and five negroes seized the Federal arsenal at Harper's Ferry, West Virginia.

"We, with our perspective dulled by familiarity," still ignored the events "gradually bringing the cleavage between the North and South to a crisis," he wrote in his autobiography, and "were still fairly confident that a peaceful solution would be found."

Dewey, who boasted in after years that he had never cast a vote, must have paid little attention to the political struggles of that year. In May the "Black Republicans" met in Chicago to become the real party of the North, succeeding the Whigs, and to nominate the next President of the country. Abraham Lincoln, a log cabin candidate with a homespun philosophy, became the candidate of the North.

At Charleston Southern Democrats assailed Douglas' theory of popular sovereignty, and the cotton states' delegates withdrew from the convention. One rump of the party nominated Douglas at Baltimore, while the Southern wing forthwith nominated Buchanan's Vice-President, John C. Breckinridge of Kentucky. The cotton states voted for Breckinridge that year, and Douglas ran second in the popular vote. But Lincoln, piling up majorities in the Northern states, without a vote below Mason and Dixon's line, won 180 electoral votes to a total of 123 for his three rivals.*

*Morison and Commager, *The Growth of the American Republic*, p. 510. The electoral vote of 1860 was Lincoln, 180; Douglas, 12; Breckinridge, 72; and Bell, 39. In terms of popular vote Lincoln received 1,866,452; Douglas, 1,376,957; Breckinridge, 849,781; and Senator Bell of Tennessee, the candidate of the National Constitutional Union, only non-sectional party in the field, 588,879.

47

Lincoln's election awakened rioting and frenzy in the South. "The people are run mad," said Alexander H. Stephens of Georgia, describing their loathing toward the "nigger-loving Black Republicans."

If the causes of the Civil War were principally economic, if they were deep and intellectual, they were attended by an orgy of emotional hate which brought matters to the boiling point. Thus George Fort Milton wrote in his life of Douglas:

Man makes much of trifles, and his history must record the whims which move him. From emergence to final conclusion, the great American crisis quickened, changed its course and was given momentum by small events and chance occurrences, neither fated nor plotted, nor of great basic weight. Much is made of the deep conflict of great social systems and yet, perhaps, six incidents, mere smudges on the face of history, did more to rouse and array the will and emotions of the two sections than did all the fundamental factors combined.*

These oddly assorted items which fanned the flames and drove the nation into war were Harriet Beecher Stowe's *Uncle Tom's Cabin;* "Bleeding Kansas"; the Dred Scott decision of 1857; President Buchanan's hate for Douglas and its consequences in politics; John Brown and Harper's Ferry; and "Bully Brooks' assault on Senator Sumner" in the Senate. The undercurrent of mighty forces was too vital, too all-engulfing, not to have set explosive eddies whirling to the surface.

Secession, first attempted by South Carolina, was an act of emotion rather than of cold logic. The South had little to gain. Slavery, until the present day, could still not have been outlawed by Constitutional amendment, for the Northern Senators could never amass the necessary votes in the face of a solid Southern bloc.† Furthermore, in the mind of Lincoln, slavery was not the issue. Long after the war began, freedom for the slaves was not contemplated by the Great Emancipator. In his view, preservation of the Union, one and inseparable, was the sole aim in the war's first stages. By secession the South lost what rights and protection it then enjoyed to preserve a balance of slave states in the new territories. To many Southerners independence became the end in itself. The geographical and industrial disparities between North and South caused a feeling, born possibly from prestige insecurities, which drove the South to feel it needed freedom to rule itself as it wished, to build a wall along the 39th parallel and end the competition from the North. The reasons calling for secession were subconscious ones, impel-

*George Fort Milton, *Eve of Conflict* (Boston: Houghton Mifflin Co., 1934), p. 237.

†Thirteen states can still block any amendment to the Constitution, since a three-quarters vote of all states in the Union is necessary to ratify any proposed alteration of the basic law of the land.

48

George Dewey, then a Rear Admiral, seated in the center and surrounded by his officers aboard the flagship *Olympia* a few days after the Battle of Manila Bay.

View of Hong Kong harbor taken in April 1898 before the American squadron sailed for Manila. The Flagship *Olympia*, with two funnels, is on the upper right of the picture.

ling the mind to seek rationalization for the overt act. In all good faith, in courage and deep patriotism, the chevaliers of Dixie left their plantations and their homes to wage a holy war for their own definition of liberty. Emotional furors killed cool reasoning, for the Republican party was ready to adopt a Constitutional amendment pledging the preservation of slavery in the Southern states. The winter of 1860-1861 found the vacillating James Buchanan packing his clothes in the White House, anxious to end his "lame duck" tenure and avoid the vexations arising from the struggle. Compromise was in the air, and Buchanan sought to do his utmost to prevent a real crisis. Throughout the land the magnitude of the crisis was not apparent. "Wayward sisters, depart in peace," was the thought mirrored by many when South Carolina voted to secede.

Young George Dewey, taking his final examinations in Annapolis that January, took the fatalistic viewpoint that if war should be declared he would be ready. When men like W. H. Seward, Lincoln's Secretary of State, thought that picking a quarrel with France or England might prevent a fight with the South, it could not be expected that Dewey, whose world had so far been bounded by schoolrooms and wardrooms, would understand the shadows on the wall.

After his examination, Dewey went home to Vermont to rest and play and await his next assignment.

Dewey was riding horseback in Montpelier on March 4, 1861, when a gangling frontier lawyer passed secretly through Baltimore to Washington for his inauguration. That day the situation was still in flux. No one knew whether the South would be enabled to secede peacefully and establish a second republic on Columbia's shores.

In his Inaugural address Abraham Lincoln made clear that the Union would be preserved. His warnings were ignored by many. Even in his cabinet there were men who believed in peace at any price. To the discerning, however, the die was cast when Lincoln stood before the half-finished dome of the national capitol and said to the South:

In your hands, and not in mine, is the momentous issue of the civil war. . . . The government will not assail you. . . . But, I hold that in contemplation of universal law and the Constitution, the union of these states is perpetual. . . . No state, upon its own mere action, can lawfully get out of the Union. I shall take care . . . that the laws of the Union be faithfully executed in all the states.

Days passed in growing anxiety and restlessness. In Charleston harbor the Federal garrison was commanded by Major Anderson, a Kentuckian, who detested the idea of secession. Surrounded by Confederate forces, he pleaded for reinforcements. Lincoln sent them, against the advice of some of his cabinet. On April 11 the Southerners called upon Anderson at Fort Sumter and demanded that he surrender. The next morning Southern guns blazed against the Federal bastion. Anderson and his men resisted all day long. Lincoln's relief ships arrived but could not put in to shore. The next day, Saturday, Fort Sumter's barracks began to burn. Anderson accepted terms and the Federal garrison marched out of the fort.

If there had been indecision in the North, if the Republicans had been opposed to following Lincoln's firmness, all doubt vanished then. On Monday morning the President called for 75,000 volunteers, and on both sides of Mason and Dixon's line young men began to appear at recruiting stations. In Montpelier the young friends of Dewey went into the county courthouse to get their blue uniforms, and in Alabama and Virginia the friends of his Southern classmates at Annapolis poured into the army offices to don the gray.

The United States, as in all her other wars, was not prepared for the new conflict. Fortunately for the North, the South was equally unprepared. The Northern states had a vast preponderance in population— some twenty million citizens to six million whites and three and a half million negroes in the South. But that margin was smaller than that which had faced the new republic in 1775 when freedom was sought from King George III.

The North was an industrial country, well knit and capable of a large industrial output. The South, with its rural areas, its cotton plantations, and its industrial backwardness, was comparable to the thirteen colonies of eight-five years before.

When Fort Sumter fell it became evident that the Northern Navy would have to adopt blockade as its grand strategy. Separation of the Old South from the states west of the Mississippi was secondary, despite its important effect upon the outcome of the war. The North had the Navy, but, like the colonies of 1775, the South outfitted privateers to prey on Northern commerce. Therefore, although the Civil War was fought predominantly on land, it was a naval war as well, of greater magnitude than any previous conflict on the seas. It brought into being radical changes in naval warfare and fighting equipment.

As war began, the Confederates seized the Norfolk Navy Yard and captured the frigate *Merrimac,* burned to the water line by the retreating Federalists, and converted it into an ironclad, big-gunned floating fortress, which terrified the North. The invention of the *"Davids,"* cigar-shaped ships carrying a submarine mine on a long pole ahead of their bows, which sank several Northern ships, was the forerunner of the submarine with its self-propelled torpedo.

In the War of the States, North and South alike built "monitor" type ships with six inches of armor plate, which doomed wooden ships and sails for combat purposes. The development of big guns with exploding shells, of fleet operations, instead of the ship-to-ship duels of earlier wars, were among the major results of the war. This revolution in naval science gave the South a chance. Had she been able to build the new-type vessels with anything like the speed and numbers achieved in Northern shipyards, the conquest of the Mississippi and the blockade along the Atlantic might never have been successfully accomplished by the Union Navy.

The United States Navy of 1861 was led by veterans of 1812; men who, Dewey said, "would be more at home in the Spanish Armada than in ships of the dreadnought class." Old, debilitated, and settled in their ideas, they were ill-equipped to fight a war which changed naval tactics and machinery. The frigates and men-of-war of the Federal Navy blew up in splinters before the onslaught of the Confederate ironclad *Merrimac*.

Wars of independence in the eighteenth and nineteenth centuries had been won, in spite of overwhelming odds, principally by the revolutionists' ability to hang on until their mother country became tired of the incessant struggle. That had occurred in 1783. The South American states had proved it too, and in that element of war-weariness lay the South's main chance.

The South was fighting for its homes, its freedom, and its way of life, just as the colonies had fought before, and in that belief resided its faith and fervor, unmatched in the North until the war was well along. The Confederate leaders, President Jefferson Davis and Admiral Franklin Buchanan, the first superintendent of Annapolis, and one of the foremost naval officers of the war, gave the South a degree of leadership in themselves. By adding Robert E. Lee, one of the greatest generals of all time, the Confederacy had leadership of inestimable importance.

Robert E. Lee of Virginia, a West Pointer, loath to leave the Union although war was apparent, became the symbol of the Southern cause. Upon him rested most of the heartache and anguish, the work and toil of the four-year war. Solely because of his unmatched skill in strategy and tactics, the South carried on its titanic fight. But on the sea the South played second fiddle to the might of Lee and Stonewall Jackson.

George Dewey frequently paid tribute to the gallantry and heroism of the Southern officers against whom he fought. And throughout his life Dewey maintained a respect and love for the brave sailors and soldiers of the South. But for none had he more regard than for Robert E. Lee, who, more than anyone else, had "given us a devil of a time."

The North had no commander to match Lee, no soldier who could inspire the loyalty given the Virginian. Grant and Sherman, even Farragut, whom Dewey loved so well, could not reach the stature of the Confederate commander-in-chief. Only one man in the North, far from the battlefield, and misunderstood and ridiculed, kept the North together. For him there was no ovation and love such as that enjoyed by General Lee. But in death and in history the White House's brooding figure rose to his rightful place.

In 1861 he was little known and less understood. In the dark years ahead he would grow, like a tree in the middle of the dark woods, which outdistances its neighbor saplings and meets the sun.

6

HISTORY IN HAMPTON ROADS

Lieutenant Dewey was taking a well-earned vacation in Montpelier when news of the surrender at Fort Sumter reached Vermont. A few days later he was on his way to duty. He reached Boston on May 10 and, sitting atop his steamer trunk and seabag in the stern sheets of a whaleboat, was rowed out to the steam frigate *Mississippi,* which was to be his home for almost two years.

A somewhat curious combination of the old and the new, with her three masts and bowsprit and a tall black smokestack amidships, she was commanded by Captain T. O. Selfridge, who was ill at ease on his first steam warship and viewed with trepidation the paddle wheels which churned the water on either side of his bridge.

The frigate, heading for the Gulf of Mexico, arrived off the Mississippi delta in 1861 to join a handful of reluctantly commanded ships blockading the port of New Orleans. Captain Selfridge, timid of steam, was equally timid of war, just as were all the other skippers of Captain John Pope's squadron. For months the ships maneuvered in the Gulf, fearful of joining combat and risking the loss of any ship. During the summer the squadron was thinned out when six of the ships were dispatched to hunt the Confederates' daring raider, the *Sumter,* which her captain, Raphael Semmes, had spirited past Federal ships off New Orleans.

The first brush with the enemy occurred in October, 1861, while the *Mississippi* was on patrol. The Southerners had converted a tugboat into an ironclad ram which had an iron prow to smash wooden ships on impact. On the evening of the twelfth the ram *Manassas* surprised the Federal ships, smashed headlong into the flagship *Richmond,* punctured her side, and frightened the rest of the squadron into hurried retreat. The *Manassas,* also wounded in the ramming, limped upstream to New Orleans under wild fire from a pair of Union sloops. This engagement, named "Pope's Run," for the squadron's flag officer, was "exasperating"

53

to the "energetic-minded officers of the Navy" and galling to the North. It was of minor consequence when compared with the less-publicized activities of the North's Atlantic fleet, which in the year 1861 captured more than 150 privateers attempting to run the blockade. But Northern morale suffered from the humiliating first encounter and needed lifting.

This lift came in November, when Flag Officer DuPont smashed the rebel positions at Port Royal Sound in South Carolina and scattered the garrison. During the next four months, by a series of brilliant engagements, DuPont secured control of a long stretch of Atlantic seaboard. In February of the next year converted gunboats commanded by Flag Officer A. H. Foote aided General Ulysses S. Grant in the capture of Forts Henry and Donelson, which opened the fight to clear the Mississippi River. Built in St. Louis, these gunboats were forerunners of the *Monitor* and the *Merrimac*. They were barges with two-inch armored casemates sloping inward at a forty-five-degree angle to inclose the guns and engines. Each ship was propelled by a stern paddle wheel and carried thirteen guns— six forty-three pounders, four seventy pounders with rifled barrels, and three eight-inch guns. These were ships in architectual transition from wood to steel. The end of the Civil War would find all navies of the world racing to build armored vessels equipped with rifled instead of smoothbore cannon.

As Grant fought southward, past Shiloh, Tiptonville, and Fort Pillow, President Lincoln, Secretary of the Navy Gideon Welles, and his brilliant assistant, Gustavus V. Fox, a former naval officer who served unofficially as chief of staff for all naval operations, determined upon a plan to breach the Mississippi from the South. "The father of waters must flow unvexed to the sea," Lincoln declared. More prosaically, he told Fox to "go ahead, but avoid a disaster," with the plan to isolate New Orleans from the rest of the South. Fox' previous naval experience had won him the admiration of active officers of the line, who knew he had been schooled at sea. "We cannot overestimate the value of his intelligent service to the country," Dewey wrote, "on meager pay, in sacrifice of private interests, for which he received hardly his fair due honor."[*]

For Secretary Welles there was less enthusiasm in the service. A white-bearded Connecticut editor, large and genial, yet possessed of a forthright tongue which won enemies all too easily, Welles was not Dewey's kind of man.

"We are familiar with Mr. Welles' character through his very voluminous diary," Dewey wrote. "It has always been amazing to me how Mr. Welles was able to do so much writing and conduct the Navy Department

[*]George Dewey, *Autobiography*, pp. 40-41.

in the midst of a great war. He was certainly a man of prodigious industry. His lack of technical knowledge would have been a great handicap if it had not been for the selection of an Assistant Secretary of the Navy whose training made him an excellent chief of staff."*

"Father Gideon," as Washingtonians called Welles, like other wartime secretaries, brought to his office little technical knowledge but great executive ability to prosecute the war. His administration of the Navy Department, with the able assistance of Gustavus Fox, made it outstanding. It "was not affected with the irritability, suspicions and insubordinations of Stanton, nor with the mild and ineffective fatuities of Halleck as chief of staff. The Navy had little of the atmosphere of graft, inefficiency and corruption that existed in the first few months of Cameron. One cannot avoid the feeling that the men at the top of the war at sea realized from the first the magnitude of the job they had to do, were flexible and experimental in finding out for themselves how to do it, were more fortunate than the War Department in picking the men to do it, and in comparison certainly did a much better job than their Army counterparts."†

Selecting the men to run the ships was the paramount task faced by Welles and Fox in the first year of the war. The seventy-eight captains on the active list at the outbreak of hostilities were veterans of 1812, mostly in their sixties, and the majority were unfitted for service afloat. Most of the skippers were more concerned with their boilers than with the enemy. Even the lieutenants were in their fifties. Subordinates of this age were likely to be afraid of authority, incompetent, and unwilling to make decisions. Welles and Fox tackled this problem first. Perhaps the timidity of the blockade, revealed in Pope's Run, helped persuade Congress, in December, 1861, to pass a law retiring all officers who were sixty-two years old or who had forty-five years of service. The number released by this law and the resignations of 321 officers to join the South gave young men in the Union Navy their chance.

David Glasgow Farragut was one of the few older officers retained in service. Born near Knoxville, Tennessee, on July 5, 1801, he had started his naval career as a boy of nine, before the War of 1812, and was close to the retirement age in 1862. Adopted by Commodore David Porter, he had served as midshipman aboard the *Essex* when it sailed around the Horn, and he had swum away from the barnacled ship when it was sunk by the British near Valparaiso, Chile. Farragut had educated himself on the sea and by reading. Between watches he studied assiduously, and by the time he was twenty was an accomplished linguist. He had served as

*George Dewey, *op. cit.*, pp. 40-41.
†Milton, *Eve of Conflict*, pp. 134–36.

commander in the war with Mexico in 1848, and had risen to a captaincy before his native state seceded from the Union. Farragut promptly left Tennessee, moved to New York, and in February, 1862, was assigned to command the Gulf squadron in which Lieutenant Dewey served.

Another of the experienced officers, David Dixon Porter, the son of Commodore Porter and Farragut's brother by adoption, was forty-eight years old and, when the Civil War began, his rank of lieutenant prevented his appointment as commander of the Mississippi squadron, despite Fox' desire. At Porter's behest Farragut was named to command, while Porter led a mortar-boat flotilla for the assault on New Orleans.

When, on February 21, 1862, the fleet arrived at Ship Island, the base maintained by the Federal squadron off the Mississippi delta, things began to happen both to the war and to George Dewey. Farragut had initiative, immense personal daring, and a complete lack of fear. Warfare, he knew, meant attrition, human expendability, and sacrifice. There was no other way. The influence of such a leader on the younger officer cannot be over-emphasized. Even if Dewey later attempted to embroider his connection with Farragut and thereby enlarge his own importance in the history of the Navy and the United States, there is ample evidence to show that Dewey lived by Farragut's precepts. Farragut, schooled in the ways of John Paul Jones, Truxton, and Decatur, became the teacher of George Dewey, whose own achievements, in turn, taught the naval leaders of World War II.

Soon after Farragut's arrival at Ship Island, Captain Selfridge left the *Mississippi* and was succeeded by Melancthon Smith, bearded and black-haired, who lighted one cigar from the end of the other and was never seen without one, whether he was in the midst of battle or resting in his cabin. The departure of six other officers, ranking Dewey, entitled the twenty-four year old lieutenant to the place of second in command. Captain Smith had no objection, but Dewey's youth, despite his black mustache and his efforts to seem older than his years, was resented by other officers in the fleet. Flag Officer* Farragut discussed the situation with Smith, suggesting that possibly an older and wiser head should be assigned the post as executive officer.

"Dewey is doing all right. I don't want a stranger here," Smith replied.

"Then we will let him stay," answered the commander.†

An assault upon New Orleans, past a pair of Confederate forts on the shores of the Mississippi and past Southern armies on the banks, was a

---

*There was no rank of rear admiral in the U.S. Navy before 1862, when Farragut was promoted to that grade.
†George Dewey, *op. cit.*, p. 51.

dangerous and exacting mission. The Confederates possessed a river defense squadron of converted gunboats and the ram *Manassas,* which had taken toll of Pope's squadron a few months earlier. At Ship Island Farragut launched into the task of fitting his fleet for action. But even while this work was going on, the entire nation, and the world, was electrified by events at Chesapeake Bay. Over the new telegraph wires hummed the story of the *Monitor* and the *Merrimac.*

On April 20, 1861, the Confederates stormed the Federal Navy Yard at Norfolk, Virginia, barely giving the retreating Northerners a chance to destroy the yard or burn their ships. One of these was the forty-gun steam frigate *Merrimac,* almost ready to embark for sea. The Northerners' haste prevented a thorough scuttling job. The *Merrimac* burned only to the water's edge, leaving a finished hull and steam-engine plant, which the Southerners salvaged by extinguishing the fire. They recovered large amounts of stores, guns, and equipment. A drydock was easily repaired, and the Confederates quickly built the hull of the *Merrimac* into the ironclad *Virginia,* modeled after the new French ironclads and the revolutionary British *Warrior.*

Lieutenant J. M. Brooks of the Confederate Navy had the idea of making a ship invulnerable with an armored wall of iron, but he lacked technical help. Blueprints for a floating battery, little more than an iron box with slanting sides on a hull, had already been drawn by a naval constructor, J. C. Porter, but the South could not build an engine capable of driving such a vessel. Brooks solved the problem. He placed the box-like iron fort on the hull of the *Merrimac* and installed a pair of seven-inch rifles, two six-inch and six nine-inch smoothbores.* The engines of the *Merrimac* had lain under the water of Chesapeake Bay for weeks, but they could still function. News of this frightful monster quickly reached the North. The United States Navy began to search for designs for an ironclad to combat the Confederate fortress. Hundreds of plans were offered. One proposal suggested India rubber sides off which shells would bounce. Only three plans proved practical. These in time developed into the *Monitor,* the *Galena,* and the *New Ironsides.* The *Monitor,* designed by John Ericcson, was the most radical. Resembling a cheesebox on a raft, she had almost no freeboard and carried but one turret, holding a pair of eleven-inch guns on the deck. She looked like a modern submarine with a revolving gun turret for a conning tower.†

*Fletcher Pratt, *The Navy: A History* (Garden City: Doubleday, Doran & Co., 1938), p. 265.
†Revolving turrets were invented twenty years before the Civil War by nineteen-year-old T. R. Timberg of New York. Used for the first time in battle by the *Monitor,* they have since become the standard armament not only of ships but of tanks and bombing planes.

The trials were almost a complete failure. The turret would not turn and the eleven-inch shot was too heavy to hoist up to the guns. Ericcson's amazing scientific ingenuity devised successful ammunition hoists and solved a thousand other difficulties. Finally, on March 6, 1862, under command of Lieutenant J. L. Worden, the *Monitor* left New York. A storm blew up in the Atlantic. For more than two days the low vessel wallowed through the giant waves, the crews expecting at every moment to go down.* There was little that was seaworthy about this first modern warship, and the wonder was that she survived the storm.

On March 8 the *Monitor* was nearing Hampton Roads when the *Merrimac,* under command of Admiral Buchanan, steamed out of the Elizabeth River into Chesapeake Bay. In the roadstead was a Yankee fleet, composed of numerous steam frigates and sailboats still in service as combat vessels. The *Merrimac* headed for the most heavily armed of these, the *Cumberland,* which had twenty-four guns throwing seventy-pound shot. Just to warm up, Buchanan exchanged shots with the Federal *Congress'* shells as if they were hailstones. Engaging the *Cumberland,* the *Merrimac* shelled her, rammed her, and caused large casualties. The *Cumberland* fought back bravely and well, despite the condition, and refused to surrender.

"Never," Lieutenant G. U. Morris shouted. "We will sink with our colors flying." She did sink, but not without giving the Navy another famous phrase and wounding the *Merrimac,* which may have decided the fate of the war the next days. For in ramming, the *Merrimac* lost her saw-tooth prow.

The *Merrimac* turned next on the *Congress* and soon shelled her into flames. The Northern ship *Minnesota* stood into the action and engaged the *Merrimac* at long range. Poor firing by the Confederate crew saved the *Minnesota.* A falling tide forced Buchanan to retire and anchor for the night. Meanwhile the *Monitor* arrived, but too late for action that Saturday afternoon. Lieutenant Worden tied her alongside the *Minnesota,* and his crew worked all night repairing damages caused by the storm so that she would be ready for battle the next day.

Word of the debacle reached Washington the next morning. Consternation reigned. President Lincoln called an extraordinary cabinet meeting in the White House, and Secretary Welles arrived to find Stanton pacing the room, hollow-eyed and despairing. Lincoln "was so excited that he could not deliberate or be satisfied with the opinions of non-professional men, but ordered his carriage and drove to the Navy Yard

*The *Monitor* actually did sink in a gale at sea in December, 1862, off the Diamond Shoals. Its hull is still visible from the surface on a still day.

to see and consult with Admiral Dahlgren and other Navy officers," Welles wrote. The cabinet members looked out the windows toward the Potomac, half expecting the *Merrimac* to come puffing up the river and lay Washington in ruins. In Stanton's view she would, single-handed, destroy every Northern ship, capture all the Northern forts, destroy Boston and New York, and levy tribute on their citizens to carry on the rebellion.

Welles alone appears to have remained unflustered by the great commotion. He pointed out to the frightened men that the *Merrimac* drew too much water to attack the Federal Army in the sounds. The *Monitor* was already in Hampton Roads, and "I had confidence in her power to resist and, I hoped, to overcome the *Merrimac*." When Stanton wanted to know what the *Monitor* was, Welles described the ship:

He asked about her armament, and when I mentioned that she had two guns, his mingled look of incredulity and contempt cannot be described; and the tone of his voice, as he asked if my reliance was on that craft with her two guns, is equally indescribable. . . . That day and its incidents were among the most unpleasant and uncomfortable of my life. . . . The events were momentous and portentous to the nation, the responsibility and the consequences of the disaster were heavier on me than on any other individual; there was no one to encourage and sustain me. Admiral Smith (who had been the deciding factor in authorizing the construction of the *Monitor*), always self-possessed and intelligent, who would have stood by me, was overwhelmed with the tidings, for his son was on the *Congress,* and, as his father predicted, when tidings reached him of the fate of that vessel, had fallen a victim.*

Fox was at Hampton Roads to await the arrival of the *Monitor* and could not help. Admiral Dahlgren, designer of the Dahlgren smoothbore eleven-inch guns, much used in the war, was "powerless and in full sympathy with Stanton in all his fears and predictions," said Welles. Nevertheless, the Secretary of the Navy continued to allay the fears of the President and his cabinet, pointing out that the clumsy *Merrimac* with its topheavy armor could not navigate open seas in safety and could be used only in Hampton Roads and the Chesapeake. But Stanton could not be calmed. He telegraphed Northern governors and mayors to float rafts and other obstructions in the harbors to keep out the fearsome *Merrimac*.

The terror created in Washington exemplified the fear all over the North that Sunday morning. But while the President and Stanton worried, the *Monitor* and the *Merrimac* were already circling in Hampton Roads, preparing for battle.

At 8:00 A.M. the *Merrimac* stood out from shore to finish off her work of the afternoon before. Buchanan had been wounded in that battle and

*Gideon Welles, *Diary of Gideon Welles* (Boston: Houghton Mifflin Co., 1925), pp. 61–62.

Lieutenant Catesby ap R. Jones was in command. As he steamed for the *Minnesota* he was surprised to see a queer little "cigar" floating toward his ironclad. The *Monitor* broke the stillness with a 170-pound shot, and a four-hour battle began.

The Southern gunners had great difficulty hitting the low *Monitor*. Even when they did, they accomplished nothing. The *Monitor's* heavy shells, however, had a large target, which they hit with regularity. While the *Merrimac* fired faster, her aim was poor, and the firing from the *Monitor* threatened to smash the weak water-line area of the *Merrimac's* armor. The *Merrimac* tried ramming. It was useless without the saw-tooth prow. When the *Monitor* withdrew to hoist up more ammunition, the *Merrimac* began a deadly fire against the *Minnesota,* but by then the the *Monitor* was back to divert her. As a leak in the *Merrimac's* bow became worse, and as the tide began to fall, Jones decided to withdraw.

Neither ship had been seriously damaged in the encounter, but the *Merrimac's* crew, having fought nearly two full days without rest, was at the end of its endurance, and Jones did not relish the prospect of staying within range of the Federal fleet for another eight or nine hours of daylight. Lieutenant Worden, on the *Monitor,* had been temporarily blinded in the encounter, but no one had been killed on either ship. The *Merrimac,* her ammunition running low, and her engines in bad repair and threatening breakdown, retired undefeated. Actually, the battle resulted in no decisive victory for either side, but terror left the North. Worden had proved that the fearsome *Merrimac* was not so dangerous after all, for Ericcson's oddly built ship proved her match. At least two ironclads were almost ready for sea, and more were on the way.

The *Merrimac* remained at Norfolk to repair her minor damages. In April she came out again, this time under the command of Flag Officer Josiah Tattnall, of "blood is thicker than water" fame.* Now a Confederate officer, Tattnall led the *Merrimac* on a hit-and-run raid, captured three sailing ships, and retired. Flag Officer Goldsborough of the Northern fleet declined to fight, preferring this time to keep the *Merrimac* contained. The wisdom of his choice became apparent in May, when the Southerners evacuated Norfolk. In the retreat the *Merrimac* was destroyed. It had no means of escape without a sure-death fight against the Northern fleet.

---

*In a Chinese-British war of 1859 Commodore Josiah Tattnall was at the mouth of the Peiho River when Admiral James Hope, the British Admiral, was being overcome by Chinese fire from the shore forts. Seeing that the English would be exterminated, Tattnall took his river steamer, the Toey-Wan, into the fray and helped the British. Then, rowing to the British flagship, he was dumped into the water by a Chinese shell. He clambered onto the English ship while his American crew helped serve the guns. Tattnall's justification for his action violating American neutrality was the famous phrase, "Blood is thicker than water."

7

TRIAL BY FIRE

$\mathcal{T}$o capture New Orleans, a feat which would secure the southern anchor of the Mississippi Valley and prepare the way for conquest of the river from both north and south, Farragut was provided with nine large ships, fifteen gunboats, and twenty mortar boats, the latter under the command of Porter. At Ship Island target practice and drill never ceased. Sides of the ships were daubed with mud for camouflage. Masts were stripped, and all spare spars, rigging, boats, and equipment were landed ashore. At the suggestion of Captain James Alden of the *Richmond,* the decks of the ships were whitewashed around the guns, so that crews could see to serve their batteries at night. For added protection against enemy shells, anchor chains were warped about the sides of the vessels. Bags of sand and coal, and nets and hammocks were hung along the wooden planks to reduce casualties from splinters. An innovation in naval warfare, this precaution proved well justified, although the crews were none too comforted, for they saw in these preparations a sure sign of deadly action ahead.

At least 10,000 Confederate troops garrisoned New Orleans, while the South's river fleet consisted of twelve ships, including the ram *Manassas* and the new heavily armored ironclad *Louisiana.* Despite her sixteen large guns, the *Louisiana's* uncompleted engines reduced her to little more than a floating fort. About thirty miles up the river from the gulf, at a bend in the channel, the Confederates held two forts: Fort Jackson on the right, or south, bank, and Fort St. Philip, opposite. St. Philip had been built by the Spaniards but had been remodeled in the nineteenth century. Fort Jackson, the stronger of the two, was constructed by the Federal Government in 1832.* Between them the batteries mounted more than a hundred guns to dominate the river. In addition, the Con-

*Joseph L. Stickney, *Life and Glorious Deeds of Admiral Dewey* (Chicago: C. B. Ayer Co., 1898), p. 138.

federates had floated a chain barrier across the channel, supported by old hulks, immediately below the guns of Fort Jackson. But this was only the first line of defense. Above the forts General Beauregard had installed batteries and earthworks in every bend and bayou to New Orleans. Small wonder a New Orleans paper in early April editorialized: "Our only fear is that the Northern invaders may not appear. We have made such extensive preparations to meet them that it were vexatious if their invincible armada escapes the fate we have in store for it."

Farragut's first division, under Captain Theodorus Bailey, whose forty-gun frigate *Colorado* had been too big to navigate the sandbar at the mouth of the river, consisted of the flag gunboat *Cayuga;* the *Pensacola,* with twenty-three guns; the *Mississippi,* with seventeen; the small sloops *Oneida* and *Varuna,* with nine and ten guns respectively; and the gunboats *Katahdin, Kineo,* and *Wissahickon.* The flagship *Hartford,* twenty-four guns, led the second division, followed by the *Brooklyn,* twenty-two guns, and the *Richmond,* carrying twenty-four. All three were screw-propelled sloops. The third division included the ninety-day gunboats *Sciota, Iroquois, Kennebec, Pinola, Itasca,* and *Winona,* Porter's mortar throwers, and the sloop *Portsmouth.*

Not one of the Federal ships was ironclad. Captain Smith had installed chains between the sidewheel paddles and the hull of the *Mississippi* for whatever protection they would offer. For days Farragut and the smaller ships waited above the sandbar while the bigger ships were dragged across. Tugs pulled the *Brooklyn* and the *Mississippi* through a foot of mud. When they reached the other side, repairs on their bottoms were necessary. All of the larger ships were trimmed heavy in the forward ends, so that if they went aground their bows instead of their sterns would stick, thus preventing them from swinging broadside to the strong current of the river.

On April 17 the last ships cleared the bar, and the squadron steamed up the river toward Forts Jackson and St. Philip. The next day Davey Porter camouflaged his twenty mortar boats with tree branches and leaves, and in the early morning darkness anchored them in the shadows of the wooden bank below the forts. The rest of the squadron remained out of range while Porter's thirteen-inch mortars opened fire. For five days, off and on, the mortars lobbed shells into the two forts, firing at ten-minute intervals all night to soften the defenders. The bombardment burned the citadel of Fort Jackson, seriously threatened the magazines, and drove the garrison to cover. From time to time the little gunboats darted ahead, blazed at the forts, and retreated when the Confederates began to find their range.

During the preliminary firing Farragut was everywhere. Rowed about the fleet in a whaleboat, he made suggestions to commanding officers, cheered them on, and saw that guns were installed properly in the foreparts of the ships or that howitzers were fitted out atop the masts with iron guards for the crews. Each day the *Mississippi* dispatched its boats to a collier below the fleet to pick up a day's supply of coal, for her bunkers had been emptied to reduce her draft in crossing the sandbar. And each night the interminable shelling continued, with a roar, a boom, and a blinding glare of light as the fuse of the lobbing shell illuminated its trajectory toward the fort. Every night, too, the Federal ships remained on the alert for blazing fire rafts of tar and resin which the Southerners sent down the river in the hope of setting the ships on fire. The rafts lighted the water from bank to bank, while the flagship's blinkers signaled orders to tow them ashore where they might burn out harmlessly.

On the night of April 20 a pair of the gunboats, commanded by Lieutenants Caldwell and Crosby, sneaked up the river toward the chain obstruction. Under cover of Porter's mortars, their little ships, *Itasca* and *Pinola,* labored for hours to cross over the chains. Just as they had succeeded, the South's forts opened fire, but the dismasted gunboats looked like the hulks supporting the chain boom and the Southern fire was inaccurate. The *Itasca* breached the chains first and steamed upstream. Then, with the current to aid his speed, Caldwell returned and smashed into the iron cable. The hulks and the chain gave way, dragging downstream, and opened a passage wide enough for any of the Federal ships to pass through.

For three more days the mortar bombardment continued, while Farragut made sure all was in order for the grand assault. Finally, at 2:00 A.M. on the morning of April 24, the *Hartford* signaled with two red lights at her peak. Led by the gunboat *Cayuga* and the *Pensacola,* the *Mississippi* fired up a head of steam and fell into the ghostly line. On the bridge Captain Smith pulled his beard and puffed at his cigar.

"Going ahead in the dark," he muttered. "Ought to be making full steam ahead in daylight, fight our way through. I cannot see in the night. . . . I'm going to leave that to you, Dewey. You have younger eyes."

The captain left the bridge to attend to the guns, while Dewey assumed his post on the hurricane deck, peering ahead at the dim, unlighted outline of the *Pensacola.* All the while the mortars lobbed shells into the forts, with little response from the weary Southerners. As the *Pensacola* passed through the broken boom of chains, she was sighted.

Dewey was near enough to the fort to hear Confederate officers ordering their men to fire upon the advancing Union ships.

From Fort Jackson deafening guns roared into the night, and on the starboard hand, from St. Philip, shellfire blazed. The *Pensacola* stopped to aim simultaneous broadsides at both forts. There was no answering fire. The *Pensacola* fired a second time. This time the fort answered. The *Pensacola,* with the heaviest armament of all the fleet, seemed unable to silence the guns. The *Mississippi* had moved above the obstructing chains by now, and was being fired upon. Dewey watched the *Pensacola* and wondered why she had stopped, despite her orders to steam full speed ahead past the batteries. He could not tell whether the shells were close or far away. Below decks Captain Smith shouted to the gun crews, directing the fire which now was blasting from all the Federal ships. Garish brilliance lighted the skies, while black powder smoke blew across the banks, stifling and hot.

In the foretop of the *Mississippi* stood an artist for *Harper's Weekly,* trying hard to keep his head and feet steady, and to see and remember everything for his sketches when and if he emerged alive. Suddenly he sighted a grayish turtle-like form heading for the ship.

"Here's a queer-looking customer on our port bow," he called. Dewey looked at once. It was the ram *Manassas* plowing through the water toward his ship.

It was his first battle, and the *Manassas* was unexpected. But Dewey coolly ordered the helm "hard a starboard" to ram the *Manassas* first. The *Mississippi,* with three times the *Manassas'* weight, could quickly put the little turtle out of commission if she could strike amidships with her bow.

Unlike the Northern infantrymen, however, who were fighting strangers, the United States Navy was fighting itself. Commander A. F. Warley, skipper of the *Manassas,* had been a Union officer. His last cruise before secession had been aboard the *Mississippi,* and he knew just how maneuverable she was. He swung his little ship toward her, barely missed her port paddle, and with a grinding lurch tore a seven-foot rent in her side. The old steam frigate listed violently, shuddered with the crash, then righted herself. Lieutenant Dewey grabbed for the port rail to keep himself from falling. A few feet below him the heavy planking of the ship had been torn apart. The inner strakes were splintered, and copper bolts had been sheared away. Fortunately, she had been filled between the frames with solid oak and was only superficially damaged.

"Sound the pumps," Dewey yelled to "Chips" standing behind him.

"I have already, sir, and there's no water in the wells," answered a veteran and completely competent carpenter.

The *Mississippi* was now well under the guns of Fort Jackson, but she was straightened out again and continued her course, firing grape and solid shot from her guns, wildly and as rapidly as possible. The Confederate forts replied. Now they were finding the range, and as the second division, led by the *Hartford,* passed the danger point, Fort Jackson's guns were losing their early wildness. A mad confusion of ships milled astern of the *Mississippi.* The *Pensacola's* pause and Dewey's swing to port against the *Manassas* had added to the confusion. Fire rafts forced the ships to dodge in and out. One raft, pushed by an unarmed Confederate tug, was rammed against the *Hartford,* and as Farragut's crew pulverized the boat with grape, flaming tar blazed into the wooden timbers of the Northern flagship.

Now the *Manassas* was on the loose again. Spotting the *Brooklyn,* it rammed her amidships. But the blow was a glancing one, and the anchor chains woven about the sides minimized the damage. By this time the *Mississippi* was out of range, while the real battle raged below. The *Brooklyn* had collided with the *Kineo.* The little *Iroquois* had been swept alongside the engineless *Louisiana* above Fort St. Philip. A murderous fire from the Southern ship killed or wounded thirty-two men, but the *Iroquois* managed to steam free. Behind her Lieutenant Crosby's gunboat *Pinola* suffered fourteen hits and eleven casualties. Three of the gunboats in the third division never passed the obstructions, and the *Varuna,* when morning came, was hard ashore, the victim of a Southern ram.

On the *Mississippi* only two men were killed and a few more wounded. As the morning light appeared, and the *Mississippi's* guns were stilled far upstream, Captain Smith spotted the *Manassas* again. "Like an assassin in the night," Dewey recalled, she was coming back for another try. Smith, taking his cigar out of his mouth, yelled at a nearby gunboat, which he mistook for the flagboat of Captain Bailey:

"I want permission to run down the ram."

At that moment the smoking *Hartford* steamed past. Farragut stood high in her rigging.

"Run down the ram," he shouted.

Smith turned to Dewey at his side. "Can you turn the ship?" he asked.

"Yes, sir," Dewey replied a little uncertainly, for the river was narrow. The helmsman spun the wheel, the *Mississippi* lumbered around, and pointed full at the belly of the *Manassas.* Warley dodged the blow but in doing so plowed fast into a mudbank. Two broadsides finished the ram, and the crew scampered out of the forward hatch onto the wooded shores seeking to avoid the deadly fire.

Captain Smith ordered a boat overboard with an officer in charge to report on the ram's condition. Five minutes later the lieutenant returned with Warley's diary and signal book and news that the stern was sinking fast. At that point the Confederate forts reopened fire on the *Mississippi,* and it became apparent that discretion was the better part of valor.

A boat was sent back to the *Manassas* armed with combustibles to set her afire. The *Mississippi* steamed upstream beyond range, past the burning bulk of the Southern fleet. Only three Southern ships survived that night. The blazing *Manassas,* floating off the shore, drifted downstream, where with a gigantic explosion, she settled under the muddy waters of the channel.

The battle had been engaged at 2:00 A.M. Five hours later the ships of Farragut's squadron were anchored at quarantine above the forts, counting their casualties. Thirty-nine had been killed and one hundred and seventy-one wounded, but the Mississippi River had been invaded, General Butler's troops were above the forts, and New Orleans was at Farragut's mercy. The fleet steamed to within fifteen miles of New Orleans and anchored for the night. Tired crews still fought to fend off fire rafts floating down the channel. The next morning, battered but invincible, the ships made their way toward the city, destroying two minor forts, Chalmette and McGehee, which opened fire as they passed.

The river was high at New Orleans when Farragut steamed in, and the guns of his ships towered over the dirt streets, threatening the old French houses by pointing down over the levee at the town. The Confederate troops had retreated the day before, leaving only an angry, impotent citizenry to surrender. The *Hartford* dispatched a few ships ahead to menace a narrow strip of land connecting the town with the mainland and prevent the sending of supplies to the beleaguered city, which had food on hand for only a few days. Captain Bailey and a lieutenant rowed ashore with a great flag, and marched through the crowds of angry Southerners to the Mint to raise the Stars and Stripes. A great roar of applause rose from the ships as it was unfurled above the city, and Dewey's heart thrilled to the spectacle.

The taking of New Orleans effectively sealed the southern end of the Mississippi. Forts Jackson and St. Philip surrendered to Porter's mortar flotilla on April 28, and Farragut sent the *Mississippi* and the *Iroquois* back to them while the rest of the fleet arranged terms for the capitulation of New Orleans.

Now, with battle over, Dewey could reflect upon his first engagement.

66

To Farragut and the Union Navy it had brought glory after months of ridicule. To Dewey it gave personal confidence and the knowledge that he had come through his first trial with honor. His steadiness under fire and his quick decision to ram the *Manassas* proved him a better officer in war than in the examination room. He had not worried about his own safety. Later, speaking with lofty unconcern, although in contradictory terms, of his emotions under fire, Dewey said:

I had little time to consider the psychology of an experience which is the source of much wonder and speculation to the uninitiated. When it comes, you are utterly preoccupied with your work; you are doing what you have been taught is your duty to do as a trained unit on a man-of-war. Only after the danger is over is it time to reflect. The wait before action is the period of self-consciousness, which ends with the coming of the first shot from the enemy or the command to 'fire' from your own side.*

Lieutenant Dewey went ashore with a group of officers to inspect the forts. "I was not deeply impressed by the damage that had been done," he recorded.† The mortar shells had cut the levee bank in spots, and mud and water covered the floors of the two batteries. Shells exploding in the soft ground had splattered dirt over all the walls of the forts, but otherwise had done little harm. Apparently the principal effect of the Federal firing had been to terrorize the garrisons, excite the men, and ruin the accuracy of their fire.

Such a hell of mortar fire, bursting shells, and confusion should have caused more destruction, Dewey felt. The rigging of the ships had been riddled, and sides of many were battle-scarred and charred, but only one had gone down. Perhaps the reason had been Farragut's theory that "the best protection against an enemy's fire is a well-directed fire of your own." Porter's mortars had disrupted the Confederates' aim, and the broadsides of the fleet had confused the enemy. But both sides' aim had been poor, and though improved in later Civil War fighting, the gunnery of naval ships was never truly accurate until the twentieth century.

After the capture of New Orleans Farragut's squadron maintained a stringent blockade upon the lower Mississippi. For weeks the Southerners tried to spirit gunboats past the Federal ships. One night one of the craft did get through.

Farragut, angered, called every commanding officer in the fleet aboard the flagship *Hartford* for a conference of war. Dewey, as Captain Smith's executive officer, went along.

"Gentlemen, be seated," Farragut began as the officers assembled in

*George Dewey, *Autobiography*, pp. 74–75.
†*Ibid.*, pp. 61–62.

his cabin. The skippers sat down while their aides hugged the bulkheads.

"How did this happen?" Farragut demanded.

A young officer from another vessel, who had been officer of the deck the night before, answered.

"It was very dark, but I could have rammed her, sir, only I was waiting orders."

That would have been a perfect answer to any man save Farragut. His long face narrowed, and he said quietly, "Young man, you had the opportunity to make a great name for yourself in your profession, but you missed it. I doubt that you will ever get another."

Farragut was right. The young officer never earned another chance and died in obscure retirement. But the warning of his idol impressed young George Dewey mightily. He remembered that lesson all his life.

Admiral Farragut lost little time after General Butler's troops occupied New Orleans to prepare for deeper invasion of the Mississippi. The *Mississippi*, however, drew too much water to make the northern sortie and was left near New Orleans to patrol the conquered city. In June of 1862 Farragut ran past Vicksburg, and Flag Officer S. P. Davis, arriving from the north with another flotilla, opened the great river from Cairo to the Gulf. Opened but not conquered, the Mississippi was still vexed, and it was not until July 4, 1863, that Grant, with naval help, took Vicksburg and ended permanently Southern rule of the waterway.

Life for the occupying force in New Orleans was made uncomfortable. On the streets, when women and children sneered and hooted at the navy blue uniforms of Federal officers, Dewey felt a personal affront. He was, however, a little happier when he made the acquaintance of some Northern families in the town, who entertained him frequently. But most of his time was spent on shipboard, fretting at the monotony of the life, half wishing he was up the river with Farragut again or in the Atlantic working hard at the blockade.

General Benjamin Franklin Butler, military commander of the city, provided some amusement from his constant arguments with the naval high command. Once the *Tennessee* steamed into New Orleans without stopping at quarantine. Butler, always fearful of a yellow fever epidemic, ordered her to spend two weeks of isolation away from the city. Commodore Henry Morris of the *Pensacola*, which, with the *Mississippi*, guarded the city, agreed readily, but he pointed out that since the crew of the *Tennessee* had mingled with the men of the other two ships, all had better return to quarantine. Butler considered what his position would be without naval support and backed down. The *Tennessee* remained the quarantine quite forgotten.

On another occasion a French gunboat sought permission to come into New Orleans. Since the port was Federal territory and the United States and France were at peace, Captain Smith agreed. When he learned of the permission, Butler was irate.

"We don't want the Frenchman around," he bellowed. Dewey was sent to inform the French captain that Butler would like to have him stay away for a few days. On the deck of the gunboat the French captain heard Lieutenant Dewey's message.

"General Butler?" he mused. "Oh yes, he is the *avocat-general*. He says I shall stay? *Voilà*, I will go," and he did.*

The British, although technically neutral in the war, were sympathetic to the South. While the implications of the Trent affair and Captain Wilkes' seizure of the Confederate emissaries Mason and Slidell or the history of the *Alabama* claims, never interested Dewey personally, one little diplomatic exchange at New Orleans did.

A certain Commander Hewitt of the British Navy arrived in New Orleans on the gunboat *Rinaldo* and became familiar with the Confederates of Creole society. Time after time Hewett invited Southern society aboard the *Rinaldo* for elaborate parties, but he never asked Federal naval officers. One evening, as if to emphasize the social insult, the *Rinaldo* band struck up a Southern song, "The Bonnie Blue Flag." Captain Smith was furious.

"Dewey," he commanded, "go over and tell that English captain we do not permit such songs in New Orleans." Slightly embarrassed, Dewey departed upon his first diplomatic mission and conveyed the request. An irate British officer grudgingly ordered his band not to play the number any more.

Intemperate as he was in chain-smoking of cigars, Captain Smith was religious to a marked degree. He hated profanity, a rare trait in any navy. Once, when Dewey was bossing a hectic job aboard ship, in the almost tropical sun, he uttered several oaths, as did the sailors.

Captain Smith heard the swearing and appeared on deck.

"Mr. Dewey," he called. "Have all the crew lay aft." On the quarterdeck Smith harangued the men and officers on the viciousness of profanity. "Hereafter, any officer caught swearing will be put under suspension," he commanded, "and any man caught swearing will be put in irons." Captain Smith turned on his heel and marched back to his cabin.

Temperance was another of Smith's fetishes not entirely shared by

*George Dewey, *op. cit.*, pp. 81–82.

his young executive officer. After months of close association on the *Mississippi,* Smith and Dewey were dining at the home of a Union officer in New Orleans. When the butler passed through the room with a tray of champagne, Smith waved it away with his ever-present cigar. But Dewey accepted a glass.

Smith walked across the room to his junior, looked down at him, and demanded, "Dewey, do you drink champagne?"

"Yes, I do. I don't very often get a chance these days," he replied.

"If I had known that, I don't think that I should have had so much confidence in you," the captain said sadly. But it seemed to make little difference after all. Dewey continued to exercise a great amount of authority on the *Mississippi,* and Smith never interfered.

Farragut's operations during the summer of 1862 were brilliant and of immense importance, although for the moment they were unsuccessful. After running the batteries at Vicksburg on June 28, 1862, he and the Northern Mississippi squadron had engaged with Confederate gunboats and river batteries on the tributaries of the Mississippi. But reinforcements on land were not forthcoming, and, although the North controlled the river north of Memphis and south of Baton Rouge, the Confederate Army dominated the vital rail and water routes through northern Louisiana to Texas.*

Congress recognized Farragut's achievements in July, commissioning him to the new rank of rear admiral. Davey Porter, who succeeded to command of the Northern squadron co-operating with Grant, also was given that rank. After Grant took Corinth in October of 1862, the Northern flotilla operated in the Tennessee and Yazoo rivers, clearing out Confederate centers of resistance, meeting success and defeat almost alternately.

Through the winter Farragut had implored General Butler and his successor, General N. P. Banks, to attack Baton Rouge, but never received co-operation from the Army. In March Farragut determined to go to Grant's aid with or without military support. Vicksburg and Port Hudson, armed to the teeth with Confederate guns, were too great a threat to the Union's control of the Mississippi. They had to be taken if the western theater of war was to be won.

Finally, General Banks agreed to make a show against Port Hudson, some hundred miles above New Orleans, almost halfway to Vicksburg. But at the crucial time Banks' men were not there, and the fleet went on ahead.

*Knox, *A History of the United States Navy,* p. 236.

It was a relief to Lieutenant Dewey to end his ceaseless practice drilling of the crew of the *Mississippi*, to get away from New Orleans with its surly crowds, and to look forward once again to action. Although the *Mississippi* was not suited for river operations above New Orleans, Porter's squadron in the North could not spare any vessels, and Farragut needed every ship he could possibly utilize. On March 14, 1863, the admiral anchored his fleet off Profit's Island, some seven miles below Port Hudson. His squadron consisted of the flagship *Hartford* with twenty-eight guns, the *Richmond* with twenty-five, the *Monongahela* with eleven and the *Mississippi* with seventeen, the little river ironclad *Essex* with seven, and three small gunboats for use as tugs to help the larger ships. Efforts to adopt twin-screw ships had for many years been turned down by the Navy. Yet in river warfare maneuverability was of cardinal importance, and so Farragut lashed the gunboats to his big ships to provide a twin-screw principle as well as to pull off the steamers if they should run aground. The *Albatross* was made fast to the *Hartford;* the *Genesee* to the *Richmond,* and the *Kineo* to the *Monongahela.* Her wide side paddle wheels making an escort alongside impossible, the *Mississippi* made the dangerous run alone.

At ten o'clock that night, with a river current of five knots keeping the ships' progress down to a walk, the little fleet moved ahead.

Port Hudson was situated on the left bank of a river bend atop steep bluffs about a hundred feet high. At the top and bases of these cliffs, Confederate guns menaced the slow ships. Through the blackness the *Hartford* steamed past the Southern batteries, and was already above the first guns when a Confederate sent up a warning rocket. Bedlam broke loose ashore. On the *Mississippi,* far in the rear, Dewey heard the Southerners shouting and soon could see them rushing between bonfires they had built upon the shore. Great reflectors placed behind each fire lighted up the Federal ships and blinded the pilots. From the high bluff a cannonade began.

At the bend, under the South's guns, the *Hartford* ran ashore and sustained a withering fire in the tops until the little *Albatross'* power pulled her free. Fighting the current, she made the bend, and fired broadside after broadside at the high guns. Then came the *Richmond,* chugging through the smoke and flame of battle, giving as much as she took from the Confederate batteries, until one shell in her engine room blew out her safety valve lever, filled the compartment with hot steam, and knocked out her steam pressure. The five-knot current was too much for the little *Genesee.* Turning around in wild confusion, the *Richmond* began to pass the fort heading downstream. Her gunners, not realizing she had turned, saw flashes on their starboard hand and returned shell for shell. Unfortunately, the guns they were answering were firing not from shore but from the frigate *Mississippi,* which scarcely expected a Federal ship to run downstream. But since fire control had not been radically improved by Dewey's constant practice at New Orleans, the *Richmond* survived the night with only eighteen killed and wounded.

The third pair of Federal vessels, *Monongahela* and *Kineo,* had even poorer luck. When a Confederate shot disabled the *Kineo's* rudder, the two went hard aground on the bank opposite Port Hudson. For twenty-five minutes, while the ships fought to get free, enemy shells dropped around them. Finally they were floated, but by that time the lashings had parted and the two ships were separated. An overheated crankpin stopped the *Monongahela's* engines, threw her out of control, and sent her drifting downstream past the forts, accompanied by the battered little *Kineo.*

It was the *Mississippi's* turn now. Captain Smith, who hated fighting at night, and Dewey, whose eyes were blinded by the smoke of coal and gunpowder, relied entirely upon the directions of the pilot. Huddled under a boat on the port side of the ship to protect himself from a shell hit, he shouted orders above the melee. He steered the *Mississippi* past the grounded *Monongahela,* while gunners fired blindly at gun flashes on the bluffs. The reflectors on shore impaired the vision of the men on the river and blocked out the fortification in the rear.

Below the fleet five mortar boats were posted to annoy the fort, but Civil War mortars, timed by hand-set fuses, were unreliable bombs. Some, whose fuses were timed accurately, exploded in the forts. Others burst high in the sky, while still others, completely out of range, landed in the river. One of them exploded on the starboard beam of the *Mississippi,* drenching her crew with water.

To add to the horror of the night a cry of "Torpedoes" went up. Then the pilot made a miscalculation. Thinking the *Mississippi* was past the shoals and ready to turn around the bend, he shouted, "Starboard the helm. Full speed ahead." The big ship veered to port. In the boiler room sweating firemen heaved coal into the furnaces with redoubled fury. With a grind and a thud the old *Mississippi* dug into the river bank.

Dewey barked orders, obeying the commands of Captain Smith—so excited now he threw his cigar overboard without lighting another. As the ship listed heavily to port, the crews of the portside guns dragged them in to even keel. The starboard guns, still trained on the flashing forts, blazed furiously, and, with engines backing hard, the paddles strained to pull the frigate off the bank. The wheels scraped through the mud, groaned, and squeaked as the boom and flash of cannon broke through the smoke and smell. The Confederates, noting the *Mississippi's* plight, trained their heaviest guns on the stationary target.

Captain Smith, recovered enough to light another cigar, opined to his lieutenant, "Well, it doesn't look as if we can get her off."

At this point a cannon ball, being heated red-hot for firing as an incendiary at the shore batteries, bounced into a forward storeroom and ignited sails and ropes stowed there. For thirty-five minutes the crew fought the blaze, while the starboard gunners continued their rapid shooting, firing a total of 255 shots in that time.* But, as Confederate practice was improving, too, the *Mississippi* absorbed merciless punishment. Finally, Captain Smith decided to abandon ship. Three port lifeboats were lowered into the current. All the starboard boats had been smashed into splinters long before.

During the evacuation a panicky orderly rushed ahead of other men to jump to safety. Dewey, who was standing by the falls, knocked the man sprawling with a well-timed uppercut. This apparently restored the frightened subordinate's courage. Five minutes later, when a wounded seaman being lowered into a boat slipped from his rescuer's hand into the river, the orderly dove overboard and pulled him back. As publicly as he had punished him, Dewey then praised the man and sent him ashore with a hearty slap on the back.†

The rest of the seriously wounded were lowered into the first boat, which carried them down river to another Federal ship. Those slightly wounded or unhurt jumped into the other two boats and headed for the nearby bank. The boats were ordered to return to the stricken ship for another load. But too long a time elapsed before they returned. Perhaps the crews were afraid. Obeying what he called an "impulse," Dewey leaped into one of the boats on the second trip. As soon as they landed, everyone dashed behind the levee except one negro cook, who stood ready to row back for a third load of sailors.

The *Mississippi* was blazing at the bow. Confederate shells pounded into her thick sides. At any minute her magazine might blow her to eternity. Dewey wrote later, "That was the most anxious moment of my career. What if a shot should sink the boat? What if a rifle bullet should get me? All the world would say that I had been guilty of about as craven an act as can be placed at the door of any officer. This would not be pleasant reading for my father up in Vermont. He would no longer think that I had done 'the rest' reasonably well. If the ship should blow up

---

*Compare this amount of shellfire with that thrown in 1943 by the cruiser *Boise* in the Solomons. The Boise fired "more than a thousand high-explosive shells and sank six Japanese ships in less than twenty-seven minutes."

†*Ladies' Home Journal*, Oct., 1899.

while I was away, and I should appear on the reports as saved, probably people would smile over my explanation."*

Luckily, the *Mississippi* did not explode at that moment. Dewey called after running crew members, told them that if a black man was willing to go back, they ought to be ready too, and persuaded some to return with the first boat. The crew of the second boat, however, seemed unmoved by his plea until, at Dewey's insistence, the acting master resorted to more persuasive means. At the point of a pistol, the crew rowed out to the *Mississippi*. That short battle, Dewey wrote afterward, had seemed about five years long.

Captain Smith had been looking for his executive officer. Together, the two searched the ship for wounded men who might have been missed in the earlier roundup. They found a cabin boy more dead than alive under a heap of bodies near a gun station. Then began the task of setting the vessel afire to save it from enemy hands. With a kerosene lamp, Dewey and Ensign O. A. Batcheller ignited a mattress in the officers' wardroom.

The officers left in the last boat with only the clothes on their backs. Captain Smith, fearing capture, threw his sword and pistols into the river. The lifeboat reached the Union ship *Richmond,* however, and Smith's precaution had been unnecessary. He was greatly upset the next day when he saw Dewey still wearing his sword. "You would not have it if you had followed your captain's example," he said indignantly.

The departure from the burning *Mississippi* followed perfect naval tradition. The men left, then the officers in inverse order of their rank, Dewey immediately preceding Captain Smith, the last to leave the ship. It was as undramatic as that, yet many of the eulogistic biographies embroidered the incident. They told how, seeing a seaman wounded and floundering in the water, the gallant Dewey plunged overboard, dragged the man to a floating spar, and got him ashore. Then, the yarn continued, he swam back to the ship, set it on fire singlehanded, and after everyone but the sixty-seven dead had gone overboard, made his way to safety through a hell of enemy fire. It is doubtful if Dewey, never one to underplay his role, would have omitted such a climax from his autobiography.

As the fire on the *Mississippi* gained headway and water whirled into the after end of the ship, her bow shook free, and the blazing derelict was carried down the river by the current. She had been turned round so that her port guns faced the fort at Port Hudson. When she was broad-

*George Dewey, *op. cit.*, pp. 96–97. It seems strange that Dewey referred in this passage to the *Mississippi* as a "boat." As every sailor knows, a boat is a vessel which can be stowed on a "ship's" deck and is used only for emergency or taxiing between warships. A naval officer like Dewey, always a stickler for proper form, would hardly have used this word himself.

side to the batteries, the fire exploded her port guns, and they issued a final defiant blast at the Confederate positions.

"She goes out magnificently, anyway, sir," Dewey said to Captain Smith. They sat in the stern sheets of the lifeboat.

The Captain bit into his cigar. Smoke and grime covered his face, and his hair hung in strings over his brows.

"I don't think so," he growled.*

Dirty and covered with smoke, they watched the ship's fires streak skyward. On the other bank a victorious Rebel yell broke over the din of battle. It was the only time Dewey heard that shout of victory, but it was once too often, he recalled. When the *Mississippi's* guns exploded in their final broadside, Dewey felt that, somehow, it compensated for the enemy's triumphant shouts.

From the deck of the *Richmond* the survivors watched the *Mississippi* shake free from the bank and float downstream, like a Ganges funeral pyre. Finally, near Baton Rouge, the ship grounded on a sandbar. A few minutes later an explosion ripped her wide apart and she sank into the mud of the Mississippi.

Farragut's attack had been a noble but disastrous enterprise. Only the *Hartford* reached the upper river. It was July 9, five days after Vicksburg fell, before General Banks' army captured Port Hudson.

In his official report of that fight Smith wrote: "I consider that I should be neglecting a most important duty should I omit to mention the coolness of my executive officer, Mr. George Dewey, and the steady, fearless, and gallant manner in which the officers and men of the *Mississippi* defended her, and the orderly and quiet manner in which she was abandoned."†

*George Dewey, *op. cit.*, p. 103.

†Soon afterward Smith was promoted to rear admiral. When he died, he left George Dewey his epaulettes and cocked hat. The Dewey collection in the Chicago Historical Society still contains a pair of rear admiral's epaulettes. With them is the sword Dewey carried in the fight and a small picture frame, containing a fragment of the stars and stripes which floated over the flagship *Hartford* at Port Hudson in 1863. Dewey's sentimental streak was intense. For example, his desire to be one with the fame of the *Mississippi* apparently prompted him, in his autobiography, to identify her as Commodore Perry's flagship on the cruise to Japan. Other authorities make it plain that the *Susquehanna* was Perry's squadron leader.

8

BLOOD ON THE ATLANTIC

$\mathcal{T}$wenty-five-year-old George Dewey returned to New Orleans a man without a ship. There he was assigned to shore duty, which, although brief, had a marked influence upon his future career. He became a prize commissioner in New Orleans to pass on the legitimacy of seized contraband, evaluate it, and sell it for the government. Since cotton made up the bulk of prize cargoes seized in the area, Dewey became an authority on the market and later invested much of his own surplus earnings in it. He also acquired a taste for good food and good living that remained with him the rest of his life.

The problem of slavery scarcely seemed to concern him. Slavery was "an accepted institution," he later wrote, and he would let others worry about the principles involved.

Dewey returned to shipboard when Captain Melancthon Smith, given command of the *Monongahela,* obtained Farragut's approval to take Dewey on as his executive officer. For a few weeks, until after Vicksburg and Port Hudson fell, he served on the sloop under both Smith and his successor, Captain Abner Read. Farragut used the vessel as flagship when he was in New Orleans, and Dewey consequently saw much of the urbane and indomitable hero. One afternoon he was asked by Farragut to accompany him on a steam launch used for reconnaissance excursions to inspect the Port Hudson batteries, still controlled by the Confederates. They steamed within range, while the old officer tried to draw fire from the emplacements. Soon the Southerners opened salvos on the little craft. Farragut remained imperturbable. To Dewey the entire venture seemed absurd. A shell landed in the river about ten feet beyond the launch. Involuntarily, Dewey jumped aside.

"Why don't you stand firm, youngster?" said the admiral. "Don't you know you can't jump quick enough?"* The launch dodged in and out

*Stickney, *Life and Glorious Deeds of Admiral Dewey,* p. 147.

among the shells. Soon another one landed close. This time Farragut dodged. A little sheepishly, he exclaimed, "Why, sir, you can't help it. It's human nature, and there's an end to it."

A few weeks later the old *Monongahela* had a close call from some Southern guns hidden in the levee banks, near Donelsonville. A field battery opened fire on the sloop as it passed. Captain Thornton Jenkins, Farragut's chief of staff, wanted to speed out of range, but Captain Read, with foolhardy courage, declared, "I've never run from any Rebel yet, and I'm not going to run now."

The *Monongahela* slowed down and engaged the battery. The ship's shells plunged into the mud of the levee, while the shore gunners rolled their own guns out of harm's way behind the mud walls to reload. Soon after the fight began a cannon ball crashed with blinding fury into a bulkhead just behind Dewey on the quarter-deck. He was knocked to the floor, stunned. Getting up, he saw Captain Read lying mortally wounded in a pool of blood. Captain Jenkins, too, was on his back. The shell had kicked over a rack of cutlasses some distance away, and one of them had flown through the air, striking Jenkins on the calf of his leg.

"When we examined the spread of the shell," recorded Dewey, "by the places where the fragments had struck, it was inexplicable how I had ever escaped without a scratch. It almost made me believe in luck. For that matter, anyone who has seen much fighting became a sort of fatalist. Evidently my time had not yet come."*

Although Captain Read's death elevated Dewey to commanding officer, he was quickly relieved because of his youth and transferred, to become executive officer, under Captain Emmons, on the *Brooklyn,* a screw sloop, half sail, half steam, which was headed for the North Atlantic blockade. Under sail she crossed the Gulf of Mexico, passed around Florida and headed for Charleston, South Carolina, where Admiral John A. Dahlgren commanded a campaign to destroy the Confederate forts.

For more than six months Union monitor-type ships had been maneuvering around Charleston harbor, never quite strong enough to capture the defenses but engaging in frequent duels with forts Moultrie and Sumter. Half a dozen new monitor ironclads under Dahlgren were assembled off Charleston when the wooden-sided *Brooklyn* arrived. She was too weak to engage in close contact with shore batteries, and Dewey was greatly relieved when he learned that Dahlgren wanted Emmons for his staff but would not hold the ship. The *Brooklyn* sailed to the New York Navy Yard and Dewey was given his first leave in more than two years.

While he was resting in Montpelier, a new development in naval de-

*George Dewey, *Autobiography*, p. 112.

structiveness made its appearance. In Charleston harbor an odd, little cigar-shaped Southern vessel, the *David,* approached the ironclad Union ship *New Ironsides* on October 5, 1863. Lieutenant W. T. Glassell in the *David* (which took its name from the story of David and Goliath) headed straight for the *New Ironsides.* Extended on a long underwater pole ahead of the *David* was a copper torpedo loaded with sixty-five pounds of explosives. The torpedo struck the Union vessel and exploded immediately. The *David's* crew, inundated by the splash, escaped from their "cigar," and all but two were captured. Those two climbed back into the *David* and escaped. The *New Ironsides* was not sunk, but her underwater hull was damaged so severely that she had to be taken to a Navy Yard for repairs.

The *David,* powered by steam, fifty feet long and seven feet in circumference, was the forerunner of the modern submarine. She could not submerge, but slid through the water with only a central cockpit appearing above water. Soon the Confederates did develop submersible craft. One of these was the *H. L. Hunley.* Her motive power consisted of eight men and a crank, which turned fins, while tanks could be flooded to let the weight of sea water submerge the craft. The torpedo was towed astern of the ship. The *Hunley* was the first real submarine. In February, 1864, it pushed a torpedo into the hull of the Union ship *Housatonic* in Charleston harbor, sinking her in five minutes. The *Hunley* was also sunk in the explosion.

The North likewise experimented with submersibles, developing the *Alligator* in the hope of finding an answer to Southern ironclads.

Dewey returned to the *Brooklyn* in the fall of 1863, expecting to resume his duties as executive officer under Captain James Alden, who, as skipper of the *Richmond,* had seen Dewey fight in the Mississippi. Washington ordered otherwise. He was assigned, instead, as executive officer on a third-rate, wooden sidewheeler named the *Agawam,* then being put into commission at the Portsmouth Navy Yard at Kittery, Maine.

The transfer was most fortunate. Had he remained aboard the *Brooklyn* he would have sailed into Mobile Bay with Farragut aboard the ship which shied at torpedoes, bottling up the Federal fleet and eliciting Farragut's wrathful shout, "Damn the torpedoes. Go ahead." Had Dewey been executive officer of the *Brooklyn* at Mobile, he would have been powerless to change its actions, but the mere fact of presence aboard the ship might have handicapped his career.

Duty at Portsmouth had two notable results. The first was his introduction to Miss Susie Goodwin, daughter of Ichabod Goodwin, war governor of New Hampshire. The leading citizen of Portsmouth, merchant in the East India business, and owner of at least a dozen merchant ships, Goodwin was also president of the First National Bank of Portsmouth and of the Eastern Railroad, later known as the Boston & Maine. For years the railroad's principal train to Boston was pulled by a Civil War-type engine called the "Governor Goodwin."

Goodwin was called "Fighting Ichabod," because at the outbreak of war he had refused to wait for the state legislature to convene and muster in the militia. Instead, he used his own money to equip the troops and speed them off to war, banking on the legislature's reimbursing him later.

The Goodwins lived in a large white house just off Portsmouth's city square, which was the social center of the town. His attractive daughter Susie was being squired by the *Agawam's* skipper, Commander A. C. Rhind, when Dewey arrived, but she was soon happier in the company of the younger officer.

The second was his arrest. One day while the *Agawam* was being fitted out by civilian workmen at the Kittery Yards, a hawser broke and the ship began to float away with the tide. The crew and executive officer pitched in to make fast another line and pull the ship back to dock. A civilian shipworker near Dewey apparently did not care if the *Agawam* floated out to sea. More hands were needed to pull, and Dewey was indignant to see an idle pair so near.

"Here you, lend a hand," he yelled at the workman, a man named Garland. "You're working for the government. Lend a hand."

Garland laughed, said he was not taking orders from any young naval officer, and proceeded about his business. It was no time for palaver, and Dewey tried action instead. Dropping the line for a minute, he ran over to Garland and landed a sturdy blow on his jaw.* The workman tumbled to the dock.

When he started to get up, rubbing his face, Dewey repeated: "I said, lend a hand." Needing no second blow, Garland helped pull the *Agawam* alongside again.

Shortly afterward Deputy Sheriff George F. Plaisted appeared with a summons for Dewey's arrest on complaint of one Garland. "Lieutenant Dewey was then a young man and felt quite grand with his stripes," Plaisted wrote later. "He looked upon me with disdain and thought a country deputy sheriff was not anybody. He was not satisfied that I could legally arrest him." The two repaired to the office of the commandant of

*Louis Stanley Young in his *Life and Heroic Deeds of Admiral Dewey*, published in 1899, tells a slightly different story. He states that Dewey struck Garland over the head with a speaking trumpet. The present account, however, is attested to by Dewey's son, who, as a boy, had heard it told many times by his grandfather Goodwin.

the yard, where Dewey was informed he must submit to civil authority. After a trial he was fined $5.00, plus $8.80 costs. "It was worth it," Dewey told Governor Goodwin, and the men laughed over their cigars. But soon the *Agawam* was ready for sea, and the double-ender, with sidewheel paddles and twin rudders on either side of the pointed stern, headed for the James River to become the flagship of Admiral S. P. Lee.

During the spring and summer of 1864 Commander Rhind fought her "as if she were a battleship" in the Peninsular campaign waged by General Butler. At Four Mile Creek the *Agawam* engaged three Confederate batteries for six days during Butler's drive on Richmond, silenced many of the guns, and retired only when her ammunition was exhausted.

Meanwhile Grant was fighting in the Wilderness, breaking the back of Lee's army. The Union Navy maintained its blockade with ever-increasing efficiency, despite the final efforts of Confederate privateers. All told, the Southern raiders captured more than 250 Northern merchantmen, skyrocketing insurance rates on American shipping so much that more than a million tons were transferred to British or other neutral registry. Because a law forbade the transfer of foreign ships to United States registry, the merchant marine was almost nonexistent until well into the twentieth century.

Only five Confederate privateers caused this downfall. Most famous were the *Florida* and the *Alabama*. Escaping through the blockade in January, 1863, the *Florida* captured thirty-seven Northern prizes before being captured herself by the Federal sloop of war *Wachusett* in Bahia, Brazil. Captain Raphael Semmes in the *Alabama* took a grand total of sixty-nine Northern ships, spreading alarm and criticism of Secretary Welles throughout the North. "Thus far the British pirate named *Alabama* sailing under Rebel colors has escaped capture," Welles wrote. "As a consequence there are marvelous accounts of her wonderful speed, and equally marvelous accounts of the want of speed of our cruisers. . . . She will become a myth, a 'skimmer of the seas' till taken, and our own vessels, of better speed and power, will be slandered as destitute of all speed."

Another time Welles wrote, "there is no little censure because fast vessels are not sent after the *Alabama*, and yet it would be an act of folly to detach vessels from the blockade and send them off scouring the ocean for this roving wolf, which has no country, no resting place but such as neutral England and France may give her. When I sometimes ask the faultfinders to tell me where the *Alabama* is or where it can be found, assuring them that I will send a force of several vessels at once to take her on being satisfactorily informed, they are silenced. Whilst these men blame me for not sending a fleet after the marauders, they and others would blame me were I to weaken the blockade in an uncertain pursuit. Unreasonable and captious men will blame me, take what course I may. I must therefore follow my own convictions."

Welles finally weakened to the demands. A special force of sixteen vessels was organized to hunt the *Alabama* and other "wolves of the sea." In June, 1864, the *Alabama* was trapped at Cherbourg, France, by Captain John A. Winslow in the sloop *Kearsarge,* who challenged the raider to a duel. Semmes accepted the dare and on Sunday morning, June 19, the *Alabama* sallied forth as French crowds lined the shores to witness the engagement. Northern gunnery proved its superiority after four bloody hours, and, leaking at every seam, the *Alabama* sank stern first into the English Channel.

But the most famous naval battle of the war was fought that year while Dewey was combating mosquitoes on the James River. On August 5, 1864, Admiral Farragut led a fleet of eighteen ships into Mobile Bay. Inside the harbor entrance, protected by a field of 180 torpedoes, or mines, lay three light gunboats and the mighty ironclad *Tennessee,* armed with two seven and one-eighth inch rifles and four six-inchers, her sides protected with six-inch armor. Farragut sent his fleet through a narrow passageway cleared in the torpedo field for blockade-runners. Four turreted monitor-type ships, led by the *Tecumseh,* edged through the mines ahead of Dewey's former ship, the *Brooklyn.* Seeing buoys marking the field, the *Brooklyn's* captain backed away from danger, swinging broadside as the other wooden ships jammed in astern. Then the *Tecumseh* struck a torpedo, and with a great blast plunged under the waves, her propellers shrieking in the air. It was a terrifying moment, but too late for retreat. Farragut, lashed to the rigging of the flagship *Hartford,* steamed ahead, past the *Brooklyn,* directly over the mines. Seamen on the *Brooklyn* yelled a warning, but Farragut roared back:

"Damn the torpedoes. Go ahead."

Mines rattled on the undersides of the *Hartford,* but all were defective, and the other Union ships followed her lead safely into the bay. Admiral Franklin Buchanan's *Tennessee* was engaged at close quarters. Six Federal ships rammed her at least once and shelled her rudder chains when they learned their shots bounced harmlessly off her six-inch armored sides. Twelve of the *Tennessee's* crew were killed and nineteen wounded in the frenzied battle which ensued, and with four guns out of commission and Northern ships closing to ram again, Buchanan surrendered his ship. The other enemy vessels were sunk or captured in the fight. Federal losses, however, were staggering. The *Tecumseh* had carried 113 men, including its brave captain, Commander T. A. M. Craven, to the bottom. Craven and the ship's pilot had come face to face at a narrow hatch of the monitor. "After you, pilot," said Craven, and the pilot was the last man to escape the foundering ship. All told, 335 Northern sailors died that day, but Farragut had captured the last Confederate seaport on the Gulf.

During the fall of 1864 the Union Navy determined to bottle up Wilmington, North Carolina, the one port available to Confederate blockade runners who were supplying Lee's army. Admiral Davey Porter was recalled from the West to accomplish the task. When he succeeded Admiral Lee in the North Atlantic squadron, he sent for Dewey to become executive officer of the *Minnesota*. Dewey remained only a day. Again his youth was held against him and he was returned to the *Agawam*. Soon afterward, however, Porter appointed him second in command of the *Colorado*, one of the same class of sail steamers as the *Wabash*, on which Dewey had made his first cruise in 1858. Although the *Colorado* was a prewar frigate of ancient design, nearly four years of Civil War had brought her almost up to date. Instead of smoothbore guns, she had been equipped with one one hundred and fifty-pounder, one eleven-inch shellgun, and forty-six nine-inchers, all modern, all rifled, and capable of meting out ample punishment to any foe.

But if the fighting power of the *Colorado* had been enhanced, her crew of 700 men was at the nadir of morale. Dewey's predecessor as executive officers had evidently been as ineffectual as her skipper, Commodore H. K. Thatcher. Dewey was given the task of whipping the crew back into fighting efficiency and discipline.

The Navy's enormous difficulties in enlisting men during 1864 led Gideon Welles to write on March 24: "We are running short of sailors and I have no immediate remedy. The Army officers are not disposed to lose good men, and seem indifferent to the country and general welfare, if their service can get along. Commodore Rowan writes that the times of the men are running out, and no re-enlistments; the Army is paying enormous bounties. Between 30 and 40 vessels are waiting crews."[*] When the cabinet met on March 25 Lincoln also showed deep concern. Welles proposed the immediate transfer of 12,000 men from the Army to the Navy. Thousands of trained seamen had changed to the Army to receive the large bounties offered, and those who remained comprised a motley assortment of bounty-jumper substitutes and foreigners, ill-mannered, ill-disciplined, who, Dewey thought, were interested only in receiving postwar pensions. Moreover, the Army opposed transfers. Welles accused General Halleck of disliking the Navy more than he loved his country.

*Welles, *Diary*, p. 545.

When Dewey boarded the *Colorado* he found more than a hundred crew members in chains on the gun deck, sentenced for minor and major infractions of discipline. Officers walking past enlisted men were assailed with profanity and abuse. On his first morning he called "all hands." A number of men failed to report. It was too cold, they said, to get out of their hammocks. This would never do. George Dewey went below to the crew's quarters and whenever he found a sailor still in his "sack," tipped him out abruptly. Thereafter, when the executive officer called "all hands," everyone reported.* But tipping men out of hammocks did not alone solve the problem. Most of the junior officers on the *Colorado* were volunteers, many of them "inferior in every way" to the men they commanded. Dewey was convinced that Porter had transferred him to the *Colorado* to make it as taut a ship as any in the squadron. He was determined to restore discipline, and although most of the crew fell in line readily, a minority remained sullen and abusive. A red-headed Englishman named Webster led the irreconcilables. A hulking bully, he intimidated the reserve officers and ruled the forecastle without resistance. Finally, when infractions continued to fill the ship's brig, Dewey ordered the ringleader Webster trussed in double irons and thrown into the hold.

Two or three days later a great commotion broke out. A frightened sentry ran on deck, preceded by noises of crashing ale bottles, which Webster, having broken free, was heaving against the bulkheads of his prison. Dewey ordered the *Colorado's* master at arms to rearrest the offender and chain him up again.

A few minutes later the frightened master reported: "Webster swears he will kill the first man who tries to come down the ladder to take him, sir."

In a twinkling Dewey grabbed a revolver and headed for the ladder. Below, Webster waited with a pair of bottles in his hand, ready to smash anybody whose feet appeared on the top rung.

"Webster," Dewey shouted from above. "This is Mr. Dewey, the executive officer. I am coming down, and Webster you may be sure of this: if you raise a finger against me, I shall kill you."†

Without waiting for a reply, Dewey began to descend, threatening with his gun. Webster waited, ready to throw, but the look in Dewey's eyes and the gun cowed him permanently. The mutinous conduct was ended. Soon the brig was empty and the *Colorado's* crew stood disciplined and ready to fight. It was a triumph which the mild Thatcher had been unable to achieve, and he wrote Washington urging the promotion of

*George Dewey, *op. cit.*, pp. 124–25.
†*Ibid.* pp. 125–27.

the young lieutenant. Again Dewey's youth stood in his way, and the Navy Department refused to advance him.*

In December, 1864, Porter assembled his fleet of more than fifty vessels, including five ironclads, at Hampton Roads, and sailed for Wilmington and the Cape Fear River. Commanding the mouth of this river, at New Inlet, was Fort Fisher, manned powerfully by the Confederates on two sides. One bastion three quarters of a mile long commanded the sea approach, and a second, one third as long, covered a neck of land leading to the river. Porter's fleet was accompanied by General Benjamin Butler and 6,500 men. The plan was to bombard Fort Fisher from the sea, while Butler and his troops attacked the bastion from the neck of land. Porter's fleet mounted more than six hundred guns, as powerful a squadron as had ever been assembled, which followed traditional American policy of arming every ship as powerfully as possible.

To meet this force the Confederates had only 1,900 men. But they had strong guns, and bombproof chambers in the forts. On the land side a field of underground mines had been planted to block invading troops.

The Federal fleet arrived off Fort Fisher in a raging gale on the night of December 23, halting twenty miles at sea, while Commander Rhind, formerly of the *Agawam,* sneaked toward the fort aboard the old *Louisiana.* She carried 150 tons of explosive. In one of the most daring acts of the war, Rhind brought the ammunition-loaded hulk under the walls of the fort, set a train of fuses, and escaped on an accompanying boat, the *Wilderness.* The resulting explosion rocked the Federal ships twenty miles away, but when they sailed in to bombard the fort they could see little evidence of any damage from the blast. Rhind's exploit, plotted by General Butler, was spectacular but without practical result. The effects of the blast were absorbed by the water.

According to Dewey, Confederates ashore thought the boiler of a blockade-runner had exploded and scarcely realized that any attempt had been made against their installations.

About noon Porter's fleet moved in to the attack on Fort Fisher. An odd assortment of ships, the squadron bungled its maneuvers by becoming confused in this almost unknown action of multiple ship movement. Shortly before one o'clock the *New Ironsides,* which was in the van, opened fire on the fort. Each ship dropped anchors from its bow and stern, and became a floating fort as it proceeded to shell the shore. Flame and smoke poured through the air as the fifty ships fired at the rate of 115 shots a minute. Porter silenced the shore guns in an hour and a quarter, but he continued a slow cannonade until 5:30, awaiting Butler's

*Stickney, *op. cit.*, pp. 149–50.

transports. They arrived too late to land that day, and Porter ordered the Northern fleet to retire for the night.

Federal casualties that first day were low. Most were caused when the Union ships' new 100-pound higher explosive Parrott guns exploded, killing their crews. "These proved to be about as dangerous to us as to the enemy and were not used again," Dewey wrote.

The next morning, Christmas Day, the fleet steamed in again, anchored, and renewed its cannonade. This time the *Colorado*, the *Minnesota*, and the *Wabash* came in closer to the fort, and with other vessels launched a slow, steady, and accurate barrage. Meanwhile, Butler and his men were landed north of the fort and proceeded to the attack. "No opposition was encountered ashore, although some of the troops advanced to within a hundred yards of the fort. Generals Butler and Weitzel, however, decided that insufficient damage had been done to the Confederate stronghold, and without making an assault re-embarked their soldiers and soon returned to Hampton Roads."* The ships' crews looked in vain for smoke and fire from the promised land assault. In the afternoon Porter signaled for many of the bombarding ships to retire from the action. The *Minnesota* and the *Colorado* were ordered to remain at anchor and to cease firing while the lesser ships steamed away.

Suddenly the shore batteries, which had been firing only spasmodically, loosed a terrific barrage on the two frigates. Ten-inch shells rained on the *Colorado*, disabling two guns, blowing out the capstan, and inflicting many casualties. Commodore Thatcher, having been ordered not to fire, was momentarily at a loss. Then, taking the decision upon himself, he ordered the *Minnesota* to protect herself, signaled the flagship why he was breaking orders, and sent Lieutenant Dewey racing down the gun deck to cry:

"Fire! Fire as fast as you can. That is the way to stop their fire."†

Thus, in the heat of battle, Dewey gave voice to Farragut's theory that "the best way to counteract an enemy's fire is to make the enemy worry about your own."

The crew of the *Colorado* frantically loaded shells and sent giant cannon balls streaking across the water to land with good effect inside the fort. A few minutes later, when Porter signaled the *Colorado* to retire, the forts were silent, and the ship limped victoriously toward the fleet.

That night the squadron retired to Beaufort, farther north along the coast, and Dewey spent his twenty-seventh birthday at sea off North

*Knox, *A History of the United States Navy*, pp. 313–14.
†George Dewey, *op. cit.*, p. 132.

Carolina supervising repair work on torn timbers as seamen cleared away the battle wreckage and prepared for another attack.

On the 12th of January, 1865, a fleet of forty-eight Federal ships and an army which General Grant this time called "a competent force properly commanded," sailed from Beaufort to make the attack Butler had failed to carry out. The ships took up position off Fort Fisher and soon silenced strongly reinforced Southern guns, while Major General A. H. Terry and 8,000 troops were landed from the transports. During the day they crept close to the fort in preparation for the attack and on the 14th the attempt was made. Monitors sailed within 800 yards of the battery to lay a bombardment of shells upon the guns facing Terry's forces. All day long the sea bombardment persisted, sometimes spasmodically, sometimes with brutal devastation. That night 1,600 bluejackets and 400 Marines were sent ashore from the ships to assail the sea side of the fort while the Army marched against the northern walls.

Dewey's request to join the landing party* was denied by Commodore Thatcher, who would automatically become flag officer if Porter were killed, and Dewey would be needed to command the *Colorado*. Much to his disgust, he was ordered to remain aboard.

The Army attacked from the north on the morning of January 15, while cheering seamen and Marines dashed up the rocks below the fort. The sailors, carrying only cutlasses and pistols, were armed as if boarding a British ship in the War of 1812 instead of a Civil War land effort. Only forty yards away from the guns of the fort, leaders of the Marine landing party halted in an angle of the wall to rally their men. The walls had been breached by the guns of the fleet, and some of the bolder sailors tried to storm the apertures. A murderous fire blew them back, leveling them with bloody toll. About one fifth of the number fell. Yet time and time again, led by Commander K. R. Breeze, the sailors and Marines re-formed their ranks and renewed the brave and hopeless attack.

Meanwhile the fleet continued its bombardment.† General Terry's troops, approaching from the north, had gained the parapets on the land side. Bombproof traverses, fifteen of them in all, protected the fort, but with the aid of accurate fire from the monitors, the troops slowly forced the defenders back. All afternoon and evening the bloody assault raged.

*George Dewey, *op. cit.*, pp. 134–35.

†During the entire bombardment, Dewey related, the fleet fired a total of some 10,000 shells, considered almost impossible at that time. With more than 160 guns participating, such a rate had never been maintained before. At the height of the bombardment, with 115 shells fired a minute, each gun was firing at a little more than a minute's interval. Since some of the monitors during the Civil War fired only every eight or nine minutes, this rate seemed magnificent at the time. In modern war a ship whose guns could fire only every minute or so would be better off at home.

As darkness fell the defense grew weaker and the fort surrendered at ten o'clock. Ensign Robley D. Evans, wounded six times during the beach assault, came back to consciousness to hear the cheers of victors in the fort and on the ships.

The fall of Fort Fisher marked the end of Confederate resistance on the sea. "Why, there is nothing left for your ships to do," the President told Welles when he heard the news. When Terry took Wilmington a few days later, Lee's supply lines were eliminated. "What Appomattox was for the Federal Army, Fort Fisher was for the Federal Navy," Dewey declared.

When peace had come, and an inventory was made in his own mind, Dewey realized that the war had brought him invaluable experience in navigation, on river and sea. Fighting the Southerners had been harder in many ways than engaging a foreign enemy. Some of the Confederate officers had been his fellows at Annapolis. On ships firing at his own had been young boys with whom, only a few years before, he had studied, argued, drunk, and smoked. It hurt, sometimes, to know you were training a gun at the heart of a boy who may have sat on the thwart ahead of you when rowing at the Academy.

"They all thought that one of them could lick two or three Yankees," he recalled of his Southern classmates. "They found out they couldn't, though. A man is a man, no matter where he was born."*

"Professionally," he wrote, "the war had meant nearly four years' training for me as an executive officer." He had served as second in command of no less than six ships, most of them among the largest in the Navy, with crews of 300 to 700 men under his command. He had survived four major battles and minor engagements too numerous to recall. Through all the shot and shell he had emerged without a scratch. The nickname of "Lucky," given him at the Academy, had been proved apt. He had seen his comrades die and one commanding officer fall dead at his feet, yet he had survived.

His training at Annapolis had been little more than "hell and discipline," he told his son. The Academy "was poor schooling beside that of serving under Farragut in time of war," he wrote in his autobiography. Now in war Dewey had found himself and, like his country, had survived the test of smoke and fire which filled him again with a sense of destiny.

*George Dewey, op. cit., p. 137.

RANK HAS NO PRIVILEGES—IN LOVE

$\mathcal{R}$. H.I.P.—Rank has its privileges—is an old naval saying which seemed completely inapplicable to George Dewey in 1865. Despite Commander Rhind's seniority, he was outranked by Dewey on Susie Goodwin's list of prospects. The letters from Portsmouth which followed the *Agawam* and *Colorado* through the latter stages of the war were matched in frequency and success only by those in George Dewey's slightly illegible hand to New Hampshire. An agreement was reached sometime during 1864 and George Dewey and Susie Goodwin were secretly engaged. George's own family knew of this turn of events, although Governor Goodwin had not been asked for his daughter's hand.

Soon after Fort Fisher Dewey was assigned to the *Kearsarge*, which in March of 1865 put into Boston harbor for repairs. Dewey arranged shore leave and went to Portsmouth. He described the visit in a letter to his brother-in-law, Dr. George Greeley, on March 20, 1865. Greeley had married George's younger sister, Mary, in 1861, and at this time was an army surgeon.

Dear Brother George,
Your kind note of Friday last is just received, for I have only returned this moment from a short visit with my sweetheart.
I spent Sunday with her there and today she came to Boston with me on a visit to her sister, Mrs. Stone, who is living in Roxbury.
I am hardly able to form an idea as to how much longer I shall be here, for I have not seen the Kearsarge since Friday. I hope, however, and think that we will be here at least two weeks longer; in the meantime I shall be in town, and very happy always to see Mary and yourself. Whenever you come, drop me a line to the Navy Yard where I shall find you and also take a look in at Parker's, say about nine in the morning, or three in the afternoon. I take my meals there, but have rooms in Chickering Building, No. 246, Washington St. My little Susy will probably remain this week and perhaps part of next, and having "been

through the mill" you can understand I anticipate much pleasure from her dear society.

I have just heard of my promotion to lieutenant commander and also of Edward's. . . .

Please excuse both blots, which have just made their appearance.* I don't know how.

Give much love to Mary and believe me

Your affectionate brother,
GEORGE DEWEY.

The promotion to lieutenant commander arrived on March 3, and encouraged by his increased income, Dewey approached Governor Goodwin to ask for his consent. The Governor listened to his request. Two sisters of Susie having previously married military officers, Governor Goodwin joked with George, saying, "What, another officer to support?" Then, laughing, the Governor took him into the stately dining room where he poured glasses of port to toast the success of the young pair.

The marriage was long delayed by the uncertainties of a naval career, and after George's brief visit in the "dear society" of Susie, the *Kearsarge* sailed with the European squadron. Dewey could well appreciate the changes in his life and in the world since he last passed Gibraltar, as a novice midshipman on the *Wabash* in 1858.

Now, in 1865, he was a lieutenant commander, a veteran of a bloody war. The year-long cruise of the screw sloop *Kearsarge*, of which he was executive officer, was a pleasant tour filled with lengthy liberty, trips to the capitals of Europe, and the association of a victorious fleet with officers of the Old World powers. Duties were routine and brief, and for the most part the *Kearsarge* officers enjoyed themselves.

The *Kearsarge* was a 1,461-ton sailing-steamer, built in a matter of weeks in 1861 after the opening of hostilities. Armed with a pair of eleven-inch Dahlgren guns, a twenty-pound rifle, six thirty-two-pounders, and two twelve-pound howitzers, she had been amply armed to sink the enemy raider *Alabama*. Now, after the war, with her wooden sides and her tall masts, she was not the latest word but was still comparable to the majority of foreign ships.

If the regular Navy officers enjoyed that cruise, some of the enlisted men did not. Many of the crew had wanted to get out of their uniforms after peace, and were discontented in the crowded forecastle. One of the most mysterious stories of Dewey's life emanated from this situation. Without record in the Navy Department files, the story of the "mutiny"

---

*Ink spots are seen on the last page of the note.

has been told in various ways. The most authentic version is attested to by Dewey's son, George, who was told the tale by his father.

A group of *Kearsarge* men refused to come on deck one day for morning muster. Below the main hatch they growled and swore, and the master at arms was powerless to force them to the deck. Refusing to come up, they refused to let anyone come down, and the junior officers were balked by the decided impasse.

"The first one down here will be killed," one mutineer yelled.

The executive officer took matters into his own hands at this point and marched right up to the ladder.

"I am Mr. Dewey," he called down. "I have two revolvers in my hand, and I'm going to shoot the first man who defies me." According to his son, Dewey did not have to go down that ladder. The men looked into his face, changed their minds, and marched on deck. The mutiny was over.

This story has been told in a more dramatic way by Dibble in a book, *"Strenuous Americans,"* which set the scene as "on the *Kearsarge* in 1886." At that time Dewey was in command of the *Pensacola* and the *Kearsarge* was on the other side of the world.

According to the Dibble version, Dewey, accompanied by the ship's clerk, went forward with a pair of guns at his side.

"Call the roll," he said.

"John Johnson," intoned the clerk. There was no answer. Dewey, who could see John Johnson below, announced that his name would be called again, and "if you don't go on deck, you will be a dead man." The name was called again, without an answer. Dewey fired his pistol and John Johnson fell lifeless.

"Now, men, the roll will be continued. As each name is called, you will answer and go on deck." The men went on deck and John Johnson's body was lowered into the sea. Fletcher Pratt has repeated Dibble's story, because, despite the fact that he describes it as "gravely suspect . . ." it "fits in perfectly with Dewey's character." No record of the incident is found in the Navy Department archives, and although Dewey was noted for his settlement of issues without report to higher authority, it seems doubtful that he could kill a man without reporting it. Nor is it credible that Dewey would neglect to discuss such an incident from the proper viewpoint in his autobiography.

The *Kearsarge* had sailed for Europe in May of 1865, soon after peace. The next summer, while in European waters, Dewey was transferred to a sister ship, the *Canandaigua*. Like all ships of the time, she moved under sail as frequently as the winds permitted. Rear Admiral Louis Goldsborough, superintendent at Annapolis in Dewey's midshipman days, assumed command of the European squadron that summer and transferred his former student to the *Colorado* as his flag lieutenant. So Dewey was again aboard the ship he had fought on at Fort Fisher in the Civil War, this time learning the duties of a staff officer and standing at Goldsborough's side at diplomatic balls and receptions of the European world.

As a lieutenant commander Dewey made friends with many British officers, and the young American's name began to spread. His social successes in England were notably attested to, as the following pieces of verse printed in an English paper indicates:

> The venturous mariner who nears old England's stormy coast,
> > Though sailing on with favoring breeze,
> Is oft engulfed and lost.
>
> So a sweet youth from that green state where sheep and lambs abound,
> > When in the Dewey bloom of youth
> He came where ships were found.
>
> Although his duty was to face the foe in stern array,
> > Did yield him to a magic grace
> That stole his heart away.
>
> Ah, luckless youth, or victimized, fly not from fate's command,
> > For many another nice young man
> Has wrecked on Goodwin's sands.

Two sailors of the *Colorado* had worked their way into the ship's brig while it was in the Mediterranean, for an offense so minor they determined to rebel. Friday afternoon, when Dewey toured the ship for the regular inspection, he heard the sailor-prisoners grousing.

"I've got some matches in my pocket that were overlooked, and I'll burn his old ship under him," one of them whispered.

Dewey slipped away, came out on deck, and rang the fire bell.

"Fire in the ship's brig," he shouted, and seamen with buckets and hoses inundated the seagoing jail. Four hoses poured water through the grating of the brig's door, and in a few minutes the prisoners were crying for help.

"Fire's out," said Dewey, "I guess their matches are pretty well soaked, now."*

The *Colorado* sailed for France soon afterward and was in the harbor of Cherbourg when the U.S.S. *Franklin* entered the port. On her main-

*Adelbert Dewey, *The Life and Letters of Admiral Dewey*.

mast was the four-starred flag of Admiral Farragut, who was on a triumphant visit to all the leading powers of Europe.

Farragut's arrival was the signal for a panoply of honors, seventeen-gun salutes, ruffles and flourishes, sideboys and bands, when he came aboard to inspect the American ships. He visited the *Colorado* and praised her efficiency and her thirty-two-piece band, the largest in the fleet. As executive officer, it was Dewey's responsibility to see the *Colorado* was shipshape. Standing by Admiral Goldsborough's side, the young lieutenant commander had one of his proudest moments when Farragut turned to his brother-in-law, Captain Pennock, commander of the *Franklin,* to say:

"Pennock, I want the *Franklin* to be just like this."*

The generous receptions held by European royalty and admiralties for Farragut lasted nearly a year. When he returned to America in 1868, his health began to fail. In 1870 the heroic admiral took his last cruise from Hampton Roads to Portsmouth, fell ill in the commandant's house there, and died on August 14.†

The *Colorado* sailed home in the summer of 1867. When she reached the Brooklyn Navy Yard, Lieutenant Commander Dewey was given leave. Susie Goodwin was more attractive than he had remembered. As soon as he arrived in Portsmouth, sets of three cards were engraved in Spencerian script. One of them read "Miss Susie‡ Boardman Goodwin"; the second "Geo. Dewey, Lieut. Comdr. U.S. Navy"; while the third announced "Mr. and Mrs. George Dewey."

On October 24, 1867, Portsmouth society drove to the Episcopal church to attend the military wedding. The colonial mansion of the Goodwins was opened wide for a gay reception. From Montpelier came Julius Yemans Dewey, no longer a poor rural doctor but the wealthy president of the National Life Insurance Company of Vermont. With him was his third wife and his two other sons, Charles and Edward, both prosperous executives of the company. Dr. Greeley and Mary were there as well, drinking toasts to the happiness of the bride and groom, the country boy

*George Dewey, *Autobiography.*

†In 1870 Dewey accompanied his father-in-law, ex-Governor Goodwin, to the commandant's house to see Farragut on his sickbed. Remembering how the admiral had sailed into battle high in the tops of the *Hartford*, Dewey was shocked to see how "pale and thin he had become. Yet, ill as he was, he retained his old-time cheerful manner which had endeared him to his subordinates."

‡In his letters Dewey referred to Miss Goodwin as "Susy"; in his autobiography he called her "Susan," while the cards announcing their engagement spelled her name as "Susie." Most earlier biographers of Dewey have stated that he was stationed at Kittery or Portsmouth in the summer of 1867 and then met Susie for the first time. Very little remains as evidence of the love of George and Susie. In his autobiography she is mentioned only in five lines.

from Vermont, now a naval officer with gold upon his sleeve, who was marrying the governor's beautiful daughter.

Orders assigned Lieutenant Commander Dewey to teach at the Naval Academy. There he assumed charge of the fourth class of midshipmen as well as the ships stationed there for training. Among the vessels was the U.S.S. *Constitution*. Some of the midshipmen barracked between her wooden decks, as crowded as the seamen in the Barbary wars, and Dewey, as their commanding officer, became her "skipper." For two years he was in command of this historic ship.

Dewey was only thirty years old, and a benedict, but to the young midshipmen, boys of ten when the great war started, he was a stern disciplinarian, an exacting taskmaster, and a veteran officer. Ruling the boys with the same iron will he exercised on shipboard, he made the fourth classmen toe the mark in a manner which undoubtedly made better officers of them than they might have been. Some of his students were later to be captains and commanders in the war with Spain. But old and aloof as he may have seemed to the midshipmen, Dewey considered himself only a youngster officer, and with Susie and the other lieutenants and their brides thoroughly enjoyed his three years at Annapolis. "Porter's Dancing Academy," it was cynically called because of Vice Admiral David Porter's penchant for social affairs, but to Dewey it was a welcome change from the "hell and discipline" he had known ten years before. Porter was relieved as superintendent in 1869 by Rear Admiral John L. Worden, skipper of the *Monitor* when it fought the *Merrimac*. Worden ended the society of Porter's regime, made the midshipmen knuckle down to studies, and tried to make Annapolis as salty as he could. But he took a liking to Dewey, as many other admirals had done, and appointed him his aide. It was Dewey's second experience as a staff officer.

In the summer of 1870 Dewey was ordered to command his first ship, the screw sloop *Narragansett*, which had been built before 1860. The *Narragansett* had originally been rated a "second class" sloop, but she was definitely and officially known as "third class" when Dewey climbed her Jacob's ladder in New York harbor. She remained there for three months without orders, while Kaiser Wilhelm waged the Franco-Prussian War. In November Prussian troops besieged Paris and captured Louis Napoleon. In January Paris surrendered, and Americans poured out funds in a collection for food to help the victims. The supplies were loaded onto three American ships to be carried to the French. Because there was no immediate use for the *Narragansett*, Dewey was given command of a sailing storeship of 500 tons, the *Supply*, and headed for the French coast.

The *Supply* arrived at Le Havre too late to be of aid. On the wharves stores from other ships lay rotting, and Dewey was instructed to take his cargo to London for sale. He brought his sloop to the East London docks and turned the cargo over to Junius Spencer Morgan, United States Ambassador to Great Britain. Dewey spent the next month having a "delightful" time through introductions made by a banker friend, Francis Blake, a former naval officer. In the summer of 1871 Dewey returned to Boston and his wife. That winter he was stationed at the Boston Navy Yard and lived in a house on Beacon Street.

A naval officer's life in those postwar years was a thing of peace and leisure. The Navy was being sold and scrapped. The monitors, with iron sheathing over green oak timbers, were rotting at the docks. In another two years all the ironclads were rusted into uselessness, and the American Navy, the North's defender in the great war, was only a fleet of twenty-year-old wooden ships, all built before the revolution in naval design.

In the late winter of 1872 Lieutenant Commander and Mrs. Dewey left Boston and reported to the Naval Torpedo Station in Newport, Rhode Island. He was promoted to the rank of commander that April 13. Ichabod Goodwin and his wife came down to Newport shortly before Christmas, for Susie was to have a child. On December 23 George Goodwin Dewey was born. Susie did not recover from the birth of her son. Five days later she died.

The Portsmouth paper on December 30 stated, under a headline reading "Sudden Death of an Estimable Lady":

Tidings were received here yesterday of the sudden death of Mrs. Susan G. Dewey at Newport, R. I. Mrs. Dewey was the beautiful and accomplished daughter of ex-Governor Ichabod Goodwin of this city, and wife of Commander George Dewey of the U.S. Navy. Her unexpected demise is a terrible blow to the venerable parents, as well as to a large circle of friends. She was a young woman of rare beauty and grace, endowed with an amiable disposition and a cheerful temperament, causing her to be loved by all who knew her.

Two days later she was buried in the Portsmouth cemetery.

The shock left her closest relatives desolated. On January 24 her mother wrote a letter* describing the family's grief:

I would have thankfully given my life to save her. She was young and beautiful, a power among her friends, an idol with her husband, and

---

*This letter, written in lavender-bluish ink, was sent to Mrs. William H. Parsons of New York. She was Anna Decatur, a granddaughter of Stephen Decatur, who burned the *Philadelphia* in the harbor of Tripoli, and beat the *Macedonian* in the War of 1812. Decatur died of wounds received in a duel with Commodore Barron in 1820.

having everything to make life desirable. The expectation of this baby completed everything. Millions of money could not have added one iota to her happiness.

I think I never knew anything like the general lamentation over her. Wherever she had lived, wherever she was known, regret and sorrow are expressed. Frank says he has never heard anything like it in Boston and Cambridge except in the case of a public character.

Oh, my dear Anna, what a good time we had in New York when you saw us there together, and in Boston, Newport and wherever we were together she was always the leader and took charge of me and told me what I must have and do, and it was my pleasure to obey. She always called me Sarah and I liked all she said and did.

The dear baby is a fine, strong child and has become the light of the house. His father is tending him by the fire in my room and feels about him as you can imagine. I have a little bed in my room and on that he takes his naps by day. Mrs. Munroe, our precious Susie's nurse, takes care of him and she is a very superior person. Captain* Dewey has left his house, and his kind neighbors on the island will superintend the packing of his furniture.

His friends in Washington have been very kind and considerate and have given him the command of the *Narragansett,* which is fitting out at Callao for the survey of the Pacific Coast, and from Panama to San Francisco.

There will be a corps of scientific men which will give him pleasant companionship. . . . It is a fine command and we are glad of anything that takes him out of his loneliness. . . . But, oh, he is so crushed. . . .

*Commanding officers of Navy ships are referred to as "captains," regardless of their actual official rank.

10

THE YEARS BETWEEN

*I*n February, wearing a black band upon his sleeve, Dewey left the United States by steamer for Panama to assume command, for the second time, of the *Narragansett*. For the next two years the sloop meandered in and out of shoals, heaving the lead, and recording depths, tides, and characteristics of the Pacific shores. From San Diego down the western coast of Lower California, north again, deep into the Gulf of California, and south to Cape Corrientes, due west to Guadalajara on the 20th parallel, the ship recorded geodetic charts, whose accuracy has made them useful till the present time.

The *Narragansett* was in the Gulf on October 31, 1873, when the merchant vessel *Virginius,* flying the American flag, was captured by the Spanish gunboat *Tornado* in the Caribbean. She was carrying a filibustering expedition to Cuba, but the presence of nine American citizens on her passenger list nearly plunged the United States into war with Spain. The crew and passengers were taken by the Spaniards into Santiago de Cuba, where a drumhead court-martial tried them and condemned and executed fifty-three of the fifty-nine on the spot. The others would have been shot also had not the British ship *Niobe* steamed into the bay under the command of Captain Lambton Lorraine. Lorraine, unwilling to await orders from home when he learned what had happened, swung his vessel broadside to the town, uncapped his guns, and announced that he would fire unless the order of execution was rescinded immediately.

General Burriel, the Spanish governor, was not afraid of war with the United States, but he hesitated to offend the British lion. The orders were revoked. Nevertheless, fifty-three persons on an American ship had been kidnaped, their flag hauled down and trampled on, and their lives taken, without due process of law. President Ulysses S. Grant immediately dispatched ships to Cuba and penned a strong protest to the Spanish Minister, who refused to receive it. Grant then ordered the American

Minister at Madrid to ask for his passport unless "satisfactory reparation" was made within twelve days. Spain, knowing the debilitated state of the American fleet, offered no apologies, and eleven days later Secretary of State Hamilton Fish cabled Madrid that if "Spain cannot redress these outrages, the United States will."

The country was in a wild state of excitement, demanding revenge and apology. Already the cause of the Cuban insurgents had been taken up by substantial majorities in America and the *Virginius* affair seemed to offer the logical and required *casus belli.** The twelve-day ultimatum expired without satisfactory action by Spain, but the American Minister did not ask for his passport, a fact which can perhaps be explained by a brief mention of the career of George Robeson, Secretary of the Navy under Grant.

When Grant was elected to the White House, Gideon Welles was succeeded as Secretary of the Navy by A. H. Borie, who held office just long enough to rename a number of ships after characters in Greek mythology. After four months he resigned, having decided he was "only a figurehead; the department is managed by Admiral Porter."†

Robeson succeeded Borie. Described as "a first-rate judge of wines, a second-rate trout fisherman, a third-rate New Jersey lawyer, and a fourth-rate secretary," Robeson came to the conclusion that money could be made in the Navy Department. He became a partner in a Philadelphia firm to which he could direct contracts for ship repairs at almost twice their original cost, and Robeson, who, according to Fletcher Pratt, was worth $20,000 when he assumed his cabinet post, retired with $324,000. Such scandals were not the only reasons, however, for the Navy's neglected state. After Appomattox Congress had refused to appropriate any funds for building vessels, and the ironclads rusted on their armor plate and rotted underneath. None was fit for action.

It is small wonder, then, that Spain thought contemptuously of America's antiquated hulks and sneered at Ulysses S. Grant's fulminations. A third threat by the administration, however, forced a compromise. As Spain was in none too healthy a state herself, she agreed to pay damages to the families of the victims and to return the ship to the United States, but offered no salute to the American flag. The *Virginius* was returned, not at Santiago but at a jungle outpost, Bahia Hondo, "battered and covered with filth."‡ She foundered off Cape Hatteras on the way home and the extent of her damage was never publicly known.

*Harry Thurston Peck, *Twenty Years of the Republic 1885–1905* (New York: Dodd, Mead & Co., 1905, 1906), pp. 534–37.
†Fletcher Pratt, *The Navy*, p. 347 ff.
‡Peck, *op. cit.*, p. 537.

News of the entire episode reached the wardroom of the *Narragansett* by way of Eastern newspapers mailed to the ship. The officers hardly analyzed their nation's state of unpreparedness, regretting only that the *Narragansett* was so far away from Cuba and from action. The skipper walked into the room. The officers rose as a man, but Dewey waved them down.

"Carry on," he said, stroking his mustache. "Why so blue?" They showed him the papers and told him they would miss the "show."

"On the contrary," he replied, "we shall be very much in it. If war with Spain is declared, the *Narragansett* will take Manila Bay."* There was no realism in Dewey's boast. He commanded a third-rate antiquated sloop, and the administration at home, knowing its weakness, had backed down. But Dewey was ready for what seemed to him a logical attack on the Philippines.

Soon after the *Virginius* affair the *Narragansett* anchored at La Paz, a little town near the southern tip of Baja, California, almost a hundred miles from the peninsula's end. About thirty miles inland from this jumping-off place was the settlement of Triunfo, where in the seventies a few Americans managed two silver mines with the help of five hundred Mexican laborers. As his ship stopped there periodically for refitting, Commander Dewey had struck up a friendship with a Mr. Brook, manager of the silver mines. A messenger brought Dewey a hastily written note from his friend. The Mexican laborers had rebelled for higher wages and were besieging the American managers in their compound. Brook pleaded for Commander Dewey to come to their rescue. The Mexican Army had a garrison of a hundred troops in La Paz, more than the small landing party of the *Narragansett,* and Dewey could not risk sending his Marines overland to Brook's relief. Instead, he dispatched Lieutenant George C. Reiter ashore with a message for the commanding general: "The American commander requests that his excellency send his troops to the immediate relief of the Americans at Triunfo. If that is not done, the commander may feel compelled to take possession of the city and the customs house, and retain possession until he receives further instructions from his government."

In company with the American Consul, Reiter conveyed this message to the Mexican district governor, adding embellishments of his own. The governor, frightened by such a belligerent message, "expressed astonishment and some petulance."†

*George Dewey, *Autobiography*, pp. 145–46.
†*Ibid.*, pp. 147–49.

"Why does your government send irresponsible boys in command of its ships to foreign ports?" he asked.*

At that moment he looked out and saw the *Narragansett* moving into position to command the main street, customs house, and the governor's own residence. The troops were sent immediately.

When New York newspapers learned of this episode, they headlined their articles, "The right man in the right place." Dewey had not considered it worth reporting to the Navy Department and soon he received the clippings in a letter from Secretary Robeson with the note: "The Department still awaits your report on this subject." A belated report was sent, and "with some anxiety" Dewey awaited a reply. The verdict was favorable, however, and his action was completely approved.

In the spring of 1875 Dewey was relieved of his command, sailed north to California, and rode the new railroad overland to New Hampshire to see his son and to rest until new orders were forthcoming.

The prospects were scarcely encouraging. By 1875 the United States fleet was in a sorry state. Only a few gunboats had been built after the Civil War; all the ships bought and converted for the conflict, all the captured ships used by the North, most of the monitors, and many of the speedily built craft, whose green, unseasoned timbers were warped and rotten, had been sold or broken up. The *Monongahela,* in which Dewey had served on the Mississippi River, had been washed ashore and back to sea again by a tidal wave on the island of St. Croix. *New Ironsides,* "fightingest" of the monitors, had burned at the dock. As the years passed, and especially after the Robeson deals, repairs became too expensive for Congress to approve expenditures for them, and those prewar ships which remained limped along in disrepair or in partial commission.

In Europe, meanwhile, armored ships were transforming the British Navy, while the American fleet, which had pioneered the revolution, could have been blown out of the water in five minutes by any of the new warships.

Even Oscar Wilde added his satire.

"I don't think I should like America," runs a line in the *Canterville Ghost.*
"I suppose because we have no ruins and curiosities," said Virginia satirically.
"No ruins! No curiosities!" answered the ghost. "You have your Navy and your manners."

Many American naval officers, discouraged by the low state into which

*This "slur" upon his maturity bothered Dewey. He was thirty-six years old at the time.

the service had fallen, retired to civilian life, but Dewey, for whom the Navy was both a career and a wife, frowned on such quitting. Whenever the question of retirement arose, he commented:

"Not until the law makes me. While you are on the active list there is always a chance for action."* Perhaps he was thinking of Farragut, sixty years old at the outbreak of the Civil War. Perhaps he was still confident of a star guiding him, the star which, having brought him grief and loneliness, must somehow bring compensation in another form.

When he reached Boston in 1875, Dewey was assigned as lighthouse inspector for the Second Naval District, a routine shore job, humdrum and dull, yet not lacking its pleasant side. He had made many friends in the city and he looked to them for recreation and solace.

In the spring of 1878 he was promoted to a higher post as naval secretary of the Lighthouse Board in Washington. Here he entered upon a gayer stage, a world of famous names and faces, and of dinners and receptions by the score. He met Senator Roscoe Conkling of New York and James G. Blaine of Maine and renewed his acquaintance with Admiral Porter. His duties on the naval boards at the time were by no means rigorous.

One of his accomplishments was to settle an argument about the use in lighthouses of lard oil, at seventy-five cents a gallon, and kerosene, at eight cents. Dewey proved his progressive trend of thought by voting in favor of John D. Rockefeller. Soon afterward, however, electricity came into use for coastal lights. Another achievement of those years made Dewey proud. He was instrumental in changing the method of paying employees —paying them directly instead of through red-tape orders on customs collectors.

He took up horseback riding again, and every afternoon, when the Lighthouse Board closed its office, he posted over the trails behind the White House or through Rock Creek Park. Frequently he cantered past a white-haired rider about whom he became rather curious, and whom he found to be George Bancroft, eminent historian and founder of the Naval Academy when Secretary of the Navy under President James K. Polk.

Reining in his horse, Dewey said, "As an officer of the Navy who owes so much to the Naval Academy which you established, I want to thank you."† The compliment pleased the old gentleman, who tipped his German cap, acquired during his days as Ambassador to Berlin, and

*George Dewey, op. cit., p. 50.
†George Dewey, op. cit., p. 152.

100

thanked the young man effusively. They became friends and rode together regularly thereafter whenever the weather permitted.

In 1881 Dewey was removed from Washington to command the *Juniata*, a sister ship of the *Kearsarge* and the *Canandaigua*, and like them, built in 1861, a mere youngster in the fleet of 1881. Since Dewey's health was poor at the time, the command was designed as a health cure. A leisurely voyage through the Mediterranean and on to the China station was planned. He welcomed the cruise, for the Orient was the only corner of the world where he had not served, but he did not relish the idea of commanding the *Juniata*. In his own words, she was "a relic of a past epoch of naval warfare, which you would have expected to see flying the flag of some tenth-rate power. She was as out-of-date as the stagecoach. Her round bottom made her roll heavily with even a slight swell, and an English sea captain at Fayal declared that he had seen her keel out of water."*

As the *Juniata* "rolled" across the Atlantic in late October, Dewey's health became much worse, and by the time she reached Gibraltar he was confined to his cabin. An English doctor, called aboard to examine him, poked at Dewey's liver, and asked if it hurt. The commander, suppressing a desire to cry out from the "excruciating twinge," said no, and sailed on to Malta, where he collapsed and was rushed ashore to the British hospital for an operation. A badly abscessed liver had nearly killed him. Dewey is said to have asked Dr. James Nicholas Dick, his British surgeon, what were his chances of surviving the operation.

"About one chance in fifty," answered the doctor. Dewey took the chance. The delicate operation was successful, but typhoid fever attacked him and he lay for weeks between life and death.

Dewey was still in the Malta hospital with a tube in his side for daily drainage the next April when he wrote his sister Mary:

My Dear Sister: . . . So I will not say much about the operation itself, except that I have been very, very ill, and on two or three occasions, very near "the other shore." At one time I fully expected to die, and nothing but an excellent constitution and God's mercy brought me through.

The climate is much like that of Florida, and we are enjoying oranges, roses, etc.—and now and then a mosquito.

Your affectionate brother,
GEO. DEWEY.

While the *Juniata* proceeded to China under a new commanding officer, Dewey toured European health resorts and spas in search of

*George Dewey, *op. cit.*, p. 154.

recovery. Mineral springs, sulphur baths, and iron water of Bad Nauheim, Bavaria, Austria, and Italy accomplished little. Finally, in February, 1884, he reached Santa Barbara, California, where, in a Montecito sanitarium, he began to regain his health. By this time America's new fleet, the White Squadron, was in preparation, but those ships which would be the pride of nineteenth-century Americans would not be George Dewey's for another fourteen years.

11

BULWARKS AFLOAT

𝒯oward the close of the administration of Rutherford B. Hayes in 1880, the American Navy consisted of an odd assortment of 142 old-fashioned ships. Only forty-eight of them were immediately available for sea duty, and only sixty-nine could possibly be considered able to enter combat operations. The feeble fleet possessed five "first-rate steam vessels," actually at least twenty-five years old and obsolete; twenty-seven second-rate ships, of which three were falling apart on shore, while seven more were listed as in "ordinary unfit for repair." Only nine of these were fit for sea. Of the twenty-nine third-rate vessels, only fifteen could, by the greatest stretch of the imagination, be considered "useful." Six fourth-rate ships, which could almost be sunk by an air rifle, and twenty-two sailing vessels, of which only five could float, made up another segment. In addition, there were twenty-four Civil War iron-clads which had managed to escape the salvage hammers, but only fourteen of these were in service. Two torpedo vessels, one unworkable, the other experimental, and a flotilla of noncombat auxiliary vessels completed the list. Dry rot in the frames made them even more vulnerable to modern pulverizing guns. The fleet ranked twelfth in the world, even below the navies of China, Denmark, and Chile.

About this time Peru and Chile engaged in a territorial dispute. Secretary of State James G. Blaine upheld Peru's side so insistently that a diplomatic crisis approached hostilities. Chile mobilized her fleet, and only when it was realized that her Navy was superior to the United States' did more tractable heads prevail. But the dangerous policy pursued by Blaine did serve to "awaken the United States to the decrepitude of the Navy" and brought on a progressive naval building program.

President James A. Garfield, Hayes' successor, appointed as his Secretary of the Navy, William H. Hunt, a Louisiana Unionist in the Civil War, who continued in office after the President was assassinated on his way to a class reunion at Williams College. Chester A. Arthur entered the White House, and in his first address to Congress said, "I cannot too strongly urge upon you . . . every consideration of the national safety, honor, and economy imperatively demands a thorough rehabilitation of the Navy." And Secretary of the Navy Hunt added, "It is a source of mortification to our officers and fellow countrymen generally that our vessels of war should stand in such mean contrast alongside the ships of other and inferior powers."

Seventeen years after the Civil War the budget of the United States Navy was $300,000,000, mostly for maintenance, a few repairs, and, according to John D. Long, some "waste." "Foreign nations," Admiral Porter complained, "laugh at us and say we can neither go to war nor defend ourselves from attack."

In Europe, meanwhile, much attention had been given to watertight compartmentation of ships to reduce the danger of their being sunk from a single shot. Foreign builders were likewise looking into the merits of high-powered, long-range rifled guns of steel, results of inventions by Armstrong in England and Krupp in Germany. European powers also bought the Hotchkiss rapid-fire gun, developed in the United States but spurned in Washington.

Between 1870 and 1875 an almost total change in shipbuilding had taken place abroad, where steel was replacing iron, although many Americans ridiculed the trend. Steel, they maintained, was merely "a high quality of iron made at greatly increased cost from cast ingots." Many Americans bitterly opposed using any European designs on the ground that it was better to experiment with indigenous American brains and material than to borrow from foreigners.

As a result, enormous differences of opinions arose as to what types of new ships should be constructed. Under Garfield's administration, Hunt appointed a naval advisory board to examine the entire problem and present its solution. Its report of November 7, 1881, urged Congress to authorize the immediate construction of thirty-eight cruisers, five steel rams, five torpedo gunboats, and ten torpedo boats. Twenty of the cruisers were to be of wood to provide jobs for woodworkers. In reply, Congress, the next August, passed a measure providing for the construction of two cruising vessels of 5,000 and 4,000 tons to be built of domestic steel and equipped with "full sail and steam power." But it made no appropriation for the program, contenting itself merely with a provision that the Secretary of the Navy appoint a naval advisory board to supervise the construction. This board, headed by Commander R. W. Shufeldt and including Commander J. A. Howell, who had topped George Dewey's marks at Annapolis in 1858, reported adversely on the construction of the larger cruisers, but proposed the building of four smaller experimental cruisers. Approving these suggestions, Congress, on March 3, 1883, authorized construction of four steel cruisers with masts and sails. These became the celebrated White Squadron, the pride of American laymen, if not of naval officers, who knew that developments in European shipyards would still leave their ships, by comparison, tiny and weak.

The squadron included the *Chicago, Boston, Atlanta,* and *Dolphin.* John Roach of Chester, Pennsylvania, had been given the contract to build them at a total cost of $2,440,000, but just after the *Dolphin* was completed in 1885, he went into bankruptcy, and the government had to take over the completion of the other three.

Except for the *Chicago,* the ships were built on conventional lines, fitted with single screws and old-fashioned machinery. The *Atlanta* and the *Boston* were 3,000-ton ships, rated at fifteen-knot sea speed, and each carried two eight-inch and six six-inch rifles. The *Dolphin,* a little dispatch ship, displaced 1,500 tons, had fifteen-knot speed, and carried one six-inch gun and a battery of smaller rifles. It was useful principally for "pleasure." The *Chicago* alone advanced maritime architecture. Two large compound engines, with cylinders standing vertically, were placed on either side of the ship, communicating power by means of walking beams to the crankshafts of the twin screws. The adoption of twin screws thus gave belated recognition to Farragut's innovation of lashing two ships together for improved maneuverability. The engine installation of the *Chicago* reverted thirty years to the designs of John Stevens for the *Princeton,* but externally-fired cylindrical boilers, similar to the design of steam sawmills in the backwoods, provided a new conception for marine machinery. She was the largest vessel of the squadron, weighing 4,500 tons, with a speed of fourteen knots, and armed with four eight-inch and eight six-inch guns, and two five-inch breech-loading rifles.

On the trial runs the *Dolphin* seemed unsuccessful, and the Navy declined to accept her. A round-the-world shakedown cruise led to a reversal of this stand, however, for she steamed 58,000 miles in 9,000 hours and required only two hours' delay for repairs. The other three cruisers all did better than sixteen knots in a one-hour run during their 1887 trials.

Congress was more lenient now, and in 1885, under the Presidency of Grover Cleveland and the Secretaryship of William C. Whitney, passed a second Navy appropriation bill, authorizing two cruisers, the *Newark* and the *Charleston,* and a pair of gunboats, the *Yorktown* and the *Petrel.*

A novel provision was introduced to provide an incentive to contractors. Builders were promised a bonus of $100 for each horsepower achieved above the blueprint specifications. Conversely, the bill provided a penalty of the same amount for every horsepower under specifications demanded by the contract. The *Newark,* built by William H. Cramp & Sons in Philadelphia, so far exceeded her 8,500 rated horsepower that she won a bonus of nearly $37,000, but the builders of the *Charleston* lost $33,000, an amount later remitted by Congress. The little *Petrel* cost her makers, the Columbian Iron Works of Baltimore, $500 below the contract price. The Navy Department had proposed to build all of the 1885 ships with compound engines, but the builders in each instance substituted horizontal triple-expansion machinery, which proved fairly satisfactory in operation.

Designs for the *Charleston* became a *cause célèbre* when the charge was made that she was copied from the Japanese cruiser *Naniwa Kan,* built in England for the Mikado. The *Charleston* was a 4,600-ton protected cruiser with four-inch armor on her deck, three-inch steel casing her turrets, and ten six-inch guns. She did, indeed, follow English plans of the Armstrong Works, which had constructed the *Naniwa Kan* at Newcastle-on-Tyne, but American builders, after inspecting the blueprints, found them quite as much like those of the Italian cruisers, the *Etna* and the *Giovanni Bausan,* and a fourth ship, probably the Chilean cruiser *Esmeralda,* all built in the same yards. The fact seems to be that the *Charleston* plans were a hodgepodge of all four, because when the Union Iron Works of San Francisco began construction, they found it necessary to alter both plans and construction frequently, at great expense.

This ship and the *Newark* were the first armored vessels of the United States Navy.

Added proof of the renascence of the fleet was shown in the establishment of the Naval War College at Newport, Rhode Island, in 1885, under the presidency of Stephen B. Luce. The college took up for the first time in American history the study of war as a technical science and gave senior naval officers training in strategy, tactics, and fleet operations. Captain Alfred Thayer Mahan, Annapolis 1859, recalled from sea duty to become professor of naval history and tactics at the college, succeeded Luce as president in 1886, and began a period of naval study and research which created literature second to none in its revolutionary effect upon world sea power.

In 1886 Congress passed another naval construction act, authorizing construction of the country's first two battleship-type vessels, the *Texas* and the *Maine.* The bill also provided for a protected cruiser, the *Balti-*

more, and a "dynamite-gun" ship, the *Vesuvius,* designed to hurl high explosives a distance of 5,000 yards from pneumatic guns. The *Texas,* a second-class battleship built from English plans, carried two twelve-inch and six six-inch guns and was fitted with a twelve-inch armor belt around the hull and a three-inch armored deck. Capable of a seventeen-knot speed and weighing 6,500 tons, she was about the size of twentieth-century cruisers.

The *Baltimore* was a twenty-knot cruiser with four-inch deck and three-inch turret protection. She carried six-inch guns, and, like the *Charleston,* was built from plans purchased at the Armstrong Works in England. Speediest of the new ships, she was fittingly selected in 1890 to carry the body of John Ericcson, designer of the first ironclad turret ship *Monitor,* to his native Sweden.

The *Vesuvius,* on the other hand, despite machinery, horsepower, and speed, failed to establish the merits of pneumatic guns, which were abandoned.

Of the 1886 ships, Armored Cruiser Number 1, christened the *Maine,* was the most famous. A 6,600-ton ship, of 9,000 horsepower, she carried ten- and six-inch guns and was protected by eleven-inch armor. Her vertical triple-expansion engines marked the change in the American Navy from horizontal engines, cramped below the water line, to those which could be protected by an armor belt.

A second pair of 4,000-ton protected cruisers was authorized the next year, the *Philadelphia* and the *San Francisco,* notable as the first built with quadruple-expansion power plants and the first vessels for which the Navy offered premiums above the blueprint speed of nineteen knots. On their trials both exceeded that rate by more than a half a knot. To these were added the gunboats *Concord* and *Bennington* and the low freeboard monitor-type vessel *Monterey,* equipped with cylindrical Scotch-type coiled boilers, another development in motive power.

In 1888 Congress authorized six more protected cruisers and two triple-screw 7,450-ton "raiding cruisers," the *Columbia* and the *Minneapolis,* which were nicknamed the "gems of the ocean." Their speed of twenty-three knots enabled them to range far and wide across the seas and to elude any stronger ships they might encounter. The protected cruisers of that year included the *Detroit,* the *Montgomery,* and the *Marblehead,* 2,000 tons each, armed with five-inch guns, and, except for their slow speed of seventeen knots, similar to twentieth-century destroyers. In the program also came the 3,200-tonners, the *Cincinnati* and the *Raleigh.* The most famed of all, however, was the *Olympia,* a white cruiser weighing 5,870 tons and firing four eight-inch guns and five ten-inch rifles. Her decks were protected by a four and three-quarter-inch layer of steel armor which was a new development.

When George W. Melville succeeded to the post of chief engineer of the Navy in 1887, his first act in his new position had been to scrap the plans for horizontal engines in the *Maine* and to provide vertical ones protected by an armor belt. The design also afforded more room for machinery, greater power, efficiency in economy of coal, and increased range. Up till now, shipbuilders spurned Navy blueprints, and revised them as they chose, but now, under Melville, who knew what he wanted, the situation changed. Plans drawn up by the Navy Bureau of Steam Engineering were followed carefully by the builders.

When the *Chicago,* the *Atlanta,* and the *Boston* were authorized, it had been stipulated that they must be built of domestic steel. Since no armor plate was then available in the United States, the government awarded a $4,000,000 contract to the Bethlehem Steel Company to produce it. Within four years the company was forced to abandon the task, and the Carnegie Corporation took over. Early armor plate, made of compound armor (one third steel face, welded to an iron backing), saw constant improvements in the next few years, as solid steel plate, nickel steel plate, Harveyized armor, and finally Krupp armor came to be accepted. Only minor refinements, thereafter, increased the invulnerability of World War fighting ships.

The "super" cruisers *Brooklyn,* 9,200 tons, and *New York,* 8,200 tons, were authorized in 1888. With eight-inch guns they were almost as big as modern heavy cruisers, although their speed was less. Two years later, the United States launched a battleship program with authorization of the *Massachusetts,* the *Indiana,* and the *Oregon,* followed in another two years by the *Iowa.* Ten-thousand-ton ships or better, with eighteen-inch steel belts and thirteen-inch turret guns, they were leviathans of the deep. These, together with the *Texas* of slightly earlier vintage, formed the battle line of the Spanish War.

To complement such improvements in shipbuilding, smokeless powder and high explosives had been developed in 1886 by two French scientists, Eugene Turpin and Paul Vieille, making possible greater range and power of armament. America's development of the new Navy in the last two decades of the nineteenth century could be traced directly to the era of the frigates and sailing ships of the line. Wooden walls had become as antiquated as sails and smoothbore guns. Steel alone could carry the added weight of big guns and modern machinery or provide the armor necessary to withstand the impact of high-explosive shells. But the principle of building various types of ships to form a well-balanced fleet remained the same as it had always been.

The battleship was the offspring of the ship of the line, a floating battery, hurling the greatest amount of steel and explosives the greatest possible distance. Three elements dictated its construction: armament, armor, and speed, but a maximum of efficiency could be achieved in only two of these elements in the same ship. The United States, which had long believed in the importance of power, sacrificed speed for size of guns and armament. American battleships were not built to outrun the enemy. They were designed to stand and fight. Armored cruisers developed during this period, on the other hand, were the forerunners of the heavy battle cruisers of World War II. Almost as powerful as a battleship, and sacrificing defensive armament for speed, they consequently had great value as hit-and-run raiders.

Protected cruisers like the *Olympia* were the grandchildren of the frigates of 1812. They were designed as commerce raiders and built in large numbers, for to American statesmen of 1890, England still seemed the potential enemy. Torpedo boats of this era, however, were new. Invention of the self-propelled torpedo, a logical development from the *Davids* of the Civil War, brought a new threat to capital ships, which would be amplified a hundredfold with the evolution of the submarine, the lurking privateer of the twentieth century. In the years after 1885 the submarine developed rapidly as a result of the experiments of Thorsten Nordenfelt and Gustave Zede in Europe and John P. Holland in the United States. The first submersible craft was invented by Cornelius Van Drebel, a Dutch scientist, in 1622, who actually rowed it under the Thames River. But none before Holland's was a practical warship. The United States Navy completed its first underwater ship, the *Holland,* in 1899, and more than twenty-five were built before 1910.

The advent of the torpedo boat and of the submarine brought on the development of a new type of ship, the destroyers. Faster than cruisers, they carried depth charges, light guns, and torpedo tubes to fight the submarine under the surface and great battleships on top.

The phenomenal resurgence of the Navy during those decades effected changes on land as well as sea. The demand for the steel plates for the first ships of the new Navy laid the foundations of the now titanic steel industry, wrote Captain Dudley Knox in his comprehensive history of the fleet. "The Navy became one of the most important adjuncts of the industrial life of the country, not through the size of orders placed but because of the constant naval demand for improvement in materials and devices. Naval specifications regularly required the best current product and often something superior, and this, together with the rigidity of naval inspection and tests, stimulated a steady advance in industrial standards which was reflected commercially to the great advantage of business at large. The unending naval quest for better performance and new possibilities, since in battle none but the best is good enough, also led ultimately to the commercial development of other great industries, such as those in electric power, oil fuel and radio."*

The national imagination was stimulated. What would these new ships mean? The public conceived of American naval pre-eminence in every corner of the world. Captain Mahan, who deplored this tendency of men to stare dazzled before the brilliance of scientific advances without noting their qualifying drawbacks, wrote, "Men's imaginations have developed abnormal agility for drawing 'mental pictures' in which fleets get about as though by magic, whereas the movement of modern fleets are in fact extremely hampered, and their scope restricted by the very elements to which they owe much of their power." Steam, indeed, provided ease of movement and speed undreamed of in the age of sail, yet, actually, because of the fuel bases and colliers needed to keep the ships under way, and because of stowage space needed for coal supplies, steam vessels were less mobile than sailing ships.

The industrial revolution had changed the American Navy, but it had done nothing for the American merchant marine. Foreign trade soared, but the tonnage of merchant ships lost to England in the Civil War had never returned. Mahan, who knew no nation could be great without a merchant marine, called the situation disgraceful.†

"What a crime that the American merchant flag does not exist in the whole world," George Dewey told his son.

---

*Knox, *History of the United States Navy.*
†Most of the statistical material in this chapter is available in public sources such as records of the Navy and of Congress. Of the published works in the field, the following have been especially useful: John Davis Long, *The New American Navy;* Frank M. Bennett, *The Steam Navy of the United States;* Fletcher Pratt, *The Navy: A History;* Dudley W. Knox, *History of the United States Navy;* Harold and Margaret Sprout, *Toward a New Order of Sea Power.*

12

ASEA IN A TUB

$\mathcal{M}$ore than two years had passed since Dewey collapsed in Malta and started his long, hard fight for health. Now, in the fall of 1884, he was in Washington again, drawn and thin, his weight below 150 pounds, and his hair rapidly turning gray. A picture of him taken at this time shows him at forty-six to be a man in middle age, his flowing mustache gray and his eyes set in dark recesses. His hair was thin at the temples, still dark on top, but gray above the ears. His slight paunchiness was gone, and there was no sag in his firm chin. He had a stern look of dignity and self-confidence.

On September 27, 1884, after twelve years as commander, he became Captain Dewey, and caught up with his Academy classmates who had been promoted before him. He was given command of the uncompleted *Dolphin*, smallest of the new White Squadron ships, but as delays in construction at Chester, Pennsylvania, kept her on the ways for another year, Dewey was offered the *Pensacola* instead. He accepted, glad to take up active duty after so long a period of rest and recuperation.

Dewey knew the *Pensacola* well. In 1862 he had guided the old *Mississippi* just astern of the *Pensacola* as she led the night attack on Forts Jackson and St. Philip. All during the next winter the *Mississippi* and the *Pensacola* were anchored side by side, guarding New Orleans, and he had long been familiar with her gun ports and the two masts which rose amid a circus-tentful of shrouds and lines from her oak deck.

Though antiquated and useless for fighting, the *Pensacola* was a luxuriously outfitted man-of-war with a fireplace in the captain's cabin. Again he made the grand tour of Europe. "As we had no commerce or interests to protect in Europe," Dewey wrote of such aimless cruises, "and were unable to protect them if we had, the presence of our squadron in European waters was perfunctory. It used to be a saying among the officers that we went from port to port to meet our wives, who were traveling ashore, and to get letters from sweethearts. One could easily have reasoned that the Navy Department, knowing that we could be of no service as an instrument of warfare, meant us to enjoy a pleasantly conducted European holiday."*

As flagship of the European squadron, the *Pensacola* carried the two-starred flag of Rear Admiral Franklin at the masthead. On the trip across the Atlantic the friendship between him and Dewey led them to call in the ship's carpenter to tear down the bulkhead between their cabins, for more companionship and a larger, more cheerful living room. Yet the long cruise and the boredom of inactivity led to quarrels over trivial incidents. The ship's carpenter was summoned again to restore the partition, after which the captain and the admiral dined in stately lonesomeness.†

During the summer of 1885 the squadron sailed to the northern fjords to avoid the Mediterranean heat. In Norway and Sweden the American officers were wined and dined ashore and returned hospitality on shipboard. They were visited by King Oscar of Sweden, who, having been a naval officer himself, enjoyed a professional chat about the navies of the world.

"This is the kind of kingdom for a man to have," he remarked. "I would rather command a man-of-war than be King of any country in the world."

Commander Bridgeman, cosmopolitan and assured, answered: "I have only tried the man-of-war, Your Majesty."‡

Knowing that the enlisted men were even more bored than the officers, Captain Dewey showed kindness and lenience in the forecastle. One of his men declared: "For the liberty breakers, the forecastle scrappers, overnight drunks, and petty offenders—he always had an exceedingly unobservant eye, and he has been noted for some difficulty he has had with his hearing apparatus when such offenders have been reported to him in the line of duty."§

Dewey usually gave lenient treatment to any one but a liar. One sailor who reeled back to the *Pensacola* after liberty at Gibraltar lied about his condition. "If you had told me candidly you took a drop too much," Captain Dewey told him, "you would be free by now. But for lying you

---

*George Dewey, *Autobiography*, pp. 158–59.
†Years later, when Franklin was retired and poor, he asked Dewey to forgive the quarrel. Dewey gladly did, and periodically afterwards sent the old admiral boxes of his favorite cigars.
‡George Dewey, *op. cit.*, p. 159.
§Adelbert Dewey, *The Life and Letters of Admiral Dewey*, pp. 494–97.

The Admiral of the Navy, George Dewey, and the second Mrs. Dewey, Mildred McLean Hazen.

get ten days in irons. Let me have the truth hereafter." And, according to the stories related by his crew members, he always did.

When the *Pensacola* arrived at Genoa on Christmas Day, the good-conduct men were mustered at the port rail ready to leave in liberty boats, but about forty of the crew had been quarantined for three months because of a little fracas a week or two before in Nice.

Captain Dewey stood on the deck, watching the liberty party leave the ship, while the quarantined sailors disconsolately smoked their pipes around the gangway. "We were looking pretty down in the mouth, I guess," one sailor recalled. The Captain "walked up and down, chewing his mustache, and every once in a while shooting a look at the men up forward." After a while he went up to the crowd and said: "You boys hop into your mustering clothes, and go off to the beach. I'll let you have a couple of the running boats when they return. Come back with the other men when you get ready. Don't raise any more trouble ashore than you can help."*

With a hearty cheer for their Captain, the men rushed for boats and shore.

At Malta a group of *Pensacola* sailors fell into a street brawl with some British tars. When the police were called, the Americans rushed to their boats and escaped to their ship without arrest. As they left behind considerable destruction to Maltese property, an apoplectic captain of the port called the next day upon Captain Dewey with the demand that he be given the right to arrest every member of the gang.

"But, sir, what can I do; how can I search out the guilty ones?" asked the diplomatic captain.

"You certainly can parade your crew before me in order that the offenders may be identified," retorted the constable.

Captain Dewey pointed at the Stars and Stripes floating above the deck and said with his usual bravado: "The deck of this vessel is United States territory, and I shall parade my men for no foreigner."†

The *Pensacola* drifted lazily through the spring of 1886 in the eastern end of the Mediterranean. The Captain spent several days in Cairo, Jerusalem, Beirut, and Athens and saw four of the seven wonders of the world.

King George of Greece was very gracious to the American captain. When the ship reached Athens, the monarch invited him to dine alone with the royal family, and toasted him with wine from Mount Parnassus.

*Louis Stanley Young, *Life and Heroic Deeds of Admiral Dewey* (Philadelphia: National Publishing Co., 1899), p. 59.
†George Dewey, *op. cit.*, p. 188.

"The next time you come, I hope you will be Admiral," he said as Dewey left that night.

"It was a source of much regret that I could not go to Greece with the *Olympia* on my way from Manila when I was an Admiral," wrote Dewey in simple naïveté in 1913, "but it meant two weeks' quarantine, and I was therefore obliged to forego the pleasure."

Later, on a summer's leave from ship duty, he enjoyed a long overland tour of Europe, visiting various capitals, London, Paris, and Geneva,* but somehow he began to believe that perhaps King Oscar had been right after all. The sea was his kingdom, even if at the moment it was not a very lively one.

The months of leisure drifted by. He alleviated the routine of the old-fashioned sloop in calm waters by ordering occasional gun drills, which the crew seemed to enjoy heartily, despite the antiquity of their equipment. As for himself, he used every opportunity to learn more of his profession. Interminably he discussed modern gunnery and seamanship with the officers of Britain. He inspected foreign warships with a professional eye upon the new guns and armor plate. Foreign books on naval science came to the cabin of the *Pensacola* and were avidly read by the light of the kerosene lamp that swung gently overhead. He studied the new possibilities of long-range guns and high explosives and taught them to his officers, who, in turn, explained these changes to the crews. After drills on the smoothbore Dahlgren guns, firing black gunpowder, they debated the fate of shells if they had been fired from rifles with the new TNT.

How long ago those days with Farragut seemed now. More than twenty years had passed since he had left the old man and sailed on the *Brooklyn* to New York, and then on the *Agawam*. It was almost that long since Susie died, and her memory was with him still. What was to come he could not know. One thing he did know—the *Pensacola* held no future. Should there be a war, what could her captain do, except sail gallantly into death, into the exploding shells of a steel-clad adversary? A minute of hell, and smoke, and flame, and the old wooden tub would disappear into the deep.

At Malta harbor, on his way home in 1889, the Captain leaned over the grilled iron fencing of his bridge and watched a gray cruiser steam to its anchorage. The red flag of the Rising Sun waved from her steel mast. She was the Japanese *Naniwa,* commanded by Captain Ito,† to

---

*In Geneva he bought a gold watch for his son, which, in 1944, still kept perfect time.
†George Dewey, *op. cit.*, p. 160. Ito, at the battle of Yahu in 1894, pulverized the wooden Chinese ships and ended forever the myth that ships of wood could stand up against steel-clad vessels.

Dewey a wholly new sight in these waters. The modern Japanese ship served but to accentuate the obsolescence of the *Pensacola*. When Dewey had served on the frigate *Mississippi* he had often dreamed of Commodore Perry's voyage to Yeddo Bay. Now Yeddo Bay had returned to him not the ancient, primitive bay of junks and sampans the *Mississippi* knew, but a bay crowded with steel fighters like this *Naniwa*, full of bucktoothed sailormen and guns menacing toward the West.

Meanwhile, Dewey's own Western world was calling, and, with glad heart, he and his crew passed Gibraltar in the spring of 1889, to end his last voyage under sail and his last sea trip for more than eight years. He was going home to see his son, now sixteen and a student at St. Paul's School, to see those new American ships he had heard of only vaguely, to help fit them out, to build a Navy which could steam on into broader seas.

13

BRIDLED AMBITIONS

*C*aptain Dewey reached Washington in the summer of 1889, hale and sturdy from his years at sea and ready for his next assignment. This was to relieve Captain Winfield S. Schley as chief of the Bureau of Equipment, a post he assumed on July 20. His first task was to acquaint himself with the naval developments that had taken place during his years at sea. The cruiser program was well under way, while the keels of the first battleships of the line had been laid. Since the Bureau of Equipment was charged with procuring and selecting fittings and parts for the shipbuilding program, Dewey, in conference with admirals, captains, and civilian experts, studied blueprints and techniques, debated policy, and learned that while on shore duty there may not be forty-hour watches through a gale, but that an eight-hour day can be filled to overflowing with interviews, paper work, and routine.

"There was nothing showy about the four years' service that followed," he commented. "The detail was not exacting, but vitally engrossing and important. In common with every other ambitious officer of the Navy, I was feeling the pulse of the new spirit and problems."*

The Republican party had returned to power that year, with Benjamin Harrison as President, Benjamin F. Tracy as Secretary of the Navy, and as Secretary of State, James G. Blaine, whom Dewey greatly admired.

"Blaine has a pen of about the heft of a capstan bar," Dewey is reported to have said of the aggressive Maine statesman. "The man at whom he directs one of his diplomatic missives does not need a searchlight to get at the meaning of it. His directness is wonderful. Epistolary obscureness—mouthing or mincing of written words—is a hateful defect in a public man."†

As Secretary of War, Harrison appointed Redfield Proctor of Vermont,

*George Dewey, *Autobiography*, p. 164.
†*Ladies' Home Journal*, Oct., 1899.

whose home in Washington became a center for New England Republicans. Six years older than Dewey, and a beneficiary of Dr. Julius Yemans Dewey's support during his early political career, it was natural for him to take the doctor's son under his wing. He introduced Dewey to the powerful and important in the capital, to Congressmen and Senators, to justices and diplomats.

A large red-faced man, heavily bearded, with deep-set eyes and prominent nose which made him look like Abraham Lincoln, Proctor was a veteran of the Civil War and had served one term as governor of Vermont, beginning in 1878. In 1891 he resigned from the War Department to represent his state in the Senate, a post he held until his death seventeen years later. It was to him, more than to any other man, that Dewey owed his start in Washington official life.

Although primarily on desk duty, Dewey took a small but, from the point of view of his own career, significant step in an inter-American crisis that arose in 1891. Don José Manuel Balmaceda, President of Chile, was accused of plotting to perpetuate a dictatorial rule, and on January 7, 1891, the Congressionalists, supporters of the Congress Balmaceda had dissolved, staged a rebellion. While the United States had no direct interest in the internal affairs of Chile, Harrison and Blaine continued to recognize the Balmaceda government, to the great fury of the rebels who were already sufficiently angered by the McKinley tariff of 1890,* and who had not forgotten Blaine's stand ten years before in the Chilean-Peru conflict. Nor were the aroused feelings of the revolutionaries soothed by the unyielding attitude of Patrick Egan, the United States Minister at Santiago, a recently naturalized Irishman who had fled his own country to escape imprisonment by the English.

In May the Chilean ship *Itata* anchored at San Diego, to obtain arms and munitions for the insurgents. Orders came from President Harrison to seize and quarantine it in port. The next day, May 6th, the Chilean crew overpowered the officers and fled to sea, taking two U.S. marshals along with them. The cruiser *Charleston* was sent in pursuit, but as the Congressionalists had by now gained control of the nation's government and its fleet, they ordered the *Esmeralda* to search out the *Charleston*.

Both ships headed for Acapulco on the Mexican coast, where the *Itata* was expected to stop for coaling. They passed at sea one still, dark night, each blacked out, crews standing by their guns, ready for action. No shot was fired, however, and when the *Itata* arrived in Chile, the Congressionalists changed their plans and surrendered her to an American squadron

*The McKinley tariff, which exacted a high tariff against South American hides, was deeply resented in the Argentine and Chile and went far to nullify the good will achieved by the first Pan-American Congress called by Blaine in 1890.

at Iquique, Chile. She was freed shortly afterward by the American courts, which held that her detention had been improper.

Indignation over the *Itata* lingered, however, and was fanned by subsequent charges and countercharges during the struggle. The climax came when Captain Schley brought the *Baltimore* into Valparaiso harbor in October and permitted an unarmed liberty party of one hundred American sailors to go ashore. A saloon brawl started, in which fifty Chilean policemen, armed with bayonets and carbines, joined the fight against the sailors. Two of the Americans were killed and seventeen or eighteen were wounded either by knives or stones. All of the sailors were dragged to jail.

Indignation in the United States rose to fever pitch, and President Harrison was ready to go to war to avenge the insult to the flag and the Navy. The cruiser *Boston* was ordered to proceed toward Chile.

Meanwhile, when Captain Robley D. Evans arrived in Valparaiso harbor on the gunboat *Yorktown* Monday, November 23, he found Schley still arguing with the Chileans about the exact alcoholic condition of the American sailors. The discussion seemed futile to Evans, who declared, "I did not agree with him [Schley] in this, for in the first place I doubted the fact, and in the second, it was not an issue worth discussing. His men were probably drunk on shore, properly drunk; they went ashore, many of them, for the purpose of getting drunk, which they did on Chilean rum paid for in good United States money. When in this condition they were more entitled to protection than if they had been sober. This was my view of it, at least, and the one I always held about men whom I commanded. Instead of protecting them, the Chileans foully murdered these men, and we believed with the connivance and assistance of armed policemen. That was the issue—not the question of whether they were drunk or sober."*

The next few weeks brought constant trouble to Evans, whose vessel was repeatedly threatened by Chilean hotheads. Additional incidents kept feeling high and added to the imminence of war, not the least of which were the Chilean government's delay in apologizing for the attack on the sailors and an accusation of bad faith against the President of the United States. Eight cruisers in the Pacific squadron were put on a war footing and volunteers stormed recruiting offices throughout the country.

To George Dewey, conflict, with its possibility of glory, seemed both certain and welcome. Meanwhile, two United States warships lay off the Argentine, ready to assist Evans in Santiago and awaiting the answer to President Harrison's demands for an apology for the accusation against

*Robley D. Evans, *A Sailor's Log* (New York: D. Appleton-Century, Co., pp. 259–60.

118

him, for indemnity to the *Baltimore* outrage, and for safe conduct to a neutral country for the defeated Balmacedaists, who were then confined in the American legation at Valparaiso.

At this point, Dewey, as head of the Bureau of Equipment, ordered a supply of coal in Argentina to fuel the American cruisers in preparation for a speedy dash around the Horn. Scarcely anything more than a routine action on the surface, taken at this juncture it appeared something more. At least it was so interpreted by the sole authority for the story, Theodore Roosevelt, who saw in it an impressive assumption of authority. In his autobiography, written in 1913, Roosevelt expanded upon the incident, even changing Dewey's comfortable quarters in the Metropolitan Club in Washington to a ship off the Argentine.

I had been struck by an incident in his [Dewey's] past career. . . . It was at a time when there was threat of trouble with Chile. Dewey was off the Argentine, and was told to get ready to move to the other coast of South America. If the move became necessary, he would have to have coal, and yet if he did not make the move, the coal would not be needed. In such a case, a man afraid of responsibility always acts rigidly by the regulations and communicates with the Department at home to get authority for everything he does; and, therefore, he accomplishes nothing whatever, but is able to satisfy all individuals with red-tape minds by triumphantly pointing out his compliance with the regulations. In a crisis the man worth his salt is the man who meets the needs of the situation in whatever way is necessary. Dewey purchased the coal and was ready to move at once if need arose. The affair blew over; the need to move did not occur; and for some time there seemed to be a chance that Dewey would get into trouble over having purchased the coal,* for our people are like almost all other peoples in requiring responsible officers under such conditions to decide at their own personal peril, no matter which course they follow. However, the people higher up ultimately stood by Dewey.†

Earlier, Roosevelt had written Dewey, "I felt very strongly that what you did showed the initiative, the decision, and the willingness to accept responsibility which it was necessary that the successor of Farragut should show. Will you write me a few lines as to exactly what it was that happened?"‡

Whether or not Roosevelt's interpretation is absolutely in accord with the facts matters little. The important thing was that the story came to

*These are the risks which must be taken," Roosevelt wrote in *McClure's Magazine* in October, 1899, "and the man who takes them should be singled out for reward and for duty. Dewey's whole action . . . marked him as one of these men."

†Theodore Roosevelt, *Theodore Roosevelt, An Autobiography* (New York: Charles Scribner's Sons, 1920), pp. 210–11.

‡This letter, typewritten in purple ink on the stationery of *The Outlook*, is now in the Dewey collection in the Chicago Historical Society.

Roosevelt's attention and made him thereafter George Dewey's stanch advocate. Finally, in 1892, Chile agreed to pay $75,000 indemnity for the *Baltimore* victims; the crisis ended, "Fighting Bob" Evans returned a hero.

Dewey served as chief of the Bureau of Equipment in the Navy Department from 1889 until the summer of 1893, during which time he visited the ways where the *Texas* and the *Maine* were being built, drafted contracts for new rifles and guns, engines and equipment for the first battleships, and, unlike his colleagues, looked with interest on the experiments of John P. Holland with the submarine.

The new ships were tonic to Dewey's hopes and dreams for the Navy and ended a feeling of frustration about his own career. Without a home or wife, he was all Navy, devoted to its cause, its champion and its defender, bound by its routine and authority, and ready always to work for its improvement.

More powerful ships were not the only changes the Navy was making in those years. A gray-haired captain named Alfred Thayer Mahan was providing it with a theory of world naval power. *The Influence of Sea Power upon History,* published in 1890, and *The Influence of Sea Power upon the French Revolution,* and *The Life of Admiral Farragut,* released two years later, became verbal shots heard around the world.

The Kaiser ordered a copy of the first work placed in every ship of the growing German Navy. Mahan's books were translated into a dozen foreign languages, and every naval officer studied them assiduously. Captain George Dewey understood better than most Americans the significance of the Mahan theory and read it with excessive care. Coinciding with the physical development of the American Navy, Mahan's works called for a new strategy of power, just as the long-range guns called for a new strategy of warfare.

Dewey was especially struck by Mahan's advocacy of peacetime concentration of fleets, a policy which that same year he tried to persuade Secretary of the Navy Tracy to adopt. At luncheon one day Tracy had asked: "Dewey, if you were Secretary of the Navy, what would you do with our ships in time of peace?"*

Dewey was well prepared to answer. "I would bring all the ships home from the European station, the South Atlantic station, and the South Pacific station, then divide them into two parts. One part I would keep on the North Atlantic station, and the other in the Pacific. Of those in the Pacific, I would keep the larger part on the West Coast, and the remainder in Asiatic waters."

Asked why, he replied, "Well, to begin with, we have no defense of our

*George Dewey, *op. cit.*, p. 161.

coasts except the Navy, and in the second place, our officers and men would have an opportunity to become acquainted with our own coasts, which they are not able to do now; and above all, we would be spending the country's money at home and giving our people a chance to see something of the Navy, which they can't do when it is scattered over all the world. We don't need to keep ships constantly on foreign stations— we have no interests there for them to protect, and there is really nothing for them to do. But if anything occurs which makes it necessary for ships to visit foreign countries, let us send a squadron of four ships instead of one, for whatever is to be done can be accomplished by four better than by one."

Mahan urged a systematic study of the art of war, a practice never followed in a fundamentally pacifist America; substitution of passive defense strategy by one of reasoned, well-planned offensives, and establishment of a policy based not on possible threat from the Atlantic side but on the new importance to America of the Pacific and Asia.

The Influence of Sea Power upon History became the naval gospel of Germany and Japan. Sir Julian Corbett, English naval historian, declared that Mahan had placed naval history upon a philosophical basis for the first time. Indeed, the volume sounded a new note in world politics, for it demonstrated conclusively the vital dependence of world empire upon sea power. Mahan pointed out the necessity and inevitability of American colonial expansion and active participation in world affairs. He recognized that force ruled international relations, and asserted vehemently the need for naval bases in the Caribbean and Pacific to guard America's coasts and commerce.

Mahan, moreover, believed in creating an offensively powerful fleet. That his influence in this matter was never fully realized was demonstrated by the largely defensive strategy employed by the Allies in the first World War and at the beginning of the second. In both wars the German powers developed their overall strategy in advance, knew what they wanted, and adapted their tactics to achieve their grand aim. Dewey alone assumed a strong offensive in the Spanish-American War, while in the Caribbean theater Sampson and Schley, following the cue of the Navy Department, sat back waiting to see what the Spanish would do. The fact that Dewey struck fast is convincing proof of his debt to Alfred Thayer Mahan.

Command of the sea is all-decisive in world power, Mahan stated in his expositions. He was a strong advocate of preparedness; saw the need of an isthmian canal, later realized at Panama through Theodore Roosevelt's aggressive policies; and believed it imperative to take possession of the maritime positions commanding the seas, which to Mahan were the "world's great medium" for trade and commerce.

It has frequently been argued that the rise of air power altered Mahan's theories. Yet the accession of Atlantic island bases from England in 1940 is witness to the fact that his belief in the necessity of island outposts was not changed by the advent of aircraft. The fight for the island bases of Japan, as well, indicate that they are as important in a world of air power as they were in 1890.

Since 1823 the United States maintained a strong foreign policy toward European powers because of the Monroe Doctrine. Yet Americans never realized that this policy was supported by England's mastery of the seas. Great Britain served as guarantor of the Monroe Doctrine when America's Navy ranked eleventh in the world. The United States, nonetheless, failed to realize the importance of the British alliance, unwritten as it was. And during the last half of the nineteenth century American foreign policy, as exemplified in the naval construction program, consisted of building a fleet designed for local shore defense together with a few fast raiding ships. The American Navy of that era was designed to wage another War of 1812 against Great Britain, the only power which the United States could fight by defending its shore and harbors and raiding British commerce.*

Mahan saw through this paradox and realized that Great Britain must not be an enemy, for America's entire foreign policy was based upon the support of the Royal Navy. This fundamental was sensed unconsciously by the State Department on half a dozen occasions between 1823 and 1900 when war was averted between the United States and England—in the Washington-Oregon border crisis of President Polk's day; in the Civil War, when Abraham Lincoln and Prince Albert preserved relations between the two countries, and in the Venezuelan affair of 1893.

But unlike England, Japan had not attained her geographic, economic, and political demands for more territory. She was a nation on the rise, whose dreams of Pan-Asia conflicted with the trade of the United States. While England protected America from a potentially hostile Germany, Japan, her twin across the Pacific, was a potential enemy.

Mahan clearly foresaw the First World War, predicting the affinity of the United States toward its future allies and the threat of Japan.

The United States fleet should predominate in the Pacific, he declared. Viewing Japan's interests in the markets of greater Asia, he wrote: "Her

* Walter Lippmann, *United States Foreign Policy: Shield of the Republic* (Boston: Little, Brown & Co., 1943).

interest in them cannot but breed that sense of proprietorship which in dealing with ill-organized states easily glides into the attempt at political control that ultimately means control by force." This possibility was veiled to most Americans for many years, despite the Twenty-One Demands upon China. But it unfolded in the seizure of Manchukuo in 1931, in the Chinese "incident" of 1937, and at Pearl Harbor on December 7, 1941.

Foreseeing that, too, Mahan wrote: "In the absence of the fleet [in the Pacific] invasion [of the West Coast] may be easy. Under present world conditions the Pacific Coast seems incomparably the more exposed of the three great divisions of the American shoreline—the Atlantic, the Gulf, and the Pacific."

Although strongly affected by Mahan's views on this and by his entire system of naval power, Dewey never put such ideas on paper. Sometimes he expressed his opinions to his friends and relatives at the dinner table, but that Mahan's views became an essential part of his thinking was revealed most strikingly when he was called upon to act. Always at these times his decisions showed acumen and knowledge, for in matters of naval diplomacy his first reaction was usually the correct one. Commodore Perry, Admiral Farragut, and Captain Mahan—these were his heroes and his guides.

Meanwhile Dewey's life was pleasant enough. He became known as an agreeable social companion, careful of his appearance—some of his friends called him "Dewey, the Dude"—popular as a high-ranking and unattached naval officer. Rear Admiral Bunce wrote of him: "There were few more popular men than . . . Dewey. He never sought popularity. It came to him. In the first place he is a fine-looking man, and he has most attractive manners. People seek him out, and whenever he is on shore he is kept busy with social engagements. At the same time he is no 'carpet-knight.' He is a fighter and a disciplinarian."*

While he moved in the society of Washington, Dewey must have inwardly smarted to realize he was growing old in parlors. From January 3, 1893, until June 30 of that year he kept a diary, written in pencil in a small leather-bound notebook. For the most part the journal was a concise, unimaginative chronicle of the weather and his habits. Seldom did a day's entry contain more than five lines. A few typical entries will suffice to indicate the events he considered worth remembering:

TUESDAY, JAN. 3. Cold and windy. Took short ride back of White House. Dined at the club and came home early. Paid all bills to date.

*Adelbert Dewey, *The Life and Letters of Admiral Dewey*, p. 405.

WEDNESDAY, JAN. 4. Cold, did not ride. Dined with Hagen. Made several calls.

JANUARY 27. Rode again . . . cold and raw. Had my hair cut.

Every three weeks the diary punctually stated, "Had my hair cut," testimony in scrawled pencilings of the regularity of Dewey's habits.

7 FEB. Cold and raw. Did not ride or make calls. Dined at the club and came home early.

10 FEBY. Unsettled weather. Took a short ride back of the White House. Went to see Modjeska in "As You Like It." Grunell's theater party.

11 FEBY. Dined at Mrs. Wallack's.

13 FEBY. Did not go out. Not very well. Tea and toast!

TUESDAY, 14 FEBY. A fine day. Passed it as usual—Rode an hour in the "White Lot." Dined at the club with Hagen and came home early.

THURSDAY, 16 FEBY. Rode two hours. Made four calls.

SAT., 25 MARCH. A fine day. Rode two hours in the afternoon. Dined at Mrs. Slater's, and took supper at Mrs. Barland's. Both very pleasant.

29 MARCH. Rode as usual after four. Dined at the club with Hagen and went to see Willard in the "Professor's Story of Love." George arrived at 11 P.M. from Princeton.

George Goodwin Dewey had entered Princeton University the preceding fall, after graduating from St. Paul's School in New Hampshire. George received the princely allowance (for that time) of $1,500 a year from his father, with extra funds forthcoming and no questions asked if there was any need, which there sometimes was. Captain Dewey was a stranger to his son, but he made sure that George had a gentleman's education. When he had been at St. Paul's, young George did not even know if he would recognize his father on the street, so seldom had he seen him.

The elder Dewey went sightseeing with his son during the next two days, perhaps remembering his own trip to Annapolis with Dr. Julius Dewey forty-nine years before when they went to the theater in New York and marveled at trains and the new steam ferryboats on the Hudson River.

The diary's entry for March 30 hinted at a slight disarrangement of his life. "Did not ride," the pencil marks stated. "George with me. Dined at home, and went to see Gloriana and Lottie Collins in the evening." Dining at home was a rare event for Dewey, and he decidedly did not enjoy the theater.

124

The next day's entry, for Friday, March 31, read, "A very fine day. Went to Mount Vernon with George. Dined at home and went to see the 'Professor in Love' at the National." His reaction to that play, which he had seen twice in three days, was lukewarm, for he wrote a different version of the title each time. Undoubtedly he had visited the play Wednesday night to find out if it was suitable entertainment for his son.

Dewey weighed himself on Tuesday, April 25, wrote in the diary, "Weigh 155 pounds." At 55 he was hard as nails, well-proportioned, riding almost daily to keep his health and figure.

George Goodwin Dewey emerged from "bicker week" at Princeton with flying colors. He was picked for the Cottage Club, one of the "big four" social groups at the university. The selection was a source of great pride to George's father. The Captain boarded the first train for New York after he heard of the honor and visited Princeton. It was more important to him, apparently, than young George's graduation, for he did not leave Washington for that ceremony. When he arrived, George's Cottage Club initiation fee was paid out of his own pocket. Dewey held court for his son's friends in a Princeton dormitory.

"This is Captain Dewey, my father," was the way young George introduced him. Unfamiliar as they were to each other, the imposing naval rank was more important than the parental association.

Dewey spent part of his visit admonishing his son to do something in the world and to make friends.

"Now at my age," he said, "I only meet acquaintances. The men you know when you are doing things are the only ones with whom you can make friends. No one ever pays any attention to men who don't do anything. They just talk and talk, and turn into bores."

He boarded the train back to Washington the next day. All the boys who had been initiated into Cottage came down to see the Captain off. Dewey put one foot on the step of the railroad car, then turned back to the college men.

"Boys," he said, waving his cane for emphasis, "you're big men now. But I doubt if any of you in after life will be any bigger." With a hearty laugh he disappeared into the car.

Dewey was relieved of command of the Bureau of Equipment in the fall of 1893, but his change of duty did not alter his way of life. He was soon attached to the Lighthouse Board, and spent the next fifteen months in comparatively easy duties. He had time to look after the internal affairs of the Metropolitan Club, particularly its cuisine, which, under his scrutiny, became the delight of its members. He also enjoyed the distinction, which some quarters may think dubious, of having introduced Scotch whisky into Washington society.

In the summer of 1893 when he was on the Lighthouse Board, Dewey made an inspection cruise aboard the U.S.S. *America.* The ship was anchored off Martha's Vineyard one sunny afternoon when its skipper, Captain Wright, went ashore to bring Dewey's son aboard to spend the night.

Dewey was pacing the bridge when two young girls rowed alongside and asked permission to visit the ship.

"Sorry, ladies," said the coxswain. "You can't come aboard. The captain is ashore."

"Wait a minute," shouted Dewey from the bridge. "This is their ship just as much as it is ours. Let them come aboard."

Dewey personally escorted the girls throughout the ship. The girls were pretty, and Dewey was gallant. Captain Wright and George Goodwin Dewey arrived a few minutes later, and bowing, Dewey introduced Wright to the girls and then turned to his son.

"And this is my younger brother, George," he said, introducing the young ladies.

"Father was a good one with the ladies," George Goodwin Dewey reminisced. "He wasn't going to let them know he had a college student as a son."

In 1895 Dewey was appointed president of the Board of Inspection and Survey, and given the acting rank of commodore. The board was charged with final acceptance of all new ships built for the Navy and the detection of any flaw in construction or performance. Inspection trips took him away from Washington a great deal during the next three years. He presided at the trials of the *Texas* and the *Maine,* and of the "super" battleships, the *Massachusetts,* the *Indiana,* and the *Iowa.* His naval uniform, for many years removed from moth balls only for state receptions, came into use again, as he stood on the bridges of 10,000-ton battleships speeding across the ocean and tested the salvos of thirteen-inch guns.

The armored cruiser, *Brooklyn,* and the protected cruisers, the *Nashville,* the *Wilmington,* and the *Delaware,* all completed during Dewey's presidency of the board, demanded visits to New York, Wilmington, Pennsylvania, and Massachusetts. Captain Willard H. Brownson and Commander William H. Emory, members of the board, usually accompanied him on these junkets, and the trio became well known as the three best-dressed men in the Navy, joking among themselves about the luggage problems involved in moving their large wardrobes. In 1896 they all journeyed to New London, Connecticut, where trials for the gunboat *Annapolis* were to be held. Dewey, arriving ahead of his colleagues, had his one pigskin suitcase carried up to his room and was rocking on the front porch of a hotel when an express wagon, loaded high with trunks, drove up.

"Ah," said Dewey, "I see that Brownson and Bill Emory have come."*

Dewey had a weakness for the latest fads—in one instance, for the brilliant yellow shoes being introduced late in the nineties. He bought a pair, the first man in the capital to wear them, and when he appeared at the bureau, his colleagues gaped at them and began to call them the "yellow perils."

In the afternoon they began to hurt. A blister had formed on his right heel, and he limped into the chief clerk's office. Falling into a leather chair, he loosened the shoelaces with a groan.

"I suppose I can't take these things off now, or those fellows will think they drove me to it," he said. After a few minutes' rest he retied the strings and limped back to his own office, his pain hidden, his pride preserved.†

His love of clothes was matched by his thrift in taking care of them, for he could hang on to a pair of old socks as long as any man. Invariably he wore silk, and during this period he wrapped the worn pairs in a little brown paper bundle and carried them to a neighbor who darned them for him.

One time he sent three pairs of a rare shade of blue. In all of Washington there was no thread to match them. She used some that almost matched, but not without Dewey's notice.

"Which of us is color blind?" he asked.

"Neither," she answered. "Where in the world did you get those weird blue stockings? Such a tint was never seen on land or sea before."

"They were brought to me from Japan," Dewey said. And when, soon after, he left for the Orient, he bought and mailed to Washington a spool of the proper shade, with the note: "Now do you think my old eyes are capable of correctly reading night signals?"

On May 23, 1896, at the age of fifty-eight, and only four years from retirement, he was given the permanent rank of commodore. Taking a leave shortly after, he spent the summer in Montpelier with his relatives and boyhood friends. One fine afternoon, as he and an old classmate, Judge Fifield, were driving through the spruce-covered hills, he commented on his life and his dwindling prospect of fame.

Ladies' Home Journal, Oct., 1899.
†*Ibid.*

"Judge [confessed the Commodore], you have had a successful record as a lawyer. You're known in this state as having accomplished something, and you can be satisfied with what you have done. With me it's different. I've always worked faithfully in the Navy, and trained myself for what responsibilities might come. But I'm approaching the years of retirement, and I'll soon be out of it all, with nothing to my credit but gradual promotions.

"I don't want war [he went on, puffing at a Havana cigar and flicking the ash over the tailboard], but without it there is little opportunity for a naval man to distinguish himself. There will be no war before I retire from the Navy, and I'll simply join the great majority of naval men, and be known in history only by consulting the records of the Navy Department, as 'George Dewey, who entered the Navy in 1854 and retired as rear admiral at the age limit.' "*

But his prophecy proved incorrect. Cuba seemed a long way off from the spruce-shaded Onion River, but the Cubans were in foment.

*John Barrett, *Admiral George Dewey: A Sketch of the Man* (New York: Harper & Bros., 1900), pp. 13–14.

14

CASTANETS RUMBLE

*T*he War with Spain has been termed a mere "diversion" offered by the Republican administration of William McKinley to distract public attention from the exorbitant Dingley tariff* of 1897, a protective barrier so high and offering such flagrant concessions to monopolies it created a furor throughout the land. Yet the forces making for intervention in Cuba were too strong, and the results of it too revolutionary, to permit such an oversimplified explanation.

Hostilities with Spain, it has often been said, might have been avoided had McKinley shown himself less susceptible to personal pressure. Theodore Roosevelt declared he was as soft as "a chocolate eclair," and more sober historians have spoken of him as "a kindly soul in a spineless body." But it is doubtful if McKinley alone could have halted what seemed inevitable, and without the liberation of Cuba by bloodshed, America's whole course would have been different. Would Germany have been able to purchase the Philippines? Would America, without them, have embarked upon world-wide commitments? Would Germany and Japan have inherited the earth?

The fact that the Cuban problem was solved by war instead of by negotiation has determined the course of half a century's history.

Actually Spain's behavior in the Cuban uprising should have been less conducive to war than the diplomatic crises involving Germany during the later years of the nineteenth century. Spain was dealing with her own colonials in a dominion tacitly recognized by the Monroe Doctrine. The German affair in Samoa had definitely constituted a Prussian threat to American rights in the Pacific islands. But as Cuba was nearer home, the issue was more acute.

America's interest in Cuba grew as the need for a transisthmian canal became more apparent. With America's need for a two-ocean fleet, a

*Morison and Commager, *The Growth of the American Republic*, p. 799.

canal was a vital necessity. Captain Mahan preached its importance. But before constructing such a channel, American control of the Caribbean was a necessity. Spain's interests in Cuba and Puerto Rico were a threat to United States policy in Latin America as well as to the United States' entire world naval strategy.

In February, 1895, goaded by misery and starvation, resulting directly from the American sugar tariff of 1894, which canceled the reciprocity treaty of 1891 with Spain, and for long rebellious against the mother country, Cuba staged an insurrection. The rebels, raiding small outposts, burned plantations, laid waste the villages, dynamited trains, and reduced the island to hopeless anarchy.* Despite the 200,000 Spanish regulars sent to put down the uprising, by the end of 1896 the insurgents controlled three fourths of the rural parts of Cuba. The Spanish governor general, who fought according to European rules, maintained control of the Cuban cities, but the ill-clad peasant troops of Maximo Gomez and Antonio Maceo continued their guerrilla-like depredations throughout the back country.

Madrid, desperately anxious to quell the uprising, then sent a new governor, General Valeriano Weyler, to Cuba with orders to proceed "at any cost." Arriving in February 1896, Weyler promptly issued the "reconcentration" order, by which all rebel sympathizers (most of the native Cubans) were to be driven into bullpens outside the cities. Without food or pure water, the victims, including many women and children, died like flies. The plight of more than 400,000 penned-up Cubans stirred the wrath of outraged people of the United States. New York papers called Weyler "the Butcher" and published pictures of filthy and emaciated Cubans lying in horrible reconcentration pens.

Despite the pressure upon him for immediate action, President Cleveland determined to preserve neutrality. It was his last year in the White House and he was reluctant to plunge into war. But when an American passenger ship, the *Alliance,* was fired upon by a Spanish man-of-war, Cleveland was compelled in his final address to Congress, on December 7, 1896, to take cognizance of the trend toward hostilities:

It cannot be reasonably assumed that the hitherto expectant attitude of the United States will be indefinitely maintained. . . . When the inability of Spain to deal successfully with the insurrection has become manifest . . . a situation will be presented in which our obligations to the sovereignty of Spain will be superseded by higher obligations which

*Peck, *Twenty Years of the Republic*, p. 531.

we can hardly hesitate to recognize and to discharge. . . . The United States is not a nation to which peace is a necessity.

Nevertheless, he maintained American neutrality to the end of his term, and on March 7, 1897, handed the reins of government to William McKinley without having recognized the belligerency of the insurgents. During the summer of 1897 the tyranny of General Weyler was intensified. American citizens were arrested and McKinley demanded their release. Still, at the opening of the next Congress, December 7, 1897, McKinley could assert that the Cubans had not gained the status of belligerency.* Nevertheless, at least forty-two secret filibustering expeditions secretly sailed from the United States to Cuba, despite McKinley's sincere efforts to prevent aid from reaching the insurgents.

McKinley's forbearance bore fruit when, in October, the government at Madrid was changed. The more liberal Señor Sagasta became the new Spanish premier, and Weyler was recalled. It looked for a time as if all trouble would die down, especially when Sagasta promised the Cubans nominal independence under Spanish sovereignty. Remembering the fate of similar promises made twenty years before, however, they refused to lay down their arms.

While McKinley and his cabinet wavered, two men in New York did not. They were Joseph Pulitzer, publisher of the *World,* and William Randolph Hearst. Hearst was a newcomer in the newspaper field and was in search of sensational news to build his circulation. "He decided," according to Henry F. Pringle, "that a war would produce the maximum number of headlines, and so he proceeded to produce the war. Pulitzer, his rival, followed his trail of red ink and gigantic type. The owner of the New York *World* did his best, but he never equaled Hearst as a maker of war."‡

In their mighty battle for circulation and "their search for the sensationalism craved by the public, these enterprising editors flooded the island with horror-hunting correspondents, and their readers' emotions were purged daily with terror and pity. The process was expensive (Hearst complained that it cost him more than a million dollars to get the United States into war), but it brought ample return in newspaper circulation. It also created a great amount of anti-Spanish sentiment which politicians seized upon to advance their personal fortunes."§

*Peck, *op. cit.,* p. 538.
†Morison and Commager, *op. cit.,* p. 800.
‡Henry F. Pringle, *Theodore Roosevelt, A Biography* (New York: Harcourt, Brace & Co., 1931), p. 174.
§Joseph Ward Swain, *Beginning the Twentieth Century* (New York: W. W. Norton & Co., 1933), p. 181.

Two days before William McKinley took the oath of office he appointed as his Secretary of the Navy, John Davis Long, Harvard graduate, distinguished citizen of Massachusetts, a brilliant lawyer, and a poet. In 1879 Long had defeated General Benjamin Butler for the governorship of Massachusetts and had clearly demonstrated his ability to select outstanding men by appointing Oliver Wendell Holmes, Jr., to the Massachusetts Supreme Court. After serving in Congress from 1883 to 1889, Long declined to run for re-election, because he did not care for the connivery he saw among his colleagues. "Congressmen are a set or ordinary men, no better no worse," he wrote in his journal. "They mean well and serve well; but their jealousies, envies, and bitternesses are innumerable."

Long had chosen Theodore Roosevelt as his Assistant Secretary, without any realization, in the beginning, that they would differ so widely in their view of America's role. Long firmly upheld McKinley's passion for peace. Roosevelt, who had privately asserted that the United States should fight every European nation with holdings in the Western Hemisphere, was of a different stamp. Cuban insurrectionists found in him their most potent ally in the American government. "No triumph of peace is quite so great as the supreme triumph of war," he said at the Naval War College on June 2, 1897.* "If we mean to protect the people of the lands who look to us for protection from tyranny and aggression," a stronger Navy must be built, a Navy, he emphasized, capable of taking the offensive. Frequently during the summer of 1897 McKinley rebuked the Assistant Secretary for his warlike utterances. Each time he promised to reform but always managed to forget his promise at the next opportunity. He watched with "contempt the efforts of McKinley to avoid the struggle. The President, he told his intimates, 'has no more backbone than a chocolate eclair.' "† He was not alone in his opinion, for a vociferous segment of the American people, many high in government and business, "desired a war and imperial expansion for their own several ends." Powerful interests eagerly advocated the annexation of Hawaii, Puerto Rico, and the Philippines. Senator Henry Cabot Lodge was among those who urged his fellow legislators to promote their accession, and now that there were new additions to the fleet Roosevelt "was anxious for something to do with his ships. . . . In the summer of 1897 Roosevelt confided to Lodge that 'it would be everything for us to take firm action on behalf of the wretched Cubans. It would be a splendid thing for the Navy too.' "‡

*Pringle, *op. cit.*, p. 171.
†Pringle, *op. cit.*, p. 172.
‡James Truslow Adams, *The March of Democracy* (New York: Charles Scribner's Sons, 1933), p. 168.

And here was where Commodore George Dewey entered the scene. He and Roosevelt had become close friends during those critical months. The Assistant Secretary's warlike attitude drew sympathy and support from the veteran naval officer, who, for his part, feared that two more years of peace would put him on a dusty and forgotten shelf. Both were abetted by Redfield Proctor, who had visited Cuba to investigate conditions and had returned to join the clique of "strenuous Republicans" insisting upon intervention. As a leader in the group, Proctor stumped the East, depicted the miseries of the *reconcentrados,* and urged upon Americans the necessity of relieving their plight.

The insurrection resulted in the destruction, by disease or by snipers' bullets, of more than 200,000 Spanish foot soldiers. Burning and pillage by both sides destroyed millions in American property. A $100,000,000 American-Cuban trade disappeared. Atrocities, even though lessened, continued, and everything that happened in Cuba was duly dramatized in the New York yellow press. As time went on appeasers of Spain seemed to have fewer adherents than before and the interventionists many more.

Official Washington remained in a quandary. McKinley still hoped for peace, Roosevelt prayed for the justification of war. Dewey wrote that though not one man in ten in Washington during those months knew that war was on its way, he himself felt "we were inevitably drifting into war with Spain."*

*George Dewey, *op. cit.,* p. 168.

15

THE RUNGS OF DEWEY'S LADDER

𝒯heodore Roosevelt was one of the leaders of a militant Republican group believing in "Manifest Destiny" and the necessity of intervention in the Cuban insurrection. Its members included Senator Henry Cabot Lodge of Massachusetts, Elihu Root of New York, Chauncey Depew, and William Howard Taft, while its advocates and sympathizers were found in the social set of Washington, among the international bankers and diplomats, and among such publishers as William Randolph Hearst, Joseph Pulitzer, and John McLean of the Washington *Post* and Cincinnati *Enquirer*. Everywhere Roosevelt preached his gospel and sought new friends. In the Navy Department he found at least seven high-ranking officers who shared his views—Captains Evans, Taylor, Sampson, Wainwright, O'Neil, Davis, and Brownson—and with them he held long consultations, plotting strategy, considering everything to put the "Navy in trim to strike quick and hard," he wrote, "if, as we believed would be the case, we went to war with Spain." Captain Mahan was consulted by mail, and George Dewey soon became a regular attendant at the unofficial sessions.

The intimacy of the two men, begun that summer, was furthered by the respect and admiration they had for one another. The author of *The Naval War of 1812* and the disciple of Admiral Farragut thought alike—both were aggressive, bold, and imperious, and in their frequent consultations they agreed on a strategy for the coming war. One of the first steps in that strategy, Roosevelt believed, remembering the Chilean affair of 1891, was to give his friend a large share in executing it.

In explaining that belief, Roosevelt later wrote of "the high professional reputation [Dewey] enjoyed, and the character he had established for willingness to accept responsibility, for sound judgment and for entire fearlessness. Probably the best way [although no way is infallible] to tell the worth of a naval commander as yet untried in war is to get at the estimate in which he is held by the best fighting men who would have to serve under him. In the summer of 1897 there were, in Washington, captains and commanders who later won honor for themselves and their country in the war with Spain, and who were already known for the dash and skill with which they handled their ships, the excellence of their gun practice, the good discipline of their crews, and their eager desire to win honorable renown. All these men were a unit in their faith in Commodore Dewey, in their desire to serve under him, should the chance arise, and in their unquestioning belief that he was the man to meet an emergency in a way that would do credit to the flag. . . . He had such a record that the best officers in the Navy believed him to be peculiarly a man of the fighting temperament and fit to meet emergencies. . . . He had shown his willingness to assume heavy responsibilities."[*]

The question of appointment was not an academic one at the moment. Rear Admiral Frederick V. McNair, commander-in-chief, would be sixty-two years old in a few months, and a successor would have to be appointed. To Long, however, there seemed little justification for upsetting naval tradition.

"War was not then—in the fall of 1897—so imminent," he wrote, "that there was reason for departing from the routine of making in the usual regular sequence the selection of two or three officers whose turn to go to sea had come."[†]

Roosevelt, on the contrary, considered the selection crucial. Rear Admiral A. S. Crowninshield, chief of the Bureau of Navigation[‡] at the time and therefore responsible for the selection of the new commander-in-chief, was not particularly well disposed toward Dewey, who characterized him as "a pronounced bureaucrat, with whose temperament and methods I had little more sympathy than had the majority of the officers of the Navy at that time,"[§] an opinion shared by Roosevelt.

Dewey's promotion to commodore entitled him to a command at sea whenever a vacancy occurred, but the turn of two other new commodores in the naval list had also come. These were Commodore E. O. Matthews, chief of the Bureau of Yards and Docks, whom Long did not wish to move because of the splendid job he was doing there,[¶] and Commodore John A. Howell, ranking man in Dewey's Annapolis class of 1858. Howell had distinguished himself in the Civil War aboard numerous men-of-war

[*]*McClure's Magazine*, Oct., 1899.
[†]John D. Long, *The New American Navy* (New York: Outlook Co., 1903), p. 176 ff.
[‡]In 1942 the name of the Bureau of Navigation was changed to the Bureau of Naval Personnel.
[§]George Dewey, *Autobiography*, pp. 167–68.
[¶]Long, *op. cit.*, pp. 176–77.

and bore the highest reputation as an ordnance expert. Above all, he was favored by Admiral Crowninshield.

Rivalry for command of the Asiatic squadron at that time would have appeared curious to a nation whose eyes were on the Atlantic seaboard. The new battleships were mobilized off Key West to control Cuban waters, while protected cruisers and gunboats seemed adequate for the Pacific station. But George Dewey, seeing opportunity in the Orient, asked for the command. He dreamed of himself in the South Pacific "with a free hand to act in consequence of being so far away from Washington," and where he "could strike promptly and successfully at the Spanish force in the Philippines," in the event of what he thought inevitable war.*

One afternoon in the fall of 1897 Roosevelt was sitting in his office in the Navy Department, disconsolately reflecting on the succession to McNair's command—he had been given to understand by Long that Commodore Howell would be chosen. Howell was cautious and bound by discipline. He would obey orders implicitly. Roosevelt had other views. He had made up his mind that Howell would never do. A letter to Long, written by a politician with considerable influence, made a strong plea for Howell. Roosevelt read it. Smashing his fist on his desk, he jumped up and rushed to the door.

"Ask Commodore Dewey to come down," he shouted to an orderly in his high-pitched voice. Then he returned to his desk and ruffled aimlessly through papers, waiting for Dewey to arrive.

In a few minutes his friend was announced. Roosevelt handed him a cigar and lighted it for him. Noticing that the door was still open, Roosevelt jumped up and slammed it shut. Returning to his desk, he told Dewey of the letter recommending his rival.

"I want you to go instead," Roosevelt said.† "What Senators do you know?"

Dewey was taken aback. Naval officers had always professed a hatred of direct political influence. Still, he did want that command.

"Senator Proctor is from my state," he began in a minute, and he told the history of Proctor's friendship for his father and himself. T. R., knowing of Proctor's powerful influence on McKinley, was overjoyed. He advised the Commodore to see his Senator immediately. Dewey put on his hat and walked over to the Senate. He wondered what he was getting himself into, as he told Proctor of his interview with Roosevelt. It was an unorthodox procedure, to say the least; yet, Dewey consoled himself, Howell had done the same thing. He was merely fighting fire with fire.

*George Dewey, *op. cit.*, pp. 167–68.
†*Ibid.*, p. 168.

136

Proctor agreed to help all he could. He met Roosevelt that night and each arranged interviews with President McKinley the next day.

Roosevelt appeared at the White House first. He talked fast and strenuously, persuading the President that Dewey was the only man who could handle problems in the Pacific. McKinley seemed convinced. Before he had a chance to change his mind, Senator Proctor, tall and spare, entered the President's office and repeated the pressure.

"I've known Dewey's father and his father before him," said Senator Proctor. "He is a real American. He's the man you want." The President agreed cheerfully and promised to do something "right away." That did not satisfy the Senator from Vermont.

"Here, write it down, Mr. President," he suggested, pushing a pad of paper across the desk.

McKinley acquiesced. "Long, appoint Dewey command Asiatic squadron," he scribbled with a pencil. Proctor tore the sheet from the pad, stood up, and thanked the President warmly.

"You'll never regret this, Mr. President," he said, and excused himself.

His next stop was at the Navy Department, where he confronted Secretary Long with the paper. That clinched matters.

A few days later, on October 21, 1897, Long called Commodore Dewey into his office and handed him a typewritten order. It read:

NAVY DEPARTMENT

Washington, October 21, 1897

COMMODORE GEORGE DEWEY, U.S.N.,
PRESIDENT, BOARD OF INSPECTION AND SURVEY,
NAVY DEPARTMENT, WASHINGTON, D. C.

SIR:

On November 30th, 1897, you will regard yourself detached from duty as president of the Board of Inspection and Survey, Navy Department, Washington, D. C., and from such other duty as may have been assigned you, you will proceed to San Francisco, Cal., and thence to Yokohama, Japan, taking passage in the steamer of the Pacific Mail Steamship Company, sailing from San Francisco on December 7th next. Upon your arrival at Yokohama you will report to Rear Admiral Frederick V. McNair, U.S.N., the commander-in-chief of the Asiatic Station, aboard the U.S.F.S. Olympia, for duty as commander-in-chief of that station, as the relief of that officer.

Respectfully,
JOHN D. LONG,
SECRETARY.

137

The ink on Mr. Long's signature was still wet as Dewey read his orders. His heart thumped violently, and he began to smile as he looked up towards the Secretary's face. It was impassive and unfriendly. Dewey's smile disappeared.

"I am glad to appoint you, *Commodore* Dewey," said Long, slowly. "But you won't go as a rear admiral. You'll go as a commodore. Perhaps," and there he paused dramatically, "you used too much political influence."

This was unheard of. Every commander-in-chief of the Pacific squadron since the Civil War had been given at least the rank of acting rear admiral to provide equality with the commanders of other fleets in Asia. The last commodore to have commanded the squadron had been Matthew Calbraith Perry, who had served before the creation of the rank of rear admiral. As a commodore in Asia in 1898, Dewey would be subordinate to the squadron commanders and officials of the other nations, "particularly in case any necessity for combined international action should arise."*

Dewey considered it a "pin-pricking slight." He drew himself erect and looked the Secretary in the eye. They were both short men, each five feet seven inches tall, and each with a more or less round face, grayhaired, and with identical long mustaches.

"Very well, sir," said Dewey coldly. "I'll be the first commodore since Perry. And he did pretty well."

In explanation he added that he had used political influence only to offset the influence exerted in Howell's behalf.

"You are in error, Commodore," Long replied. His use of "commodore" cut Dewey's pride. "No influence has been brought to bear on behalf of anyone else."†

A few hours later, however, Mr. Long found the letter written for Howell and wrote a note to Dewey acknowledging that fact. But it made no difference, for Dewey sailed to the Orient with a commodore's pennant in his luggage.

The story of the method by which George Dewey received the command of the Pacific squadron has become a *cause célèbre* in American history. The account given here is corroborated by the autobiographies of Dewey and of Theodore Roosevelt and by George Goodwin Dewey, who received his information from Roosevelt, Dewey, and Proctor. In Mr. Long's notable *The New American Navy*, published in 1903 (by no means merely a defense of his administration, but a comprehensive, authorita-

*George Dewey, *op. cit.*, p. 173.
†*Ibid.*, p. 169.

tive and interesting account of the building of America's fleet after 1882), is given a completely different version of the episode. He emphasizes his approval of Dewey's appointment, adding:

The Asiatic squadron, in case of war with Spain, offered the larger probable opportunity for distinction, although the European squadron was a choice flag command of the Navy, and included Spanish waters. I decided to give Dewey the Asiatic and Howell the European station, and this arrangement, on my submitting it to President McKinley, who had made no suggestion in the matter and who always left such matters to the Secretary, was approved by him. I remember his simply saying to me, in his characteristically pleasant way, "Are you satisfied that Dewey is a good man for the place, and that his head is level?," to which I affirmatively answered. Political or personal influence had nothing to do with his selection, which was entirely my own.

Dewey "gave immediate evidence of the fact that the department was warranted in placing faith in him," Long wrote, by his quick application and study of the Far Eastern situation, and his research into problems of the Philippines and perusal of charts and maps to fit him for his new command. When he relieved McNair, he assumed command of "a thoroughly efficient and well trained force, and the credit for this condition is largely due to McNair. When the latter arrived in Washington he stated that he had turned over to Dewey plans for an attack . . . which were similar in many respects to those afterward followed."

It would have been natural for an administrator to want to participate in the fame of Dewey, indeed it would have been unpopular after 1898 to admit having opposed Dewey's selection. On the other hand, Long was honest and scrupulous. Perhaps both accounts are true. Perhaps Roosevelt and Dewey, convinced that Long had made up his mind to choose Howell, did the Secretary an injustice, and the collusion of the Assistant Secretary, the Senator, and the Commodore may have been completely superfluous. Certainly, John Long was one of America's most incorrupt and honorable statesmen. He loathed graft and chicanery in politics, and the political pressure in support of Dewey perhaps irked him too much to grant the usual promotion with the command. It is possible also that his suppression of that part of the story in 1903 deliberately sought to omit anything that might harm Dewey's public prestige.

Dewey's appointment met with considerable opposition in other quarters. People recalled his unflattering soubriquet of the "commodore ahorseback," and "Dewey the Dude." Congressmen from California protested against the appointment, desiring it for favorites of their own, but the Assistant Secretary remained firm in his support of Dewey. After a delegation which was urging its favorite son for the command had spoken, Roosevelt exclaimed vehemently:

"Gentlemen, I can't agree with you. We have looked up his record. We have looked him straight in the eyes. He is a fighter. We'll not change now. Pleased to have met you. Good day, gentlemen."*

"I knew that in the event of war Dewey could be slipped like a wolf-hound from the leash," T. R. wrote in 1913. "I was sure that if he were given half a chance he would strike instantly and with telling effect; and I made up my mind that all I could do to give him that half chance should be done. . . . All that was needed with Dewey was to give him the chance to get ready and then to strike, without being hampered by orders from those not on the ground. Success in war depends very largely upon choosing a man fit to exercise such powers, and then giving him those powers."†

Dewey remained in Washington a little more than a month after he received his appointment, finishing his business in the Bureau of Inspection and Survey, and preparing his personal affairs for two years at sea. Piqued though he was by the refusal of a promotion, he remembered Perry reverently and made himself ready to be a worthy successor to his hero if opportunity came. Busying himself with investigations of the Pacific squadron, he learned that its stores of ammunition were actually below peacetime standards, for the supply that had been ordered,‡ had failed to arrive. The only other ship which could carry explosives was the U.S.S. *Charleston,* then under repair at Mare Island and not expected to sail for another six months. Dewey appealed to Roosevelt, who at once ordered the U.S.S. *Concord,* nearly ready for sea on the West Coast, to carry as much of the needed supply as possible. Though too small for all of it, Dewey persuaded her commanding officer in San Francisco to overload her and skimp on other supplies, and by altering her course and stopping in Hawaii for more provisions, she could carry extra pounds of ammunition.

The Commodore also visited the office of Naval Intelligence in Washington for information about the Philippines. The last material available dated back to 1876. Then and there Dewey decided to establish his own intelligence system in the Far East. He bought every book on the subject then in print, and it was these which filled the boxes he watched being loaded aboard the *Gaelic* that December 7 in the year 1897.

The Metropolitan Club gave him a farewell dinner Saturday evening,

*William Draper Lewis, *The Life of Theodore Roosevelt* (Philadelphia: John C. Winston Co., 1919).
†Theodore Roosevelt, *Autobiography*, pp. 213–14.
‡George Dewey, *op. cit.*, pp. 170–171.

November 26, at which both leading officers of the Navy and prominent
civilians toasted his success with these verses:*

> Ashore afloat, on deck below,
> Or where our bull dogs roar,
> To back a friend or breast a foe,
> We pledge our Commodore.
>
> We know our honor'll be sustained
> Where e'er his pennant flies,
> Our rights respected and maintained,
> Whatever power defies.
>
> And when he takes his homeward tack,
> The Admiral's banner won,
> We'll hail the day that brings him back,
> And laud the duty done.

Over the cigars Dewey waxed reminiscent.

"My chance has come," he said to a Navy captain next to him, almost
as if he were talking to himself and not to a dinner companion. "And I
owe it largely to Theodore Roosevelt. Why he took such an interest in my
application, I don't know. There were three applicants, you know, and
my claim was not the best. The Assistant Secretary overcame all opposition. . . . And, now, I go."

After a pause he added, "You know, Farragut didn't get his chance
until he was over sixty, but he took it, and . . . ." The Commodore realized
how it sounded. He laughed embarrassedly. "What am I saying?" he went
on. "Farragut and I!"†

No record remains of another farewell paid by the Commodore that
November to the house on K Street where the "three widows of Washington" held their brilliant court. The ladies were Mrs. Washington Mc-
Lean, widow of the founder of the Cincinnati *Enquirer* and the Washington *Post,* and her two daughters, Mary and Mildred. Mildred, born in
Cincinnati in 1850, had been married at the age of nineteen to William
Babcock Hazen, a brigadier general in the Civil War, twenty years her
senior. Hazen was stationed in the Northwest, where Mildred had a baby
girl who died during an Indian uprising against an Army fort. Then, for

*This verse was prepared by Archibald Hopkins. Numerous versions of the third stanza
exist. Mark Sullivan, in *Our Times*, gives it as:
> And when he takes the homeward tack,
> Beneath an admiral's flag,
> We'll hail the day that brings him back,
> And have another jag.

†Young, *Life and Heroic Deeds of Admiral Dewey*, p. 97.

sake of contrast, they were transferred to Vienna, where he served as military attaché of the American Embassy, and where his wife's beauty and fashionable dress attracted considerable attention at the Hapsburg court.* After some years of officialdom in Washington, where the Hazen home, given Mildred by her father, became a center of capital society, Hazen died.

Dewey had known them both at the height of their social success, but long years at sea on the *Pensacola* had interrupted the connection, and by the time he returned in 1889, Mildred was a widow. The two developed a close friendship in the next eight years, yet their names were never linked, for by then Mrs. Hazen was much sought after by men far more prominent than Dewey then was.† She had committed herself to none.

Perhaps, like Dewey, she, too, had a sense of destiny ahead.

*While in Vienna, Mildred, under the influence of the Hapsburg society, embraced Catholicism.
†One of her suitors, Mildred wrote, was Bellamy Storer, a Roosevelt intimate who later married Maria Longworth, the aunt of T. R.'s son-in-law, Nicholas Longworth.

16

GUEST MOST HONORABLE

On Christmas Day, after a seventeen-day voyage, Commodore Dewey stepped from the gangplank of the Pacific mail steamer *Gaelic* into the streets of Yokohama. "Seventeen days," Dewey explained to his son, "because we dropped a day when we crossed the 180 degrees of longitude." Dewey unlimbered his legs after the long journey by sightseeing on shore, and even such a superficial inspection brought forcibly home to him the changes that had taken place since Perry's visit fifty years before.

The next day, his birthday, he left for Nagasaki, where the *Olympia* was stationed, but before embarking he mailed a letter to his son, in which he wrote cheerfully, "I am sixty years old today and you were twenty-five on the 23rd. We are getting on."

The *Gaelic* sailed out of Yeddo Bay, where Perry and the old *Mississippi* had anchored forty-four years before, and steamed southwest past the Japanese islands. Dewey watched snow-capped Fujiyama disappear below the horizon, and he peered westward at the hills behind Mississippi Bay, named after his Civil War steam frigate. He promenaded on deck as the steamer churned through the Totomi Sea, past Cape Shionomi, by Toso Bay and Shikoku, Kyushu, and headed northward past Kagoshima Bay for Nagasaki.

Making port on New Year's Eve, the Commodore slept on shore that night and early the next morning boarded the *Olympia,* lying in the roadstead. The flagship's white sides glistened in the sun, and smoke rose lazily from her smokestacks.

Fore and aft her tall masts slanted upward but, unlike the heavy spars on the *Pensacola,* they carried no sails. Both ahead and astern of the superstructure a gun turret was mounted, each containing a pair of eight-inch, rifled cannon, long-ranged and accurate. She also carried ten five-inch rapid-fire guns to supplement her main batteries. A pair of mighty triple-expansion engines gave her a speed of more than twenty-one knots, a record rate at that time. Her bow, unusual in design, protruded at the water line and receded as it rose from the water. Anchor chains hung in graceful festoons aft of the starboard prow, while the port chain stretched taut into the water, tugging on a bower anchor.

Dewey was thrilled as he looked at her sleek lines and thought of the heft of her 5,870 tons of steel, compared with the wooden walls and cast-iron smoothbores of the steam sloop *Pensacola*. The complete modernity of his flagship thrilled his sailor's heart as he made ready to step upon her four-inch armored deck.

Rear Admiral McNair received him, and together the officers inspected the ship and went over the squadron records. Dewey spent Sunday resting and reviewing the ship's documents. On Monday, January 3, decks were cleared for the ceremony of relieving command.

At nine o'clock the crew of the *Olympia* lined up on the starboard side of the quarter-deck in their dress blues, while officers stood at attention in front of the men. Admiral McNair with his staff marched aft to face the flag. Commodore Dewey marched to the deck a minute later, accompanied by his flag lieutenant, his flag secretary, and his aide. Visiting officers from the squadron's other ships saluted their new commander-in-chief. Sideboys stood stiffly by the port rail, and the *Olympia's* band played the "Admiral's March."

Admiral McNair stepped forward, and spoke briefly. First thanking his men and officers for their co-operation, he then turned to his successor and proudly informed him of the squadron's first-rate condition. Then he read his orders to sail the next day on the *Coptic* for the United States. Finally, he gave his last command, ordering the flagship's captain, Charles V. Gridley, to haul down the two-starred admiral's flag. A gun began to fire slowly, in salute to the retiring commander-in-chief, and as the last of the thirteen volleys sounded, the blue flag began its descent from the masthead.

Commodore Dewey stepped up to McNair and saluted him. Returning the salute stiffly, McNair turned and walked back to his staff. Dewey put on his glasses, took his orders from his breast pocket, and read them through. Then, replacing the sheet, he directed Captain Gridley to break his commodore's pennant at the mast. The broad blue flag was hoisted to the peak. As a quartermaster made fast the halyard, the salute gun began to fire again, eleven shots for the new commander-in-chief.

The ceremonies were over. The *Olympia's* crew was marched forward, while the Marine guard and band moved to the gangway to render proper honors to officers leaving the ship.

Commodore Dewey and Admiral McNair walked aft to the commander-in-chief's cabin, where McNair turned over his keys and records. The long official letter transmitting the files and records contained "no hint of the pregnant events then pending," Dewey recalled. "An account of the uneasy state of affairs in Korea, of some anti-missionary riots in China, of the seizure of Kiaochow Bay by the Germans one month earlier, the attitude of the Japanese, and some minor international matters were treated of; but in no manner was there any forecast given of the work in which the squadron would soon be so vitally interested, while the only mention of the Philippines was a short paragraph to the effect that 'for some time the newspapers have contained accounts of a rebellion in progress in the Philippines'; but that no 'official information has been received in relation thereto, and no information of any sort that shows American interests to be affected.' In fact at that time the Philippines were to us a *terra incognita*—no ship of our service had been there for years."*

The next day Commodore Dewey boarded the *Coptic* to bid farewell to his predecessor, and then went ashore to begin his formal calls. Punctiliously he paid his respects to the consuls of England, Germany, and the other foreign powers represented at Nagasaki, and to the senior officers of European and Japanese ships in the harbor. He also visited the Russian Admiral Donkasoff, senior ranking officer in the bay, aboard the Czarist ship *Painyot Azora,* where he received his first foreign salute of eleven

*Beginning on January 1, 1898, perhaps because he foresaw the importance of the coming months, George Dewey kept a diary. The first volume was kept faithfully every day of 1898. The second volume was continued daily through the year of 1899 until November 3. Brief as the entries were, they formed the outline to be used later for a complete account of Dewey's command of the Asiatic squadron.

In 1904, at Dewey's instance, his aide, Commander Nathan Sargent, U. S. N., compiled an account of Dewey's participation in the Philippines' engagements of the war with Spain. It was written "from official records in possession of Admiral Dewey and of the Navy Department, and from personal memoranda and recollections of the Admiral and of the commanding and other officers who served with him in the Manila campaign," according to Sargent's foreword.   On the title page of this 197-page account, Admiral Dewey wrote in his own hand: "Commander Sargent has written this description of the operations of the squadron I had the honor to command in 1898–99, at my instance and while in daily association with me. I believe the statements of facts to be as correct as is possible in any historical account. (Signed) George Dewey, Admiral of the Navy."

Admiral Dewey wrapped the document in a piece of brown paper and wrote thereon: "Not to be published until after my death. George Dewey." The account was obviously prepared as the official record of Dewey's command in the Philippines. Eulogistic and editorialized, it shows conclusively that Dewey handled to perfection the battles and diplomatic difficulties confronting him.

For many years the document was lost among the vast bulk of Dewey's papers and souvenirs. It was unearthed by his son, George Goodwin Dewey, in 1934, and has never before been shown to anyone except a few close friends of Dewey's only descendant.

The following chapters concerning Admiral Dewey's activities in the Philippines are based largely upon this hitherto unpublished account. When quotation marks are used without further explanation, they indicate direct quotations from the Sargent record of 1904.

guns. On January 11, after close inspection of his own ship, he pronounced her fit, and on Saturday, January 15, at 11 A.M., the *Olympia* weighed anchor, saluted the Russian and English flagships, and left the harbor. She sailed north and east, through the straits of Tsushima, where Admiral Togo would smash the Czarist fleet in 1904, and headed east to the western entrance of Shimonoseki Strait between the islands of Kyushu and Honshu. After a delay of one night, caused by thick weather, the flagship steamed through the Inland Sea and, discharging her pilot at Kobe, proceeded to Yokohama, where she anchored at 3:30 A.M., January 18.

At dawn the *Olympia* fired thirteen guns for the Japanese rear admiral and paid similar salute to the city itself. Then Commodore Dewey put on his dress uniform to receive a Japanese captain who came to pay his respects. In the afternoon he called upon the Japanese admiral and went ashore to meet the governor of the province and foreign consuls. The next day he returned the Japanese captain's call, and as the latter's guest went ashore for dinner and saw a geisha dance.

His first weeks were marked by scrupulous observance of all the naval and diplomatic proprieties, for he was determined to shine both as naval commander-in-chief and as diplomat. Japan in 1898 was an awakening nation. Alert to the "menace" of the West, and bent on equality with it, she was feverishly building an industrial might. British shipyards turned out steel cruisers for the young Japanese Navy. Even in the 1890's Japan was looking with eager eyes toward a Pan-Asiatic federation dominated by Nippon.

Mahan had sensed the threat in 1892 when he wrote *The Influence of Sea Power upon History* and urged American control of a string of island bases to the Orient. Dewey, too, realized the need. Like Theodore Roosevelt, he was learning to think in terms of world power and prestige, even before the day of empire had dawned.

Roosevelt had urged some type of action against Japan in 1897. Cleveland's refusal to annex the Hawaiian Islands had seemed sheer folly to the Assistant Secretary of the Navy. On April 22, 1897, he assured President McKinley that the Japanese were viewing those islands with "covetous eyes." Japan, he said, had sent a cruiser to Honolulu. That move had been checked by dispatch of the U.S.S. *Philadelphia* there.

On May 3 Roosevelt wrote to Captain Mahan: "If I had my way, we would annex those islands tomorrow. If that is impossible I would establish a protectorate. . . . My own belief is that we should act instantly before the two new Japanese warships leave England. I would hoist our flag over the island, leaving all details for after action. I believe . . . we should build a dozen new battleships, half of them on the Pacific Coast.

. . . I am fully alive to the danger from Japan."* That letter was written in 1897, before America had a single Pacific outpost.

Dewey's own interest in the growing power of Japan was intensified by his personal affinity to Commodore Perry. As he attached himself in history to the star of Farragut, so he hoped that the deeds of two commodores would be linked for all time in the annals of American relations with the empire of the Mikado. And when he dictated his report to his aide in 1904 he said: "The forecasters of the future have predicted that the Pacific Ocean will be the theatre of the twentieth-century struggle between nations for commercial supremacy, and that the country which commands the commerce of the Pacific will control the commerce of the world. What a commentary upon the fateful working of these events, that of these two American commodores, one with his masterly management of Japan should have been the instrument of giving his country the entering wedge to this great trade, and that the other in conquering for her an Eastern Empire should have assured her the trade routes of that commerce for all time."

This same report contains no hint of anything save friendship and respect for the Japanese government, yet Dewey was aware of Japan's growing threat, and often asserted in private his views that her warlords would one day attack the United States.

"He felt we would have to fight Japan some time," his son declared. "Father told me it is coming, and when it comes this great nation of ours will set back Japan 1,000 years. They hate us, and next to the Germans they were the most unfriendly to us. It is coming sure."

Dewey's desire to foster American-Japanese relations was revealed in his great care for all proper etiquette. "The commodore was aware of the fact [his aide wrote] that for years it had been customary for the commander-in-chief of our squadron, as soon as possible after his arrival, to ask for an audience with the Emperor of Japan; and he fully realized the importance of observing this and every amenity which in any degree would tend to retain good will of a rather sensitive nation. He determined, therefore, to request the audience without delay, and in this decision he was actuated both by consideration of the proverbial friendliness of the Japanese toward the people who had brought them out of medieval darkness and by the perhaps more interested motive of one who might need and whose duty it was to cultivate the good offices of their government." The custom had been neglected in latter years, but Dewey arranged an appointment with the Emperor for January 24.

*Pringle, *Theodore Roosevelt*, p. 171.

Owing to the illness of the Empress, however, it was postponed and Dewey did not appear at court until February 4.

While he waited at Yokohama, the Commodore made it his business to become acquainted with Japanese food and customs, as well as to watch the diplomatic games of the foreign powers whose fleets were stationed there. "Affairs are very unsettled in the Far East," he wrote his son in January, "and I expect my tour of service out here will be very interesting. The Germans, Russians, English, and Japanese are playing a big game of bluff since it remains to be seen who will take the big pot. We are fortunate in being out of the game. All we have to do is look on and see that our interests do not suffer."

On January 23 he wrote George a fatherly letter, chiding him for misspelling Yokohama. ""It is Yokohama, not Yokehama as you addressed your last letter," the Commodore wrote. "You must write on both sides of your letter paper as they charge double postage over half an ounce. . . . I am glad you have so many pleasant homes to visit. It is not good for a man to live altogether with men. I know this well from a long experience."

The Commodore enclosed a "slip" from a Japanese English-language newspaper. Headlined "The New American Admiral," it discussed Dewey's arrival to assume command, and called him "one of the strongest and finest looking men in the United States Navy, while his record of service is a splendid one." After outlining Dewey's naval career, it stated "he must have had a somewhat busy time of it, and in that capacity must have formed a pretty good acquaintance with most of the more modern style of craft now to be found in the U.S. Navy list. . . . It may be confidently predicted that it will not be long before he receives authority to hoist his pennant as rear admiral." Despite the compliments, Dewey added to his son, "they have not much to write about although great events are formulating at their very doors. There is not much 'freedom of the press' in Japan."

"I like this station more and more," he wrote to George in his next letter. "The people grow on one and the cheapness of nearly everything makes even a poor man rich. Yesterday I lunched at the Grand Hotel and paid for luncheon and a quart of excellent table claret a dollar and a quarter Japan money, or sixty-two and a half cents of our money. I receive my pay in gold and exchange it for Japanese paper and silver at the rate of two for one. That is, my gold dollar is worth a little more than two Japanese dollars and the latter goes rather farther than a gold dollar does in New York. And everything else is equally cheap. A jinricksha is fifteen cents (seven and a half) an hour. You should read up on this interesting country. Lafcadio Hearn's *Glimpses of Unfamiliar Japan* is as good as anything. I am reading just now his *Out of the East.*"

"Great fleets of war vessels are watching each other out here, all working for the same end, trade. We have very great interests here and in China, and I am happy to say they are increasing. Our trade with both Japan and China is very large."

The Commodore inherited two Chinese servants from Admiral McNair. He engaged two more himself. Their cheap wages and their efficiency amazed him. One of them, Ah Mah, returned to the United States and remained his loyal manservant for many years.

On February 3 he departed for his long-awaited audience with the Emperor. Accompanied by his personal aides and fleet staff, he boarded the morning train to Tokyo, where they called upon Mr. Buck, the United States Minister, and then paid their respects to Baron Sammonija, grand master of ceremonies at the imperial palace. Dewey had prepared himself for this moment with great care. He had studied intently the records of Commodore Perry's conferences with the Japanese, he had read every book available about the people, and had studied closely those with whom he had come in personal contact—among them a Japanese servant who had remained with him several years and had silently disappeared.

A delegation of Japanese naval officers awaited him at the palace. Their ranking officer was a commander, whose walk, as he approached Dewey, seemed familiar. It was, without doubt, his former servant.

"I looked him hard in the eye, and I am sure he realized that I recognized him," Dewey said. (Nor was he the only one of his kind. We know now that planting officers as servants in the United States was only part of the master plan pursued for many years before Pearl Harbor.)

The pattern was never completely unfolded for George Dewey. Yet, unlike other Americans, he comprehended the 300-year-old drive of Japan to conquer the world. Launched in 1592 by the war lord Hideyoshi, who attempted to conquer Korea and China, the campaign was nurtured along until 1941 by the Japanese religion of Shinto and the warrior code of Bushido.

After Commodore Perry's visit in 1854, Lord Hotta, Japan's leading statesman, advised his Emperor to make friends with the white race, as a step toward the goal of Japanese world domination. Hotta proposed alliances with other nations and a policy of "friendly deception" while mastering the industrial developments of the Western World. Japan learned from Captain Mahan the necessity of developing sea power. Her war with

Russia in 1904 was calculated to guard her flank for the inevitable blow at China. Her acquisition of Pacific island bases, unsinkable aircraft carriers, after the first World War was designed to augment her naval might. After she became one of the three great naval powers in 1927, Baron Tanaka formulated a blueprint whose pattern blossomed on December 7, 1941. Known as the "Tanaka Memorial," it urged the cynical violation of treaties, deception, and a policy of "blood and iron." To carry out the grandiose program Tanaka stated: "We have to face the United States, which has been turned against us by China's policy of fighting poison with poison. In the future, if we want to control China, we must first crush the United States, just as in the past we had to fight the Russo-Japanese War. But in order to conquer China, we must first conquer Manchuria and Mongolia. In order to conquer the world, we must first conquer China."

The Emperor received Dewey with great cordiality. The reception "bore little of an Oriental character," Dewey reported, "and barring the surroundings, the decorations of the palace, and the costumes and occasional genuflections of the servants, its scene might as well have been at Berlin, St. Petersburg, or any European capital."

The Emperor, in full uniform, resplendent with ribbons and medals, was flanked by a host of aides, court chamberlains, and gentlemen-in-waiting. The apparent cosmopolitanism of the imperial couple led the Commodore to note again, in his persistent drawing of parallels between himself and Perry: "What a contrast in the reception of the two American commodores who at an interval of but forty-four years had cast anchor in the Gulf of Yeddo. The one, regarded with an apprehensive consternation only rivaled in degree by the cataclysmic changes in beliefs, customs, and national policy of which he was the precursor, the other, welcomed with all the amenities of civilization; the one, after vexatious delays allowed to meet the representatives of an invisible and impotent Mikado, the other received openly by an Emperor who was that anomaly in the Far East—a constitutional monarch; the one, landing in a country hidden in Oriental isolation, the other, debarking in a thriving port open to the commerce of the world and being transported to Tokyo by railway. The world has seen great changes in its time, but none more radical than the extraordinary *bouleversement* of all the practices and preconceived ideas of Japan such as followed the memorable visit of Commodore Perry."

Dewey thought the audience a great success. Before returning to Yokohama that afternoon, he called upon the Japanese Ministers of Foreign

Affairs and of the Navy to pledge cordial relations between the two countries in the best diplomatic manner.

Meanwhile, he anxiously awaited ammunition for his squadron, whose stores of shell and powder were precariously low. The *Concord* had brought thirty-five tons of munitions, but thirty-seven tons more were necessary to bring the squadron's stores up to even minimum requirements. The Navy Department had not as yet thought it important to expedite the shipment.

On February 11, one day after the transfer of munitions from the *Concord* to the *Olympia,* Commodore Dewey headed his little fleet across the China Sea to Hong Kong. This move, according to Sargent's account of 1904, "made upon his own volition, is a clear indication of the trend of the Commodore's thoughts at this time, and seems but the logical result of his strategic studies. Should war result, he had but one aim in view—to take the initiative and attack. Meantime he chose the nearest port to his quarry as the most advantageous position from which to watch the progress of events, and when the moment should at last arrive, to strike."

Scarcely a seer was needed to know that the American squadrons should take position near the Philippines. Most of Dewey's fleet was already in Chinese waters, and his instructions from Theodore Roosevelt had been specific enough for him to know that it would be his duty to deal with the Spanish fleet as soon as trouble started. Just two weeks before, on January 25, Dewey had received a cable from the chief of the Bureau of Navigation, ordering him to "retain until further orders the crew of the squadron whose terms of enlistment have expired," instructions which gave evidence that relations between Washington and Madrid were not improving.

When Commodore Dewey arrived at the British colony of Hong Kong six days later, on February 17, he heard astounding news.

17

THUNDERBOLTS ARE FORGED

On the twelfth of January riots broke out in Havana. Mild at first, they increased in violence the next five days. Mobs broke the windows of newspaper offices and threatened American citizens. On January 23 Fitzhugh Lee, Consul General at Havana, cabled Captain Charles D. Sigsbee, commanding officer of the *Maine,* then off Key West, that protection was necessary. In order to divert suspicion of his plans, Sigsbee accompanied all his officers ashore that night to attend a dance and informed crew members that the *Maine* would leave in the morning for New York.* The next day the battleship sailed for Cuba, while Secretary Long, in Washington, wrote in his journal, "I hope with all my heart that everything will turn out all right."†

The *Maine* arrived in Havana on the 25th. Captain Sigsbee had but one wish, he wrote, "to be friendly to the Spanish authorities, as required by my orders." Accordingly, he prepared to salute the Spanish flag and admiral. "But such salutes are given only when it is known they will be returned. I, therefore, deemed it prudent to determine this point, although the visit of a Spanish officer to my ship would ordinarily be thought sufficiently convincing. So, in the course of conversation with the Spanish officer . . . I said, 'I am about to give myself the honor of saluting your national flag; from which battery will the salute be returned?' He replied, 'From the Cubaña battery.' With that assurance both salutes were fired and returned."‡

Captain Sigsbee and five officers attended a bullfight the next Sunday, where they were greeted circumspectly, if with scant friendliness. One leaflet, assailing the "Yankee pigs" for sending a man-of-war to Cuba,

---

*Charles D. Sigsbee, "Personal Narrative of the Maine," *Century Magazine*, Nov. and Dec., 1898.

†Lawrence Shaw Mayo, *America of Yesterday as Reflected in the Journals of John D. Long.* (Boston: Atlantic Monthly Press, 1923).

‡Sigsbee, *op. cit.*

and urging all Spaniards to throw out the Americans, was stuffed into Sigsbee's hand. When later published in the United States it aroused great feeling. The *Maine's* captain blandly continued his social calls and courtesies, and all seemed well.

Such was the situation on February 8 when United States newspapers printed a private letter from Señor Dupuy de Lome, the Spanish Ambassador at Washington, written to a friend in Havana, stolen in Cuba, and sent to Hearst. Besides revealing bad faith in Spain's dealings with the United States, it contained a sharp criticism of President McKinley.

"McKinley is weak and a caterer to the rabble," de Lome had written, "and, moreover, a cheap politician, who wishes to leave a door open to himself and to stand well with the jingoes of his party."* The Spanish government immediately disclaimed all sympathy with de Lome's sentiments and promptly recalled the Ambassador, but he was furiously denounced in the press, and demands for intervention thundered through the United States Senate.

Secretary Long, obliged to cancel a dinner engagement at the de Lome residence on February 10, noted in his journal that day "an unfortunate occurrence. So it is that little things are obstacles that throw great movements off the track, and sometimes lead to disaster."†

Ill-advised as the de Lome letter was, it might have been forgotten but for a tragedy in Havana Bay. A little before ten o'clock on the evening of February 15, Captain Sigsbee was writing in his cabin on the *Maine*. The battleship's officers were lounging in the wardroom amidships, and up forward crew members were talking, writing, singing, and getting ready for bed. Suddenly a thunderous blast rocked the ship. The bulkheads of Sigsbee's cabin crumpled in as another blast shook the ship. A bloody sailor ran down the smoke-filled passageway from the bow. The forward end of the ship was shattered in the explosion, and the rest of the vessel was ablaze. Fewer than a hundred of the *Maine's* crew of 335 escaped unwounded. They pulled the injured into boats as the blazing ship settled on the shoal.‡

Shortly after midnight McKinley received a cable from Captain Sigsbee, narrating briefly the loss of the ship and the death of two officers and 264 enlisted men. "Public opinion should be suspended until further report," he took care to add.

It was the news of the *Maine* that greeted Commodore Dewey when

*Peck, *Twenty Years of the Republic*, p. 540.
†Mayo, *op. cit.*
‡Pratt, *The Navy*, p. 363.

153

he reached Hong Kong on February 17. The next day a carefully worded telegram from Secretary Long reached him:

> MAINE DESTROYED AT HAVANA FEBRUARY 15TH BY ACCIDENT, THE PRESIDENT DIRECTS ALL COLORS BE HALF-MASTED UNTIL FURTHER ORDERS. INFORM VESSELS UNDER YOUR COMMAND BY TELEGRAPH.

The American squadron's colors drooped sadly at half-mast, while all the foreign ships in the harbor lowered their ensigns in sympathy. Messages were brought by their captains, and European representatives in other Oriental cities cabled condolences. All united in "horrified amazement" at such an act in time of peace.

On February 17 President McKinley appointed a naval court of inquiry, headed by Captain William T. Sampson, to investigate the origin of the blast, but "Remember the Maine" insistently rang out over the country.

On the afternoon of February 25 Theodore Roosevelt became acting Secretary of the Navy, while his superior went home for a rest. Roosevelt was evidently on Long's mind, for he wrote in his journal, "T.R. is so enthusiastic and loyal that he is in certain respects invaluable. Yet I lack confidence in his good judgment and discretion. He goes off impulsively."*

When Long returned to his desk the next day, a copy of a cablegram from Roosevelt to Dewey lay upon his desk:

> ORDER THE SQUADRON EXCEPT THE MONOCACY TO HONG KONG. KEEP FULL OF COAL. IN THE EVENT DECLARATION OF WAR SPAIN, YOUR DUTY WILL BE TO SEE THAT THE SPANISH SQUADRON DOES NOT LEAVE THE ASIATIC COAST, AND THEN OFFENSIVE OPERATIONS IN PHILIPPINE ISLANDS. KEEP OLYMPIA UNTIL FURTHER ORDERS.

Since the *Olympia* had previously been ordered to return to the West Coast of America, to be replaced as flagship by the *Baltimore,* then in Honolulu, Roosevelt's cable was calculated to make certain that the Asiatic squadron should not be reduced in striking power at such a critical juncture.

Dewey lost no time in executing the orders. He had already formulated plans of action to be followed as soon as he received a free hand. A cablegram to expedite the arrival of the *Boston* and *Concord,* both at sea, was dispatched. The United States Consul at Manila was requested in a coded cablegram to obtain all possible information concerning the fortifications, submarine mines, and general defenses of Manila Bay, and to inform

*Mayo, *op. cit.*

Dewey of every movement of the Spanish fleet. Dewey also considered the effects of a possible proclamation of neutrality by the British and other governments, for he was 7,000 miles from any home base, and provisions and fuel must be arranged for. Although without instructions from the Navy Department, he immediately began discreet negotiations for the purchase of supply steamers with full cargoes of coal.

Back in Washington the effect of Roosevelt's action on Secretary Long was less happy. "The very devil seemed to possess him," Long wrote in his journal on February 26. "Yesterday afternoon he has gone at things like a bull in a china shop. It shows how the best fellow in the world and with splendid capabilities is worse than no use if he lacks a cool head and careful discretion."

As the month of March dragged on, anger in the United States rose steadily and events marched to their now seemingly inevitable conclusion. The press became even more warlike, and Spanish flags were burned by huge crowds assembled to demand vengeance and to stampede McKinley into action. Knowing war was probably unavoidable, the President nevertheless waited while the Navy Yards worked night and day to make the fleet ready. Torpedoes and mines were bought from foreign nations to protect the harbors of the East Coast. On March 8 Congress unanimously appropriated $50,000,000 to be placed at McKinley's disposal for national defense. The Spanish Junta countered with a $40,000,000 loan from the Bank of Spain. Mobilization in the United States began March 11. The next day Captain Charles E. Clark steamed out of San Francisco in the battleship *Oregon* on his epic and unprecedented cruise around Cape Horn to join the Atlantic battle line. Spain offered the Cuban insurgents an armistice on March 12, which the Cubans haughtily turned down. On March 14 Admiral Cervera and the Spanish Atlantic fleet left Cadiz for the Canary Islands, and the same day Senator Redfield Proctor's inflammatory report on Spanish atrocities in Cuba was headlined on front pages from coast to coast.

The divers finished their investigation of the *Maine's* sunken hull, and on March 21 Captain Sampson delivered the verdict of his naval court to Secretary Long. Made public seven days later, it stated carefully, but categorically, that the *Maine* had been destroyed from external causes, apparently by a submarine mine; that the plates of the ship had been blown inward and its keel driven up through its deck—the reverse of the effects which would follow an internal explosion.* No attempt to fix responsibility was made. Spain, countering with her own report, argued

*Peck, *op. cit.*, p. 543.

that the *Maine* blast was from internal causes, but by now no one in the United States cared to listen to that version.

A dozen years after the Spanish War, the *Maine* was raised and a more thorough naval investigation was made, in which the findings of the Sampson commission were sustained. The *Maine's* hulk was then towed into the Atlantic Ocean and sunk without an inspection by any other nation. Doubt of the cause still persists, but at a time when a newspaper publisher could order a foreign correspondent to sink a hulk in the Suez Canal to halt a Spanish fleet, almost anything could happen—and did.

Commodore Dewey worked twenty hours a day. Early in March, when the *Boston,* the *Concord,* and the *Raleigh* reached Hong Kong, he ordered them immediately into drydock for complete overhauling and repairs. All the ships were fully fueled and provisioned, the crews were drilled daily, and machinery was kept ready to move at a moment's notice. Dewey personally inspected every detail, supervised plans to unload all combustible material from the vessels, and insisted on the highest efficiency of the crew.

In the absence of an intelligence system the Commodore formed his own by obtaining the assistance of O. F. Williams, the Consul at Manila, who reported every scrap of information he could glean. "While, naturally, not technical, it was of immense value to the squadron." His courage in remaining at Manila, despite threats against his life, impressed Dewey greatly. He was able to report to the Commodore the mounting of six new guns on Corregidor at the entrance to Manila Bay, the planting of submarine mines there, the number of Spanish ships in the harbor, and Spanish efforts to fortify Olongapo at Subic Bay.

His reports, Sargent declares, "were redolent of the prevailing atmosphere of excitement and suspicion, and form an interesting *olla podrida* of intelligence concerning ships and defenses, menaces of murder to Americans, progress of the various insurrections, preparations of the fleet and forts, clandestine visits to the Consul's quarters, threats against his safety, and extravagant rumors of all sorts, not the least of which was the story that the United States government had implored the Pope to intercede and to save us from destruction by the army and navy of Spain." The last rumor was so thoroughly believed that it was proclaimed in all the churches of Luzon.

In addition to Williams, Dewey enjoyed the services of an American businessman whose name has been lost to history, who made numerous "business" trips from Hong Kong to Manila to investigate certain matters upon which special light was desired; and of his own aide, Ensign F. B. Upham, who, in civilian clothes, frequently impersonated a world

156

traveler by going from ship to ship in the harbor of Hong Kong to pick up information. From steamer crews arriving from the Philippines, Upham learned that the Spaniards were compelling ships to employ Spanish pilots in the waters of Manila Bay to steer them through alleged mine fields.

"A specious bluff," the Commodore grunted at this report.

Despite the lack of a professional intelligence system, Dewey gained a remarkable knowledge of the defenses of Manila. He wrote Secretary Long a frank and confident letter on March 31, predicting with uncanny assurance what he would be able to do as soon as war began.

SIR: 1. On the receipt of your telegram of February 26, the Olympia, Raleigh and Petrel were at this port, and the Boston and Concord were at Chemulpo, Korea. The two latter vessels were ordered here at once and arrived five days later.

2. Since that time the vessels have been kept full of the best coal obtainable, provisioned and ready to move at 24 hours notice. From inspection made during the past month, I find the squadron in a high state of efficiency.

3. I have been in communication with reliable persons in Manila and am able to give you what I believe to be a true account of the defenses of that place, which are as follows:

(a) The cruiser Reina Christina, of 3,500 tons.

(b) The wooden cruiser Castilla, of 3,342 tons.

(c) The gunboats Juan de Austria and Isla de Luzon, of 1,130 and 1,030 tons respectively.

(d) About twelve armored tugs and launches for river service.

(e) A battery of five or possibly six six-inch guns on Corregidor Island at the entrance to Manila Bay, 27 miles from the city. These guns have only been mounted during the last month. There is a clear channel on each side of the island, one two, and the other five miles in width.

(f) A small and weak battery at Cavité, the naval station, seven miles by water from the city.

(g) Batteries similar to the last along the waterfront of the city itself, and a small fort at the entrance to Pasig River.

(h) About 10,000 soldiers of all ranks in all the islands, of which half are in the vicinity of Manila. The Islands are now in a state of insurrection and my informants state that even the Spanish soldiers, which constitute only a small part of the whole, are disaffected. Both ships and forts are in need of ammunition.

4. I believe I am not overconfident in stating that with the squadron now under my command the vessels could be taken and the defenses of Manila reduced in one day.

5. There is every reason to believe that with Manila taken or even blockaded, the rest of the Islands would fall either to the insurgents or

to ourselves, as they are only held now through the support of the navy and are dependent upon Manila for supplies.

6. Information has just reached me that there are 5,000 armed rebels in camp near Manila, who are willing to assist us.

> Very respectfully,
> Your obedient servant,
> GEORGE DEWEY,
> Commodore, U.S. Navy, Commanding
> U.S. Naval Forces on Asiatic Station.*

The resources of the Spanish defenders were later found to have been underestimated by more than two gunboats and fifty-seven heavy shore rifles, but in his confidence, Dewey had been more than correct. Dramatically enough, his letter arrived in Washington after May 1. The same assurance he voiced in a letter to his son, written a few days later:

The news today is decidedly warlike and I have made my arrangements for a descent on Manila as soon as war is declared. As you can fancy, I am very busy. The Baltimore should be here in ten or twelve days, as she sailed from Honolulu on March 25. . . . I wish you would send me six cases of Whitteman Bros. and Co. shoe polish for patent leather shoes. Send by paid express to Navy Pay Office, San Francisco, and write Pay Inspector Griffing and ask him to send me by one of the China steamers....

Another thing, in case anything should happen to me during the war, you will become my sole heir to between $80,000 and $90,000. I wish you to pay your Aunt Mary Greeley during her life the sum of five hundred dollars a year, $500.

I don't expect anything will happen, but it is well that you should know my wishes.

It looks to me today as if war was inevitable. I have written the Dept. that I expect to capture the Spanish ships and reduce the defenses of Manila in one day. With much love,

> Your affectionate father,
> GEORGE DEWEY,

P.S. The polish comes in small round boxes and is a paste.

To his sister, he scrawled in pencil:

I have seven men-of-war all ready for action, and should war be the word I believe we will make short work of the Spanish reign in the Philippines. The insurgents are ready to rise at our first gun, and long before this reaches you we may be masters of Manila and Philippine cities. But, after all, war is a terrible thing, and I hope some way out of the dilemma may be found without resorting to the very last course. . . . My health continues good although it is taxed to the utmost, and my one prayer is that I may hold out until we have finished our work. . . . I be-

*Archives of the Navy Department.

158

lieve I am not overconfident in saying that with the force under command I could enter the Bay of Manila, capture or destroy the Spanish squadron and reduce the defenses in one day.*

Throughout the month of March coal and ammunition had been Dewey's overpowering concerns. One seemed almost as unobtainable as the other. On March 11 he cabled Long:

FOR THE SQUADRON TO OPERATE IN PHILIPPINE ISLANDS IT IS DESIRABLE THAT AMMUNITION AND COAL SHOULD BE SENT FROM SAN FRANCISCO IMME-DIATELY. OTHER GOVERNMENTS HAVE BOUGHT ALL GOOD COAL.

The Secretary replied the next day:

YOU ARE AUTHORIZED TO CONTRACT FOR THE DELIVERY OF 5,000 TONS OF COAL AND LESS AT SUCH PLACE AS YOU DECIDE UPON. ORDER GOOD COAL FROM ENGLAND IF NECESSARY.

Immediately, Dewey sealed his preliminary negotiations for coal and bought the entire cargo of the steamer *Nanshan,* then on the way from Cardiff, Wales, with 3,000 tons of coal. He then decided it would be wise to purchase the *Nanshan,* since in the event of hostilities he might find himself without a collier. A cable to the Department requesting permission to do so crossed one from Long ordering him to buy the ship. Long's cable read:

CHARGE TO SPECIAL APPROPRIATION. SEND THE RECEIPT TO THE DEPART-MENT. ENLIST FOR SPECIAL SERVICE IF POSSIBLE ONE YEAR UNLESS SOONER DISCHARGED THE CREW. DETACH AND ORDER TO ASSUME COMMAND OF EACH AN OFFICER. ARM IF POSSIBLE. WAR MAY BE DECLARED. CONDITION VERY CRITICAL.

The Department reinforced Dewey's little squadron by ordering to Hong Kong the new revenue cutter, the *McCulloch,* which had reached Singapore on a round-the-world shakedown cruise. Among her passengers were John T. McCutcheon and Edward W. Harden, newspaper correspondents for the Chicago *Tribune* and the New York *World,* respectively, who had thought they were on little more than a pleasure cruise.

The financial side of Dewey's arrangements for coal and ships was ably handled by the fleet's paymaster, Pay Inspector D. A. Smith, whose energy and business qualifications stood the Commodore in good stead, and who made complete preparations for future supplies, whatever complications might ensue from war and the neutrality of other powers. He was espe-

*Adelbert Dewey, *Life and Letters of George Dewey,* pp. 190–91.

cially successful in his relations with the British. Yet, because Dewey did not quite know where they would stand, he sought the help of Lieutenant C. P. Rees, officer of the *Monocacy,* a United States river steamer of Civil War vintage then in Shanghai, in enlisting the services of a Chinese merchant who could insure both an immediate and a future supply of coal and provisions. An isolated spot on the South China coast was selected as a base where supplies could be loaded and repairs made.

Here again Dewey showed his foresight and ingenuity. He gloated in 1904, when Rear Admiral Luce, who had not credited Dewey with having made any provision for such a base, wrote a critical article on the Spanish War in which he said, "The defeat of the American squadron at Manila . . . would have been a disaster the extent of which it would be difficult to compute. Failure to gain a decisive victory even, would have been almost as bad as actual defeat, for the American commander had actually no base to fall back upon."

Authorized by Washington on April 9, Dewey purchased another coal steamer, the *Zafiro,* but he disagreed with Long's orders to arm the colliers. Armed, they would be liable to the restrictions of neutrality laws invoked against American men-of-war, Dewey reasoned. Instead, he registered the *Nanshan* and the *Zafiro* as American merchant steamers and cleared their papers for Guam—an almost mythical port of call at that time—thus freeing them for a mission to English, Chinese, or Japanese ports for any supplies he might need. The crews were retained. Indeed, the English sailors looked forward eagerly to an adventurous descent upon the forces of Spain. But in order to integrate their operations with the rest of the squadron, Dewey stationed an American officer and four enlisted men on each collier to follow battle signals and fleet maneuvers.

Another suggestion sent by Long in early April aroused even greater objection. "I received a rather surprising cable from Secretary Long," Dewey wrote in his autobiography. "He reminded me of the well-known international law that after the outbreak of hostilities further supplies and coal could not be obtained at the neutral ports, except to enable me to proceed home. He concluded as follows: 'Only the Japanese ports are available as storehouse. Should advise storehouse at Nagasaki, Japan, for the base of supplies or supply steamer to accompany the squadron.' "*

Dewey, who believed he had already overcome the potential difficulties of neutrality, thought the advice not only gratuitous but wrong. Japan, he reasoned, would be the last nation on earth to violate neutrality for the benefit of the United States. He cabled Minister Buck at Tokyo:

*Adelbert Dewey, *op. cit.,* pp. 190–91.

Air view of Cavité. Sangley Point is in lower left corner, Cavité just above. The Spanish ships were lined up from the western end of Sangley Point to Cavité.

(Lower) Air view of the city of Manila looking southwest. The breakwater was built after Admiral Dewey's exploits in the Philippines.

AM INFORMED IN CASE OF WAR WITH SPAIN, JAPANESE PORTS CAN BE USED
BY THIS SQUADRON AS BASE FOR SUPPLIES AND COAL. IS THIS CORRECT?

To which came the answer:

PORTS CANNOT BE USED AS BASE FOR SUPPLIES AND COAL. JAPAN WOULD
CONCEDE NOTHING BEYOND STRICT NEUTRALITY.

"If I had acted on the Secretary's advice," Dewey commented, still nursing his dislike for Long, "not only should we have given a sensitive nation offense, but our squadron might have suffered a good deal of inconvenience."†

All was not preparation for war in Hong Kong harbor, however. The Hong Kong Club offered amusement to officers and ladies, and there were dinners, dances, and races in the colony.

Part of the social life, however, cast a sinister shadow, reflected in Washington by what was at best a German plot to side with Spain. Germany was at the height of her colonial expansion program. The twentieth-century German fleet was in the process of construction, and the Kaiser had schemes for the peaceful conquest of a sizable overseas empire. Germany had little interest in Cuba, but in the Philippines she saw the possibility of aggrandizement. Spain was receiving little benefit from the islands in the Far East, and while no positive proof exists of German designs on them, circumstantial evidence points strongly to the fact that Spain was willing to sell them to the Reich.

During the spring of 1898 Prince Henry of Prussia was in command of the German Asiatic squadron. He arrived in Hong Kong harbor on March 8 in the battleship *Deutschland*.

It was Prince Henry who cabled the Kaiser a few weeks later:

THE PHILIPPINES HAVE DECIDED UPON REVOLT AGAINST SPAIN, AND WOULD
GLADLY PLACE THEMSELVES UNDER THE PROTECTION OF A EUROPEAN
POWER, ESPECIALLY GERMANY.

From that cable stemmed the German troubles faced by George Dewey for several months in Manila Bay. The existence of the document, however, was never known to Dewey. To him, Prince Henry seemed "a charming companion, under forty, full of life and vigor, a thorough sailor who had really worked through all the grades from midshipman to rear admiral, and although brought up in the trammels of court etiquette, was ready to cut adrift from conventionalism whenever circumstances demanded such a course."

*Adelbert Dewey, *op. cit.*, p. 191.

Prince Henry's readiness to drift away from conventional naval etiquette involved him in a spirited diplomatic contest with the Commodore.

The round of entertainment for the Prince seemed endless. One dinner was given by the Prince himself, aboard his ship, to which he invited the British major general, Wilsone Black, and the commanders of British, Russian, and American men-of-war. At the end of the meal, in accordance with diplomatic custom, the host proposed toasts to the heads of the various governments represented, each toast given standing, as the band played the appropriate national anthem.

At such ceremonies the host usually drank to his own sovereign, then to the leaders of the other countries represented, in the order of the rank of the senior officers present. Prince Henry correctly proposed a toast to the Kaiser, then to Queen Victoria. The remaining ranking guests were Commodore Dewey and a Russian captain, Dewey's junior in rank. Unfortunately, not only did the Prince drink first to the Czar of Russia and then at the last toast to the President of the United States, but the *Deutschland's* band played "Hail Columbia." The double slight was not overlooked.

"Your Highness," suggested Dewey, "May I call your attention to the fact that 'The Star-Spangled Banner' is our national air and not 'Hail Columbia.' I shall be delighted to send you a copy of the former."

Dewey pointedly left the dinner at an early hour and immediately dispatched a copy of "The Star-Spangled Banner," which the German band scrupulously played the next morning. But the Commodore remained convinced that the slight against his nation had not been accidental.* Other incidents served to confirm his view that there was malice in the Prussian's actions. After the arrival of the *Deutschland,* fights between German and American sailors, and also between German and British sailors, became so frequent that the British governor of Hong Kong was compelled to take a hand by issuing an order that, since the Germans "belonged to a friendly nation and were guests at a friendly port," it should be the pleasure and duty of enlisted men to treat them as such.†
One British petty officer, drinking with a Prussian soldier, enjoyed re-

---

*Peck has given a slightly different version of Prince Henry's slighting order of toasts. The German Prince used the French form, calling the countries in alphabetical order. But, according to that procedure, the toasts should have been to *l'Allemagne* (Germany), *l'Angleterre* (England), *les Etats-Unis* (the United States), and lastly *la Russe* (Russia). Peck states that Commodore Dewey promptly led his officers from the dinner, although it is not corroborated by the Sargent-Dewey account. According to Peck, Prince Henry later apologized by saying that he had forgotten the French word for the United States and was thinking of the German translation, *Vereinigte-Staaten,* which would follow Russia in the alphabetical order.

†Hugh Rodman, *Yarns of a Kentucky Admiral* (Indianapolis: Bobbs-Merrill Co., 1928), p. 238.

venge. The German proposed a toast to the Emperor and the Englishman politely joined him. Then a second toast was proposed by the German.

"To the Emperor," he shouted and drained his stein again.

"What about the Queen?" asked the Englishman.

"To the Emperor," shouted the German, drinking another half pint.

"Well," said the Englishman, "if you won't drink to the Queen, then up comes your Emperor," and he pushed his fingers down the German's throat.*

When convinced finally that Prince Henry's snub had not been directed at him but at his country, Dewey gave orders that no American officers should accept invitations to the balls and dinners being given for the Prince. It became an open scandal. The Prince soon noticed the conspicuous absence of the Americans and asked the reason.

"Your Royal Highness should be aware of the cause of it," his hostess replied, "for you are the cause."

Prince Henry seemed genuinely stunned when he learned the explanation. The next morning he stopped off at the *Olympia* on his way to the German flagship, and in civilian clothes rushed up to Commodore Dewey to apologize. No offense had been intended, he said, and only his lack of naval experience caused the slight.

The Commodore met frankness with frankness. "Prince Henry, I have always liked you, and now I do so more than ever," he replied. After that the two met often, and though they disagreed on international topics, they were always frank in their discussions. One afternoon Commodore Dewey was in Prince Henry's cabin on the *Deutschland,* enjoying a cigar and a glass of Liebfraumilch.

"The powers will never allow the United States to annex Cuba," said the Prince.

"Your Highness, we do not wish to annex that island," answered the Commodore, taking his administration's line. "But, we cannot suffer the horrible condition of affairs which obtains at present in that island, and which is happening at our very doors. And we propose to put a stop to it." The words were said slowly, deliberately. The Prince smiled skeptically, for all the powers at that time were maneuvering in China waters, ready to grab whatever territory any other power would permit. Only five months before the Germans had seized Kiaochow Bay in the North.

"And what are you after? What does your country want?" he asked.

With a twinkle in his eye, thinking of Germany's "lease" of Kiaochow, Dewey threw the Kaiser's own words back to the Prince. "Oh, we need only a bay," he said.

*Rodman, *op. cit.*, pp. 239–40.

A second diplomatic tussle with Prince Henry occurred when one of a party of *Deutschland* sailors visiting the *Olympia* was recognized as an American deserter. He could not be arrested in his German uniform, but he was put off the ship, and Dewey began a useless correspondence with the German rear admiral demanding his surrender. Prince Henry blandly replied that as a German subject and a seaman in the German Navy the man could not be surrendered.

The Dewey-Sargent account dismissed these matters more casually than did Hugh Rodman, executive officer of the *Raleigh,* who wrote: "In my own mind I have sometimes wondered if this were not a studied and intentional slur on the part of Germany, and a forerunner of other impertinences which characterized her actions at Manila and elsewhere during the Spanish War and which showed so conspicuously during the World War. At any rate, the German officials met their match in Dewey, who, if he may not have used the conventional diplomatic language, still left nothing to the imagination, and usually called a spade a spade."*

The German attitude in Hong Kong merely reflected the policy of the Wilhelmstrasse. The Kaiser's strategists could hardly be expected to understand how the inexperienced volunteers of the United States might hope to defeat more than 200,000 Spanish regulars in Cuba, and the Kaiser himself saw in an American defeat the chance to achieve longed-for colonies in Brazil and in the Philippines.

In Europe Germany found friends of Spain in Italy and France, whose citizens had invested heavily in Spanish bonds, and in Austria, for the Spanish Queen Regent was a Hapsburg. Calling at the British Embassy in Washington on April 6, a joint representation of these powers approached Sir Julian Pauncefote, dean of the diplomatic corps, to help them frame a note to McKinley, urging nonintervention. Under orders from the home office to proceed cautiously, Pauncefote helped tone down the spirit of the message, and the powers contented themselves with suggesting that "they earnestly hope that further negotiations will lead to an agreement which, while securing the maintenance of peace, will afford all guarantees for the re-establishment of order in Cuba. The powers do not doubt that the humanitarian and disinterested character of this representation will be fully recognized and appreciated by the American nation."†

McKinley replied in equally polite terms. He recognized the good will prompting the representation, and added his hope for peace, so "terminating the chronic condition of disturbance" in Cuba which so deeply

*Rodman, *op. cit.,* pp. 238–39.
†Peck, *op. cit.,* p. 550.

164

injured the interests and menaced the tranquility of the American nation. The government of the United States appreciated the humanitarian and disinterested character of the communication made on behalf of the powers named, he wrote, "and for its part, is confident that equal appreciation will be shown for its own earnest and unselfish endeavours to fulfill a duty to humanity by ending a situation, the indefinite prolongation of which has become insufferable."

The note and answer were summarized in the New York *World*: "Said the six Ambassadors: 'We hope for humanity's sake, you will not go to war.' Said Mr. McKinley in reply: 'We hope if we do go to war, you will understand it is for humanity's sake.' And the incident was closed." Again Germany failed in its efforts to avenge the Samoan affair, despite the fact that, except for Great Britain, Europe was unanimously on the side of Spain. The continental press screamed in headlines and cartoons against the Yankee "pigs" and predicted a speedy disaster for the American republic in a contest with the might of Spain. On April 4 the Pope was reported to have issued a plea to Spain for peace. The next day the United States Consuls in Cuba were recalled. On April 11 McKinley, wearied by the war of nerves, sent a message to Congress asking powers "to take measures to secure a full and final termination of hostilities between the government of Spain and the people of Cuba . . . and to use the military and naval forces of the United States as may be necessary for these purposes. . . . In the name of humanity . . . I have exhausted every effort to relieve the intolerable condition of affairs which is at our doors."*

Theodore Roosevelt was jubilant. Congress convened in joint session and a few hours later passed a resolution declaring Cuba was and ought to be free and independent and directing the President to use force to implement his demand upon Spain to withdraw and put an end to the atrocities in that island. Accordingly, McKinley cabled United States Ambassador Woodford in Madrid the text of an ultimatum to the Spanish government. But the Spanish Ambassador in Washington had already asked for his passports. Diplomatic relations were severed.

On April 21 the Queen Regent of Spain, attended by twelve-year-old King Alfonso XIII, addressed the Spanish Cortes in a pathetic, yet noble and courageous speech. She was greeted with frenzied cheers as she pleaded for devotion to the century-old pride of Spain.

On the same day Rear Admiral William T. Sampson, in command of the Atlantic squadron, sailed to blockade the Cuban ports. Twenty-four hours later the United States cruiser *Nashville* captured the Spanish ship *Buena Venture,* first prize of the war.

*Peck, *op. cit.*, p. 555.

In faraway Hong Kong Commodore Dewey had been holding his eager men in check for several weeks and had encouraged his officers to counteract frightening stories of the impregnability of Manila, the great strength of its forts, and the vast extent of its mine fields. Everyone, it appeared, knew that Dewey was sailing there, and it was freely predicted that the fleet was headed for certain death. Large bets were placed in the exclusive Hong Kong Club, with heavy odds against the Americans. According to Dewey, not a single member would put up a shilling on his success. The British were openly skeptical. A few days before war had broken out, a group of officers of the Royal Navy entertained the officers of Dewey's squadron at the club. "A pleasant evening was passed," Sargent reports, "and the greatest cordiality prevailed."

After the Americans left, someone said, "What a very fine set of fellows. But unhappily, we shall never see them again."

The last week in Hong Kong was a busy one. The gunboat *McCulloch,* commanded by Captain D. B. Hodgson, had arrived on April 17. On the nineteenth Commodore Dewey ordered the sides of every vessel painted battle gray. On the twenty-first Secretary Long cabled the commander-in-chief:

THE NAVAL FORCE OF THE NORTH ATLANTIC STATION ARE BLOCKADING CUBA. WAR HAS NOT YET BEEN DECLARED. WAR MAY BE DECLARED AT ANY MOMENT. I WILL INFORM YOU. AWAIT ORDERS.

Dewey was fighting against time. The *Baltimore,* with half of the fleet's ammunition, had not arrived. Late on the twenty-second, however, Captain N. M. Dyer headed the cruiser's white bow into the harbor and sighted the gray hulls of the squadron. The somber aspect shocked the *Baltimore* sailors, but a riotous welcome revived their spirits. Their ship was then rushed into drydock for debarnacling and battle-gray paint.

Aboard the *Baltimore* Commander B. P. Lamberton, a Southerner who had been ordered to relieve the ailing Captain Frank Wildes of the *Boston,* was left without a post when Wildes begged to remain for the duty ahead. Dewey kept both by appointing Lamberton his chief of staff. Lamberton was of a "sunny, hopeful and tactful disposition" and proved of immeasurable assistance to the Commodore in days to come. Captain Gridley of the *Olympia,* also ill, refused to leave, and Dewey "could not find it in his heart to replace him."

Lieutenant Rees, who had helped arrange for the remote Chinese base, was to serve as Gridley's executive officer. Joseph L. Stickney, a newspaperman, who had been trained at Annapolis and had been sent out to cover the campaign by the New York *Herald,* became one of Dewey's aides, serving him loyally and well. He emerged as one of the Commodores most distinguished biographers.

Dewey had been told to await orders, but that became impossible. On April 23 an English boat rowed out to the *Olympia* with a letter to Dewey from Governor Wilsone Black:

Sir: I have the honor to inform you that I have received information from the Secretary of State for the Colonies that a state of war exists between Spain and the United States of America, and that I am directed to give immediate notice to the commanders of all ships of war belonging to either of the belligerents within the waters of this colony that no warlike stores nor any coal beyond what may be necessary to carry such ships to the nearest port of the country to which they belong may be taken on board after receipt of this communication and that such ships of war must put to sea as soon as possible.

I therefore beg to request that you will be good enough to comply with these instructions as regards the taking in of warlike stores and coal and that you will further be good enough to leave the waters of the colony with all ships under your command not later than 4 P.M. on Monday the 25th instant.

I have the honor to be, Sir,

Your most obedient servant,

W. BLACK,

Major General Administering the Government.

Beneath the official signature was a highly informal note penned by the governor. "God knows, my dear Commodore," he wrote, "that it breaks my heart to send you this notification." Dewey wrote in reply:

SIR:

I have the honor to acknowledge the receipt of Your Excellency's letter of the 23rd instant, and to inform you that the requests contained therein will be complied with, although I have not been informed by my government that war has yet been declared.

Thanking you for the many courtesies I have received at your hands, I have the honor to be

Your Excellency's obedient servant,

GEORGE DEWEY, Commodore U.S. Navy,

Commanding U.S. Naval Force on Asiatic Station.

Dewey's plans were all completed, and he knew what he must do. Six ships of his squadron were sent ahead to Mirs Bay, a Chinese port thirty miles away, where neutrality provisions would not be enforced. In the Sunday afternoon sunlight American sailors cheered the ships as they weighed anchor. The cruisers *Boston* and *Concord,* the gunboat *Petrel,* and the supply ships *Nanshan* and *Zafiro* made up the advance group.

Dewey planned to utilize all the time afforded him by the British governor, since notification of a state of war had not yet reached him. He rushed work on the *Baltimore,* and sent for the United States Consul at Manila, who had served him so heroically in supplying intelligence, and whose knowledge of the mines and fortifications in Manila Bay would be needed. Despite threats against his life, Williams did not leave until the twenty-third.

Among those who bid Dewey farewell was Prince Henry, who said, with a sly smile, "Well, Commodore, good luck. I may send some ships to Manila—to see that you behave."

Dewey was equal to the barb and directed his own: "I should be delighted to have you do so, Your Highness. But permit me to caution you to keep your ships from between my guns and the enemy."

No word had arrived from Washington on Monday, and at 10:00 A.M. Dewey cabled Long that he was sailing for Mirs Bay to await orders and that he would keep in touch with Hong Kong by tug. Five minutes later the war-gray flagship steamed from the harbor, followed by the *Raleigh,* limping because of a breakdown in a circulating pump, and the *Baltimore,* fresh in her new gray coat. The *Raleigh* anchored at the Kowloon dockyard opposite Hong Kong for overnight repairs and rejoined the squadron at Mirs Bay the next day.

That afternoon the Commodore personally supervised the distribution of ammunition from the *Baltimore* into the magazines of his other ships. Every ship was cleared for action. Wooden tables and chairs were thrown overboard and the crews held extraordinary drills in sub-caliber target practice and at battle quarters. The entire squadron was put on a war footing that night, with armed watches on every ship, and lights blacked out.

Ensign Caldwell had remained behind in Hong Kong. At 12:15, two hours after the *Olympia* had sailed, a cable was delivered into his hands. Immediately he boarded the chartered tug *Fame* and steamed across the China Sea to Mirs Bay.

At seven o'clock that evening Caldwell hailed the *Olympia* and went aboard. He found Dewey seated in his cabin at a green felt-covered table, studying a chart of the Philippine Islands.

"Here is a cable from the Secretary, sir," Caldwell said, laying the envelope upon the table.

Commodore Dewey opened the envelope and unfolded the white sheet:

WAR HAS COMMENCED BETWEEN THE UNITED STATES AND SPAIN. PROCEED AT ONCE TO PHILIPPINE ISLANDS. COMMENCE OPERATIONS PARTICULARLY AGAINST THE SPANISH FLEET. YOU MUST CAPTURE VESSELS OR DESTROY. USE UTMOST ENDEAVOUR.

18

PASSAGE TO DESTINY

*T*he two houses of Congress convened on Monday, April 25, 1898, and by unanimous vote declared war against the Empire of Spain. The next day President McKinley issued a proclamation announcing that a state of war had existed since April 21.

The United States entered upon hostilities with an army of less than 28,000 officers and men,* whereas Spain had more than 200,000 soldiers under arms in Cuba alone. The disparity made little difference, however. President McKinley's call for 125,000 volunteers was answered within a few days, recruits were trained in a few weeks, and some of them participated in the land battles in Cuba.

America was better prepared at sea, where in almost every category the new Navy was superior to Spain's. The United States had four new battleships: the *Iowa, Indiana, Massachusetts,* and *Oregon;* Spain had only one, the antiquated *Pelayo.* After the *Maine* was sunk in Havana harbor, the United States fleet included one second-class battleship, the *Texas.* It was matched on the books of naval theorists by the Spanish battleship *Christóbal Colón,* but as the *Colón's* gun turrets were not mounted during the war, she was never used.

The United States, with two new fast ships, the *Brooklyn* and the *New York,* was equal in armored cruisers to the three older Spanish cruisers, the *Infanta Maria Theresa, Almirante Oquendo,* and *Vizcaya,* all in poor repair. Eleven American protected cruisers outnumbered Spain's three. America held a twenty-one to twelve edge in unprotected cruisers and gunboats, although there were twenty-five more Spanish gunboats in the Philippines which never saw action. Only in torpedo-carrying vessels did Spain possess an advantage of seventeen to eight, but this was counteracted by six modernized American monitors, a class which Spain did not possess.†

*Morison and Commager, *The Growth of the American Republic,* p. 802.
†Knox, *A History of the United States Navy,* p. 332.

Commodore Dewey commanded seven ships of war in the Asiatic squadron, and although his fleet was superior to the Spanish Philippine squadron, he had less of a margin than he had assumed March 31 when he wrote Secretary Long that he could reduce the defenses of Manila and capture the Spanish fleet in one day. The ships lined up as follows:

The flagship *Olympia,* commanded by Captain Charles V. Gridley. A 5,870-ton ship, with four-inch protective armor on her decks, and carrying four eight-inch guns, ten five-inchers, and twenty-one rapid-fire small-calibre rifles.

The *Baltimore,* commanded by Captain N. M. Dyer. A cruiser of 4,413 tons, carrying four eight-inch rifles, six six-inch guns, and eight rapid-fire rifles in the secondary battery.

The *Raleigh,* commanded by Captain C. B. Coghlan. A 3,213-ton ship, carrying one six-inch rifle, ten five-inch guns, and twelve rapid-fire rifles in the secondary battery.

The *Boston,* commanded by Captain Frank Wildes. A 3,000-ton cruiser, carrying two eight-inch guns, six six-inchers, and six rapid-fire smaller rifles.

These were the big four. In addition, the squadron included the gunboats *Petrel,* skippered by Commander E. P. Wood, and *Concord,* commanded by Commander Asa Walker, with ten six-inch guns between them; and the *McCulloch,* a revenue cutter with only small secondary guns, commanded by Captain D. B. Hodgson. The *Zafiro* and the *Nanshan,* unarmed supply ships, made up the train.

All told, the American fighting squadron totaled 19,098 tons and possessed fifty-three guns larger than four-inch, and fifty-six under that size. Eight torpedo tubes in the fleet gave added punch. The squadron was manned by 1,456 officers and men.

Six hundred miles from Mirs Bay, the seven-ship Spanish fleet of Rear Admiral Don Patricio Montojo y Pasaron waited in the Philippines. Its largest vessels were the cruisers *Reina Christina* and *Castilla,* the latter constructed of wood. The *Reina Christina* carried six 6.2-inch guns, while the *Castilla* had four five-inchers and a pair of 4.7-inch rifles. The remainder of the Spanish fleet was composed of little ships, none as large as 1,200 tons, and none carrying more than four 4.7-inch guns and secondary batteries apiece. They were the *Isla de Cuba,* the *Isla de Luzon,* the *Don Antonio de Ulloa,* the *Don Juan de Austria,* and the *Marqués del Duero.* Four more small ships, twenty-five gunboats, and numerous auxiliaries were in the squadron, but were not engaged during the war.

Commodore Dewey knew that the American fleet's supremacy would be more than offset by the weight of Spanish shore guns at Corregidor and Manila. According to Captain Mahan, one shore-based gun was the equal of four guns of similar caliber afloat, a sobering thought for the sixty-year-old Commodore. But Dewey had done his utmost to perfect the squadron, and now, in his own thoughts, he had only "to do the rest."

Every detail of tactics and strategy had been thoroughly discussed and plotted by the Commodore in Hong Kong.* Every ship captain knew each detail of how and when to act. Indeed, months before, Dewey and Roosevelt had outlined the plan to be followed when war should come. When Long's cablegram arrived, Dewey simply proceeded to execute his plans. But few in the United States had taken much thought of the Spanish position in the Orient. Americans thought only of Cuba; the Philippines and Dewey's squadron received scant attention. It seemed a very new idea, therefore, when, on April 17, in Boston, a youthful lawyer from Indianapolis addressed guests at a Middlesex Club banquet:

"What should be the policy of the war? It is our military duty to strike Spain at her weakest point before we strike her at her strongest points. Cuba must fall . . . but that will be only when Spain is conquered. . . . In the Pacific is the true field of our earliest operations. There Spain has an island empire, the Philippine Archipelago. It is poorly defended. Spain's best ships are on the Atlantic side. In the Pacific the United States has a powerful squadron. The Philippines are logically our first target." Albert A. Beveridge spoke militantly and angrily, as if no one would appreciate the wisdom of his plan.†

But almost at that very moment Consul Williams was making for the *Olympia* in Mirs Bay, China, bringing slightly disconcerting news. The Spanish squadron had gone to Subic Bay, thirty miles north of Manila, he informed the Commodore. "It was the natural position for them but we had credited them with appreciating this, and the move necessitated caution." Dewey informed his commanding officers that the squadron must be prepared to fight either in Subic Bay or at Manila.

With favoring winds and a calm sea, they steamed southward toward Bolinao Bay, at the northern tip of Luzon Island. The men and ships were drilled in daylight and darkness for coming action. They practiced battle drills, fire-fighting, repairing injuries. Iron and canvas were

*The measure of Dewey's early preparations was summarized in later years by Rear Admiral Hugh Rodman, who served on the *Raleigh* in the Philippines campaign. "Dewey was in every respect an ideal officer for the command of our ships in Asiatic waters," Rodman wrote. "Cool, devoid of fear, efficient, and forceful, he had the respect and confidence of every officer and man who served under him. Prior to leaving Hong Kong every contingency which might arise was considered and studied, and plans made to meet each one, so that when the time actually came to engage the enemy's fleet, we had a prearranged plan which fitted the case perfectly."

†Claude G. Bowers, *Beveridge and the Progressive Era* (Boston: Houghton Mifflin Co., 1932).

built up as shields for the gun crews, lengths of heavy sheet chains were faked up and down over buffers of awnings to give added protection to the ship sides and ammunition hoists. Every stick of woodwork which could be spared was thrown overboard to keep down hazards of fire or splinters.* The men performed this task with such enthusiasm that they threw over their own mess tables and had to eat off the decks for weeks.†

In the evenings the band of the *Olympia* cheered the men with patriotic airs. One Thursday night, when it struck up "Yankee Doodle Dandy," the young sailors stopped eating, dropped their forks, and sang with a zest that boded well for conduct in the trial to come.

Blacked out, the ships steamed through the tropical waters in a phantom line of invisible black, the churn of propellers and the luminous phosphorescence breaking at the bows the only signal of their onward course.

One night Dewey had read to his men an incendiary letter written by the Archbishop of the Manila See and published by the Spanish Governor General, Don Basilio Augustin Davila:

Spaniards [the fanfaronade said]: The North American people, constituted of all the social excrescences, have exhausted our patience and provoked war with their perfidious machinations, with their acts of treachery, with their outrages against the law of nations and international conventions. The struggle will be short and decisive. The God of Victories will give us one as brilliant and complete as the righteousness and justice of our cause demand. Spain . . . will emerge triumphantly . . . humiliating and blasting the adventurers from those states that, without cohesion and without a history, offer to humanity only infamous traditions and . . . united insolence and defamation, cowardice and cynicism. A squadron manned by foreigners . . . is preparing to come to this archipelago with the ruffianly intention of robbing us of all that means life, liberty and honor. . . . The North American seamen undertake, as an enterprise capable of realization, the substitution of Protestantism for the Catholic religion. . . . Vain designs, ridiculous boastings! . . . The aggressors shall not profane the tombs of your ancestors, they shall not gratify their lustful passions at the cost of your wives' and daughters' honor. . . . Filipinos, prepare for the struggle and unite under the glorious Spanish flag . . . let us fight with the conviction that victory will crown our efforts. . . .

The crews greeted the message with catcalls and amusement. The *Olympia's* ship paper, *The Bounding Billow*, answered the accusations with ridicule, and the Americans swore to prove the "braggart" Spaniards wrong.

*The Spaniards did not take this precaution. As a result, fires started on the Spanish ships were far greater than those caused on American ships by similar hits.

†Stickney, *Life and Glorious Deeds of Admiral Dewey*, p. 34.

Land was sighted early Saturday morning, April 30, when as day broke, the mountains of Luzon rose through the tropical mists. Commodore Dewey signaled the *Boston* and the *Concord* to steam ahead at full speed to reconnoiter Subic Bay. A group of fishing boats was spotted off Cape Bolinao, and the *Zafiro* was dispatched to overhaul them and learn the whereabouts of the Spanish fleet, but as the fishermen knew nothing, the supply vessel returned toward the *Olympia* to report. Misjudging his distance, the helmsman swung straight across the flagship's bow. A collision seemed inevitable, when Lieutenant Strite, on the *Olympia's* bridge, swung the flagship's helm hard over, clearing the little *Zafiro* by less than three feet.*

Soon afterward an officer thought he heard shots far to the south. Had the *Boston* and the *Concord* run into opposition? Signal flags were run up the mast of the *Olympia.* The *Baltimore* raced ahead to support the advance units. At half-past three the rest of the squadron caught up with the three vessels off the entrance to Subic Bay. With relief, the Commodore read their signal flags, saying that no enemy had been seen. Dewey turned to Commander Lamberton, standing on the bridge beside him.

"Now we have them," he said with supreme assurance. The men on the *Olympia,* looking up at the bridge, saw a serious, composed officer, walking quietly beside the rail. The Commodore's white cap sat low over his frosty gray hair, and his broad shoulders made him seem more athletic and robust than one would expect in a man just under five feet seven inches tall. Now and then he drew his fingers over his eyes or rolled the ends of his mustache The men drew confidence from his face. In him they saw fixity of purpose, confidence, and certainty.†

This was his pose of leadership, the pose which would cause his men to see in him their goal, and, in their admiration for his iron will, forget themselves and their fears. The Commodore walked the bridge all afternoon long, standing in sight of his men as a symbol, like the figurehead on the *Olympia's* bow, of the invincibility of their arms.

Yet in his own heart there were qualms.‡ His knowledge and his past experience warned him of perils ahead. It had been thirty-six years since the old *Mississippi* steamed past Forts St. Philip and Jackson, and thirty-four years of comfortable peacetime duties had elapsed since his last ordeal of steel and shell at Fort Fisher, when the *Colorado* stood up before

---

*Stickney, *op. cit.*, p. 33.

†Barrett, *Admiral George Dewey*, pp. 197–201.

‡"George," Dewey told his son, "I did not know whether I would just blockade the Philippines or fight the Spanish fleet."

Confederate guns. Now, as an elderly man, less than two years from retirement, he was approaching the most grueling test of his life.

Farragut had known no fear when he stormed Southern forts or sailed headlong through torpedoes at Mobile Bay. But that was more than thirty years before. Torpedoes were more efficient in 1898. Could Dewey emulate his master and sail boldly through the mine field between Corregidor and El Fraile Islands at the entrance to Manila Bay? Could he hope that none would explode, as none had exploded under Farragut's *Hartford?*

"What would Farragut do?" he wondered as he stood on the bridge that afternoon of April 30. The risks he was preparing to meet seemed immeasurably greater. Should he blockade the coast indefinitely and bottle up the Spanish fleet, or should he strike? As he gazed at the mountains and watched a new moon rise above them, he thought of his father's admonition: "You must do the rest yourself," and remembered Theodore Roosevelt's faith in him. There could be only one answer. Farragut's words of thirty-four years before rang in his ears: "Damn the torpedoes. Go ahead!"

The Commodore called to Captain Gridley and ordered him to slow down and signal the other vessels that every captain was wanted aboard the flagship for consultation. The meeting in the Commodore's cabin, four miles off Luzon, was brief. The commanders of the *Boston,* the *Concord,* and the *Baltimore* repeated their statement that no Spanish ships had been seen in Subic Bay.

"Very well, gentlemen," said the Commodore simply. "We shall enter Manila Bay tonight. You will follow the motions and signals of the flagship." That was all. There were no discussions, no questions, no written orders. Every contingency had been discussed before.

Lieutenant William Winder, Dewey's nephew, who was aboard the *Baltimore,* saluted him. "Commodore, I have always made it a policy never to take advantage of our being related," Winder said. "But in this instance I should like to make an exception. We think the bay is mined. I should like to be given the privilege of commanding the *Zafiro.* She has the largest displacement of any of our ships. I could soon find out if the bay is mined, and if it is, I should have cleared a way for the squadron. Sir, this is one chance I have to become famous."

Commodore Dewey understood perfectly. He looked fondly at his nephew for a minute, then he answered:

"Billy, I have waited sixty years for this opportunity. And much as I like you and know you are a fine officer—mines or no mines, I am leading

174

the squadron in myself. Good luck, my boy." Winder saluted his distinguished relative and returned to his ship.*

On the Spanish side, however, desperation was in the air. On April 25 Admiral Montojo had sailed his squadron for Subic Bay, thinking it a better position for defense, but when it arrived there, he learned that no preparations had been made. Four 5.9-inch guns, which should have been mounted a month before, were lying on the beach. American sailors could have mounted them in twenty-four hours, but Montojo reasoned there was not time.

Only a few mines had been planted, and although the eastern end of the entrance had been blocked by sinking three old hulks, the bay was virtually defenseless. At first Montojo planned to hide there, hoping that the American squadron would sail past without investigation, and be ambushed by a sudden sortie, but a cable from the Spanish Consul at Hong Kong, which reached Montojo April 28, informed him:

THE ENEMY'S SQUADRON SAILED AT 2 P.M. FROM THE BAY OF MIRS, AND ACCORDING TO RELIABLE ACCOUNTS THEY SAILED FOR SUBIC BAY TO DESTROY OUR SQUADRON AND THEN WILL GO TO MANILA.

That was enough for Montojo. He did not wish to anchor his ships in the deep water at Subic where the crews would drown after the ships were sunk. He held a council of his captains and all agreed to return to Manila, where shore batteries were more powerful, and "where the water was more shallow so that after the ships were sunk the crews could get ashore." The Spanish high command in the Philippines evidently held little hope of defeating the American invaders. But, instead of anchoring before Manila, where the shore guns were strongest, the Spanish fleet stopped at nearby Cavité, to save the capital city from shelling.

The gloom of a tropical night settled over the United States fleet as it steamed steadily for the entrance of Manila Bay. All lights were masked, save for those that dimly shone on the taffrails of each ship, visible only to the vessel immediately astern. Officers and men stood ready at the guns. At eleven o'clock a light shower passed overhead, and heavy cumulus clouds obscured the new moon.

Manila Bay is a spacious body of water, some twenty miles across, opening northward from a narrow entrance. On either side of the inlet are high volcanic peaks, covered with tropical foliage. Several islands guard the water passage. Corregidor and Caballo, dividing the entrance into two channels, are the major islands in the entranceway. Between the

*Stephen Decatur VII, a close friend of the late Captain William Winder and of George Goodwin Dewey, is the authority for this incident. Winder related it to Decatur.

two are two channels, known as Boca Grande, or the great mouth, and Boca Chica, the little mouth. Boca Chica has a navigable width of two miles, while Boca Grande would be twice as wide, except for another small rocky island, El Fraile (The Friar), which reduces the channel to about three miles. Both Corregidor and Caballo, being high and rocky, afford perfect opportunities for harbor defense.

The Spaniards, however, "with natural procrastination, which seems inherent in their nature, had delayed fortifying these islands until war appeared inevitable." They did mount enough guns during the spring of 1898 to put up a lively battle. They had mined the passageway with much publicity to deter any hostile fleet from attempting to break through, but the very publicizing of the mine field gave Commodore Dewey cause for suspicion. He and Lamberton had thoroughly discussed the subject of Manila mines while they were still in Hong Kong and had decided that "the submarine mines in Boca Grande might be safely considered a negligible quantity." Dewey remembered how the Suez Canal had been mined a dozen years before. For weeks ships refused to go through until an Italian admiral, reasoning that the Egyptians were too unskilled to lay mines properly, steamed through without an explosion and lifted the blockade. With this knowledge, Commodore Dewey reasoned that the depth of water in Boca Grande would make the planting of mines a difficult proceeding for any but experts. It was unlikely that the Spaniards would have skilled engineers in Manila, he thought. Furthermore, contact or electrical mines would soon lose their efficiency in tropical waters. The publicity campaign concerning the mines seemed like a cry of "wolf" to Dewey, and he decided to ignore the potential dangers.*

*Lieutenant John M. Ellicott, one of the officers aboard the *Baltimore*, in an article, "The Defenses of Manila Bay" in the *Proceedings of the U.S. Naval Institute* (June, 1900), stated: "In the face of all evidence the existence of mines at the entrance to the Bay can scarcely be doubted. A chart was captured at Cavité with lines of torpedoes marked on it in Boca Chica and off San Nicholas shoal, and with marginal memoranda about the spacing and number of mines. In the articles of capitulation signed by the governor of Corregidor, it was stated that mines existed in Boca Grande. The testimony of nearly every Spanish officer interviewed by the writer was to the same effect. If these mines were contact mines, they had become innocuous from barnacles or seaweed or badly adjusted moorings; if they were electro-controlled, the firing devices had not been installed, or were defective."

This opinion was emphatically denied by Rear Admiral Bradley A. Fiske, who, as a young lieutenant, was aboard the *Petrel* in the battle. Admiral Fiske told Mark Sullivan (*Our Times*, p. 316) that there were no mines. "I had requested Dewey before we left Hong Kong," he wrote, "to give me the job of pulling up the mines in Manila Bay, but was told there were none. Subsequently I found this to be true. I found mines and electrical apparatus under construction in the Cavité arsenal, but none had even been finished."

This view is in contradiction to the statement of Commander Sargent and Dewey in the 1904 account. Most of the histories written of the battle state that mines were planted, although all agree that none of them exploded.

176

It was nearly midnight when the hills of Manila loomed close above the American ships. The *Olympia* headed for the Boca Grande passage. Through the darkness the Commodore could see shadows of the land, and aided by compass bearings and soundings, he inched his way toward the mine field.

The other ships, all in one column now, followed their leader. El Fraile was passed at a distance of about half a mile, and still no mines broke the tropic stillness. The flagship changed her course to NE by N, and she inched her way ahead. Officers and men waited breathlessly at the guns. Corregidor and El Caballo were pitch dark, without a sign of life.

Tension stretched to the breaking point as everyone waited for the first mine to explode or for the first defense gun to blast into action. The heat was intense. In the boiler rooms the black gangs sweated as they threw coal on the fires. Men were talking in whispers on the *Olympia's* bridge, anxious and a little frightened.

The Commodore looked at Captain Gridley and said in a loud voice, so the men could hear:

"A fine night for a smoke, eh, Gridley? It's a pity we can't light up."*
That lessened the anxiety and men breathed more easily.

Only spasmodic flashes in the hills showed that the Spaniards were awake. The squadron had been spotted, but still no guns flashed and still no torpedo boats dashed through the inkiness to loose torpedoes at the invading fleet.

Then, at ten minutes past midnight, when the leading ships had all passed Corregidor, the batteries on El Fraile opened fire. One heavy shell exploded between the *Petrel* and the *Raleigh*.

"Well, well," said the Commodore to Captain Gridley, "They did wake up at last."

Guns on the *Boston*, the *Concord*, the *Raleigh*, and the *McCulloch* immediately returned the fire. White flashes of light shattered the dark. Three volleys blasted the El Fraile battery into silence. That was all. No more shots were fired. The Spanish command, not expecting that an enemy fleet would show the "foolhardiness" to enter an unlighted and unknown channel at midnight, had given no orders to defend the channel. Later the Americans were informed that they had been seen clearly entering the bay, but that the commanding officers of the entrance forts had "for some extraordinary reason" never given orders to open fire. The Caballo batteries, with their three six-inch breech-loading guns, could have sunk any of the United States' unarmored ships with one direct hit. But they did not fire a shot.

*Young, *Life and Heroic Deeds of Admiral Dewey*, p. 223.

The squadron was past the entrance channel. The submarine mines were still lying unexploded in the water. Perhaps they had rusted out of commission in the salt water. Possibly they were in the wrong places or sunk. The American fleet was in the bay, twenty-four miles south of Manila, where the ships of Spain lay waiting for the dawn.

The Commodore ordered all ships to lower their speed. At four knots the squadron slid through the calm waters. The batteries had been passed. It was a more miraculous deed than any of Farragut's, and Commodore George Dewey, his faith and confidence justified, stepped into his cabin for a few winks of sleep.

19

MARS IS A MARINER

At four o'clock the Commodore walked to the *Olympia's* bridge and scanned the shadows of the hills. He had lost his white naval officer's headgear and wore a gray tweed traveling cap instead. Mess attendants circulated among the men lying at their guns. With sleepy murmurs the gunners rose, stretched, and reached for the mugs of steaming coffee handed around.

The battle squadron headed for Manila at a four-knot speed, while the supply ships, escorted by the *McCulloch,* left the squadron and sailed to the outer reaches of the bay. The six fighting ships reached the outer limits of the Manila anchorage at a few minutes before five o'clock. Behind the hills the darkness thinned. Black turned to deep blue, and, with the suddenness peculiar to tropical climates, the dawn broke fast over the sea. Between the squadron and the town of Manila a large fleet of merchant ships rode at anchor. Accepting a pair of binoculars from Lieutenant Brumby, the Commodore searched for the Spanish ships, which he had expected to take a stand before Manila. None were in sight.

He gave orders to swing the squadron parallel to the Manila shore and head for Cavité. As the gray ships passed the city, 400 yards apart, shore guns at Manila broke the early morning silence.

It was 5:05 A.M., Sunday morning, May 1, 1898.

Headed by the flagship, the United States battle line, in order of position, included the *Baltimore,* the *Raleigh,* the *Petrel,* the *Concord,* and the *Boston.* The Spanish guns were aimed at the center of the squadron. One heavy shell, striking only ten or fifteen yards astern of the cruiser *Baltimore* would have hit her, if successful, square on the water line and done serious damage even before the battle was joined.* Fortunately, most of the shells from the thirty-nine heavy guns of the Manila and

*Rodman, *Yarns of a Kentucky Admiral,* pp. 241–42.

Luneta batteries passed far above the American ships, ricocheting in the bay two miles beyond. Disdainfully the flagship ignored the fire.

Commodore Dewey stood with Captain Lamberton on the bridge. Just behind them Lieutenant Calkins, the ship's navigating officer, and Lieutenant Rees, the executive officer of the *Olympia,* stationed themselves, to watch the helmsman and the chart and to repeat to the Commodore the reports of the leadsmen as they heaved their lines to measure the depth of water beneath the ship. Captain Gridley was stationed high in the conning tower to direct firing.

While the land shells splashed harmlessly beyond the American ships, two great surges of water leaped high in the air almost two miles ahead of the squadron. These were submarine mines exploding. The dull roar reached the flagship. Turning to Lamberton, the Commodore said: "Evidently the Spaniards are already rattled."

Only the *Boston* and the *Concord* replied to the shore guns, each dropping a pair of shells on the forts. At 5:10 lookouts in the *Olympia's* tops saw the Spanish squadron forming an irregular crescent in front of Cavité. The battle line swung to starboard to head straight for the enemy.

Admiral Montojo's seven ships rode at anchor across the mile-long entrance of Bacoor Bay. The batteries of Cavité and Sangley Point guarded them at the western end, and the shallow beaches of Las Pinas prevented attack from the east. Two 5.9-inch rifles were installed at Sangley Point, while immediately behind the point another 4.7-inch cannon was installed at Cañacao. Montojo, fearing damage to Manila, had foresworn the aid the capital city's thirty-nine shore guns might have given him.

The American ships moved toward Cavité. Then the *Olympia* signaled, "Prepare to engage the enemy." Flags on every ship verified the command. Gun crews slammed shells into their guns, and the click of breech locks closing broke the stillness. Then came the signal all were waiting for: "Engage the enemy." Simultaneously, all over the squadron, mastheads burst into brilliant fields of red, white and blue.* Bands struck up "The Star-Spangled Banner." Officers and men stood at awed attention, saluting "as if on parade," and at the final sustained tone a mighty cheer echoed above the ships.

"Remember the Maine" was shouted from a hundred throats. It was 5:40 A.M. The *Olympia,* about 5,000 yards from the Spanish ships, followed a converging course, which kept the Spanish ships on her starboard bow. The American squadron headed toward them at a speed of eight knots, as the Spanish ships, unable to find the range, fired widly. Geysers splashed in the water near and far.

*Rodman, *op. cit.,* p. 242.

At 5:41 Dewey looked up at the conning tower. In a calm voice of assurance, heard throughout the ship, he said:

"You may fire when you are ready, Gridley."*

The Commodore seized hold of a stanchion on the bridge. An eight-inch rifle in the *Olympia's* forward turret roared as black powder belched from the muzzle. The *Olympia* lurched and rolled with the recoil of the big gun. It was the signal for a general outburst. Shells from the five other American ships plunged through the air. The first volleys missed their mark, but the smoke and the noise upset the Spanish gunners. Their answering salvos landed far out of range.

As the first shot rent the air, the *Olympia* turned to starboard, and with the squadron following astern now at distances of 200 yards, kept the Spanish ships on the port side. The port batteries of every American ship blazed destruction. When the *Olympia* reached a point about 1,500 yards north of the tip of Sangley Point, she made a complete circle to starboard and headed back to rake the Spanish ships from her starboard side. Five runs were carried out between 5:40 and 7:35 that morning.

The American fleet coursed past the Spanish vessels at distances ranging from 3,000 to 2,000 yards, the length of each run being about two miles. After the fourth trip, which ended at the eastern end of the course, Lieutenant Calkins notified the Commodore that the water was deeper than was indicated on the chart. Since Dewey wished to approach as close to the enemy as possible without running aground, the fifth run was carried out at less than 2,000 yards from the ships and shore batteries of Admiral Montojo.

Smoke blackened the white uniform of the commander-in-chief and clung to the sweat on the gunners, bared to the waist, as they rushed to load and fire, load and fire. The pointers and trainers stood by the guns, turned wheels back and forth, kept their sights on the Spanish ships. Behind them shell boys rushed across the decks to ram in shells and to catch the hot cases springing out as breech locks were pulled clear. Below decks sweating ammunition handlers carried shells and powder bags to the powder hoists. In the engine rooms black gangs heaved coal through the insufferable heat. Altogether, 1,456 sweating men raced through their well-known duties that hot morning, with the discipline of an afternoon of routine drill in an open, peaceful sea.

Explosions roared to the hills and echoed back across the bay, stinging the ears and jarring the teeth with each booming report of the guns.

*The popular version of the deathless statement is "You may fire when ready, Gridley." This is more concise, more dramatic perhaps, but Dewey insisted stoutly that he had put in the two extra words. He was not thinking of posterity at the moment.

Smoke covered the ships and only when they ceased fire to turn and begin a new run against the Spanish ships did they emerge from the cloud.

On the *Boston* gunners shed their jumpers, then their pants, finally their underwear, and by the end of the fourth run they wore only shoes. Every twenty minutes they were served whisky and water which they gulped down as they worked and swore.*

During the second run, when the *Olympia* was still untouched by enemy fire, a Spanish torpedo launch headed out from the point behind Cavité. Stickney, the Commodore's newspaper aide, called Dewey's attention to her.

"You look after her," Dewey barked back. "I've no time to bother with torpedo boats. Let me know when you've finished her."

Gunners in the secondary rapid-fire batteries turned their small guns on her, spattered her with spray, and blew her out of the water. She sank bow first, as her crew splashed toward shore.

The American fire was concentrated on the *Reina Christina*, flagship of the Spanish fleet. On the third run Admiral Montojo bravely charged the *Olympia*, whose eight-inch guns, trained accurately on his ship, tore into her stern, killed twenty Dons, and partially disabled her steering gear. Another volley struck the forecastle, shattered four of the secondary guns, and knocked their bleeding crews to the deck. A third shell smashed through the after orlop, another severed the mizzenmast. The Spanish ensign and Admiral Montojo's flag plunged into the sea. A sailor raced to replace them on another spar. In the sick bay, awaiting medical attention from blood-spattered doctors, lay eighty wounded Spaniards. An eight-inch shell from the *Olympia* smashed through the hull and exploded violently in the hospital. Not a man survived.

The *Reina Christina* had had enough and staggered back, wounded and on fire, to the protection of the other ships. Sailors fought desperately to put out fires on the stern and in the ammunition rooms. Cartridges began to explode, and Admiral Montojo ordered the magazine flooded to end the danger. A smaller gun from the *Olympia* knocked out the *Christina's* starboard bow gun as she retreated. Her broadside guns were still in action, but shells from the American ships played havoc with the crews. Man after man dropped to the deck. The wounded cried piteously, and fires broke out in new spots with almost every American shot. Then Montojo gave orders to abandon ship. As the sea cocks were opened and water poured into the *Reina Christina's* hull, the unwounded sailors lowered boats and struggled manfully to drag their injured fellows into

*Orders against profanity had been issued, but no one, least of all the commander-in-chief, observed them, according to witnesses.

182

them. The admiral, accompanied by his officers and a sailor carrying his pennant, rowed to the cruiser *Isla de Cuba,* where he again raised his flag. The gallant Captain Don Luis Cadarso, commander of the sinking Spanish flagship, although injured, was still directing the rescue of his men when another shell ripped through the superstructure and killed him.

Meanwhile, Spanish shells thundered through the *Olympia's* rigging. When some of the men on the bridge ducked, the Commodore shouted, "Don't dodge, boys; they can't hit you after they're past." Just below the bridge a gun was firing regularly at the enemy, and as the vessel turned on one of its runs, the muzzle swung around to maintain its train upon the Spanish ships. The Commodore stood at the starboard side, staring ahead. Suddenly an aide seized him by the coat and thrust him back. Angrily Dewey tried to wrench himself free, but at that point the gun belched smoke and blackened the rail where he had been standing.* The concussion would have knocked him down.

During the second run Lieutenant Rodman, on the *Raleigh,* went below to cheer the ammunition gang and tell them the battle was going well. As he neared the powder room he heard a fiddle playing. The powder men, wearing abbreviated gunny sacks, combined their ammunition passing with a hula dance. "There'll be a hot time in the old town tonight," they sang.

"Men," Rodman said. "Things are coming our way. We've got 'em on the run. I don't know what that tune is you were playing, but it's a corker. Keep it up. I want the music to reach the upper deck. Go on with the dance, and I know we'll have ample powder and shells to keep the guns going."†

Captain Coghlan had ruled that no profanity should be used during the battle and that all orders should be given in the identical language of the drills. On the third run, observing that the Spanish ship *Castilla,* apparently undamaged, was beginning to find the range of the *Raleigh,* he leaned over the bridge and yelled at Rodman, who was directing fire.

"Rodman, do you see that blankety-blank white ship that's raising hell at our expense and turning his whole damned battery on us? Give him hell and keep it up."

"Captain, I don't find some of your words, or your exact orders, in the drill manual," Rodman said, as he trained a gun on the *Castilla.* "But I understand what you mean."

Ladies' Home Journal, Oct., 1899.
†Rodman, *op. cit.,* pp. 243–44.

"You do what you're ordered to do, and do it damned quick," roared the captain.

"Aye, aye, sir," said Rodman, and a six-inch gun blasted a shell straight and true to explode under the after bridge of the *Castilla*. It wiped out a five-inch gun and a six-pounder, wounded all the gun crews, and killed or wounded every officer on the bridge. A Spanish lieutenant of marines who had left the bridge a moment before, later told Rodman of the damage from that shell, adding that it was the first shell which had struck the *Castilla* during the action.* It was only the first of many, however. Other American ships turned their attention to her, riddled her with shot, and set her ablaze. With twenty-three of her crew killed and eighty wounded, she was abandoned and sunk.

On the fourth run the Commodore was looking over the *Olympia's* starboard side when a six-pounder from a Spanish ship hit the flagship's plates six feet beneath his feet, denting it in a few inches, and shaking him up slightly.† Five other Spanish shells hulled the *Olympia* during the fight, but virtually no damage was sustained.

The *Baltimore*, just behind, fared less well. Five shells smashed into her hull, one of them entering the side just forward of the starboard gangway. It tore into the ship above the main deck, through the hammock netting, down through the deck planks and steel deck, and bent the deck beams in an officer's stateroom off the wardroom. From there the shell bounded up through the after engine room, struck against the cylinder of a six-inch gun, which was disabled by the blow, then continued its erratic course to smash into a box of three-pounder ammunition, strike a ladder, and fall without exploding on the deck. The American ammunition, however, did explode, and the blast slightly wounded Lieutenant F. W. Kellogg, Ensign N. E. Irwin, and six enlisted men stationed in the room.

The squadron began its fifth run to the west at 7:15 A.M. In the middle of it Captain Gridley approached the Commodore to report that only fifteen rounds of five-inch ammunition remained in the magazines. Without any exact knowledge of the damage to the enemy fleet, Dewey anxiously ordered his ships out of range, where ammunition could be redistributed among the fleet. At 7:35 the signal came to cease and retire "for breakfast." This wording added greatly to Dewey's later fame, especially when newspaper accounts of the battle declared that the unruffled Commodore had debonairly interrupted the fighting to give his men their breakfast as usual.

*Rodman, *op. cit.*, pp. 244–45.
†Dewey saved the steel section of the hull, and it is now in the Chicago Historical Society.

184

Some of the men protested. One gunner yelled to Commander Lamberton, "For God's sake, Captain, don't stop now. Let's finish 'em up right off."*

As the squadron withdrew from the range of fire, the smoke lifted slightly and enabled the Commodore to judge more accurately the effects of his 114 minutes of shooting. The distress of the Spanish ships was evident. Many were on fire, explosions from their bursting magazines sounded across the bay, some were obviously sinking, and one or two were limping behind Cavité Point. They had stopped shooting altogether, and only poorly aimed shells from the three shore guns continued to land far beyond the American fleet. Later it was learned that these had been mounted so that they could not be trained on targets closer than 2,000 yards, on the assumption that "no enemy would venture within this distance."

Ah Mah, the Commodore's personal attendant, brought his chief a cup of hot coffee, while Bob, the Chow dog Dewey had bought at Hong Kong, rushed up to the bridge happily wagging his tail.

"Well, Ah Mah," said Dewey. "What you think?"

"Very fine, Commodore," answered the Chinese servant. "Just like target practice."

As the fleet passed into the bay, American gunners gave a wearied cheer and collapsed on the decks. Below, smoke-blackened engineers had been at their posts in the fiery heat of the engine rooms of the fleet since midnight, and the coal heavers had been locked in the depths of the ship, for battle hatches had been battened down. The temperature according to one of the stokers,† had reached almost 200° Fahrenheit, and ventilating pipes did little to relieve it. The roar of the engines and of shells almost burst the engineers' heads. Each time a gun fired, the ships' lunge sent men careening into scalding pipes. Heat from the furnaces seared their hands and wrists, and singed their hair. The only water was in an old pork barrel. The firemen plunged their hands in it to cool them off and used it to moisten their parched mouths as well. For 114 minutes of battle the men in the suffocating engine rooms expected every moment to be their last. Now and then apprentice boys came to the ventilating pipes and yelled down news of the fight. Frequently firemen collapsed from the heat and were carried on deck for fresh air. "I shall never forget those few hours I spent in front of the furnaces in Manila Bay," said Stoker Twitchell. "It seemed to me the longest day I ever lived."

*Stickney, *Life and Glorious Deeds of Admiral Dewey*, p. 47.
†He was Charles H. Twitchell of the *Olympia*. His story appears in Adelbert Dewey's *Life and Letters*, pp. 370–74.

When the fleet withdrew, the men in the boiler rooms came on deck, grimy, sweat-covered, and exhausted. They looked around the decks, frightened, expecting to see blood running through the scuppers from piles of dead and wounded. But they saw none. No one on the *Olympia* had been scratched. Safe in the outer bay, the Commodore called all commanding officers to a consultation aboard the flagship, while the sailors rested at their posts and devoured sandwiches and hot coffee.

One by one the captains reported their casualties: Captain Dyer of the *Baltimore*: five hits, eight slightly wounded; Commander Wood of the *Petrel*: one hit, none injured; Captain Wildes of the *Boston*: four minor hits, no wounded; Captain Walker of the *Concord*: no hits, no injuries. The score was flashed to the fleet from the *Olympia* signal flags, and at every announcement of "0 killed, 0 wounded," a cheer swept through the squadron. The *Baltimore's* score: "0 killed, 8 wounded," brought the greatest yells, for she had emerged from the fray smoke-blackened and with lifeboats in shreds.

Shortly afterward Dewey learned that the information given him about an ammunition shortage was wrong. Gridley had been told that only fifteen rounds of eight-inch ammunition remained, whereas, in reality, only fifteen rounds had been fired, leaving eighty-five rounds in the ammunition racks. At eleven o'clock, therefore, the little squadron returned to attack once more. This time the *Baltimore* led, to save the remaining shells aboard the *Olympia*. At 11:16, guns roared again but the Spanish ships still afloat had taken refuge behind Sangley Point. Only the *Don Antonio de Ulloa* remained at anchor in the roadstead, bravely returning the American fire. In a few minutes American shells found her range, and, smothered by shells, she sank with colors flying. The Spanish shore batteries, unable to achieve the range, were soon silenced as well.

Now the mopping up began. The *Olympia* signaled the *Concord* to destroy a large transport, *Mindanao*, which had been beached on the eastern shore, while the *Petrel*, whose light draft permitted her to navigate shallower water, was ordered to enter the harbor of Cavité and destroy any ships left there.

Gallantly the officers and men on the little *Petrel* headed into the harbor to fire six-inch shells at the government building. Only a few shots were necessary. The Spanish flag came down, and a white flag of surrender floated in the noonday breeze. At 12:30 the *Petrel* signaled that all Spanish forces had surrendered, and firing ceased. But as the vessels were not completely destroyed, Lieutenant E. M. Hughes boarded a whaleboat with seven men to set them on fire. Four, including the *Don Juan de Austria*, the *Isla de Cuba*, the *Isla de Luzon*, and the *Marqués del Duero*, had been abandoned in shallow water. Two others (out of commission) which had not engaged in the fight also lay in the harbor. These were the *General Lezo* and the *Correo*. All were burned. Only the armed transport *Manila* was spared, to be floated and serve for many years as an American gunboat in Asiatic waters.

All afternoon the *Petrel* worked at her task, and by 5:20 rejoined the squadron with a string of tugs and launches in tow.

Secretary Long's order to "capture or destroy" the Spanish fleet had been executed to the letter. Dewey's prophecy that he could reduce the defenses in one day was borne out, even though Manila's thirty-nine shore guns remained unscathed. The city, however, was demoralized. Shore firing had long since ceased, and when the *Olympia, Baltimore,* and *Raleigh* steamed toward the city in the early afternoon, the flagship anchored unconcernedly off the Luneta battery in full range of Spanish guns. Consul Williams left the *Olympia,* boarded the *McCulloch,* and crossed to a British ship moored near the Pasig River to hand the English captain a message from the Commodore to the British Consul, then representing American interests in the islands. It asked him to warn the Spanish captain general that if another shot were fired at the American ships, the Commodore would "destroy the city," that any and all torpedo boats which might have sought safety in the Pasig River must be surrendered at once, and that if the American Navy were allowed to share the Manila cable, Commodore Dewey would permit the Spanish to use it, too.

The Spanish official willingly agreed not to reopen hostilities unless it became apparent that Dewey was aligning his ships in position to bombard the city.

On the other terms the captain general was less amenable. He advised Dewey that his honor would not permit him to surrender any torpedo boats, even if there were any in the river, nor could he accede to the request for American use of the cable. Unperturbed, Dewey ordered the *Zafiro* to drag for the cable, pick it up, and cut it in two. This was done that night, and the next morning Manila was isolated from the outer world. Another cable, open to Cebu, but not beyond, was severed on May 23.

The cutting of the cable became one of the most controversial of all Dewey's actions in the Philippines. His consequent isolation, of course, made him the master of the situation, out of touch with Secretary Long, and able to manage affairs as he desired. His own explanation was that his squadron carried no telegraphic equipment which would permit it to pick up the cable and use it from shipboard, and that he cut the cable to prevent the Spaniards from calling for reinforcements. Furthermore, he added, cutting the cable seemed the easiest way to avoid future claims by the company in the event that revolution spread through Manila and unauthorized persons sent messages without paying for them. Nevertheless, by putting himself solely in command and eliminating telegraphic communication, he strengthened his own authority in Manila and could act without reference to possible interference from Washington.

In the final inventory of the action certain assets and liabilities were revealed. Lieutenant John M. Ellicott, a naval intelligence officer who published a report of the battle, showed that 141 hits had been scored upon the Spanish squadron, and that 167 Spaniards had been killed and 214 wounded, a total of 381 Spanish; there were only eight minor casualties on the United States side. The *Reina Christina,* with 130 killed, was hit at least thirty-nine times, possibly more; the *Castilla* suffered forty hits; the *Ulloa,* thirty-three; the *Don Juan de Austria,* thirteen, and each of the other vessels, five or less. No record was made of the total number of shells fired by the American ships, although no authority has ever tried to claim that the percentage of hits was anything but low.

In the earlier minutes of battle American marksmanship was exceeded in wildness only by that of the terror-stricken Spanish. During the first hour the Commodore stormed on his bridge because of the waste of ammunition. Bradley Fiske, who was aboard the *Raleigh,* wrote: "Everybody was disappointed at the great number of shots lost. Our practice was evidently much better than that of Spaniards, but it did not seem to me that it was at all good. . . . Our gunners fired too fast, I thought." The American gunnery had at least been good enough to justify Montojo's belief that he had no chance of victory.

The one-sidedness of the battle has undoubtedly detracted from Dewey's reputation. Some of his critics have charged that his one great battle gave him no right to a position among the great naval heroes. Certainly, as Dewey was the first to admit, if the Spaniards had fought to their best ability the victory could not have been so cheap; probably also, as Admiral Fiske has stated, if Admiral Montojo had utilized the great shore guns in Manila, he could have sunk every one of Dewey's ships. Nevertheless, it is uncontested that Commodore Dewey made his pre-battle plans with all the thoroughness of a Farragut or of a Nelson; that his entrance into Manila Bay was as coldly calculated and courageous as Farragut's at Mobile; and that his daring made possible the great success which he achieved. He himself declared that "the battle of Manila Bay was won at Hong Kong." The 1904 account stated:

To us it seems almost incomprehensible that the guns of Caballo and Corregidor failed to fire on our ships; that when our vessels were hampered by the narrow waters of the entrance, there was no night attack from the many small vessels possessed by the Spaniards; and that during the action neither the *Isla de Cuba* nor *Isla de Luzon,* each of them protected with armored decks and fitted with two torpedo tubes, made any attempt to torpedo our ships. But, as at all times during the war, the Spaniards lacked initiative; their courage was indisputable, but undirected courage alone does not conduce to successful war.

Admiral Dewey's success was due to his exhaustive preliminary studies of the situation, to his careful foresight and preparation at Hong Kong, to his wise consultations with his captains and their mutual consideration of every contingency which might arise, to his analytical diagnosis of all the ominous rumors of Spanish preparation, and finally to his celerity and virtual surprise of their position at an hour when he was least expected.

The element of surprise was perhaps the outstanding contributor to the victory. Although the Spaniards knew that Dewey was on his way, apparently they never believed he would dare attempt an entrance by night. Admiral Montojo was at a ball in Manila when Dewey passed Corregidor. Many of the Spanish officers stayed overnight in the capital and rowed out to their ill-fated ships after the battle had been joined.

Even in the morning the American fleet gained the advantage by holding its fire until the Commodore and Gridley were ready, and then opening such a concentration of shells that the Spaniards became demoralized. That tactic was another borrowed by Dewey from Farragut, whose policy Dewey stated as "the best defense against enemy fire is superior fire of your own." That creed has been expressed in various ways, but no matter how it is stated it recognizes the fact that in battle the din and fury of rapid explosions is almost as terrorizing as actual hits.

It was one of the ironies of this extraordinary war that the Spanish admiral, Don Patricio Montojo y Pasaron, ordered home to Madrid to stand court-martial for his failure, should have later called upon his chief antagonist to defend him. In a letter addressed to Dewey he wrote:

To His Excellency,
Rear Admiral Dewey.

MY DEAR SIR:

With all my consideration and special respect, I present my earnest thanks for the amiable reply which you took the occasion to send to my letter, regretting also that the circumstances in which we find ourselves do not permit me to convey my feelings by conversation.

Being called to Madrid to make answer to charges which may be made against me, principally for going to Subic and for the loss of my squadron at Cavité, I have to defend myself from the calumny which may be raised against me; for this purpose it would be of the greatest utility and much force if I were able to offer the highly valuable testimony of the authorized opinion of yourself, the distinguished commander-in-chief of the squadron which I had the honor of engaging.

For this purpose I am compelled to put on record:

1. That the port of Subic was without shore fortifications or submarine torpedoes at its entrance.
2. That the destruction of my squadron, given the superiority of yours, would have been far more complete at Subic than at Cavité because, the depth of the water being much greater in the former port, ships and men would have sunk, causing great loss of life.
3. That you did not find us unready at the entrance of Manila Bay and still less so at Cavité, and if fortune did not favor the Spaniards it was not for lack of valor but principally because we had poor ships.

I know that my temerity in making this request of you is very great; but invoking the fact that we belong to the same profession and remembering that you have more than once had the kindness to praise my conduct, I force myself to believe that this will be well received.

The affair has an immense importance for me, since it is closely related to my honor and professional reputation.

I have another request to make of you, and that is in favor of Captain Del Rio, old and sick, late naval commandant at Subic, and the officers, sailors and soldiers who are with him in the power of the insurgents, and very badly treated. If you would consent to arrange for their transfer to Manila, continuing as prisoners, they would be satisfied.

For my part, after begging your pardon a thousand times, for the liberty which I am taking, I hope that you will kindly grant my request for which your faithful servant will be eternally grateful.

PATRICIO MONTOJO.

Dewey's answer, not without subtlety, read:

MY DEAR SIR:

It gives me pleasure, replying to your letter to record my testimony in favor of a gallant foe.

1. In regard to the port of Subic, it was carefully reconnoitred on the 30th of April by three of my ships, two of which made the complete circuit of the bay without finding anything to oppose them.
2. Your statement as to the probability of greater loss of life in a deep bay like that of Subic than in shoal water as at Cavité, appears to me to be incontrovertible.
3. Although without accurate knowledge as to the condition of your ships, I have no hesitation in saying to you what I have already had the honor to report to my goverment, that your defense at

190

Cavité was gallant in the extreme. The fighting of your flagship, which was singled out for attack, was especially worthy of a place in the traditions of valor of your nation.

In conclusion, I beg to assure you that I very much regret that calumnies have been cast at you, and am confident that your honor cannot be dimmed by them.

With assurances of my highest consideration,

Very sincerely,
GEORGE DEWEY
Rear Admiral U.S.N.
Commanding Asiatic Station.

To his own men, however, he made no excuses for the Spanish defeat.* When the last echo of battle had died down that May afternoon, and only the smoking hulks of the Spanish fleet marred the tropical peace, the Commodore assembled his officers in his cabin to thank them for their skill and bravery, and added solemnly:

"Gentlemen, a higher power than we has won this battle today."

Hardly a single sign of battle remained as the tropical sun sank below the hills of Luzon and the *Olympia's* band played the soft tones of "La Paloma," a message of peace to the hundreds of Manila residents who crowded to the shore to see the conquering ships. Manila had endured a day of fear and horror. Now at evening civilians crowded around the batteries of shore guns, as if there were no war.

As the tropical night swiftly engulfed the city, the Commodore tossed a half-smoked cigar into the bay, then rubbed his eyes, and went below to his cabin. Sitting down at the green felt-covered table, he took out his little leather-bound diary and wrote:

SUNDAY, MAY 1. Reached Manila at daylight and immediately engaged the Spanish ships and batteries at Cavité. Destroyed seven of the former including the *Reina Christina* and *Castilla.* Anchored at noon off Manila.

He crossed out the word "seven," and above it wrote "eight." The Commodore pulled at his mustache and reread the entry. He put a little cross after the word *"Castilla,"* and at the bottom of the page, after another cross to mark the footnote, added "Also one large steam transport."

Then he went to bed.

*Many historians attribute the victory to the simple fact that the Spaniards neglected target practice. (Captain John Russell Bartlett in *The Century Magazine*, Oct., 1898.)

20

SHOTS HEARD ROUND THE WORLD

𝒯he dawn that lighted up Manila Bay May 2, 1898, broke over a new world. Overnight the United States had entered a new era, all unknowing, as a world power. The Stars and Stripes which flew from Maine to California the day before now spanned 7,000 miles of sea to wave over an island empire in the Orient. The day of continentalism was over.

A week passed before full details of the battle and its outcome were known, a week of suspense and disturbing reports filtering through from Spain. Before the second phase the captain general of Manila had sent a cable to Madrid, saying,

> AT DAYBREAK THE ENEMY TOOK UP POSITIONS, OPENING WITH A STRONG FIRE AGAINST FORT CAVITE AND THE ARSENAL. OUR FLEET ENGAGED THE ENEMY IN A BRILLIANT COMBAT, PROTECTED BY THE CAVITE AND MANILA FORTS. THEY OBLIGED THE ENEMY WITH HEAVY LOSS TO MANEUVER REPEATEDLY. AT NINE O'CLOCK THE AMERICAN SQUADRON TOOK REFUGE BEHIND THE FOREIGN SHIPPING ON THE EAST SIDE OF THE BAY. OUR FLEET, COVERING THE ENEMY'S SUPERIORITY, NATURALLY SUFFERED A SEVERE LOSS. THE REINA CHRISTINA IS ON FIRE, AND ANOTHER SHIP, BELIEVED TO BE THE DON JUAN DE AUSTRIA, WAS BLOWN UP. THERE WAS CONSIDERABLE LOSS OF LIFE... I CANNOT NOW GIVE FURTHER DETAILS. THE SPIRIT OF THE ARMY, NAVY AND VOLUNTEERS IS EXCELLENT.

Other dispatches got through that day before the *Zafiro* cut off communication with the rest of the world, but on May 2 Washington heard that the Spanish fleet had been severely drubbed. Senator Redfield Proctor, whose sponsorship of Commodore Dewey seemed vindicated, wrote to President McKinley, "I feel well this morning. You may remember that you gave, at my earnest request, the direction to Secretary Long to assign Commodore George Dewey to the Asiatic squadron. You will find you made no mistake; and I want to say that he will be as wise and safe, if there are political duties devolving upon him, as he is forcible in action."*

Secretary Long, jubilant, commented in his diary that everyone was rejoicing, but the silence from Manila after the first day gave rise to doubts and fears. The Spanish government, despite its own unfavorable information, continued to spur its people's hopes with false reports of an American repulse.

Finally, on May 4, Manila time (May 5 in the United States), the Commodore sent the *McCulloch* to Hong Kong with the news. Aboard were Edward W. Harden filing for both the New York *World* and Chicago *Tribune*; John T. McCutcheon of the Chicago *Tribune*; Dewey's temporary aide, Joseph L. Stickney of the New York *Herald,* and Lieutenant Brumby, who was to file the Commodore's official messages. The newspaper releases were not censored. Dewey stipulated only that no mention of future moves should be discussed and that his own messages should be dispatched first. When the *McCulloch* reached Hong Kong on May 6, the correspondents scrambled over the side to race for the cable office. Harden reached it first and thrust his message at the girl behind the desk. Stickney dashed past him into the manager's office. A few minutes later Brumby entered sedately and filed the official messages in code. Harden convinced the cable manager, after a little argument, that his message had been filed before Stickney's. Dewey's report, of course, was sent first, but since the Commodore had ordered it to be read back for verification at every relay point, it was greatly delayed. At the first station where there were two cable lines, Harden's cable went ahead and reached New York at 3 A.M. on May 7. Newspaper offices went wild, newsboys dashed through the streets of Chicago and New York shouting of the victory, and not Dewey, but James Keeley, managing editor of the Chicago *Tribune,* conveyed the momentous news to the President and Secretary of the Navy by long-distance telephone at 3:30 A.M.* It was mid-morning before Commodore Dewey's message reached the Navy Department.

In his journal for that day, Long wrote:

First thing this morning are two telegrams from Commodore Dewey, confirming the story of his overwhelming victory at Manila: the utter destruction of all the enemy's vessels, eleven in number, and the suppression of the forts. He has the city at his command. The country is wild with enthusiasm over this victory. The President, of course, is delighted. We are actively engaged in preparing reinforcements of men, munitions of war and supplies for the Asiatic squadron.

*George Dewey, *Autobiography*, p. 228.
*Mark Sullivan, *Our Times, 1900–1925* (New York: Charles Scribner's Sons), p. 319 ff.

In all such great events the praise or the blame, as the case may be, is very unequally distributed. This is a glorious achievement, redounding specially to his credit. No man could have done better or deserved more. Had the enterprise failed, it would have been ruin. Yet, in either case, the responsibility runs out to an infinite number of others. Nobody now thinks of my four immediate predecessors who have brought the Navy up to the condition it now is. Nobody thinks of the patience and thoroughness with which our ships have been equipped and armed, and our ordnance brought to the highest state of efficiency by officers here at home whose names will never be mentioned. Little thought even is given to the officers and men who, by their gallantry and skill, have won the immediate victory.*

Long's entry reveals not only his rather grudging recognition of Dewey, but the administration's sudden plans to capitalize upon the victory by sending troops and reinforcements to the Philippine Islands. There appears to have been little advance consideration of the step. Instead, weeks passed before the President made up his mind whether the country should accept the Philippines as a dividend of the war. Then England, not McKinley, made the decision.

On June 3 the President, through his new Secretary of State, William R. Day, notified John Hay, American Ambassador in London, that his plans for peace would allow Spain to keep the Philippines, except "for a port and necessary appurtenances to be selected by the United States."† On June 14, however, he indicated to Hay that the question of the rights of the insurgents must be recognized and that therefore the United States must reconsider its earlier statement. In July he asked Hay's opinion about the advisability of the June 3 plan, to which Hay replied that "the British government prefers to have us retain the Philippine Islands, or failing that, insist on option in case of future sale."‡ The United States kept the islands, therefore, not so much because of a farsighted policy of its own but because of England's preference that America, rather than Germany or Japan, take the islands. Yet neither McKinley nor Dewey knew what to do with the lands which had fallen into the power of the United States on May 1. Dewey thought the Filipinos entirely capable of self-government, but after the Spanish fleet was destroyed he made no move to sail away. He apparently had no intention of launching his country on a policy of imperialism. Nonetheless, a line in one of his cables to Secretary Long contained a significant suggestion which altered American policy.

*Mayo, *America of Yesterday as Reflected in the Journals of John D. Long.*
†Tyler Dennett, *John Hay: From Poetry to Politics* (New York: Dodd, Mead & Co., 1933), p. 190.
‡*Ibid.*, p. 191.

194

Dewey's first message, written immediately after the battle, merely listed the Spanish ships destroyed and requested the department to "send immediately from San Francisco fast steamer with ammunition." The second cable, however, written May 4, and received by Long simultaneously with the first, added a potent suggestion:

> WE CONTROL BAY COMPLETELY AND CAN TAKE CITY AT ANY TIME, BUT HAVE NOT SUFFICIENT MEN TO HOLD. . . . I CAN PROVIDE THE SQUADRON COAL AND PROVISIONS FOR A LONG PERIOD. GREAT EXCITEMENT IN MANILA. SCARCITY OF PROVISIONS, OUTBREAK IMMINENT. WILL PROTECT FOREIGN RESIDENTS.

His suggestion that the city could be taken unconsciously helped determine McKinley's future action. Washington assumed it had no choice but to follow up Dewey's success. "At a moment when the American people were wild with delight over the brilliant triumph of their young Navy, popular disappointment would have been intense if the victorious fleet had thereupon turned around and skulked home. Sober-minded critics would, moreover, have condemned the whole expedition as a useless raid without any bearing on the course of the war," wrote Archibald Cary Coolidge—a useless raid, however, only if one considered pointless the complete destruction of Spain's Asiatic fleet.*

The jubilation created by the victory had its first effect on Dewey on May 7 when he received the following cable from Secretary Long:

> YOU ARE ASSIGNED TO COMMAND THE U. S. NAVAL FORCE ON THE ASIATIC STATION WITH THE RANK OF REAR ADMIRAL. HOIST THE FLAG OF A REAR ADMIRAL IMMEDIATELY.

Later that day the Secretary dispatched another cable to the new rear admiral:

> THE PRESIDENT, IN THE NAME OF THE AMERICAN PEOPLE, THANKS YOU AND YOUR OFFICERS AND MEN FOR YOUR SPLENDID ACHIEVEMENT AND OVERWHELMING VICTORY. IN RECOGNITION HE HAS APPOINTED YOU ACTING REAR ADMIRAL AND WILL RECOMMEND A VOTE OF THANKS TO YOU BY CONGRESS AS A FOUNDATION FOR FURTHER PROMOTION. THE CHARLESTON WILL LEAVE AT ONCE WITH WHAT AMMUNITION SHE CAN CARRY. PACIFIC MAIL STEAMSHIP COMPANY'S STEAMER PEKIN WILL FOLLOW WITH AMMUNITION AND SUPPLIES. WILL TAKE TROOPS UNLESS YOU TELEGRAPH OTHERWISE. HOW MANY WILL YOU REQUIRE?

Congress was quick to join in the praises, by passing a special act increasing the authorized number of rear admirals from six to seven in

*Archibald Cary Coolidge, *The United States as a World Power* (New York: The Macmillan Co., 1921).

order to create a vacancy for Dewey. On May 16 the Congress adopted a joint resolution of thanks, reading in part:

> *Resolved* by the Senate and House of Representatives of the United States of America in Congress assembled, that in pursuance of the recommendation of the President the thanks of Congress and of the American people are hereby tendered to Commodore George Dewey, U.S.N., commander-in-chief of the United States Naval Force on the Asiatic Station, for highly distinguished conduct in conflict with the enemy as displayed by him in the destruction of the Spanish fleet and batteries in the harbor of Manila, Philippine Islands, May 1, 1898. That the thanks of the Congress and the American people are hereby extended through Commodore Dewey to the officers and men under his command for the gallantry and skill exhibited by them on that occasion.

Amid the many congratulatory cables which reached the Philippines from friends, political leaders, admirers, and complete strangers were two which the new rear admiral particularly prized: One was from Theodore Roosevelt, then a lieutenant colonel in the Rough Riders regiment: "Every American is your debtor!" The other was signed "Mildred McLean Hazen."

Commodore Winfield Scott Schley, commander of the Flying Squadron in the North Atlantic, declared Dewey's victory "must deservedly take its place side by side with the greatest naval victories of the world's history."* Henry Cabot Lodge, Republican Senator from Massachusetts, said it compared favorably with that of Lord Nelson at Aboukir on the Nile, and the mantle of Farragut was unreservedly draped about Dewey's broad shoulders. Vermont, the hero's home state, passed a flowery resolution of eulogy. Montpelier went wild at a gigantic celebration on May 9, and the brothers and sister of the Admiral found themselves heroes, too. A group of rich Vermonters subscribed a fund for a marble statue of the Admiral to be erected in the statehouse, next to that of Ethan Allen.† Boston named a square for him, and his old school, Norwich University, quickly started plans to construct a new building, to be known as Dewey Hall.

Again in July, hero worship reached a frenzy in Congress. Senator Lodge introduced a resolution that a jeweled sword be given the Admiral and bronze medals commemorating the Battle of Manila Bay awarded to all his men. It was passed without debate, and a committee was appointed to supervise competitive bidding for the finest design. Tiffany and Com-

---

*Sullivan, *op. cit.*, p. 323.
†Adelbert Dewey, *The Life and Letters of Admiral Dewey*, p. 402.

pany of New York won the contest with designs for a twenty-two-carat gold-hilted sword, with appropriate decorations of oak leaves and acorns, a grip of sharkskin, and the initials "G.D.U.S.N." studded in diamonds. On the damascened blade of thin steel appeared the inscription: "The gift of the Nation to Rear Admiral George Dewey, U.S.N. In Memory of the Victory at Manila Bay, May 1, 1898."* Its only drawback was that it was too heavy for practical use, and was worn only at White House receptions.

Honorary degrees were heaped upon the Admiral by Princeton and Pennsylvania among many others. Norwich University conferred upon him the degree of Master of Military Science, and dozens of other institutions, large and small, made him a doctor of "everything but divinity."†

The victory had its effect outside the United States. Until May 1, 1898, the American Navy had been ignored as a major force. After its lopsided triumph over Spain, America's naval reputation swelled immeasurably. Bradley Fiske, who had sailed from Hong Kong with the squadron April 27, had noted with what contempt Europeans of the colony had treated Americans. When he returned to Hong Kong soon after the battle, he found their "whole manner and attitude toward us had suddenly become quite as toward equals."‡

The effect of the battle upon the war was, of course, crucial. While the victory lifted American morale to the heights, it plunged Spain into despair. Serious peace riots rocked Madrid on May 6 and 7, and the Germans, who had considered intervention, quickly changed their minds. The May Day victory, above all, settled definitely the fate of Spanish rule in the Philippines. From the moment the American flag flew over Cavité, the fall of Manila and of the entire archipelago became a certainty.

After May 1, 1898, America became a world power whose Asiatic interests menaced Japanese dreams of Pan-Asiatic domination. Captain Mahan realized the fact. Theodore Roosevelt understood it, and as a result sponsored construction of the nation's greatest fleet and sent sixteen battleships to Tokyo Bay in 1907 to show the Mikado the power of the United States. But as Walter Lippmann has pointed out, "From the day when Admiral Dewey sailed into Manila Bay until the day when General Wainwright surrendered Corregidor [April, 1942] the United States never made a sustained and prudent, or remotely adequate effort to bring its obligations and its power into balance."§

*This inscription was supposed to be changed to "Admiral George Dewey" before the sword was presented to him on the steps of the Capitol in Oct., 1899, but it never was.
†Adelbert Dewey, op. cit., p. 401.
‡Sullivan, op. cit., p. 324.
§Lippmann, United States Foreign Policy, p. 28.

Few Americans realized the true import of Dewey's triumph. To a country making ready to give its hero the wildest ovation ever accorded any man, Spain's defeat merely eliminated a great worry. If Dewey with his unarmored cruisers could sail boldly into the heart of a European power's greatest overseas territory and smash her ships and forts, there was nothing to dread. The rest of the war would be, as Mr. Dooley said, "a picnic." May 1 created from the conflict of a few hours a naval hero to rival England's Lord Nelson. Without a life lost it launched the nation on a new course of world responsibility, which would later exact its price.

21

FIGHT FOR THE SUN

At Manila hard work still remained for the American squadron. On the evening of May 1 a steam launch put out from the shore for the *Olympia*. The Commodore watched the boat heading for his ship and, fearful of a torpedo attack, ordered his men to train their searchlights and guns upon the craft. Its mission proved to be a peaceful one, however, for it carried a Spanish official who requested permission to proceed to Corregidor and instruct the commanding officer not to fire upon any American ships. The Commodore approved, but ordered the Spaniard to return to the *Olympia* after giving his orders.

The next morning the Spaniard was put aboard the *Raleigh* as a hostage. The *Raleigh* and the *Baltimore* then steamed to Corregidor to demand the surrender of the entrance batteries. If the guns at Corregidor should treacherously attack the American ships, Captain Coghlan, on Dewey's orders, was to kill the Spaniard. As the Spanish forces had been cowed into complete submission, the island batteries surrendered without protest. The *Boston* and the *Concord* landed men at Corregidor and El Fraile the next day to disable the guns, destroy the ammunition, and carry the breech plugs to the American squadron.

On the morning of May 2 Commodore Dewey saw the Spanish flag flying over the Cavité arsenal, where the day before a white flag of surrender had flown. Indignant, he dispatched Lamberton on the *Petrel* to demand the formal surrender of the arsenal. Lamberton went ashore at 9:30, giving orders to Commander Wood that if he did not return within one hour, the *Petrel's* guns should start shelling. On reaching the arsenal he found Spanish soldiers and sailors under arms, insisting that they had not surrendered but had only declared a "temporary truce."

Lamberton marched up to the Spanish commandant, Captain Sostoa, and demanded an immediate surrender, but gave the Spaniards until noon to lower their flag and deliver up their arms. Captain Sostoa demurred. He needed time to submit the matter to Madrid, he insisted. This was refused. Then he asked for time to advise with authorities at Manila. Lamberton refused again, informing the Spaniard that only an unconditional surrender of officers, men, and arms would be considered. Then the American officer returned to the *Petrel*. As noontime approached, the *Petrel's* men were preparing to shell the white brick buildings, but at 11:35 the flag of Spain was lowered, and a white flag again floated above the fort. Officers and men marched out of the arsenal in a few minutes and began the seven-mile walk to Manila. Perhaps imperfect knowledge of each other's language caused a misunderstanding of Lamberton's terms, but he did not prevent the evacuation. The American fleet could not be hampered with prisoners, and the Spaniards were small menace in Manila. That same day the *Petrel's* men occupied the arsenal at Cavité and dismantled the guns of Sangley Point and Cañacao. Manila Bay was thus under complete control of the Commodore from Vermont.

Under Commander Wood, the Cavité navy yard was promptly organized for the repair and maintenance of American ships. Then a blockade of Manila was established. More than twenty Spanish gunboats remained uncaptured, and every American ship stayed on twenty-four-hour alert against surprise attack.

The British Consul, E. H. Rawson-Walker, who had represented American interests in the Spanish city, paid an official call to the *Olympia* at noon, May 2. In appreciation of his many courtesies to the United States after April 21, Dewey invited him to stay aboard for luncheon, and while the two were sitting on the after deck, discussing the state of affairs in Manila, an officer reported to the commander-in-chief that Spaniards were manning the Manila shore batteries. A bosun's pipe sounded general quarters, and men stood by the guns, but it was only a precaution. Dewey, convinced there would be no firing, unconcernedly escorted Rawson-Walker to his cabin for a leisurely meal, during which the two agreed that the possibility of outbreak should be avoided. That afternoon, to avoid misunderstanding of American intentions, the squadron moved to permanent mooring positions off Cavité, where it could not possibly be considered in position to shell the city. Merchant vessels were assigned anchorages outside the zone of possible naval operations and were informed of the regulations. In addition, the *Concord, Callao, Manila,* and *McCulloch* were assigned as patrol ships, to board every ship entering the bay to see that it was informed of the blockade and given a clear understanding of the provisions. Lookouts on the *Olympia* scanned the horizon twenty-four hours a day, and at the glint of a sail or a trail of smoke over the horizon gave the signal for investigation of the newcomer.

One night in May the *McCulloch* was sent to overhaul a small craft spotted coming out of an inlet in the bay. Quickly captured, it proved to be the Spanish gunboat *Leyte,* which on May 1 had escaped up a river, where its commander had hoped to find refuge. Running short of provisions, however, he had finally been obliged to try his escape. He surrendered peaceably. The next day Dewey was discussing the capture with newspapermen. The *Leyte* would be renamed and commissioned as a United States boat, he said.

"What will you call her, sir?" asked a newspaper correspondent.

"I have made a suggestion to Lamberton which I think a good one," he replied. "You know they have just given the names of two colleges, Harvard and Yale, to two of the merchant cruisers which have been pressed into the Navy."*

"Well, here we have the *Leyte* and the *Callao.* Those names are hardly suitable, I think, in view of the new fashion. I think I shall recommend to the Secretary that the *Leyte* be renamed the 'Massachusetts Institute of Technology,' and the *Callao,* the 'Pennsylvania College of Physicians and Surgeons.' "

Despite the pleasantries aboard, the months of blockade were trying. The greatest vigilance had to be maintained at all times against some sudden move, for more than a thousand surviving officers and men of Montojo's fleet were sitting in Manila in enforced idleness. A Spanish army of 13,000 was stationed in the city, and scores of merchant ships, yachts, launches, and coastwise vessels lay at anchor in the harbor. It seemed almost certain to Dewey that the men of Montojo's squadron, chafing under their defeat, might attempt some desperate measure. Their apparent inertness seemed to Dewey merely a device to lull him into fancied security. Rumors of attack which never materialized were frequent. Filipino insurgents notified the commander-in-chief on May 20 that the Spaniards planned to move against Cavité that night. The *Petrel* and the *Callao* were consequently moved to a position commanding the navy yard, where they waited all night with crews at the guns ready to open fire at a second's notice. Black gangs on the other ships kept fires burning, and sailors waited for a flash from shore to slip their anchors and steam into battle. But nothing happened.

A month later Spaniards were reported to have amassed a fleet of torpedo boats to attack the squadron. Night watches were doubled, and everything was made ready to resist assault. Commander Asa Walker, whose bushy beard won him the name "an explosion in a mattress fac-

*Barrett, *Admiral George Dewey,* p. 123.

tory," steamed the *Concord* around the bay at 3:00 A.M. to search for the boats. None were found.

When the *McCulloch* returned from Hong Kong on May 10 with cable messages and news from home, it brought wires of congratulation from every community of America, but more important was the commission from Secretary Long appointing the commander-in-chief a rear admiral. The higher rank was already necessary and its value apparent, for foreign men-of-war had begun to arrive, and Dewey would need all the prestige possible to control the diplomatic situation.

"Colors" on the *Olympia* had added significance, therefore, at eight the next morning. When the national ensign of the United States was raised, a blue admiral's flag with two white stars was also hoisted to the masthead, and the Commodore's broad blue pennant was in the Admiral's sea chest.* Already the British ship *Immortalite,* commanded by Captain Edward Chichester, had arrived, and from him the Admiral received the first salute of thirteen guns in recognition of his promotion.

Significantly enough, the first foreign man-of-war to enter Manila Bay under the blockade was the German cruiser *Irene,* which arrived the morning of May 6. Coming from Nagasaki, she had been informed of the American victory by a British steamer as she approached the Bocas entranceway, but chose to ignore both Dewey's regulations and the international usage which required that neutral warships might enter blockaded ports only on sufferance and through the courtesy of the blockading nation.

During the next two days other neutral ships arrived, including the French cruiser *Bruix,* and the Japanese cruiser *Itsukushima.* Requested to anchor clear of the line of fire from the Manila batteries, all observed the courtesies required of the situation by reporting to the *Olympia* and following the requests of the American commander-in-chief. On May 9, at the unusual hour of 3:00 A.M., the German cruiser *Cormoran* entered the bay. A steam launch was dispatched to stop her and ascertain her nationality, but she ignored the signals and proceeded toward the city of Manila. Commodore Dewey sent a blinker code to the *Raleigh,* which, blacked out and invisible, steamed close aboard the German ship and fired a shot across her bow. The German commander was "quickly brought to his senses." He not only stopped his engines but threw them hard astern. When an American boarding officer visited his vessel, his manner showed that he fully realized the narrowness of his escape. Dewey was willing to believe the *Cormoran's* action was either "a mistake," or

---

*Dewey flew this flag every May 1 from the flagpole of his Washington home to celebrate the anniversary. It is now on display in the Dewey room at the Chicago Historical Society.

evidenced "ignorance of naval rules of action," but as the weeks went by, he began to view it as the forerunner of a series of annoyances engineered by the Kaiser's fleet to precipitate trouble.

On May 13 Rear Admiral Dewey dispatched two cables to Secretary Long, one showing his readiness to capture Manila itself, the other indicating his interest in his officers and his unselfish desire that they receive their share of recognition for the exploits of May 1. The first one read:

> THE SQUADRON THANKS THE PRESIDENT FOR YOUR MESSAGE IN YOUR TELEGRAM OF MAY 7. I AM MAINTAINING STRICT BLOCKADE OF MANILA BY SEA AND BELIEVE REBELS ARE HEMMING IN BY LAND. GREAT SCARCITY OF PROVISIONS IN THE CITY. I BELIEVE THE SPANISH GOVERNOR GENERAL WILL BE OBLIGED TO SURRENDER SOON. I CAN TAKE MANILA AT ANY MOMENT. TO RETAIN POSSESSION AND THUS CONTROL THE PHILIPPINE ISLANDS WILL REQUIRE, IN MY BEST JUDGMENT, WELL-EQUIPPED FORCE OF 5,000 MEN, ALTHOUGH UNITED STATES TROOPS SENT BY PEKIN WILL BE VERY USEFUL TO RELIEVE THE OLYMPIA OF GUARDING CAVITE. UNITED STATES TROOPS SHOULD MAKE PROVISION FOR EXTREMELY HOT, MOIST CLIMATE. SPANISH FORCE IS ESTIMATED 10,000 MEN. THE REBELS ARE REPORTED 30,000 MEN. I SHOULD SUGGEST THE [CRUISER] CHARLESTON OR PEKIN BRING A FEW OFFICERS AND ABOUT 100 MEN, PARTLY ENGINEERS DEPARTMENT, TO MAN TRANSPORT MANILA AND CAPTURED VESSELS. I AM LOADING MANILA WITH ORDNANCE FROM THE SPANISH MEN-OF-WAR. I PROPOSE TO ASSIGN LIEUTENANT COMMANDER SINGER TO COMMAND. CAPTURED ON MAY 12 THE SPANISH GUN VESSEL CALLAO ATTEMPTING TO RUN BLOCKADE; RELEASED ON PAROLE OFFICERS AND MEN. I HAVE PLENTY OF COAL FOR THE PRESENT AND CAN PURCHASE MORE IN CHINESE PORTS. WILL HOLD FREQUENT COMMUNICATION WITH HONG KONG. ONE BRITISH, ONE FRENCH, TWO GERMAN, ONE JAPANESE MEN-OF-WAR HERE OBSERVING.

The second, shorter message read:

> I THANK THE PRESIDENT FOR MY PROMOTION. FORCIBLY RECOMMEND THAT COMMANDER LAMBERTON, CHIEF OF STAFF; CAPTAIN WILDES, THE COMMANDER OF THE BOSTON; COGHLAN, COMMANDER OF THE RALEIGH; GRIDLEY, COMMANDER OF THE OLYMPIA; DYER, COMMANDER OF THE BALTIMORE; WALKER, COMMANDER OF THE CONCORD; WOOD, COMMANDER OF THE PETREL, WITHOUT WHOSE AID I COULD HAVE DONE NOTHING, EACH BE ADVANCED TEN NUMBERS.

During the next six weeks the German fleet began to arrive in force, and with every new member that entered Manila Bay, German arrogance increased. "Day by day," Sargent reported, "they exercised an increasing disposition to ignore his rights and authority, significant when viewed in terms of the naval superiority of the German squadron to the American." During June the German fleet was joined by the *Kaiserin Augusta*, flying the flag of Vice Admiral von Diedrichs, the *Kaiser*, the *Deutschland*, the *Prinzess Wilhelm*, and the transport *Darmstadt*, carrying 1,400 sailors.

The *Kaiser* arrived after dark June 18, completely disregarding a launch sent to board her, and anchored off Manila. The next morning she steamed across the Cavité to report to Admiral Dewey. The *Darmstadt* meanwhile sought permission to transfer her men to the other ships. Admiral Dewey granted it, although use of a blockaded port for such action might justly have been withheld. But the courtesy was unappreciated and abused. The men who provided von Diedrichs with a large landing force were kept aboard for almost a month and trained ashore almost daily at the entrances to the bay.

Dewey, as the junior in rank, had paid von Diedrichs the first courtesy call, during which, in view of Germany's slight commercial interests in the islands, it seemed pertinent to the American Admiral to inquire "why so large a force had been assembled off Manila."

Von Diedrichs drew his heels together with a Prussian click and pompously replied: "I am here by order of the Kaiser, sir."

The aggressiveness of the Germans was in direct ratio to the superiority of their squadron. The *Kaiser* and the *Deutschland*, though old battleships and not formidable in their own class, could nevertheless have blown the unarmored American cruisers to wreckage with their ten-inch guns. Dewey's task in Manila would probably have involved fewer indignities at the Germans' hands if his squadron at that time had included a ship of the *Oregon* class. As it was, his authority was flouted in every conceivable way. German officers were soon on most cordial terms with the Spaniards in Manila, who paid them marked courtesy and openly asserted that the German squadron would intervene for Spain. Von Diedrichs officially visited Governor General Augustin Davila in Manila, and the Spaniard returned the call to the *Kaiserin Augusta* at night, staying two hours, although twenty minutes was the official length of a formal visit. Governor Davila was saluted by the *Kaiserin's* guns, and other Spanish officials were similarly saluted by the German squadron. German ships landed supplies of food and clothing for the Spanish in distinct violation of neutrality. Once Prince von Lowenstein of the German intelligence department, who had spent many weeks in the islands, was brought aboard von Diedrichs' flagship. The admiral's attempt to conceal this visit was frustrated by a heavy sea, which forced the Prince's boat to seek refuge on a British ship, whose officers informed Dewey.

One day von Diedrichs haughtily asked for permission to visit the Cavité naval yard. Admiral Dewey agreed, but insisted, to the German's evident displeasure, upon escorting him personally. While they were looking at the Spanish guns at Sangley Point, the German remarked scornfully, "They were not ready." The insinuation that Dewey had taken unfair advantage of the Spanish by attacking before they had completed all their defense installations was hardly tactful under the circumstances. The German squadron offended in other ways as well. Its officers frequently visited Spanish troop outposts to watch them fight the insurgent Filipinos and to examine all the military installations around Manila. Landing boats took soundings of the water's depth off the mouth of the Pasig River, and a party of seamen occupied the lighthouse at the river's mouth for several days, for what purpose Dewey never learned.

In a dozen ways their ships ignored conditions of the blockade. They followed American vessels close astern, shifted their own positions without authority, ran in and out at all hours, and finally, without permission, established a temporary base at Mariveles harbor, opposite Corregidor, where they landed men, ostensibly for drill, and took possession of the quarantine station. Von Diedrichs moved into a large mansion recently deserted by Spanish officials, and the Germans remained in complete possession of the deserted outpost for several days.

Movements noted in the *Olympia's* log will indicate the activities of the German fleet: "On June 27 the *Irene* returned from Mariveles. During the first watch at night the Germans shone a searchlight at the entrance to the bay, and the *Kaiserin Augusta* left her Manila anchorage and stood down the bay. The next day the *Kaiser* steamed in and anchored just beyond her assigned berth. On June 29 the *Irene* got under way, steamed about the upper bay and returned. Later she left the harbor again. The *Prinzess Wilhelm* anchored and the *Cormoran* weighed anchor and steamed to Mariveles."

On June 30 the first of Dewey's reinforcements arrived. The three transports, bringing 2,500 men and escorted by the cruiser *Charleston,* made a welcome addition to the Admiral's fleet. As the *Charleston* passed through Boca Grande, the *Kaiserin Augusta* weighed anchor and followed close behind, "dogging their heels after a fashion that could be explained only as an attempt to be gratuitously offensive."* That same afternoon the German collier *Trinidad* arrived with coal for the German squadron. Dewey's permission for coaling, grudgingly asked, was reluctantly given. During the next few days the German fleet was in constant movement, its ships entering and leaving the harbor, without any acknowledgment whatever of the American right to board them and make sure of their identity.

One incident brought Admiral Dewey's forebearance almost to the

*Barrett, *op. cit.*, pp. 109–12.

breaking point. At a moment when the Germans knew the American squadron was on the alert against a rumored torpedo attack, a strange launch headed for the *Olympia*. Searchlights were turned on the launch, but it made no move to stop and steamed straight on.

Admiral Dewey rushed to the side of the bridge. "If it doesn't stop, fire on her!" he shouted. A six-pound shot was hurled across the water over the mast of the German launch. Still it came on. The Admiral ordered: "Fire again, and fire to hit."

The six-pounder was joined by a brisk fire of small arms. Spray splashed over the bows of the launch. The launch halted, its coxswain waved a German flag in the glare of the *Olympia's* searchlight, and very shortly afterward a picket boat from the *Olympia* brought the German lieutenant aboard the flagship. Frightened but angry, he protested to an American ensign:

"Why do you fire on me? This is a launch from the German admiral's flagship." Without answering, the officer led him to Dewey's cabin.

"Do you know what you have done?" Dewey demanded, his face red with anger. "Do you know that such a rash act on your part is against all rules of war and might have brought serious trouble to your country and mine? It would have been easy for a Spanish boat to hoist a German flag and sink the *Olympia* if we failed to stop it. There is no excuse for such carelessness!" Then a bit more quietly, "Present my compliments to your admiral and ask him to direct his officers to be more careful in the future."*

The German's explanation that he had come to seek permission for coaling early the next day hardly convinced Admiral Dewey, who saw in the episode a German attempt to test the readiness of the American fleet. When von Diedrichs protested the Americans' right to board all vessels entering the bay, Admiral Dewey insisted it was not only his right but his duty. He could see no reason why neutral men-of-war could possibly object to the procedure.

"As a state of war exists between the United States and Spain," Dewey pointed out, "and as the entry into this blockaded port of the vessels of war of a neutral is permitted by the blockading squadron as a matter of international courtesy, such neutrals should necessarily satisfy the blockading vessels as to their identity. I distinctly disclaim my intention of exercising or claiming the *droit de visite* of neutral vessels of war. What I do claim is the right to communicate with all vessels entering this port now blockaded with the forces under my command. It could easily be possible that it was the duty of the picket vessel to notify incoming men-

*Long, *The New American Navy*, pp. 112–13.

of-war that they could not enter the port, not on account of the blockade, but the intervention of my lines of attack."

Still denying that right, von Diedrichs notified Dewey that he would call a conference of all the senior officers of neutral ships at Manila to decide the issue. The only officer who attended was Captain Chichester; the others, recognizing the validity of Dewey's position, refused to waste time over the matter. Captain Chichester, however, wishing to settle the question in von Diedrichs' mind, had brought a few volumes of international law, passages from which he read aloud.

"I don't see how I can join you in this protest," the Englishman said. "I've been looking up all the authorities, and I find that this American admiral is so deadly right in everything he does that if we make a protest we shall only show that we know nothing at all about international law."*

He added that his own government had in fact instructed him to concede much more than Dewey had ever required, and he had given all his captains instructions both to report to the Admiral immediately upon entry into the harbor and to satisfy fully any inquiries he should make before joining other British ships.

The next time von Diedrichs called upon Chichester the Englishman was seated at his writing table reading a large red book. The German made the mistake of asking what it was.

"That," said Captain Chichester, "is a book on naval etiquette."

"Indeed," said von Diedrichs. "I wasn't aware such a book existed."

Captain Chichester already knew that.

"Ah," he cried with suspicious eagerness. "Let me present it to you. You really ought to read it. I'm sure you must need it awfully. You will learn an immense deal from it."†

The Englishman was unduly optimistic. German slights continued, while Admiral Dewey's impatience mounted. On July 5 he hoisted his flag on the *McCulloch* to make a personal reconnaissance of the German positions around Mariveles. Steaming down to the entrance channel and passing around the German vessels anchored there, he left without communicating in any way. The implied threat was too subtle for the German admiral, however. The next day the insurgents informed Dewey that the Germans were intervening at Subic Bay. Since Dewey's policy had been to allow the insurgents to weaken the Spaniards as much as possible, he did not intend to tolerate German aid to the Spanish. He immediately sent the *Raleigh* and the *Concord* to Subic Bay, where a force of Spanish troops entrenched on Isla Grande were besieged by the Filipinos. The

*Peck, *Twenty Years of the Republic*, pp. 582–83.
†Barrett, *op. cit.*, p. 113.

German cruiser *Irene* had called upon the Spanish commander there earlier and had notified the Filipinos that they would not be allowed to use a small steamer in their attack. It was an unheard-of proceeding in the absence of a Spanish-German alliance. The *Irene* was entirely without authority, nor were German interests at stake.

Sailing from Cavité at midnight, July 6, the *Raleigh* and the *Concord* arrived at Subic Bay at daybreak of July 7 and steamed in, cleared for action, with their crews at battle stations. Just as they entered the bay the *Irene* departed, in its haste slipping the cable of her anchor, rather than daring to take time to hoist it from the bottom.

A German officer later reported that the officers on the *Irene* were certain that the American ships were ready to start a war then and there, and her commander knew his ship was no match for the *Raleigh* and the *Concord* combined. Perhaps he remembered Admiral Montojo's fear of the "deep water" in Subic Bay. At any rate the Germans fled. After a few shots fired by the American at the fortifications of Isla Grande, the Spaniards promptly surrendered, and the island was taken in the name of the United States, while the Filipinos captured the 579 Spanish defenders.

To all the German infractions of the blockade Dewey, much to the astonishment of his own officers, remained outwardly impervious, lest by embroiling his little fleet in a battle with the superior German forces he undo the accomplishments of May 1. On July 17, however, a second relief expedition of 3,500 men, commanded by General F. V. Greene, arrived at Manila and brought with it a considerable force of field guns. By then, moreover, Dewey was sure of the support of the five English ships in the harbor.

Three days later he resolved on a showdown, when the *Cormoran*, an old offender, steamed into the bay. Determined that she would not pass his flag without stopping, Dewey called his flag lieutenant to the bridge.

"Mr. Brumby," he ordered. "I wish you to go on board the *McCulloch* and stop that vessel; mind you, sir. Stop her."

The *McCulloch*, with Brumby aboard, headed for the *Cormoran*, whose commander, doubling his speed, made for the northern part of the bay. The *McCulloch* followed for several miles, her signal flags reading "I wish to communicate" hoisted at the masthead. Not until she came within range and shot across the bow of the German ship did the German commander realize that his "trifling maneuvers had better cease and that Admiral Dewey's orders should be respected."

The next day a staff officer from the German squadron boarded the *Olympia* with a list of grievances from von Diedrichs in his hand, and was ushered into Admiral Dewey's littered cabin.

The room was literally inundated with large round wastebaskets which Dewey whimsically adopted as filing cabinets and filled with letters cables, newspapers, magazines, and presents in disorderly piles.

The German lieutenant, a little startled by the untidiness, recovered well enough to salute the Admiral and Lieutenant Brumby. In "a particularly precise, Prussian manner," and with constant reference to his memorandum sheet, the Prussian recited "His Excellency's" protests.

Dewey stood silently throughout the long harangue, but his complexion, Brumby noted, changed from white to red and back again as his anger rose. He restrained himself with the utmost effort until the young German came to his last protest, the affair of the day before. Not only, he complained, had German ships been boarded in the bay, but American vessels had signaled important news to communicate when, as a matter of fact, there was no news. When he finished his recital the Admiral began to speak calmly and softly "in that particularly suave manner which those who are best acquainted with him recognize as meaning mischief."

"And does 'His Excellency' know that it is my force and not his which is blockading this port?" asked the Admiral.

"Yes, sir," answered the German lieutenant.

"And is he aware that he has no right here except such as I choose to allow him, and does he realize that he cannot communicate with that city except by my permission?"

A noncommittal shrug of the aide's shoulders served for answer.

"One would imagine, sir, that you were conducting this blockade."

"Oh no, sir." The German shook his head.

Dewey's voice was becoming higher, but still he spoke deliberately.

"If the German government has decided to make war on the United States, or has any intention of making war, and has so informed your admiral, it is his duty to let me know."

The young German was startled. The Admiral raised his hand and pointed a finger under his visitor's nose.

"Do you want war with us?" he shouted, his voice rising in pitch and intensity until it could be heard in the officers' quarters below.

"Certainly not," replied the German. He was beginning to understand the power and determination of his adversary.

"Well, it looks like it. And you are very near it; and—" his voice was a storm breaking across the thundering waves "—and, you can have it, sir, as soon as you like."

The interview was over. The aide backed away in consternation. "Your Admiral seems to be much in earnest," he said to Lieutenant Brumby, who replied, "Yes, and you can be certain that he means every word he says."

After that the Germans submitted without further protest to the daily boardings, and von Diedrichs remained quiet, not, perhaps, because of Dewey's words alone, but because of what he learned from Captain Chichester, whom he rushed to see as soon as his shaking aide had reported the stormy interview on the *Olympia*.

On the *Immortalite* Captain Chichester was urbanity itself. Von Diedrichs asked him a pointblank question:

"Have you instructions as to your action in case of actual hostilities between myself and the American squadron?"

"Yes," said Chichester, "I have."

"May I ask, then, to be informed as to the nature of those instructions?"

"There are only two persons here who know what my instructions are," answered the Englishman. He paused, to let the words sink in. Then, with devastating implication, in a quiet, steady tone, he went on: "One of those persons is myself. . . . The other is Admiral Dewey."*

Despite the lesson, Admiral von Diedrichs made one more attempt at intimidation—on August 13, the day of the assault on Manila by American forces, which he may have hoped would be unsuccessful. As Dewey's ships moved from Cavité toward the Manila batteries that morning, the German fleet moved toward a position just behind the United States squadron, which would then lie between his own vessels and the shore batteries. Whether he intended to start firing or not will never be known. Captain Chichester, alert to the maneuver, moved his ships, too, and sailed between Dewey and von Diedrichs. The German saw the purpose, continued his course beyond the American ships, and watched the battle from the far side of the bay.

Chichester's co-operation during those weeks at Manila became the basis of a lasting personal friendship between him and Dewey and had important repercussions on future Anglo-American relations as well. Indeed, it might be regarded as a major factor in the realignment of American naval policy, for it was after the Spanish-American War, when Great Britain displayed such friendship to the American cause, that the idea of a possible third war with England disappeared from American strategy. The Navy was no longer designed as a coastwise defensive force, equipped with speedy raiders to destroy the far-flung commerce which only Great Britain possessed.

After the capture of Manila neutral foreign warships gradually dispersed, leaving the bay to the control of the American fleet, which had

*Peck, *op. cit.*, p. 584.

210

grown to fifty-two ships, the greatest squadron ever assembled in the Orient. Among the first to leave was the French admiral, to whom, on a parting visit, Admiral Dewey said, "I wish particularly to thank you for your strict observance of neutrality and of the rights of the blockading squadron during your stay in these waters. I especially appreciated it, if you will allow me to say so, sir, because I am aware that French sympathies have not been altogether with us."

The Frenchman, acknowledging the tribute, replied, "And, Admiral, you must let me congratulate you that in all your conduct of affairs here, you have not made a single mistake."

The Admiral's reply, known all over the bay within fifteen minutes, won a significant and approving smile.

"Oh yes, I have," said Dewey. "I made one," pointing his finger across the bay at the *Kaiserin Augusta*. "I should have sunk that squadron over there."

22

TWILIGHT'S RED GLARE

*I*n the Atlantic the war was as slow in starting as that in the Philippines had been lightning-quick. Rear Admiral William Thomas Sampson, commander-in-chief of the Atlantic fleet, had left Key West, Florida, the evening of April 21 and in less than twelve hours had begun blocking Cuban ports. The blockade dragged on for weeks, while sailors grew listless from inaction. At Hampton Roads Commodore Winfield Schley waited with his flying squadron, ready to sail for any Atlantic port to do battle with Cervera, whose fleet had left the Cape Verde Islands on April 29. Experienced Navy men realized that Cervera could not dare battle before putting in for fuel and repairs after his long Atlantic crossing, but to politicians and to the public, fear of a sudden descent by Spain's fleet was as real as the panic the morning after the Confederate ironclad *Merrimac* had destroyed Northern vessels in the Civil War.

Puerto Rico, a Spanish possession in the West Indies, was Cervera's logical goal. Admiral Sampson arrived there on May 12 with ten ships, including two battleships, two cruisers, and two monitors, which had been towed most of the way for the use of their heavy guns,* to find no sign of the Spanish squadron. He bombarded and silenced the forts of San Juan in a speedy action that resulted in the death of one American sailor, then sailed back toward Key West.

At Fort de France, the Spanish admiral, learning of Sampson's impending visit to Puerto Rico, had changed his plans and put in at Curaçao to recoal his ships. He arrived there May 14, and slipped away the next day to be lost again for two more weeks. That fortnight saw a true war of nerves, abetted eagerly by newspapers which printed every rumor about the whereabouts and imminent threat of the enemy fleet. Coast watchers reported "seeing" the enemy fleet almost every day, even as far north as

*Knox, *A History of the United States Navy*, pp. 342–44.

Maine, but usually it developed that the warships reported by the imaginative watchers were fishing boats or clouds.

American naval forces continued the blockade of Cuba during Sampson's junket to San Juan, and the cable from Cienfuegos on the northern coast was heroically cut by blockading ships under shore fire. When Sampson returned to Key West, May 18, he met the flying squadron under Schley, which had finally been sent south, and while the senior officer led a large force two hundred miles east of Havana to reconnoiter, he ordered Schley to see if Cervera was at Cienfuegos. If not, Schley was to blockade Santiago, the Spaniard's only alternate port. Finding no Spanish ships at Cienfuegos, Schley proceeded to Santiago, which he reached May 26. The high hills circling the harbor effectively concealed the Spanish vessels, and shortage of coal in a heavy sea led Schley to start back for Key West to refuel. This so-called "retrograde movement" lasted for twenty-seven hours and laid him open to severe criticism. When the sea grew calmer, he returned to Santiago.

When Sampson heard of Schley's temporary departure from Santiago, he sped in anger to the port with his own forces. In the United States newspapers, which served as unofficial chiefs of staff for the conduct of the war and which had never favored Sampson's appointment, brought out the issue between the two men, to the greater glory of Dewey, who without fanfare had destroyed an entire Spanish fleet.

On May 31 Schley boarded the battleship *Massachusetts* and, with the *Iowa,* commanded by Captain Evans, closed to within 7,000 yards of Santiago harbor, from which he bombarded the forts and Spanish ships beyond the hills. Sampson arrived June 1 on the cruiser *New York,* accompanied by the *Oregon,* famous for its epic run around the Horn. Commanded by Captain Clark, she had sailed from San Francisco March 12 and under forced draft had plowed around the tip of South America, had then steamed north, and had reached Florida on May 24 after a sixty-four-day journey. Now her twelve-inch guns arrived to augment the American squadron.

A gloomy prospect of long blockade faced the American ships, for in the face of strong shore batteries, underwater mines, and Cervera's fleet, Sampson did not choose to emulate Farragut and Dewey by forcing the entrance for a finish fight. The approach of the hurricane season added to his problems. To prevent dispersal of his fleet by bad weather and the escape of Cervera's ships under cover of it, Sampson planned a bold, dramatic action that would effectively bottle up the enemy's squadron. Before dawn on June 3 Lieutenant Richmond Pearson Hobson boarded the old collier *Merrimac,* loaded with 2,000 tons of coal and with a series of detonating charges around her hull, and steamed into the narrow harbor entrance to sink the hulk and bar passage to any ships. With a crew of seven picked volunteers, he entered the channel. When the *Merrimac's* bow touched bottom at the first bend, he swung her tiller so her stern would swing around and block the narrowest part of the entrance, but just as he reached that point, the Spanish forts awoke and opened a blistering fire on the ship. One shell disabled the steering gear. The *Merrimac* floated past the narrow entrance and sank in relatively deep water beyond, leaving a wide enough channel for ships to leave or enter the port. Miraculously, Hobson and his men escaped the withering Spanish fire and the explosion of their own derelict and swam about until they were picked up by Admiral Cervera himself, who, impressed with the gallant action, and pleased that it had failed, quickly arranged for their exchange to the American fleet.

The blockade was interrupted periodically to test the strength of shore installations. On June 6 the entire American force bombarded the batteries for two hours at close range. It suffered no casualties and silenced the Spanish guns in thirty minutes. On other days individual ships briefly exchanged shots with the shore guns to test their alertness and to try to improve their own accuracy. Each night the dynamite ship *Vesuvius*, equipped with pneumatic guns, sailed under the hills to propel 200-pound projectiles of guncotton over the hills at the hidden Spanish fleet, but as her range was limited and as her novel guns were notoriously inaccurate, little was accomplished.

Admiral Sampson then asked for troops to help him capture Santiago. "If 10,000 men were here, city and fleet would be ours within forty-eight hours," he cabled.* Spain had approximately 13,000 troops in Santiago, roughly the number which garrisoned Manila on the other side of the world. The contrast with Dewey's request was notable. He had asked for only 5,000 troops.

While these events were taking place in the Atlantic, the Spanish, so near to complete defeat, attempted one supreme effort to recapture Manila. As early as May 12 the Navy Department had asked Dewey if he needed a supply of submarine mines to defend Manila Bay in the event that a Spanish force should be sent out to attack him. At that time Cervera's destination was unknown and it was not beyond the realms of possibility that he might sail around the Horn for the Philippines. But Dewey, recalling the uselessness of the Spanish mines off Corregidor and believing that the deep water would make American mines equally unavailing, declined the offer.

*Knox, *op. cit.*, p. 350.

214

A week later a new rumor reached Washington, and on May 20 Dewey was notified that a Spanish admiral, Cámara, with the *Carlos V,* the *Pelayo,* and the *Alfonso XII,* together with a fleet of transports, had left Spain for the Far East. To the cables that reached him via Hong Kong and the *McCulloch,* he confidently replied:

I DO NOT CONSIDER SUBMARINE MINES PRACTICABLE HERE, ON ACCOUNT OF GREAT DEPTH AND WIDTH OF BAY AND ENTRANCE. IF ATTACKED BY SU-PERIOR FORCE, THE SQUADRON WILL ENDEAVOR TO GIVE GOOD ACCOUNT OF ITSELF. THE AMERICAN BARK SARANAC WAS CAPTURED OFF ILOILO, PHIL-IPPINE ISLANDS. UPON THE ARRIVAL OF THE CHARLESTON WITH AMMUNI-TION, I PROPOSE TO RECAPTURE AND TO CLEAR THE ISLANDS OF SMALL SPANISH GUN VESSELS. WHEN IS CHARLESTON EXPECTED TO ARRIVE? I RE-QUEST YOU WILL SEND TO THE ASIATIC STATION THE BENNINGTON AND YORKTOWN IF POSSIBLE. WILL BE MORE USEFUL THAN THE PHILADELPHIA. HOW MANY TROOPS COMING HERE ON PEKIN? WHEN EXPECTED TO ARRIVE? I REQUEST SEND PROVISIONS FOR THE SQUADRON, 2,000 MEN FOR THREE MONTHS. ALSO SMALL STORES.

About the same time soap was running low, and Dewey asked for 60,000 pounds, as well as for 20,000 pounds of tobacco and 2,000 suits of white clothing for his men.

During the next week Washington, becoming more concerned about the progress of Cámara's squadron, notified Dewey on May 27 and 30 that two monitors, the *Monterey* and the *Monadnock,* would be sent to reinforce him. Sending monitors, with their low freeboard, across the Pacific was a risky experiment. Ships of that type had never made a long ocean voyage, and the Navy Department took a chance necessitated by the shortage of more modern men-of-war.

While the threat from Cámara was still vague, Dewey worried because of the pressure exerted by the growing German fleet. Fearing that another battle might be forced upon him either by Spaniards or Germans, he cabled Secretary Long on June 12 asking that the departure of the monitors "be expedited." The cable was received in Washington June 17, and the next day Long replied:

THE SPANISH FLEET, TWO ARMORED CRUISERS, SIX CONVERTED CRUISERS, FOUR DESTROYERS, REPORTED OFF CEUTA, SAILING TO THE EAST, BY THE UNITED STATES CONSUL AT GIBRALTAR. IF THEY PASS SUEZ, EGYPT, WILL CABLE YOU. THE MONTEREY AND COLLIER SAILED FOR MANILA FROM SAN DIEGO ON JUNE 11. THE MONADNOCK AND COLLIER WILL FOLLOW JUNE 20 IF POSSIBLE. COULD YOU NOT HAVE VESSEL AT HONG KONG TO RECEIVE NOTICE CONCERNING SPANISH FLEET PASSING SUEZ? SECOND DIVISION OF THE ARMY EXPEDITION, ABOUT 3,500 MEN, IN FOUR STEAMERS, SAILED FROM SAN FRANCISCO AT NOON, JUNE 15. THE ARMY ESTIMATES THEY WILL MAKE AVERAGE SPEED 10 KNOTS PER HOUR, AND TOUCH TWO DAYS AT HONOLULU. SUSTAINED SEA SPEED SEEMS DOUBTFUL.

American agents throughout the Middle East forthwith began to harass Cámara as much as possible. Neutrality provisions in British possessions were invoked to prevent him from coaling, largely through the effort of Ambassador John Hay in London, who persuaded the English to delay Cámara's progress by raising diplomatic technicalities. When the Spaniard arrived at Port Said on June 26, Secretary Long cabled Dewey an itemized account of his strength:

CAMARA'S FLEET ARRIVED OFF PORT SAID JUNE 26 AND IS REPORTED BY OUR AGENT THERE AS FOLLOWS: PELAYO, CARLOS V., AUDAZ, AIRES, 10 GUNS, ISLA DE PANAY, 3 GUNS AND THREE UNARMED TRANSPORTS, COLON, COVA-DONGA AND SAN FRANCISCO. THEY WILL COAL IMMEDIATELY TO BE SUPPLIED BY CORY BROTHERS, WHOSE AGENTS ARE SAVON BAZUI. THE BOTTOM OF SHIPS APPARENTLY FOUL. A TELEGRAM FROM LIEUTENANT SIMS, NAVAL ATTACHE AT PARIS, JUNE 25, SAYS THAT SPECIAL AGENT NOW AT CARTAGENA REPORTS ONE TRANSPORT CARRIES MUNITIONS OF WAR, AIRES AND PANAY EACH ONE REGIMENT OF INFANTRY, AND SAN FRANCISCO ONE BATTALION MARINE INFANTRY. AUXILIARY FLEET HAS 20,000 TONS OF COAL. ALL CRUIS-ERS UNARMED EXCEPT RAPIDO, PATRIOTA, AND AIRES. THE UNITED STATES AUTHORITIES IN EGYPT HAVE PROTESTED AGAINST CAMARA TAKING COAL AND HE WILL BE DELAYED AS MUCH AS POSSIBLE. THE DEPARTMENT HAS ASKED THE STATE DEPARTMENT THAT ALL OF THE U. S. OFFICIALS ON THE ROUTE TO MANILA SHOULD RECEIVE ORDERS TO DELAY CAMARA AS MUCH AS POSSIBLE. RAPIDO AND PATRIOTA WERE FORMERLY NORMANNIA AND COLUMBIA, AND REPORTED EACH TO CARRY FOUR 6.2 INCH, FOUR 4.8 INCH, TWO 3¼ INCH, AND FOUR 37 MM. REVOLVING CANNON. OTHER REPORTS SAY MORE, BUT THAT IS DOUBTFUL. WE HAVE NOT THE PARTICULARS OF AIRES' BATTERY. CAMARA IS REPORTED NOT A VERY EFFICIENT MAN, BUT HE MAY HAVE GOOD OFFICERS.

The State Department's efforts were most helpful. Ethelbert Watts, United States Vice Consul at Cairo, protested vehemently and effectively to Lord Cromer, English adviser to the Egyptian government, against the stay of the Spanish squadron in Egyptian waters, whereupon the Egyptian government refused to sell Cámara more coal than enough to return to Spain. Since he had that much already, he was firmly requested to leave Port Said within twenty-four hours.

America was nervously watching the progress of Cámara's squadron. William Randolph Hearst, who, as one of the chief fomenters of the war, believed it his duty to see that it was carried to a successful conclusion, telegraphed Arthur Brisbane,* then in Egypt, to buy a ship "at any cost" and sink it in the Suez Canal, to block Cámara.

Cámara lingered in Port Said, endeavoring to enlist stokers to coal his

*George Dewey, *Autobiography*, p. 360. Mrs. Dewey identified the Hearst correspondent as Arthur Brisbane.

ships, but when Watts objected, the Egyptian government refused the Spaniard such a right, and he finally sailed away. He did not return to Spain, but continued on through the Suez Canal, stopping at the port of Suez, at the head of the Red Sea, July 1. When Egyptian authorities warned him away, he anchored five miles off the harbor, outside the three-mile limit and Egypt's control. Although coal had been refused him, he was still able to continue his voyage, for his colliers accompanied his fleet and could easily recoal the vessels in one of the Arabian ports of the Red Sea, where he loitered for seven days.

Admiral Dewey had no intention of making Montojo's mistake of waiting inside the bay to be attacked by Cámara's superior squadron. The *Pelayo* and the *Carlos V* alone approximated the entire tonnage of Dewey's fleet, and the Spanish guns, besides, could throw far more shells than the Americans. Dewey formed two possible plans of action. In Corregidor he saw a natural spot for a defensive action. There his fleet could attack the Spaniards as they maneuvered through the narrow entrance channel in a drawn-out column. If any American ships were damaged they could retire behind the rock to avoid complete destruction, while other United States ships continued to blast the Spaniards.

Dewey's second and more probable plan of operations was to sail among the southern Philippine islands and send small scouting vessels ahead to spot the Spanish fleet. As soon as it arrived he proposed to sally forth in a nautical ambush and attack the superior Spanish forces while they were strung out in scattered formation, hampered by their transports, and before they had an opportunity to recoal from their long journey.*

Newspaper correspondents in Manila Bay, slightly nervous about the advance of Cámara, asked Dewey what he would do if the Spaniards arrived.

"*Do?*" he answered. "Why go out and meet them and win another victory or a monument."†

But he had no opportunity, nor did the provocation arise. An army of 17,000 Americans, commanded by General Shafter, reached Cuba on June 20. Admiral Sampson urged an immediate assault of Santiago by ships and troops, an enterprise, which, based on the land and sea co-operation so thoroughly effective in the Civil War, might readily have conquered Santiago and Cervera's fleet. But Shafter, overestimating the size of the Spanish force, insisted upon landing at Daiquiri, twenty miles to the east, an operation which consumed five days in disembarking all

*Such tactics, employed by the Japanese Admiral Togo against the Russians in Tsushima Straits, resulted in the almost complete destruction of the Czar's fleet in 1905.
†Young, *Life and Heroic Deeds of Admiral Dewey*, p. 225.

troops and supplies, because many of the thirty-two army transports refused to come closer than twelve miles from shore.

The Army was ready to move and proceeded against Santiago on June 30. The next day Colonel Leonard Wood and Lieutenant Colonel Theodore Roosevelt led the Rough Riders on a heroic and triumphal charge up San Juan Hill, gaining control of a commanding height only three fourths of a mile from Santiago. The town, surrounded on the north and east, was ripe for plucking, but Shafter attempted to persuade Sampson to attack with the fleet. "The Navy," he said, "can now operate with less loss of life than I can."* He then informed the War Department that he could not attack the town and must retire his troops some five miles. Sampson, who had urged a joint action by Army and Navy to take the town, was irked by Shafter's stand, but to settle the dispute the two arranged a conference to take place at Daiquiri on the morning of July 3.

Sampson sailed eastward in the *New York* at nine o'clock that morning, leaving the blockading squadron under the temporary command of Commodore Schley.

It was an unfortunate time for his conference, for Cervera, informed by the Spanish general that Santiago was indefensible, had decided on a bold flight through the American squadron to avoid having his ships included in the surrender terms. Against such overwhelming odds, his heroic sortie was nothing short of suicidal. The torturous channel at the entrance forced his ships to file out one by one at ten-minute intervals. As soon as they emerged they would run headlong into the American battleships and cruisers off the entrance, yet he attempted the flight and sallied forth on the flagship *Maria Theresa* into a barrage of American guns. The *Iowa,* commanded by "Fighting Bob" Evans, fired the first shot at 9:35. Sampson heard it five miles away. The *New York* immediately turned westward in pursuit of the battle. The entire American squadron then began to fire upon the lone Spaniard. Powder from the guns blacked out the sky, and the ships had to maneuver in a dense cloud with visibility almost zero. The *Maria Theresa* headed straight for the cruiser *Brooklyn,* flagship of Commodore Schley, to whose starboard lay the *Texas,* commanded by Captain Philip, the *Iowa,* and the *Oregon.* As she headed southwest toward the *Brooklyn,* the three battleships turned to port to bring their guns to bear on her. In such close quarters the likelihood of collision was imminent, but if all the American ships turned in the same direction, the chances of a mixup were minimized. Schley, however, turned to the east at top speed through the black smoke.

Captain Philip, on the bridge of the *Texas,* suddenly saw Schley's

†Knox, *op. cit.,* p. 354.

218

vessel speeding right for his bow. The *Texas* could not turn east without hitting the *Iowa* and the *Oregon*. Philip had assumed that Schley would reason as he did and turn away from the other ships. For a moment it looked as if two American ships would be put out of the battle, but the *Texas* engines backed full speed astern, and they missed each other by inches. Meantime, the *Maria Theresa* was racing to the west and two more Spanish ships, the *Vizcaya* and the *Colon,* emerged from the harbor, following their flagship's lead. The American ships, firing madly through the smoke and din, paralleled their course further offshore. The *Brooklyn* lost ground after its eastward turn, but with its superior speed soon caught up with the fight and poured shells at the leading Spanish ships.

The *Iowa* raced 2,200 yards astern of the *Maria Theresa,* showering her with twelve-inch shells, while the *Brooklyn,* almost abreast of Cervera, dropped eight-inch shells on the flagship, which in less than an hour was blazing in the stern. When her steam pipes broke, escaping steam imperiled the crew. Then, her skipper, Captain Concas, having been seriously wounded, Admiral Cervera assumed personal command. Realizing the plight of his ship, he ran her ashore at 10:30, six miles west of Santiago, just as magazines began to explode and fires blanketed the ruined ship.

The *Vizcaya* and the *Colon* had avoided the American fire during its concentration on the *Maria Theresa* and had fled to the west, with the United States squadron in full pursuit. The speedy *Oregon* forced on all draft and kept even with the normally faster cruiser *Brooklyn,* followed by the *Texas* and the *Iowa.* Turrets of all four ships blasted at the fleeing Spanish vessels, while their after guns concentrated on a fourth, the *Oquendo,* which was no match for the American fire. At 10:35, only an hour after battle had been joined, she ran ashore half a mile west of the *Maria Theresa* and hauled down her colors.

The battleship *Indiana,* her boilers out of order, tried to keep up with the chase. Beside her, off the entrance of the bay, the converted yacht *Gloucester,* commanded by Lieutenant Commander Wainwright, awaited his chance. As executive officer of the sunken *Maine,* Wainwright had refused to go ashore in Havana, vowing he would not land on Cuban soil until he could do so with a party of Marines. Now his moment had come. As the destroyers *Pluton* and *Furor* appeared in the entrance channel, his guns, joined by those of the *Indiana* and by the secondary stern batteries of the *Oregon, Iowa,* and *Texas,* fired rapidly at their target. By this time Admiral Sampson in the *New York* had arrived. Under overwhelming American fire, the light Spanish ships succumbed. The *Pluton* scurried ashore, and the *Furor* sank after only a few minutes.

Now the American squadron concentrated its fire on the lumbering *Vizcaya,* which caught on fire a little after eleven. As she turned ashore to escape the shelling, a violent explosion blasted red and yellow smoke high into the air. The Spanish ensign at the stern dropped down, and sailors on the *Texas* shouted in triumph.

"Don't cheer boys, the poor fellows are dying," Captain Philip called out.* They quieted down as the *Texas* renewed the chase after the last Spanish ship, the speedy *Colon,* which had outdistanced the American squadron and was beyond range of the *Brooklyn's* guns. For almost two hours she raced away from her pursuers, until her supply of good coal gave out, forcing her captain to use a poorer grade from bunkers filled in Santiago. The steam pressure dropped, and the American ships closed in. From far astern thirteen-inch shells of the *Oregon* splattered the water around her. A pair of big shells lobbed over her masts, and with a great rending sound the wind rushed in to fill the vacuum created by the shell's trajectory. Realizing she was doomed, Commodore Paredes ran her ashore.

The battle, which had raged for three and a half hours, cost Spain seven ships sunk, 323 men killed, and 151 wounded. The American ships, on the other hand, were only slightly damaged. Their sides were blackened and many of their lifeboats were shattered by the explosion of shells, but the good fortune which had attended the fleet at Manila Bay operated at Santiago on July 3. One American was killed and one wounded. Never had a naval war been fought with so little loss of life.

The battle of Santiago virtually ended further Spanish resistance in the Atlantic as well as Admiral Cámara's cruise.

In the 1904 account Dewey claimed partial responsibility for Cámara's retreat. On June 27 he had cabled Secretary Long:

> HAVE RECEIVED INFORMATION CADIZ SQUADRON PASSED GIBRALTAR FRI-
> DAY MORNING, JUNE 17, BOUND EASTWARD. SHALL THE MONADNOCK AND
> MONTEREY ARRIVE IN TIME? IN MY JUDGMENT, IF THE COAST OF SPAIN WAS
> THREATENED, THE SQUADRON OF ENEMY WOULD HAVE TO RETURN.

In 1913, however, Dewey wrote that that cablegram reached the Navy Department "a few hours after the board of strategy had advised that Commodore Watson" be dispatched to the Spanish coast. Secretary Long wired Dewey on June 29 stating that Watson, with the *Iowa, Oregon, Yankee, Dixie, Newark, Yosemite,* and four colliers, was "preparing

---

*Frederick J. Bell, *Condition Red; Destroyer Action in the South Pacific* (New York: Longmans, Green & Co., 1943), p. 7. Captain Bell says he was told by a gunner who was there that Captain Philip had had a headache all through the battle of Santiago and actually said, "Belay that goddam racket. This is no madhouse."

with all possible dispatch to start for the Spanish coast. The Spaniards know this." Coupled with Sampson's victory, the threat alone forced Cámara to start home on July 8 and caused so much alarm in Spain that efforts to obtain peace were made through the French Ambassador, M. Jules Cambon.

In Cuba American troops which had survived through battle were dying in large numbers from yellow fever. Some 350 Americans died of battle wounds, and 2,560 succumbed to the fever. But despite the fatalities from poor sanitation and "embalmed bully beef," improperly packed, all that remained of the light-hearted war was General Miles' invasion of Puerto Rico, renowned to Finley Peter Dunne readers as Miles' "Midnight Excursion and Picnic."

The Atlantic theater of the Spanish-American War created heroes but none to compare with the Admiral in the Philippines. The glory of Sampson and Schley was greatly dimmed by the bitter dispute over credit for the victory and by earlier criticism of both men—Schley for his "retrograde movement" in June and his eastward turn during the battle of Santiago on June 3, Sampson for his absence at the crucial moment.

Perhaps the nearness of the Atlantic squadron to the Navy Department handicapped the commanders, a difficulty which Dewey, by cutting the Manila cable, managed to avoid. The Navy Board, composed of Rear Admirals Sicard and Crowninshield, Captain Barker, and Captain Mahan, was competent, but its absence from the scene of war necessarily hampered the movements of the fleet, for it ordered detailed maneuvers which would have been better left to the judgment of the commander-in-chief.

But if the two leaders failed to receive highest acclaim, at least the Cuban theater brought fame to some of the other officers: Lieutenant Rowan, who carried "the message to Garcia" through the Spanish lines; Captain Philip of the *Texas* for his compassionate "Don't cheer boys, the poor fellows are dying"; Lieutenant Richmond Hobson for his exploit in scuttling the *Merrimac* at Santiago; Captain Clark for his record-breaking run around the Horn; and Theodore Roosevelt for his attack on San Juan Hill.

Captain Charles V. Gridley, who lives in Dewey's order, "You may fire when you are ready, Gridley," did not live to enjoy his renown. The strain of the battle overtaxed Gridley's already weakened condition and he was adjudged too ill to continue his duties. On May 26 he left Manila Bay. He died at Kobe, Japan, on his way home.

The unquestioned hero of the entire war, however, was the man who in 114 minutes of battle had struck the first decisive blow.

23

OUR FLAG SHALL BE THERE

*E*milio Aguinaldo arrived in Manila Bay on May 19, 1898, aboard the American vessel *Nanshan*. The Filipino leader's career had been a stormy one. Born in Cavité of Chinese and Tagalog parents, he was educated at St. Tómas University in Manila, and while still a youth became mayor of old Cavité. In 1895, after the mysterious death of a Spanish sergeant named Seville, apparently his rival for the affections of a beautiful native girl, Aguinaldo disappeared. The next year, at the outbreak of an insurrection against Spain, the latest in a long history of rebellions, the diminutive half-breed emerged as the nominal leader, but the affair ended with his acceptance of a $400,000 bribe from the Spanish and a promise to persuade his fellow revolutionists never to rise again.

The spring of 1898 found him in Singapore, ready to sail to Europe to enjoy his fortune, which he had refused to divide with his fellow revolutionists on the grounds that Spain might fail to keep her promises of more liberal rule and a fund for a new uprising would then be necessary. When war between Spain and the United States seemed certain, he boarded the first boat for Hong Kong, hoping to sail into Manila with the American squadron.

Waiting in Hong Kong until May 6, when the *McCulloch* arrived with the news of the May Day victory, he asked Lieutenant Brumby's permission to go to Cavité. Without authority for such a step, Brumby refused, but reported to the Admiral the desire of Aguinaldo and several other insurgent leaders to come to the Philippines. Since the insurgents might be of some aid, Dewey sent Ensign Caldwell to Hong Kong with orders to bring back Aguinaldo and a few of his colleagues. Edwin Wildman, Vice-Consul General at Hong Kong, who accompanied the leader on the return trip, remarked later on his imperiousness and on his manner of an exiled monarch returning to claim his hereditary rights. At that time, according to Wildman, Aguinaldo dreamed of a native government, "independent," but "under American advisers."*

When the little man called upon Admiral Dewey he "appeared much discouraged at the situation, so much so, in fact, that he requested the Admiral to let him leave again for Japan," but Dewey requested him to remain, allowing him to establish headquarters in the Cavité arsenal, where he promptly opened negotiations with his Filipino friends. In only a few days he rallied a thousand men to his cause. Soon their visits became such a nuisance to the Marine officer in charge of the arsenal guard that Dewey ordered Aguinaldo to remove his headquarters to Cavité town. Within a week he informed Dewey he had a force sufficient to battle the Spaniards and persuaded the Admiral to lend his men some condemned arms, a few Mauser rifles, abandoned by the Spanish at Cavité, and an obsolete smoothbore gun. This he wished to float across the bay for a western attack on Manila, but the Admiral demurred.

Dewey's policy was to allow the Filipinos to fight the Spanish on the neck of land leading to Cavité, thus forcing the Spaniards back toward Manila. The insurgents began their advance from Cavité near the end of May. Every night firing on shore marked their slow progress toward the city five miles away, and every night they made a little progress toward Manila.

From the very first the status of Aguinaldo offered a perplexing problem, and Washington, in a quandary because it did not yet know whether the United States would take the Philippines or give them independence, determined to do nothing which would bind its future course. On May 26 Secretary Long cabled Dewey as follows:

YOU MUST EXERCISE DISCRETION MOST FULLY IN ALL MATTERS, AND BE GOVERNED ACCORDING TO CIRCUMSTANCES WHICH YOU KNOW AND WE CANNOT KNOW. YOU HAVE OUR CONFIDENCE ENTIRELY. IT IS DESIRABLE, AS FAR AS POSSIBLE AND CONSISTENT WITH YOUR SUCCESS AND SAFETY, NOT TO HAVE POLITICAL ALLIANCES WITH THE INSURGENTS OR ANY FACTION IN THE ISLANDS THAT WOULD INCUR LIABILITY TO MAINTAIN THEIR CAUSE IN THE FUTURE.

Dewey replied to this message on June 3:

RECEIPT OF TELEGRAM OF MAY 26 IS ACKNOWLEDGED, AND I THANK THE DEPARTMENT FOR THE EXPRESSION OF CONFIDENCE. HAVE ACTED ACCORDING TO THE SPIRIT OF THE DEPARTMENT'S INSTRUCTIONS THEREIN FROM THE BEGINNING, AND I HAVE ENTERED INTO NO ALLIANCE WITH THE INSURGENTS OR WITH ANY FACTION. THIS SQUADRON CAN REDUCE THE DEFENSES OF MANILA AT ANY MOMENT, BUT IT IS CONSIDERED USELESS UNTIL THE ARRIVAL OF SUFFICIENT UNITED STATES FORCES TO RETAIN POSSESSION.

*Edwin Wildman, *Aguinaldo* (Boston: Lothrop, Lee & Shepard Co., 1901).

Again on June 14 Long wired Dewey to make sure that he was not committing the nation to an alliance it might not wish to honor:

> REPORT FULLY ANY CONFERENCE, RELATIONS, OR CO-OPERATIONS, MILI-TARY OR OTHERWISE, WHICH YOU HAVE HAD WITH AGUINALDO AND KEEP INFORMED THE DEPARTMENT IN THAT RESPECT.

Dewey received the cable some days later. It was not until June 27 that his answer reached the Secretary:

> RECEIPT OF TELEGRAM OF JUNE 14 IS ACKNOWLEDGED. AGUINALDO, INSUR-GENT LEADER, WITH THIRTEEN OF HIS STAFF, ARRIVED MAY 19, BY PERMIS-SION, ON NANSHAN. ESTABLISHED SELF CAVITE, OUTSIDE ARSENAL, UNDER THE PROTECTION OF OUR GUNS, AND ORGANIZED HIS ARMY. I HAVE HAD SEVERAL CONFERENCES WITH HIM, GENERALLY OF A PERSONAL NATURE. CONSISTENTLY HAVE REFRAINED FROM ASSISTING HIM IN ANY WAY WITH THE FORCE UNDER MY COMMAND, AND ON SEVERAL OCCASIONS I HAVE DE-CLINED REQUESTS THAT I SHOULD DO SO, TELLING HIM THE SQUADRON COULD NOT ACT UNTIL THE ARRIVAL OF THE UNITED STATES TROOPS. AT THE SAME TIME, I HAVE GIVEN HIM TO UNDERSTAND THAT I CONSIDER IN-SURGENTS AS FRIENDS, BEING OPPOSED TO A COMMON ENEMY. HE HAS GONE TO ATTEND A MEETING OF INSURGENT LEADERS FOR THE PURPOSE OF FORM-ING A CIVIL GOVERNMENT. AGUINALDO HAS ACTED INDEPENDENTLY OF THE SQUADRON, BUT HAS KEPT ME ADVISED OF HIS PROGRESS, WHICH HAS BEEN WONDERFUL. I HAVE ALLOWED TO PASS BY WATER RECRUITS, ARMS AND AMMUNITION, AND TO TAKE SUCH SPANISH GUNS AND AMMUNITION FROM THE ARSENAL AS HE NEEDED. HAVE ADVISED FREQUENTLY TO CONDUCT THE WAR HUMANELY, WHICH HE HAS DONE INVARIABLY. MY RELATIONS WITH HIM ARE CORDIAL, BUT I AM NOT IN HIS CONFIDENCE. THE UNITED STATES HAS NOT BEEN BOUND IN ANY WAY TO ASSIST INSURGENTS BY ANY ACT OR PROMISES, AND HE IS NOT, TO MY KNOWLEDGE, COMMITTED TO ASSIST US. I BELIEVE HE EXPECTS TO CAPTURE MANILA WITHOUT MY AS-SISTANCE, BUT I DOUBT ABILITY, THEY NOT YET HAVING MANY GUNS. IN MY OPINION, THESE PEOPLE ARE FAR SUPERIOR IN THEIR INTELLIGENCE AND MORE CAPABLE OF SELF-GOVERNMENT THAN THE NATIVES OF CUBA, AND I AM FAMILIAR WITH BOTH RACES.

The Admiral was handling the problem with the greatest delicacy, distinguishing with care between friendly assistance, which would help his own cause, and outright alliance, which would have implied recognition of belligerency and the corporate rights of a Filipino state. To Aguinaldo, however, untutored in the nuances of diplomatic usage, Dewey's early friendship seemed tantamount to recognition of him as a chief of a state.

Dewey was especially careful never to put anything in writing, a step which permitted Aguinaldo later to allege that he had received from the Admiral numerous promises of sovereignty. During the early days of the

The Battleship *Maine*, one of the United States' first ships of the line, sunk in
Havana Harbor February 17, 1898.

The U.S.S. *Dewey*, named for Admiral George Dewey, and launched in 1934.
This destroyer, sleek and fast, is typical of World War II "tin cans."

Filipinos' warfare against Spain, it was necessary to negotiate with Aguinaldo concerning the disposition of Spanish women and children taken prisoners by the insurgents. Dewey had received a request from Governor General Augustin Davila early in June asking him to secure passage through insurgent lines for several Spanish families. Aguinaldo promptly granted the request in a classic letter:

DEAR SIR:
I would have great satisfaccion in pleasing you what you are asking me to allow the free return to Manila some Spanish families resident in Pampanga specially the General Mr. B. Augustin's.
I must remember you that the said province my forces have not taken yet, but only surrounded; reason for which I see the impossibility to may garantee the free pass that you ask.
Notwithstanding I give to my subordinates terminat orders that as soon as they get in their hands the said families, not only keep the habit consideration among the civilizes nations, and also treat them as friends and carry them to Manila, as soon as the way will be safed from any risk, so as the families and their conveyers and the plan of operations would allow. I am, Dear Sir,

Yours respectfully,
E. AGUINALDO.

A few days later, quick to make use of his growing feeling of importance, he appeared aboard the *Olympia* in uniform to pay formal respects to the American commander-in-chief. Carrying a gold-mounted cane, which Spaniards considered the symbol of a field officer's authority, and accompanied by his staff dressed in homemade uniforms, Aguinaldo assumed the airs of the leader of a state. Dewey was amused, but he took pains to forego any military honors to the ragamuffin band that might be construed as official recognition.

Skirmishes between Spaniards and Filipinos continued almost daily. On May 29, after a fierce assault against the Spanish garrison in Bakor Church in Old Cavité,* halfway to Manila, the Spaniards surrendered. The insurgents then installed several old cannon in Cavité and peppered the Spanish positions so violently that the Spaniards fled back toward Manila. It was hard to understand how 13,000 Spanish troops with modern equipment could have failed to annihilate the 1,000 or more Filipinos, but the insurgents' guerrilla tactics kept their losses low, and the Spaniards, probably to avoid casualties, adopted the Fabian policy of withdrawing toward Manila, apparently waiting for the American armies to come and conquer them. The insurgents fought so well that

*Stickney, *Life and Glorious Deeds of Admiral Dewey*, pp. 76–81.

by the end of May Cavité province was cleared of Spaniards. In Manila, nearly surrounded, panic spread, especially among the European Consuls, who appealed to Admiral Dewey to evacuate all their subjects. Dewey at first planned to quarter the refugees in Cavité, but then, fearing congestion when American armies should arrive, he arranged to have the Consuls charter fourteen steamers in the bay as temporary quarters. One group, together with almost five hundred Chinese, was permitted to sail for Amoy, China, on an English steamer. Ten of the other vessels were reserved for English, French, German, and other European civilians. The last three were reserved for Spanish women and children and placed under the protection of English, French, and German men-of-war in the bay. Dewey also arranged safe conduct for several hundred Spanish wounded to a hospital ship. Indeed, although Manila was a city at war, and commercially isolated from the rest of the world, in every instance not affecting the blockade, Admiral Dewey granted requests for privileges with a liberality which surprised neutral onlookers.

Whatever his ultimate plans, Aguinaldo issued a proclamation in May calculated to maintain a friendly American attitude:

> The Great North American nation, the cradle of genuine liberty, and therefore the friend of our people, oppressed and enslaved by the tyranny and despotism of its rulers, has come to us manifesting a protection as decisive as it is undoubtedly disinterested towards our inhabitants, considering us as sufficiently civilized and capable of governing for ourselves our unfortunate country. In order to maintain this high estimate granted us by the generous North American nation, we should abominate all those deeds which tend to lower this opinion, which are pillage, theft and all sorts of crimes leading to persons or property, with the purpose of avoiding international conflicts during the period of our campaign.

Relations grew strained only after American land reinforcements began to lay plans for taking Manila without insurgent help. The first troops arrived aboard three transports on June 30, escorted by the cruiser *Charleston,* a welcome addition to Dewey's fleet.* A second contingent of 3,600 soldiers arrived aboard four transports under command of General F. V. Greene. News of the victory at Santiago was brought by the Japanese Cruiser *Naniwa Kan.* Admiral Dewey's reaction was curious. "Do you believe," he asked a newspaperman, "that the American people

---

*On the passage the *Charleston* captured Guam. Dewey immediately urged Secretary Long, in a cable dated July 1, 1898, to fortify Guam.

will still remember us for what we have done, and not put us behind those who were at Santiago?"*

General Greene's men were landed the next day at Paranaque, a position more than halfway from Cavité to Manila, which the insurgents had reached in their drive. For some strange reason the Spaniards did not molest the landings. Adhering to their agreement not to shell the American fleet unless it shelled Manila first, the Spaniards watched silently and without opposition for four days while American soldiers were landed with their supplies. The Americans took up positions just beyond the sandy beach in a place guarded against sudden attack by rice paddy fields and dense tropical underbrush. Encampments were established there, within range of the Spanish fieldpieces but beyond the range of Mauser fire, and still the enemy made no move to interrupt the leisurely establishment of tents, camp equipage, ammunition dumps, and guns.

By then, despite their flimsy arms and organization, the insurgents had pushed along the beach almost to the outer fortifications of Manila and had invested the city on the inland side as well, an advance which enabled American troops to camp within a few miles of the city, within easy striking distance of the Spanish forts. But Aguinaldo's successes increased his arrogance and his demands. Having captured a number of small boats and junks, he formed a miniature navy to transport troops around the bay for operations on either side of Manila, movements of which Admiral Dewey was kept informed by a native named Gonzaga, "a little fellow who worked on the railroad and used to paddle down the bay in a banco at night and tell me about the movements of the insurgents."†

Soon Aguinaldo's little fleet adopted a national flag, designed after the rising sun of Japan, which had aided Aguinaldo in his revolutionary career.‡ As the tiny ships steamed about the harbor with the new flags flying in the wind, Admiral Dewey became more and more annoyed. One day a Filipino steamer left Cavité and crossed the bay with a load of troops. To meet his regulations that every ship receive his permission before leaving anchorage, the Filipino steamer headed straight for the *Olympia,* but its inexperienced skipper failed to turn, and the boat seemed ready to crash into the side of the American flagship. Dewey, on the afterdeck at the time, boiled over. In the face of a seemingly inevitable collision he ordered the sailors to man the guns, but just as the men were ready to blow the boat out of the water, the Filipino pilot veered away.§

*Barrett, *Admiral George Dewey*, pp. 22–23.
†Wildman, *op. cit.*
‡Aguinaldo, after forty years of exile in Japan, returned to the Philippines with the Japanese conquerors in 1942.
§Barrett, *op. cit.*, pp. 171–73.

After repeated excursions in which the insurgent "navy," sailed too close to the *Olympia,* Dewey ordered all the native captains to report aboard the *Olympia.* When the ragged, nondescript group of naval officers appeared on the quarter-deck, the American Admiral read them the riot act.

The Filipino flag, he told them emphatically, was not recognized by the United States, and the presence of the little boats around the American squadron was not desired. As the warning was translated by a Filipino interpreter, one of the native captains grumbled a few words in native dialect.

"What did he say?" demanded Dewey of the interpreter.

"He says, sir, that he'll get even with you."

Dewey turned red with fury.

"Throw that man overboard," he shouted. Two brawny American sailors picked up the little native captain and heaved him high over the starboard rail. Dewey started toward his cabin as the native splashed in the bay. For a few days thereafter the Filipino captains took care to stay away from the *Olympia.*

On the whole, Dewey had great regard for the capacities of the natives, whom he considered well able to govern themselves. But for Aguinaldo, who had once been bribed with Spanish gold, he entertained ill-concealed contempt. Perhaps an insurgent leader of a different order might have changed the whole subsequent course of the Philippine campaign.

On July 25, when Major General Wesley Merritt arrived at Manila Bay, the two officers sat at luncheon in the Admiral's cabin and discussed their plans. Dewey advised the general that any attack on Manila should be delayed at least until the monitor *Monterey's* arrival. The Germans were "behaving nastily" and there was possible danger of intervention by von Diedrichs. Aguinaldo, too, was beginning "to show the cloven hoof."

More important, however, the commander-in-chief was quietly conducting negotiations with the Spanish governor for the peaceable surrender of Manila, which had for some time been without food as a result of the blockade enforced by insurgent lines on the land side and by the guns of Dewey's fleet at sea. As early as May Governor General Augustin Davila had intimated to the British Consul Rawson-Walker his willingness to surrender the town. But without sufficient forces to occupy it himself, and unwilling to allow the insurgents to do so, Dewey had not considered the proposal. In July Rawson-Walker became very ill and in the second week of August he died. Monsieur Edouard André, the Belgian Consul at Manila, assumed his duties as intermediary between the enemy commanders, and now that troops were arriving, Dewey was ready to broach the subject of peaceful capitulation. M. André saw Davila, who seemed more than willing. On August 1, however, Madrid relieved Davila of his command, appointing General Jaudenes to succeed him. The change convinced Dewey's chief advisers, Lamberton and Brumby, that a heated battle for the city could not be avoided.

General Merritt agreed with them but was willing to defer to Dewey's judgment and agreed to suspend operations until it was evident whether the Spanish were sincere in their talk of peace.

Meanwhile, the newly arrived troops grew restless for action. Upon Merritt's accession to command, arrangements to move the insurgents out of the Americans' way were begun. Under General Greene's diplomatic pressure, Aguinaldo and the insurgents abandoned the shore trenches in favor of American troops, who found their predecessors' shallow rifle pits incorrectly placed for attack and who immediately dug deeper and more formidable trenches about 100 yards nearer the Spanish garrison in San Antonio Fort. For three days, although only 1,000 yards away, they were unmolested. Then, realizing the threat of the American position, the Spanish opened fire during the night of July 31. To the Navy, it seemed just like all the previous skirmishes between the insurgents and the Spaniards, but to the green recruits the sudden explosions were terrifying. The Spaniards maintained a brisk musketry and artillery fire for two hours without advancing from the fort, and killed ten and wounded thirty Americans. American strategy called for no attacks until the proper moment, and Generals Merritt and Greene ordered their men not to return the fire unless the Spanish sallied forth. During the next week the Spaniards opened fire three nights without an American countermove. Four thousand more Americans, under General Arthur MacArthur, landed that week. The troops chafed at the restraint, anxious to attack, but Dewey, who had spent weeks perfecting his plans, did not propose to have them upset by premature action. He urged delay until ammunition dumps were piled on land and until the *Monterey,* with her two twelve-inch and two ten-inch guns, was overhauled to help in the bombardment, and perhaps even help fight the German fleet as well.

Negotiations for a peaceful surrender of the city continued. M. André, the Belgian Consul, cajoled and argued with Spanish General Jaudenes to convince him of the futility of resistance. Manila was starving. Its defenses were weak, its army was in an exhausted condition, and since news of Admiral Cámara's return to Spain, Spanish morale was utterly destroyed. Despair stalked among troops and civilians alike. But since General Augustin Davila had been replaced because of his despairing reports to his government, his successor was committed to at least a token defense in order to save face.

Jaudenes, therefore, although refusing to consider capitulation without the formality of an attack, agreed that the Manila batteries would not fire upon the United States squadron if it in turn refrained from shelling the city. He arranged, in case of surrender, to fly a white flag from a selected spot inside the walls. As a prior signal it was agreed that Dewey would fly the flags indicating "D.W.H.B." meaning "Surrender." Sketches of the signal flags and of the building from which the white flag would fly were given both parties to this unusual agreement. Through M. André, Admiral Dewey warned the Spaniard that the generosity of surrender terms would depend largely upon the brevity of resistance. Parleys with the low-spirited defenders continued until the day of the actual attack.

August 10 was selected as invasion day. Forty-eight hours before, Dewey and Merritt wrote General Jaudenes a letter, politely informing him of the coming assault:

SIR:

We have the honor to notify Your Excellency that operations of the land and naval forces of the United States against the defenses of Manila may begin at any time after the expiration of forty-eight hours from the hour of receipt by you of this communication, or sooner if made necessary by an attack on your part.

This notice is given in order to afford you an opportunity to remove all noncombatants from the city.

With equal politeness Jaudenes replied:

GENTLEMEN:

I have the honor to inform Your Excellencies that at half-past twelve today I received the notice with which you favor me, that after forty-eight hours have elapsed you may begin operations against this fortified city, or at an earlier hour if the forces under your command are attacked by mine.

As your notice is sent for the purpose of providing for the safety of noncombatants, I give thanks to your excellencies for the humane sentiments you have shown, and state that, finding myself surrounded by insurrectionary forces, I am without places of refuge for the increased numbers of wounded, sick, women and children, who are now lodged within the walls.

Very respectfully, and kissing the hands of your excellencies,

FERMIN JAUDENES
Governor General and Captain General of the Philippines.

The Americans answered this profuse communication on August 9:

The inevitable suffering in store for the wounded, sick, women and children, in the event that it becomes our duty to reduce the defenses of the walled town in which they are gathered, will, we feel assured, appeal successfully to the sympathies of a general capable of making the determined and prolonged resistance which your excellency has exhibited after the loss of your naval forces, and without hope of succor.

We therefore submit, without prejudice to the high sentiments of honor and duty which your excellency entertains, that surrounded on every side as you are by constantly increasing force, with a powerful fleet in your front, and deprived of all prospect of reinforcement and assistance, a most useless sacrifice of life would result in the event of an attack, and therefore every consideration of humanity makes it imperative that you should not subject your city to the horrors of bombardment. Accordingly, we demand the surrender of the city of Manila, and the Spanish forces under your command.

In his next reply Jaudenes omitted "kissing your excellencies' hands," and informed them that the Manila council of defense was unable to authorize a capitulation.

But taking account of the most exceptional circumstances existing in this city which your excellencies recite, and which I unfortunately have to admit, I would consult my government if your excellencies will grant the time strictly necessary for this communication by way of Hong Kong.

The American commanders promptly rejected this request and made ready for the attack August 10. In his correspondence Dewey had taken care that a veiled hint of bombardment and shelling the town was changed to the phrase "reduce the defenses of the city."*

"It is necessary for us to remember that we are making history," he told newspapermen discussing the question. "If we left in words which implied no respect for noncombatants, women and children and property, we would be censured for it by the future historian." All responsibility for any bombardment would therefore rest upon the enemy.

Preparations for the onslaught were made on August 9. Admiral Dewey ordered all foreign men-of-war and commercial steamers away from the anchorages off the city. The English and Japanese ships shifted their anchorages to Cavité, near the United States squadron, but the Germans moved north of the city, where Dewey considered their position a possible menace to his own maneuvers. During that day the American fleet cleared for action. Boats and extra gear were landed at Cavité, the *Concord* and the *Petrel* were sent across the bay to the vicinity of the German

*Barrett, *op. cit.*, pp. 150–51.

ships, more or less as a counterthreat, and the next morning they moved between the Germans and the city.

The morning of August 10 dawned clear. The American fleet stood at general quarters, with steam up and battle flags rolled at the mastheads, ready to break out at a signal. Flags went up on the *Olympia,* and all over the squadron eyes turned to read the message.

"The attack is postponed," it read. An audible murmur of disappointment spread from ship to ship at more delay after 102 days of weary waiting. Worse than that was the ignominy of steaming out for action and returning to port without firing a shot. Dewey, however, maintaining his composure, merely sighed and remarked that it was "too bad" the Army, "after doing its best," was not ready.* What he said to Captain Lamberton in his cabin is not known.

Two more dreary days passed, while soldiers sweated on the mosquito-ridden beaches and sailors sweltered on shipboard. On the twelfth it was announced the assault would be delivered the next day. It rained at intervals that humid night. No one slept. On August 13 the sky cleared, and a refreshing breeze swept across the water.

The fleet got under way at 8:45 and steamed to its appointed positions off the city. As the gray *Olympia* slipped her moorings and headed north, bluejackets on the *Immortalite* swarmed to the rail while the British band struck up the air of "Under the Double Eagle," Dewey's favorite march. It was at this point that the English squadron, following the American ships past the city, slipped between them and the German ships, which had raised anchor and were heading south.

The American ships steamed slowly, majestically across the bay. As they approached the city, every man went to his battle station. The *Olympia,* the *Raleigh,* the *Petrel,* and the *Callao* took up positions off Fort San Antonio, two miles south of the city of Manila, where they commanded the fort, its magazine, and the Spanish entrenchments. The *Charleston,* the *Boston,* and the *Baltimore* steamed to a point opposite the Luneta battery, while the *Concord* and the heavily armed monitor *Monterey* steamed in nearer the city's batteries. General Merritt directed land movements from the *Zafiro,* which had been detailed as his general headquarters for the attack.

The Admiral, calmly puffing at a cigar on the *Olympia's* bridge, watched the Army's troops advancing through fields and along the beaches. At 9:35 he gave the signal to fire. With a roar the *Olympia's* eight-inch guns sent shells whining into the fort. The four ships off Fort Antonio maintained a steady, slow bombardment for an hour, without an answering

*Barrett, *op. cit.,* p. 149.

shot from the batteries. The warships off the city held their fire, waiting for the enemy to start the battle, but General Jaudenes kept to his promise. Neither the Manila nor the Luneta batteries fired once on the American ships.

The little *Callao*, commanded by Lieutenant Bon Tappan, and the smaller *Barcelo*, skippered by Naval Cadet White, moved close to shore, just ahead of the advancing soldiers, and swept the beaches and Spanish trenches with their machine guns. The men followed, racing from one point of cover to the next, meeting little opposition on the way. At 10:32 they reached the parapets, and the ships ceased fire. With the final rush the troops swarmed over the earthworks and bayoneted their way through the defenses. The red and yellow Spanish flag came tumbling down. An American flag went up, and as it floated above the fort, bluejackets sent up lusty cheers from the ships.

The *Olympia*, with the *Petrel* and the *Raleigh* just astern, headed for the city a few minutes later and arrived off the Pasig River at eleven o'clock. The signal flags "D.W.H.B." flew at her mast. Firing of small arms and fieldpieces echoed from the southern edges of the city, but no white flag floated from the doomed fort. Men on the flagship scanned every building in the town for a sign of it. Finally, at 11:20, the Admiral made out the flag of surrender fluttering from the southwest bastion of the walls, and a mighty cheer echoed above the ships as Lieutenant Brumby, Colonel Whittier, and Consul André jumped into a small boat to arrange preliminary terms of capitulation.

"You have given me no orders, sir," Brumby called out as he left.

"I leave it all to you," the Admiral replied airily. "Do whatever you think best. Whatever General Merritt wants will be acceptable to me."*

As American units steadily advanced through the southeast part of town, the Spanish soldiers threw their guns away and retreated into the city. The insurgents of Aguinaldo, deprived of a final fight against the capital city, stormed up to the American lines in order to march in with the United States troops.

Brumby returned to the flagship at 2:20, bringing with him capitulation terms. The ships, which had been cruising at slow speed, ready to fire in the event of renewed fighting, dropped anchor off the city. Presently, catching sight of a Spanish flag still flying high from the citadel, the Admiral sent Lieutenant Brumby, with two signal boys as an escort, ashore once more, carrying the largest ensign to be found aboard the *Olympia*. Pushing his way through panic-stricken mobs and Spanish sol-

*Barrett, *op. cit.*, pp. 154–55.

diers, still carrying their guns, Brumby entered the citadel, marched to the plaza, and hauled down the Spanish colors.

At 5:43 the men on the ships saw the Stars and Stripes rise above the government building. The guns of every ship fired a twenty-one gun salute. In the plaza a band from an Oregon regiment struck up the national anthem as American officers and men stood at attention, saluting the American flag flying for the first time in history over an Oriental empire.

The next morning Admiral Dewey formally notified the commanders of foreign squadrons that the city had been occupied and that the port was open. Manila was his.

In view of the long wait and the thorough preparations for a major offensive, it had been exceedingly easy. In all, ten American soldiers were killed and sixty-eight wounded. Almost 13,000 Spaniards had surrendered, and more than 20,000 stands of arms were recovered by the Americans. The details of the surrender were worked out by a commission representing the Army, the Navy, and the Spanish. Captain Lamberton represented the Admiral. The terms allowed officers to retain their side arms, horses, and private property, but all enlisted men were to lay down their guns, while the city, its inhabitants, churches, educational establishments, and all property were placed under the "safeguard of the faith and honor of the American Army."

Inspecting the town two days later, the Admiral found everything tranquil and orderly. Civilians had resumed their peaceful occupations, and, save for American sentries, there was no indication that a sovereignty of 377 years' duration had been changed.

On August 13 (August 12 in Washington), just before the Army had stormed Manila, a peace protocol had been signed between the United States and Spain which provided that the United States, pending the conclusion of a treaty of peace to determine the control and disposition of the Philippine Islands, occupy and hold the city of Manila, the bay, and harbor. Ironically enough, if the Manila cable had been intact the attack on the city would never have occurred. "No interruption to the fateful progress of affairs," was therefore offered, the report of 1904 editorialized. "To those who for three months had been awaiting such a consummation, it was a matter of infinite satisfaction that the result was due to the guns of our fleet, to the bravery of our troops, and to the threatened demonstration on the Spanish coast rather than to the efforts of diplomacy."

The *Zafiro* left for Hong Kong the next morning with a cable announcing the second victory. Two days later the *Monadnock* arrived, bringing news of the armistice. For the first time in months the ships were lighted at night. The broken cable, brought up from the bottom of the bay, was spliced together, and once more Manila could speak directly to the outer world. The war was over.

On the twenty-second the *Zafiro* returned with provisions and mail for the squadron. Among the messages was one from President William McKinley:

RECEIVE FOR YOURSELF AND FOR THE OFFICERS, SAILORS AND MARINES OF YOUR COMMAND MY THANKS AND CONGRATULATIONS AND THOSE OF THE NATION FOR THE GALLANT CONDUCT ALL HAVE AGAIN SO CONSPICUOUSLY DISPLAYED.

"The grand result had now been achieved." The conquest of the archipelago had been swift and cheap. The toil of consolidating an empire remained ahead.

24

NO REST FOR A HERO

Of the 7,083 islands of the Philippine archipel-
ago, most are merely rocks jutting above the sea. Only 466 are more than
one square mile in size. In 1898 their eight million native inhabitants
coped with the hazards of fevers, volcanoes, tropical jungles, and wild
animals, but the mineral and vegetable assets of the islands offered promising prospects for an exploiting and civilizing western power. Gold,
copper, tin, platinum, and iron lay beneath the tropical growths. Sulphur,
gypsum, and marble in rich abundance waited for development. Pearl
fishing, rice paddies, and sugar-cane plantations had flourished under
Spanish rule, yet on the whole the vast potentialities of their possessions
were never realized by the Spaniards. Indeed, the natural resources of the
islands were so little known that the United States scarcely interested
itself during the fighting of the Spanish War in acquiring the lands.
Even when the peace protocol was signed, the government had not
decided whether to keep the Philippines, give them independence, restore
them to Spain, or turn them over to some other European power.

After the battle of Manila Bay President McKinley had seriously
considered retaining one island as a naval base, and Admiral Dewey suggested Manila and the island of Luzon, largest in the islands. Notwithstanding, few Americans were ready to take on the responsibilities that
ownership involved. The United States had fought the war primarily for
Cuba, although Dewey's victory quickly launched a movement to annex
the new-won lands.*

Dewey, who from the very first appreciated the importance of establishing a co-operative program, was confirmed in his view when, shortly

---

*Location of the Asiatic squadron at Manila immediately forced the construction of
Pearl Harbor as a halfway station and naval base in the Pacific. On July 7, 1898, the
Senate adopted the Newlands resolution annexing the Hawaiian Islands. Meanwhile a
move to rename the Philippines the Dewey Islands failed, and, as a compromise, the
seashore drive in Manila was named Dewey Boulevard. In 1942 the Japanese changed
this to "Peace Boulevard."

after August 13, as a result of American refusal to allow the insurgents to share in the final assault on the city or to occupy it jointly, his relations with Aguinaldo underwent a radical change. From that day the native leader and his men transferred enmity from Spain to the United States preparatory to a new revolt.

On August 20 Dewey cabled Secretary Long:

> I TRUST IT MAY NOT BE NECESSARY TO ORDER ME TO WASHINGTON. SHOULD REGRET VERY MUCH TO LEAVE HERE WHILE MATTERS REMAIN IN PRESENT CRITICAL CONDITION.

A week later the Navy Department informed him:

> THE PRESIDENT . . . WILL RESPECT YOUR WISHES AND NOT DIRECT YOU TO LEAVE YOUR PRESENT DUTY. HE DESIRES YOU TO COMMUNICATE TO GENERAL MERRITT YOUR VIEWS UPON THE GENERAL QUESTION OF THE PHILIPPINES, WITH SUCH INFORMATION AS YOU HAVE, AND TO TRANSMIT TO THE PRESIDENT IN WRITING BY THE QUICKEST METHOD* THE SUBSTANCE OF YOUR SUGGESTIONS TO MERRITT.

The Admiral remained aboard the *Olympia* in Manila Bay for nearly a year longer, never leaving the islands, although every ship and every officer was afforded brief rests and change of climate in Hong Kong. When the *Olympia* went to China for a change of scene, Dewey transferred his flag to the *Boston* and remained at his post. "Whatever merit there was in untiring devotion to work while there was work to do," he wrote, "I might rightfully claim as an expression of gratitude for the honor which my country had bestowed upon me."†

The peace commission met in Paris on October 1. For America, Judge William R. Day, retiring Secretary of State; Senator Cushman K. Davis, Senator William P. Frye, Senator George Gray, and Whitelaw Reid served as commissioners. Señor Don Eugenio Montero Rios, President of the Spanish Senate, represented the beaten power of Spain.

For more than two months the commissioners argued. At times it appeared that a settlement could not be agreed upon, and that war must be resumed. America was still uncertain about its course concerning the Philippines, and Spain insisted that the islands be returned to her dominion. At this point Aguinaldo proclaimed himself dictator, and insurgents announced that they would slay every Spaniard they could seize. The British government meanwhile learned that Spain was preparing to sell the islands to a European power. During November, in fact, Spanish

*Possibly by hand of Merritt.
†George Dewey, *Autobiography*, p. 287.

bonds rose because of a report that she would turn them over to France, whereupon England maintained that no nation other than Great Britain or the United States should have the Philippines. The mounting pressure of events convinced McKinley that there was no road back: America must become an overseas power. On December 10, 1898, a peace treaty was signed which provided that Cuba, Puerto Rico, Guam, and the Philippine Islands should go to the United States* and that Spain be paid $20,000,000. By this America acquired a string of outer bastions in the Caribbean and Pacific.

If the native insurgent element bulked large in the United States' decision to buy the Philippines, the problem grew as time went on. No sooner had General Merritt's troops taken Manila on August 13 than Aguinaldo's forces became a threat. Since they controlled the water system outside the city, they used it as a bargaining factor to win concessions, and when they were persuaded to withdraw, on September 14, they continued their agitation. Aguinaldo established headquarters for his "government" at Malolos, about twenty-eight miles from Manila, from which he issued a plea to President McKinley on November 15, protesting against many wrongs, some real, more imagined, and asked for a clarification of America's intentions toward the islands.† The answer came December 10 with the signing of the peace treaty, when the Filipinos learned definitely that their dreams for independence were not to be realized.

On December 21 President McKinley issued an order to Secretary of War Alger which acknowledged the acquisition of the Philippines by the United States but provided that in exercising its powers the military government of the islands should assume the role of friend rather than conqueror. Nevertheless, tension increased daily. General E. S. Otis, military governor of the islands, commanded almost 50,000 soldiers to enforce order, and Admiral Dewey seized all the little steamboats of the Filipinos' "navy," which had been transporting troops and supplies about the islands.

The die was cast when Aguinaldo, now a self-styled dictator and military commander, on January 6, 1899, broke off friendly relations with the United States Army in the Philippines, listing a long series of grievances as his reasons. The next day, Admiral Dewey, who thought conciliation still possible, cabled the Secretary of the Navy urging establishment of a commission to stop the coming conflict.

*Peck, *Twenty Years of the Republic*, pp. 605–607. Soon after the peace treaty was signed, Spain sold the Caroline, Pelew, and Ladrone Islands, except for Guam, to Germany. Guam had been captured with a few shots from the *Charleston* on June 21, 1898.
†Stickney, *Life and Glorious Deeds of Admiral Dewey*, pp. 299–303.

This important message was marked "Secret and confidential." It read:

NOTWITHSTANDING THE PROCLAMATION OF THE PRESIDENT AFFAIRS ARE
VERY DISTURBED IN PHILIPPINE ISLANDS. THE NATIVES ARE EXCITED AND
FRIGHTENED, AND BEING MISLED BY FALSE REPORTS SPREAD BY SPANIARDS
WHO SHOULD BE RETURNED TO SPAIN AS SOON AS POSSIBLE. STRONGLY URGE
THAT THE PRESIDENT SEND HERE AS SOON AS POSSIBLE SMALL CIVILIAN COM-
MISSION TO ADJUST DIFFERENCES. THIS SHOULD BE COMPOSED OF MEN
SKILLED IN DIPLOMACY AND STATESMANSHIP.

At the same time Dewey wrote his friend, Senator Proctor: "This appears to me an occasion for a triumph of statesmanship rather than of
arms. Should the President decide to do as I suggest, I hope that you will
be a member of the commission. These people are afraid of us, Navy and
Army, but would listen to you while they would not to us. They should
be treated kindly, exactly as you would treat children, for they are little
else, and should be coerced only after gentler means of bringing them to
reason have failed."

Such a commission was appointed by McKinley on January 12, composed of Jacob Gould Schurman, president of Cornell University; Professor Dean C. Worcester of the University of Michigan; Charles Denby,
former minister to China; Admiral Dewey; and General Otis. Before they
could sail, however, the hand-picked "Philippine Congress," composed
of his followers, voted Aguinaldo, on January 20, authority to declare war
at any time. The fact that his party was a minority mattered little. He
hoped that by creating parliamentary forms and dummy congresses he
could persuade the world that he was the chosen leader of all the Philippines. During the fall of 1898 he had gone so far as to send a commission
to Washington to agitate for concessions, but his opponents, composed
of merchants and many influential families, undermined his claims by
sending delegations of their own.

Both groups had strong support in the Philippines, as well as in the
United States. On the North American continent the issues of imperialism and expansion were fought vigorously between two sets of partisans.
During January it appeared more than likely that the Senate would not
ratify the acquisition provisions of the peace treaty, for, Democrats and
Republicans alike, the latter led by Senators Hale of Maine and Hoar of
Massachusetts, opposed expansion. Aguinaldo unwittingly acted in a
manner which prevented the immediate freeing of the islands; for while
the Senate debated, on February 4, Filipino insurgents outside Manila
attacked American sentries.* They were repulsed in a bloody battle, at

---

*Evidence that the attack of February 4, 1899, was premeditated is plentiful. On the
night before it occurred, Aguinaldo's representative in Washington, D. C., hastily entrained
for Canada.

the cost of fifty American and more than a thousand Filipino lives.

By February 6, when the peace treaty came to a vote in Washington, the attack of the insurgents insured its passage. Some who had opposed annexation now saw the national honor at stake and resolved that natives of the Philippines must be tamed before they could be considered ready for self-government. Even William Jennings Bryan, arch foe of expansionism, lent his support to the treaty. Even so, it was barely ratified by the necessary two-thirds majority, and the Republican administration did not know until after the Senate clerk had begun to call the roll how the vote would go.*

Operations against the insurgents proceeded on land under the command of General Otis, General Ovenshine, and General Arthur MacArthur. In the preliminary engagements around Manila Bay the American fleet's big guns aided. The natives, outnumbered, fell back, their casualties many times greater than those of the American troops. Even the Filipino "sharpshooters," strapped in trees to snipe at the United States soldiers, accomplished little.

A few days after the initial uprising the insurgents rose in the island of Cebu. German residents there promptly took advantage of the opportunity by raising the German flag over their houses and business buildings. Admiral Dewey, however, met the needs of the situation by ordering the *Petrel* to the island, where the sight of her guns persuaded the Filipinos to surrender and the Germans to haul down their flags.

Fighting in the country around Manila continued throughout February. The United States fleet was always busy. Joint operations were planned by the Admiral and General Otis, and troops were transported to vantage points by smaller vessels of the squadron. Water communication was almost the only way in the mountainous, densely forested terrain, where tropical undergrowth impeded all movement.

Late in February General King arrived to command reinforcements against the growing revolt, paid his respects to the Admiral, then went up the Pasig River to his headquarters at San Pedro Macati. The next Sunday Dewey, lunching nearby, suggested that the party, consisting of several ladies, board his steam launch and go up river to call upon the general. While Dewey and his friends were waiting at the general's headquarters, shots peppered the building, zinging against the stone walls and splattering on the zinc roof. It was a dangerous moment, but Dewey's composure quieted the ladies,† and without further delay, they all started

*Peck, *op. cit.*, pp. 611–12.
†Barrett, *Admiral George Dewey*, pp. 181–85.

240

back for Manila. A little way downstream their boat was fired upon, and water sprayed the occupants before they steamed out of range.

On February 15 Aguinaldo issued a proclamation from his seat at Malolos, warning that insurgent troops would kill all foreigners found in the islands. "Philippine families only will be respected," Aguinaldo stated. "They should not be molested, but all other individuals of whatever race they may be will be exterminated without any compassion."* "War without quarter to the false Americans who have deceived us. Either independence or death," he cried. The insurgents fired Manila on Washington's Birthday, and American troops, attempting to fight the flames, were shot at as they worked. Fire hoses were cut to hamper them further. Curiously enough, only the native quarter of the city suffered serious damage.

During the following months small bands of guerrillas roved down from the hills in forays against American troops and kept up their struggle until March 23, 1901, when Aguinaldo was finally captured by Colonel Frederick T. Funston in one of the most gallant exploits of American history.

Meantime George Dewey's fame grew. His absence from home whetted the appetites of Americans who created a hero they had never seen, and the continued bickering between the friends of Sampson and Schley contributed further to the adulation of the one unquestioned hero of the war. His dispatches to the Navy Department, concise, modest, and to the point, enhanced his reputation with the people, who demanded fresh honors for him. To meet the clamor, Representative Livingston of Georgia introduced a resolution in the House of Representatives in December seeking to create the rank of Admiral of the Navy. Greeted with cheers and enthusiasm at first, the resolution headed for a slow death in committee. But in February, 1899, another Dewey hero-worshiper, Representative Moody of Massachusetts, added a rider to the Navy appropriation bill, then under consideration, providing that Dewey be appointed Admiral of the Navy.†

Livingston's original resolution was thereupon exhumed and passed by the House. The Senate concurred on March 2, 1899. President McKinley was "authorized to appoint, by selection and promotion, an Admiral of the Navy, who shall not be placed upon the retired list except upon his own application; and whenever such office shall be vacated by death or otherwise, the office shall cease to exist." By its terms the Admiral was entitled to remain on active duty until his death, or if he chose to

---

*Stickney, op. cit., pp. 330–31.
†Adelbert Dewey, The Life and Letters of Admiral Dewey, p. 389.

retire, to draw full pay of $13,500 a year, plus allowances, for the remainder of his life. It was an unprecedented move. Farragut and Porter had both been admirals, entitled to four stars, but they had been admirals *in* the Navy. Dewey therefore outranked his famous predecessors.

President McKinley immediately forwarded Dewey's name to the Senate, and the appointment was confirmed, but owing to a typographical error, it read Admiral *in* the Navy. A later bill corrected the mistake. Theodore Roosevelt reappointed Dewey in 1902 and this time saw to it that the word was *of*.

Notification of his appointment reached Dewey in Manila on March 4, accompanied by two cables from Secretary Long conveying both his own and the President's congratulations. That same day the American commission to the Philippines arrived aboard the cruiser *Baltimore* and established headquarters in Manila. It began its studies at once, but it was March 20 before the first official meeting was held. Dr. Schurman was named chairman, with powers to draw up a proclamation to the Filipinos stating the aims and desires of the United States. Issued April 4, it contained eleven articles. First, it stated, the supremacy of the United States must and will be enforced. It promised the "amplest liberty of self-government," reconcilable with just, stable, effective, and economical administration; guaranteed civil rights to the Filipinos; promised their welfare and advancement; and forbade exploitation. It guaranteed an honest civil service in which natives would be employed; promised fair and equitable collection of taxes and a "pure, speedy, and effective administration of justice"; and pledged the construction of roads, railroads, public works, public schools, and general development of trade.*

Praised by half the natives as a promise of fair and enlightened administration, the proclamation was branded by Aguinaldo's junta a "tissue of generalities." Nevertheless, some of his lieutenants met with other Filipino leaders to determine whether Americans would grant more concessions, and under a flag of truce treat with the natives to achieve the "pacification" of the islands. Rumors that Aguinaldo's cabinet favored acceptance of the American proclamation and sought peace filtered throughout the archipelago during April. More and more of his followers left him to return to peaceful ways of life, and though the wily leader still maintained an army, the end of the insurrection seemed near. The need for Dewey's continued presence diminished, and he was soon called home.

Later, when the United States Senate investigated the background of the rebellion, Dewey was harried by questions designed to show what

*Stickney, *op. cit.*, 366.

242

comfort he might have given Aguinaldo during the blockade of Manila Bay. And at a hearing of the Senate's Philippines committee in 1901, the Admiral publicly admitted he had used the Filipinos to "help drag our chestnuts out of the fire," by letting them attack the Spanish troops before the American Army arrived, because the expediency of war demanded such action. But when he was asked by a member of the committee: "Did you at any time, Admiral, recognize his government or his independence?" Dewey answered quickly:

"Oh, never. Certainly it never entered my head that they wanted independence."*

His defender from all attacks proved to be none other than Secretary John D. Long, who wrote, so far as Dewey was concerned:

. . . no apprehension that he had been or would be indiscreet existed. In battle he had proved himself to be a cool, courageous commander-in-chief; in diplomacy he had already displayed judgment and tact, and the President was willing for the time to leave the handling of matters in the Philippine Islands in his hands.†

Of Aguinaldo's open letter, written on January 1, 1900, and asserting that Dewey had promised freedom for the Philippines, the Admiral declared:

That statement is a tissue of falsehoods, I never promised him directly or indirectly, independence for the Filipinos. I never treated him as an ally, except so far as to make use of him and his soldiers to assist me in my operations against the Spanish. He never uttered the word 'independence' in any conversation with me or my officers. The statement that I received him with military honors or that I saluted the Filipino flag is absolutely false.

When Aguinaldo came to Cavité he never thought of independence. That was an idea that came into his head later. His one desire was to be allowed to fight, that he might destroy the power of the friars. I allowed him to go ashore, but he was very uncertain as to the kind of reception he would get. He was so timid that I had to urge him to remain after he got there. The assertion that I made Aguinaldo any promises is a pure fabrication. Why, at that time, Aguinaldo never thought of asking, much less demanding, promises or presuming to dictate terms of any kind. He is not a smart fellow in a general sense, but the shrewd half-castes of Manila made use of him to further their ambitious schemes, for Aguinaldo was supposed to bear a charmed life. The natives believed that he possessed the power of the Anting-Anting, that he was impervious to a bullet. . . . They had a large force, but not many arms. If we could have had

*Long, *The New American Navy*.
†*Ibid*.

5,000 men there early enough, there would not have been any trouble—we could have controlled them absolutely. The unfortunate part of the whole situation was that the importance of Aguinaldo at that time was enormously magnified, and he soon realized it. His advisors, Mabini and his associates, were also quick to understand and take advantage of it. I have seen Mabini's statement that I asked Aguinaldo if he could control the island, in which case I offered to arm his forces. I never asked him any questions of the kind, nor made him offers and promises. Most of Mabini's assertions are absolutely false, and what truth he writes is misleading.*

On May 1, 1899, Dewey received a telegram from the President:

ON THIS ANNIVERSARY OF YOUR GREAT VICTORY THE PEOPLE OF THE UNITED STATES UNITE IN AN EXPRESSION OF AFFECTION AND GRATITUDE TO YOURSELF AND THE BRAVE OFFICERS AND MEN OF YOUR FLEET, WHOSE BRILLIANT ACHIEVEMENTS MARKED AN EPOCH IN HISTORY WHICH WILL LIVE IN THE ANNALS OF THE WORLD'S HEROIC DEEDS.

His health, none too good when he left America eighteen months before, had been worn down by the hot, wet, and feverish climate. His command of a fleet seven thousand miles from home, threatened by Germany for so many weeks, and the slow, wearisome mopping up of Filipino insurgents were irksome and began to pall. He wanted to be back in the nation's capital instead of in a little bay at the ends of the earth. The field of glory had yielded its riches. He wanted to enjoy the harvest.

The *Olympia* made ready to sail on the afternoon of May 20. American sailors lined the rails of every ship, watching their flagship's preparations. Captain A. S. Barker of the *Oregon,* who was to relieve the Admiral of his command, stood on the bridge watching the crew hoist the last boats aboard. Bright signal flags flew at the masthead of every vessel, spelled out "Bon Voyage," "Good-By," and "Happy Sailing."

At 4:00 P.M. the ship's bell of the *Olympia* struck eight bells. The Admiral, in a starched white uniform, turned to Captain Lamberton and said quietly:

"Weigh anchor."

A deck winch ground into action, and the great chain dripped rusty water as it rose from the bay. When the anchor broke the surface, crews left behind cheered lustily at the home-going sailors who scrambled up the rigging to man every yardarm and wave their white sailor hats in farewell.

Slowly the *Olympia* got under way and rode majestically past the other

*Wildman, *Aguinaldo.*

ships. "Hurray, hurray," shouted the men of the *Oregon,* farthest out in the bay as the flagship steamed on the way.

From every ship guns roared their seventeen salutes. Then the band of the *Oregon* played "Home, Sweet Home." Merchant vessels dotting the harbor dipped their flags. Farther out in the bay, where the black British cruiser *Powerful* lay at anchor, the *Olympia* steamed by to the roar of another salute, and the *Olympia's* band, at the last firing, responded with "God Save the Queen," while the Englishmen played "Auld Lang Syne."

A lump choked the Admiral's throat as he stood on the bridge, looking back at the green hills of Luzon, which had always reminded him of Vermont. He would never again, he thought, stroll along the pathways of Cavité, never watch the sun rise over the walls of old Manila, or step out of his cabin to smell the air sweet and moist, cool for a few minutes after the rain. Manila was fading in the distance, and the ships with their bright flags were growing smaller. The salutes continued, scarcely audible now. Only a few puffs of white smoke showed that the adieus were still being made.

Soon she entered the Boca Grande channel, passed the spiked guns of Corregidor and El Fraile, and steamed between the steep rock hills into the China Sea. The American squadron was hull down on the horizon, but a few white clouds of smoke still puffed in the air and disappeared. These were the shore batteries of Manila, saying the last word of farewell.

25

STAR-SPANGLED ADMIRAL

The *Olympia*, white again, with her four-starred Admiral's flag at the peak, entered the harbor of Hong Kong on Tuesday, May 23. This time Dewey did not have to make the first calls. Foreign ships, commanded by lesser officers, fired their salutes, and the British, Russian, Japanese, and French captains promptly crossed the bay to pay their proper respects. Gracious, assured, and punctilious, he returned all the calls, as usage dictated, within twenty-four hours, then went ashore to the Peck Hotel, while his ship was dry-docked for repairs.

After two weeks, during which he participated somewhat reluctantly in social affairs and dinners, he made preparations to depart Tuesday, June 6. Dignitaries in uniform and richly gowned ladies crowded the quarter-deck of the *Olympia* to bid the Admiral good-by, and as the cruiser sailed out of the harbor, guns gave him full honors. A carnival spirit filled the bay. Cheers and whistles split the air. The *Olympia* band played "Auld Lang Syne" and "God Save the Queen" in final salute to the British governor, then fell silent as the ship began her leisurely cruise around the southern shores of China, past Indo-China and Siam. On June 11 she reached the Malay states and dropped anchor in the harbor of Singapore. More ceremonies followed. The Admiral had tea at the British Government House with Sir Charles and Lady Mitchell, while the ship's officers sipped Pim's Cup Number 2 at the Raffles Hotel, and crew members gulped gin slings in the waterfront saloons.

A few days of sight-seeing, races, colonial teas and dinners, then on again, without haste, despite the impatient eagerness of bluejackets, many of whom had been four years without a sight of America. On July 6, a blistering, cloudless day, the ship reached the Gulf of Aden and entered the Red Sea. She arrived at the Suez Canal six days later, paused at Port Said for coaling, and entered the Mediterranean the next day, steaming northwest, past Crete and Greece, into the Adriatic Sea.

246

Dewey's return to the Mediterranean had for him the quality of a triumphal procession. He had entered it first without fame, as a midshipman on the *Wabash*, an unknown student learning his profession. He had returned in the eighties, in command of the *Pensacola*, proud of his four stripes, but ashamed of his antiquated ship. Now, with gold braid "up to his elbow," his every movement was the subject of universal notice. The honors, salutes, and courtesies were equaled only by the ceremonies Admiral Farragut had enjoyed forty years before.

But this was not merely a personal triumph. The contrast between his previous visits to the Mediterranean and this trip reflected the contrast between the United States of 1887 and the United States of 1899. In those twelve years Dewey had risen from moderate rank to a position of supreme naval importance, but his advancement personified even more notably the rise of his country.

"Fine weather," Dewey wrote in his diary on July 19, as his ship sailed through the Adriatic. "At noon passed Lissa—the scene of the naval battle between the Austrians and Italians thirty-three years ago (20 July)." At Trieste, where the ship anchored the next morning, Dewey began again the regular routine of calls, salutes, and courtesies. He was entertained by the United States Minister the next evening in the Hotel de la Ville at a dinner attended by all diplomats of highest rank, and as the port was cool, gay, and pleasant, the Admiral remained there until August 1. He walked on shore, drove about the countryside sight-seeing, visited the Empress' stud farm at Uffizi, where four hundred fine thoroughbreds were being raised, and was host at a dinner for twelve aboard the *Olympia*.

Interviewed by an enterprising foreign correspondent of the New York *Herald* in the lobby of the Hotel de la Ville on July 27, Dewey was asked whether the recent recall of Admiral von Diedrichs as commander of the German Pacific fleet could have been made as the Kaiser's gesture of friendship to the United States. Dewey replied bluntly:

He was relieved from his Manila post in accordance with an arrangement of long standing, and because his time was up, not as a concession made in friendliness to the American government. The German policy is to prevent other powers from obtaining what she cannot accept herself. We need a large and thoroughly equipped Navy that can cope with any other power. That is the only way to block such activities. Our next war will be with Germany.*

Needless to say, his words made the front page. Washington was aghast. The report "annoyed his friends here beyond measure," wrote the Wash-

*The New York Herald, July 28, 1899.

247

ington correspondent of the New York *Times*. "No one believes he said anything of the kind, and all point to his long record of discreet utterances and refusal to be drawn into any discussion of public affairs as indicating the improbability that he would not break loose in such startling fashion."*

Secretary Long said simply, "I do not believe it." Herr von Mumm, German Ambassador to the United States, hastened to the State Department and was closeted with Secretary Hay for two hours.

Another reporter reached the Admiral on July 30 and asked him if the New York *Herald* story were true. "I long ago gave up denying or affirming newspaper reports," Dewey replied.

No mention of his explosive prophecy appeared in the diary. His entry for July 27 merely said, "Drove two hours in the afternoon. Am in better health." Perhaps his chest was feeling lighter.

After his return the Admiral freely admitted to his friends that he had made the statement attributed to him. "But what would you tell the President if he asks you?" they demanded.

I would tell him simply this: "Yes, Mr. President, I said it, and I firmly believe it; for it is coming surely. And God willing, I'll fight in it."

The warning, printed on the front pages of nearly all the newspapers in the country, greatly shocked the American people, who never knew how much Dewey had suffered from the German squadron at Manila Bay. The Trieste statement was the first of many that caused minor crises for the State Department between 1899 and 1917, when Dewey's prophecies were finally proven inexorably correct.

While Dewey was still in Italian waters or visiting at Italian ports, the Atlantic squadron of the United States fleet left Bar Harbor for Caribbean maneuvers before meeting the *Olympia* at sea to escort the hero up the Hudson River. America was preparing for his home-coming. Triumphal arches, etched invitations on gold plates, and gold plaques were ordered. Tiffany and Company's silversmiths had been working for months on a large gold cup, eighteen inches high, ornately embellished with bas-relief and inscriptions. Ten thousand dollars in twenty-dollar gold pieces were melted for its manufacture. They also tooled the ten-thousand-dollar jewel-encrusted Congressional sword which would be presented in Washington. A nationwide campaign, launched by New York papers to collect dimes for a gigantic loving cup almost six feet high, produced coins from 70,000 schoolchildren and grateful adults. The heroic cup, made of the melted dimes, was etched with pictures of the Admiral of Manila Bay and engraved with expressions of glowing praise.

The New York Times, July 30, 1899.

248

The eagerness of the city of Columbus, Ohio, to entertain the hero resulted in a large gold plaque invitation. "Christopher Columbus on October 12, 1492, made possible the achievement of George Dewey on May 1, 1898," it read, "and the capital city of Ohio which perpetuates the great discoverer requests the presence of the Great Admiral as its guest." A similar plaque, prepared by the Grand Army of the Republic, gave Dewey full credit for healing the sectional wounds of the Civil War and invited him to the annual G.A.R. encampment at Jacksonville, Illinois. Gold eyeglass cases, gold paper cutters, elaborately patterned cigar boxes, porcelain commemorative plates, miniature busts of the Admiral, miniature hats and epaulets, all inscribed to honor Dewey, were turned out by the nation's craftsmen as presents from grateful citizens.

The town of Three Oaks, Michigan, prepared a silken United States flag, inviting him to the unveiling of the "Dewey cannon." "Dewey dolls" were manufactured by the thousands, and thousands of metal coins were minted, gilded, and stamped with a portrait of the Admiral on one side and a soap advertisement on the other. More than twenty firms handed out thousands of these good-luck pieces to schoolboys. Men pinned them to their lapels.*

Beer mugs with the Dewey crest or with pictures of the "Hero of Manila Bay" graced the counters of china stores from Cutler, Maine, to LaJolla, California, and were quickly bought up. Paper weights, Dewey canes, Dewey inkwells, Dewey candlesticks, "Our Hero" letter openers, Dewey spoons, watch fobs, hats, and hundreds of different types of badges and commemorative medals were turned out by novelty concerns for a hero-worshiping public. The Piccadilly Club in Cincinnati, Ohio, sent the Admiral a loving cup. So did the city of Savannah, Georgia. St. Louis, Missouri, presented him with an ornate silver punch bowl, complete with ladle. The number of different kinds of trophies, souvenirs, relics, and assorted items of pure junk beggars description.†

The tributes took other forms than metal or china. Reams of verse poured from the pens of poets—or what passed for poets. No estimate of the amount of verse extolling George Dewey has ever been made. Every paper in the country printed scores of lines written by professionals and amateurs alike, and no one can calculate the number of poets whose words failed to see the light of day.

*William S. Dewey, "Commemorative Store Cards of Admiral Dewey," *The Numismatist Magazine*, March, 1939.
†Virtually the only souvenir that could not be produced was the United States postal stamp. Federal law forbids the likeness of living persons on postage. But after his death Dewey was immortalized, with Sampson and Schley, on a four-cent stamp.

Perhaps the most popular effusion was written by a Kansas lawyer, Eugene Ware, whose pen name was "Ironquill." Appearing in the Topeka (Kansas) *Capital* soon after May 1, 1898, it was quickly snatched up all over the country and almost rivaled the song "There'll Be a Hot Time in the Old Town Tonight" in its popularity:

> Oh, dewey was the morning
> Upon the first of May,
> And Dewey was the Admiral
> Down in Manila Bay.
> And dewey were the Regent's eyes
> Them orbs of royal blue,
> And dew we feel discouraged?
> I dew not think we dew!*

Anticipating a portion of what lay ahead, the Admiral wrote his son, "How I dread the show and would give anything to escape it all. But suppose that would be impossible. However, I shall take just as little of it as is possible."

The day before sailing from Gibraltar, September 10, 1899, on the last lap of his journey, he wrote young George:

MY DEAR SON:

We leave here tomorrow for New York. I am allowing plenty of time as one of our screws is partially disabled and it would never do to be too late.

I expect to anchor off Tompkinsville on the 28th and shall look for you soon after. Bring your bag and be prepared to stay aboard for a day or two.

The committee has informed me that the annex of the Waldorf-Astoria is reserved for my use while the guest of the city. I expect to go to Washington to receive the sword on Tuesday 30 Oct., after that to Montpelier for a reception. After that to get out of everything I can. My health is improving and I hope to be all right before reaching New York. I am much pleased at the manner you have staved off the interviewers. Mr. John Barrett sent me advance sheet of his sketch of me. Very good.

I like, rather, Murat Halstead's Life of Adml. Dewey.

> With love,
> YOUR AFFECTIONATE FATHER.

The transatlantic passage was uneventful, but the *Olympia's* partially disabled condition required sixteen days for the crossing. Finally, when the excitement of the nation and of the *Olympia's* crew had been whipped to the boiling point, the flagship reached Sandy Hook, at seven o'clock

*Sullivan, *Our Times*, p. 322.

250

on the cloudy morning of September 26. Later the clouds thinned, the sun came out, and small boats clustered around the white ship, carrying dignitaries who clambered aboard to be the first to welcome the hero home.

The *Olympia* anchored in the midst of the United States Atlantic fleet. Nearby rode the *Iowa,* the *New York,* the *Texas,* and the *Brooklyn,* which had destroyed the Spanish fleet at Santiago. Their captains, many of them Dewey's seniors before Manila Bay, at once embarked in their boats to approach the white *Olympia* and pay their respects to the new head of the Navy. Rear Admiral William T. Sampson was the first.

Accompanied by the entire fleet, the *Olympia* sailed up to Tompkins-ville the next day, where anchor was dropped and more visits began. Governor Theodore Roosevelt, with the governors of Vermont and New Jersey, called. The steamboat *Petrel,* which had served so gallantly at Manila, brought Boss Richard Croker of Tammany Hall and Chauncey Depew, head of the New York Central, as well as the Admiral's son, George. Sir Thomas Lipton, on the *Shamrock,* also exchanged calls. That night, as the hero looked past the Statue of Liberty toward Brooklyn Bridge, he saw, in thirty-six-foot letters, the brilliant sign:

WELCOME DEWEY

The visits continued through October 26, but the real celebrations started on Friday, October 29. "A fine day," the Admiral noted in his diary, and a red-letter day, too, for it was the only entry of that year written in ink. At one in the afternoon a "grand naval parade" in Dewey's honor got under way. Sirens shreiked, whistles blew, and foghorns blared into the din. The Atlantic squadron, led by the *Olympia,* steamed up the west side of the city, past the European passenger docks. Around the great men-of-war little tugs, motorboats, yachts, and dories struggled to keep up with the grand procession, while crowds lined the docks and spilled onto the roofs of buildings all along the shore. The flotilla steamed northward to Grant's tomb at 125th Street, where the *Olympia* turned and headed down river again.

At 106th Street she dropped anchor and saluted the city, her guns scarcely audible against the cacophony of noises from thousands of ships, factories, and voices. The next morning the Admiral arose at six, as usual, breakfasted in his cabin with Captain Lamberton, and at 7:45 left the flagship. A team of black, sleek horses took him to the Waldorf-Astoria, where rooms awaited the official party. Later in the morning a parade of more than 35,000 men in uniform and civilian clothes formed north of

156th Street and marched down Fifth Avenue. In the line filed Army troops, bluejackets, veterans of 1861, and civic organizations, interspersed with a dozen bands that played the marching songs of John Philip Sousa —"Tenting Tonight," "The Battle Hymn of the Republic," and other favorites. For three hours they moved down Fifth Avenue until, at 23rd Street and Fifth Avenue, they reached the Dewey Arch, an imposing mass of white, rising more than seventy feet above the street. A temporary structure, it was intended as a model for a permanent marble arch for which a million-dollar subscription drive had already begun.

The first of its kind erected in this country to honor a hero, it was inspired by the triumphal arch of Titus in Rome. Flanked by twenty-eight tall white columns, topped by Corinthian capitals and large balls, it was surmounted by a quadriga, representing Victory at Sea, in a boat towed by four seahorses emerging from the surf, while scenes of the naval victory at Manila Bay embellished the central archway. The Chicago *Inter Ocean* declared that "All who have seen the monumental arches of the Old World agree that in originality, grace, animation, spontaneity, and symmetry, the Dewey Arch is worthy of perpetuity. . . ."*

The man it was built to celebrate rode down the avenue the morning of October 30, leading the triumphal parade. Behind his coach Governor Theodore Roosevelt rode on horseback, followed by perfectly groomed sailors, soldiers, and Marines. Crowds of more than 100,000 citizens lined the sides of Fifth Avenue all the way, standing for hours with flowers in their hands to toss at the conqueror. At 23rd Street the Admiral, with his party, left his coach to mount the stand and return the incessant salutes of men passing in review. Until five in the afternoon they stood there. Then came speeches and ceremonies and the presentation of a giant key to the city, but the crowning award was the Tiffany loving cup of gold embossed with pictures of the victory.

Dewey had prepared himself for wild scenes of welcome, but he had hardly expected anything like this.† The reception committee, formed of leading citizens from every state in the nation, kept the Admiral up late that night at a reception in the Waldorf-Astoria. Sunday was given over to milder eulogies by the committee members and the fashionable of the city, and early Monday afternoon, in charge of a committee from Washington, he boarded a special train for the nation's capital.

Curious crowds stormed railway stations all along the route to watch the special train speed by, and at Washington more than 5,000 citizens

*Sullivan, *op. cit.*, pp. 339–40.
†"It was a perfect ovation," he wrote in his diary that night. "My emotion was indescribable."

were massed at the Union Station to welcome him. Close to the carriage reserved for him stood a fringed phaeton in which sat three ladies. As the Admiral in his heavy blue uniform, with gold up to the elbows and epaulets pointing high above his wide shoulders, walked out of the station, they were the first to catch his notice. He greeted Mrs. Washington McLean first, with a courtly salute, but his eyes were on Mildred McLean Hazen, wearing gay feathers in her hat.

A "Pastel Lady" she was often called, because of her delicate smallness and her slimness. She was forty-nine that day, but to the hero of Manila Bay her flawless complexion and the tilt of her head made her seem more like thirty.

The ladies had evidently made their plans, for Mrs. Washington McLean immediately offered the Admiral the use of Draper House during his stay for the official ceremonies.

Dewey demurred, "I should never allow three charming ladies to discommode themselves for my sea-dog comfort," he protested.

But as the charming ladies had already moved out of their home and were very insistent, the Admiral agreed to accept their hospitality.

A parade was waiting. His hostesses rode off in their carriage, while George Dewey settled himself in his own, and with his son at his side, he rode under escort to the White House. There President William McKinley and the cabinet waited to do him fresh honors. Secretary Long was fulsome in his praise and guided the lion of the hour through introductions to the officials whom he had never, as a commodore, met before. After dinner, on a stand near the Treasury Building, the Admiral and his staff reviewed a torchlight procession of men and flags, and shortly before midnight Dewey, his son, and staff rode to 1707 K Street, N.W., to the McLean home, where the Admiral went to a much-needed rest.

A great reviewing stand, erected on Capitol Hill and draped in flags and bunting, was the scene next morning of the climax of the welcome home—the presentation of the gold sword of Congress. Thousands gathered in the open space for the ceremonies, Congressmen and Senators crowded behind the principal speakers on the platform, and President McKinley himself was waiting when the Admiral's carriage drove up. A great roar broke from the crowd as the white-haired Admiral, his full-dress hat in his hand, mounted the steps to the stand. The President walked down a few steps to escort him to his seat. Secretary Long followed, carrying a long case.

A hush fell as the Secretary stepped forward to read a speech he had been weeks preparing for the august occasion. In slow, scholarly tones he read the words which epitomized in every respect the universal admiration, awe, and love which the people felt for the Admiral.

"My dear Admiral," Long began, and he turned to the hero with a courtly bow. "Let me read a few extracts from our official correspondence, covering less than a fortnight's time, and now known the world over." He then gave to the public the significant messages that had passed between Hong Kong and Washington, and Manila and Washington. Then Long went on:

In these few words what a volume of history; what a record of swift, high, heroic discharge of duty! You went; you saw; you conquered. It seems but yesterday that the Republic, full of anxiety, strained its listening ear to catch the first word from those distant islands of the sea. It came flashing over the wires that May morning as the sun bursts through the clouds, and filled every heart with the illumination of its good cheer. In the twinkling of an eye your name was on every lip; the blessing of every American was on your head; and your country strode instantly forward, a mightier power among the nations of the world. As we welcome you back, there comes back into the vivid picture of that time, with all its hopes and fears, and then with all its swift succeeding triumph and glory.

Let me now read the Act of Congress in pursuance of which we are here:

"*Resolved,* by the Senate and the House of Representatives of the United States of America in Congress assembled, That the Secretary of the Navy be, and he hereby is, authorized to present a sword of honor to Commodore George Dewey, and to cause to be struck bronze medals, commemorating the battle of Manila Bay, and to distribute such medals to the officers and men of the ships of the Asiatic Squadron of the United States under command of Commodore George Dewey on May 1, 1898, and that, to enable the Secretary to carry out this resolution, the sum of $10,000.00, or so much thereof as may be necessary, is hereby appropriated of any money in the Treasury not otherwise appropriated."

It was by this solemn enactment, approved by the President, that the people of the United States made provision for putting in material form one expression of their appreciation of your valor as an officer of their Navy, and of your great achievement as their representative in opening the door to a new era in the civilization of the world. The victory of Manila Bay gave you rank with the most distinguished naval heroes of all time. Nor was your merit most in the brilliant victory which you achieved in a battle fought with the utmost gallantry and skill, waged without error, and crowned with overwhelming success. It was still more in the nerve with which you sailed from Hong Kong to Manila Harbor.

. . . No captain ever faced a more crucial test than when that morning, bearing the fate and the honor of your country in your hand, thousands of miles from home, with every foreign port in the world shut to you, nothing between you and annihilation but the thin sheathing of your ships, your cannon, and your devoted officers and men, you moved upon the enemy's batteries on shore and on sea with unflinching faith and nerve, and before the sun was halfway up the heavens had silenced the guns of the foe, sunk the hostile fleet, demonstrated the supremacy of American sea power, and transferred to the United States an imperial cluster of the islands of the Pacific. Later, by your display of large powers of administration, by your poise and prudence, and by your great discretion, not only in act but also in word, which is almost more important, you proved yourself a great representative citizen of the United States, as well as already its great naval hero. . . . It may be your still greater honor that you struck the first blow, under the providence of God, in the enfranchisement of those beautiful islands . . . so that generations hence your name shall be . . . a household word, enshrined in history. . . .

By authorizing the presentation of this sword to you as the mark of its approval your country has recognized therefore, not only the rich fruits which, even before returning from your victory, you have poured into her lap, but also her own responsibility to discharge the great trust which is thus put upon her and fulfill the destiny of her own growth and of the empire that is now her charge. . . .

It is my good fortune, under the terms of the enactment of Congress, to have the honor of presenting to you this beautiful sword. If during the many coming years which I trust will be yours of useful service to your country it shall remain sheathed in peace, as God grant it may, that fact will perhaps be due more than to anything else to the thoroughness with which you have already done its work. I congratulate you on your return across the sea in full health of mind and body to receive it here! here in the national capital; here on these consecrated steps where Lincoln stood; here, standing between the statue of the first President of the United States and him who is its living President today; here in this beautiful city adorned with the statues of its statesmen and heroes, the number incomplete until your own is added; here among this throng of citizens, who are only a type of the millions and millions more who are all animated by the same spirit of affectionate and grateful welcome. I cannot doubt that it is one of the proudest days of your life, and I know that it is one of the happiest in the heart of each one of your fellow countrymen, wherever they are, whether on the continent, or on the far-off islands of the sea.

Now, following the authorization of Congress, I present this sword of honor which I hold in my hand—my hand!—rather let it go to you through the hand of one who in his youth also periled his life and fought for his country in battle, and who today is the commander-in-chief of all our armies and navies, the President of the United States.

President McKinley arose and received the sword from the Secretary. He turned it over in his hands, passed it to the Admiral, then took it back again, and carefully snapped it into place on the Admiral's sword belt at his left side.

The parade that followed lasted for more than an hour, while the Admiral stood at attention beside the President reviewing the steady march. That night the White House was lighted up for a gala dinner of eighty guests. Every cabinet member, every Supreme Court justice, seven governors, numerous senators, including Redfield Proctor of Vermont, and many diplomats and officials were the honored guests. The Admiral, his son, and his brother Charles represented the Dewey family at the all-male gathering, while Lieutenant Brumby and Caldwell, a lieutenant now, attended Dewey as they had daily for more than twenty-one months.

Over cigars the President asked for a complete personal account of the Manila campaigns. Reluctantly at first, then growing interested in his subject, the Admiral told his experiences. When he came to the German troubles, the listeners leaned forward in their seats. Little of that part of the campaign had been heard in Washington. President McKinley emphatically declared that not a single vestige of any report concerning the affair of von Diedrichs had been transmitted to him. Nor did the Navy Department files contain references to it.

"No, Mr. President," Dewey answered proudly. "As I was on the spot and familiar with the situation from day to day, it seemed best that I look after it myself at a time when you had worries enough of your own."[*]

In the account of 1904 Dewey approved the following words which indicated his pride in his accomplishments, a pride which was amply repaid that night in the home of the President.

His fortunate isolation, and the delays and uncertainties of communications with him, had forced the Navy Department to leave matters to his discretion to a much greater extent than would have been the case had the cable been intact. Governments rarely recognize the fact that their agents at a distance, if at all worthy of confidence, are infinitely better capable of forming correct judgments in emergencies than are the home authorities possibly thousands of miles away; yet the temptation to interfere is ever strong, and can rarely be resisted. His fortunate cutting of the cable saved Admiral Dewey from such interference and left him in undisturbed possession of Manila Bay where he exercised his sovereignty with a force and discretion which can only inspire commendation.

From time to time . . . he had dispatched a vessel to Hong Kong to

George Dewey, *Autobiography*, p. 252.

256

transmit a brief account of operations, or to forward some suggestion with regard to governmental policy in the Philippines; but these communications were confined to such concise messages as could be sent by cable, and for the entire period of his service in Manila Bay, not a half dozen written reports can be found in all his official correspondence. .

The many questions resulting from the destruction of the Spanish fleet, the enforcement of the blockade, the operations of the insurgents, the protection of the refugees, and the presence of so many foreign men-of-war, were passed upon by the Admiral and his decisions executed without recourse to the advice or direction of Washington. He dominated the situation, and his fame as an administrator is as firmly established by the conduct of affairs after the battle of Manila Bay as is his skill as a strategist and tactician by the preparation and celerity antecedent to it.

The verdict of Admiral Dewey's countrymen coincides with that of the French admiral who so impressively informed him that he had made no mistakes.

Those are the final words of the 1904 account prepared by Commander Sargent at Dewey's suggestion. Approved by him as being "as correct as is possible in any historical account," they show the version of his position in history which he wished to perpetuate. The words of praise were written by Commander Sargent, who, naturally enough, wished to please the Admiral. The simple acceptance of them by the Admiral as being "as correct as is possible," may cause the modern reader at times to wonder at the apparent disparity between the frequent reiterations of Dewey's modesty with his ready acceptance of such sycophancy.

On Wednesday, October 4, the Admiral visited the Navy Department and the White House for more consultations. That evening he dined at Beauvoir with Mrs. Washington McLean and her daughters. The brief diary contains no mention of the conversation, yet entries for the next few days showed how matters were progressing. On the fifth of October he moved into a new office in the Navy Department, made several calls in the afternoon, and returned to 1707 K Street to receive numerous visitors. On Saturday he called upon General Miles. The next day he rode through the rain to church and lunched at Beauvoir with Mrs. McLean and Mrs. Hazen.

A special train took the Admiral's party to Vermont, Monday evening, where the state had prepared gigantic ceremonies. The Admiral received the degree of Doctor of Laws at the University of Vermont, and at Montpelier on Thursday he reviewed a parade of militia. The Senate, in classical tradition, placed a laurel wreath upon his brow, while the governor, mayor, and 40,000 Vermonters paid tribute to the native son who had risen to such heights of fame. Small boys in Vermont no longer aspired to storm Ticonderoga in the brown uniform of the Green Mountain Boys; they yearned now to wear the blue and gold of naval heroes.

The grand procession continued throughout New England. On Saturday Boston did its best to outdo the other receptions by naming a square in Dewey's honor and presenting him with a jeweled sword, Admiral Farragut's pennant, a watch, and the freedom of the city. The state militia passed in review, and the governor held a banquet for 217 guests at the Algonquin Club. Returning to Washington the next week, Dewey established himself in sumptuous quarters in the Everett House. But 1707 K Street seemed to hold far more attractions than any other spot in the city.

The strain of being the nation's number one hero was beginning to tell, but the demands never ceased. He was importuned to make a triumphal tour of Southern cities, besieged by hundreds of callers every day, both at the Navy Department and at Everett House, and he would, it seemed, never finish with the clamor. His digestion was becoming bad, the strain of calling on a dozen people a day, receiving as many more, shaking hands, accepting eulogies and congratulations was almost too much. Only at the McLean mansion did George Dewey find rest and relaxation. There he could unbend and forget that he held the spotlight of the world. And there, one Sunday evening, as he and Mildred talked of the proposed Southern tour, Dewey spoke of "how he dreaded it," and she answered:

"I would not go if I were you. Don't go. Nobody takes more interest in you than Mamma and I, and we both think it would be too great a strain after your anxieties in the Orient."

"Do you take an interest?" he asked suddenly.

"Oh, very great," she answered.

They were sitting upon a sofa in the tapestried ballroom.

"How great?" demanded the Admiral, a little eagerly, as he made an imperceptible motion toward Mildred's end of the sofa.

Mildred paused for a minute, then answered:

"More than I can well explain."

"Do you take enough interest, to say that——" He stopped, reached out his hand and lifted hers from the cushion, "——do you mean that you will be my dear wife, and let me love you all I wish?"

The words were out now. His long loneliness was ended, and Susie was almost forgotten. But not really forgotten perhaps, for Mildred was Susie, too. She was short and slim as Susie had been. She was dark-haired and deep-browed, and her vivacity, social success, and her sympathy were the qualities he had loved in Susie.

"Yes," she said quietly, "and—thank you, too."

With that the Admiral leaned over and kissed her hand. Then he pulled her to him, put his arm around her firm shoulder, and kissed her face.

"Thank God," he said.

In a couple of minutes, he added:

"Can't I see your mother?"

"I doubt it," she said, "Mamma is taking a bath."

"Try," he insisted. Mildred got up and started for the stairs. "I'll go ask," she said.

Mildred ran upstairs and found her mother just out of the bath, in a long white peignoir, with her hair braided down her back.

"Darling," said Mildred, "Admiral Dewey wants to speak to you."

"Dear, I'm not dressed properly," said Mrs. McLean. Then she noticed her daughter shaking, her face flushed like a schoolgirl's.

"He really wishes it, dearie," said Mildred. Mrs. McLean went to the top of the stairway, and the Admiral of the Navy bounded up the steps like a boy of nineteen. He stopped a step below the old lady, with Mildred below him, her hand clutching his arm.

"Dear Mrs. McLean," he began, "this dear little lady [he still did not call her Mildred] has promised to be my darling wife!"

Mrs. McLean gasped. Then she leaned down and kissed the Admiral's forehead.

"God bless you. I give her to you," she answered, her voice tremulous. "She is my dearest possession." And there the three stood, Mildred with one hand in George's and the other in her mother's.

Mildred recalled that she did not sleep a wink the "livelong night."* The Admiral returned to Everett House. Before he retired he opened his diary and in pencil wrote: "Sunday 29 Oct. Unsettled, later clear. Lunched at the country club with Jesse Brown. Dined at Mrs. McLean's. Engaged." (He was at the bottom of the left-hand page, and the word "engaged" had to run up diagonally across the sheet to find room.)

The next day his diary stated that he drove with Mrs. Hazen for two hours in the park and that evening went to the theater. Their engagement was announced to the papers at once. It was not until Thursday, however, that his entries in the diary referred to his fiancee as "Mildred," instead of "Mrs. Hazen," and the next day he gave up his diary entirely.

The news of the engagement surprised the entire country. The press

*This account of Dewey's proposal was told by Mrs. Dewey to her close friend Elizabeth Ellicott Poe, to whom she said, "I always wanted to make some record of George's asking me to marry him. . . . Perhaps in the years to come the people will be interested in knowing how so great a man did ask his wife."

hounded the engaged pair for information about the wedding date, but it did not have long to wait. On November 9, 1899, they slipped off, with only a few friends, to St. Paul's Roman Catholic Church in Washington, where at noon they were joined in matrimony by Monsignor Mackin.

The Admiral left a brief wedding luncheon to attend a conference at the Army-Navy Club. As he was entering the building a newspaperwoman stopped him and asked: "Admiral, forgive me for asking you, but are you going to marry Mrs. Hazen? My paper—"

Dewey interrupted her with a gruff, "No, I am not."

She gasped.

"But why not?" she asked.

"Because," and his eyes twinkled with mirth, "I just married her this noon."

The couple left Washington that evening for a hectic four-day honeymoon in New York City, for the Admiral could not go into the street without attracting a crowd of well-wishers and autograph seekers. On November 14 they returned to Washington, to the house at 1747 Rhode Island Avenue, N. W., the gift of the people to the Admiral, made possible by a fund of $50,000 raised during the summer. This was not an unprecedented gift; both Grant and Sherman had been presented with homes by the grateful people after the Civil War. Both had later sold them when their fame dimmed and creditors became more numerous than autograph hunters. The gift of the Dewey house sprang from a spirit of gratitude. It was to end in public misunderstanding and anger, and in personal sadness.

Deeded to the Admiral in October, it was ready for him when he returned from his honeymoon, but by that time the nation's press noted that Mrs. Dewey was a convert to Catholicism. The American Protective Association, an anti-Catholic organization, had been active for some time, and feelings against papacy ran high throughout America. They had a new vent now, in their hero's wife, and, as Mark Sullivan has written, Dewey learned "that a public which has made a man a hero has, by the essential nature of that act, established with him a relation of watchful guardianship which regards itself as justified in frank discussion and admonition about matters which as to men not heroes, have the sanctity and immunity of personal intimacy. Indeed, stronger than that, it was as if the American public had elected itself to be Admiral Dewey's bride; and as if the Admiral had committed bigamy; or, at best, it was as if he had procured a divorce abruptly and without just cause."[*]

The storm first broke when he decided that he would like to deed the

*Sullivan, *op. cit.*, p. 332.

house to his son. The Admiral consulted an attorney who informed him that the laws of the District of Columbia and the terms of the gift would prevent him from doing so. It would be necessary, they said, first to convey the house to Mrs. Dewey, who in turn could convey it to George Goodwin Dewey. Papers to effect the first transfer were drawn up. On November 21 the nation's press announced that the house had been conveyed to Mildred. Then the campaign of abuse began. Stories declared Mrs. Dewey's intention of making the house the center of papacy in the country. Two days later the correct story of the plan to provide for George Goodwin Dewey's accession to title was printed, but it was too late. There was more talk, often about Mrs. Dewey's jewels, which were undoubtedly many and brilliant, and always about her religion.

All in all, the first months of their married life were not happy for the Deweys. The public clamor and gossip, ill-founded though it was, hurt both the Admiral and his wife more than the public ever knew. Dewey could not understand the reason for the whispering attacks, particularly because his adulation from the public had been, and still was, tremendous. Invitations to appear at cities everywhere continued to flood his desk. He was asked to make speeches all over the nation. Letters of congratulations, trophies, and presents still swamped the postman who called at 1747 Rhode Island Avenue. Hundreds of citizens came, at all hours literally, to visit the house which they had helped provide. Thirty babies were named after him.

The anomalies of the situation were too complex for the forthright Dewey, though Finley Peter Dunne summed up the situation succinctly in Mr. Dooley's words, with his usual genius for making a point, "Raypublics ar-re not always ongrateful. . . . On'y whin they give ye much gratichood ye want to freeze some iv it or it won't keep."*

The pendulum of feeling, which had swung so far, was moving back to normal, yet in the process it struck at both George and Mildred Dewey. Not all the press was hostile, but all members of it seemed to find it necessary to "cover the news," by reporting the assaults. The New York *Times* complained that the whole affair made Americans look ridiculous in the eyes of foreigners, and "this abrupt substitution of the cold shoulder for the warm heart argues a want of steadiness in our makeup."†

The Chicago *Inter Ocean* declared that the switch of feeling "shamed the name of gratitude and discredited the intelligence of the American people," while William Randolph Hearst sprang to Dewey's defense to

*Sullivan, *op. cit.*, p. 340.
†*Ibid.*, p. 341.

point out that the very persons who were then lambasting the Admiral would be the first to demand his services if the country needed them against any foe.

Possibly the fact that it was a Presidential year offered the best explanation of the perplexing attacks.

26

PRESIDENTIAL ASPIRATIONS

While the unprecedented fervor of Dewey idolatry was at its height, the people, not satisfied by the creation of the highest naval rank in history for him, wished to elevate their hero still higher. During the summer of 1898 the cry "Dewey for President" swept the land. Political leaders, for reasons of their own, eagerly considered the possibilities. Republicans opposed to President McKinley saw in Dewey the ideal, unbeatable opponent. Democrats opposed to William Jennings Bryan's "free silver" and anti-imperialistic position were not unfavorable, while many independents, admiring the Admiral's completely nonpolitical, nonpartisan background, promised a large vote for him.

While Dewey was still in the Philippines, Colonel Watterson, publisher of the Louisville *Courier-Journal** and Joseph Pulitzer of the New York *World* publicly launched Dewey-for-President booms. The *World* went so far as to dispatch a political expert to Manila to sound out the Admiral's views. With typical bluntness, Dewey declined the honor:

I would not accept a nomination for the Presidency of the United States. I have no desire for any political office. I am unfitted for it, having neither the education nor the training.

I am deeply grateful for many expressions of kindly sentiment from the American people, but I desire to retire in peace to the enjoyment of my old age.

The Navy is one profession, politics another. I am too old to learn a new profession now. I have no political associations and my health would never stand the strain of a canvass. I have been approached by politicians repeatedly in one way or another, but I have refused absolutely to consider any proposition whatever. This is final.†

*Sullivan, *Our Times*, p. 324.
†Adelbert Dewey, *The Life and Letters of Admiral Dewey*, p. 426.

As final the people treated it. The Dewey booms died down, and the American people turned to other candidates.

No naval officer had ever aspired to the Presidency. Men of the sea had traditionally stayed clear of politics, and Dewey's refusal won the esteem of other officers in Manila Bay. The night before he left the Philippines, at a farewell dinner to his captains aboard the *Olympia,* he had mentioned the boom, and all had advised him "not to consider it for a moment."* Two weeks before Christmas, in 1898, the Admiral wrote his brother Charles in Montpelier about the strong letters from home urging him to become the Democratic candidate for President. "I had rather be an Admiral ten times over," he commented.

Unfortunately, the finality of the Admiral's decision was not so unequivocal as he had stated in faraway Manila. When he returned to New York in October, 1899, when he saw thirty-six-foot letters of electricity blazing on the Brooklyn Bridge, and when he realized the magnitude of his reception, ambition flared up in him.

As the *Olympia* lay at anchor in New York's harbor, even before Dewey went ashore to his public, a long, sleek yacht drew near. Three top-hatted citizens stepped into a motor tender and came aboard to pay their respects to the conquering Admiral. The yacht was the *Corsair.* The men were J. P. Morgan, William Randolph Hearst, and Richard F. Croker, "boss" of Tammany Hall.

Morgan came straight to the point.

"Admiral Dewey," he said, "we want you to run for President." The Admiral, taken aback by the blunt demand, answered with equal directness.

"No, sir," said the Admiral, "I am a Navy man and I don't want any part of it."

At this point the experienced Croker, who had handled temperamental candidates before, interposed forcibly, "Admiral, we're going to run you, and meanwhile, don't you say nothin'."

Nevertheless, Dewey stood firm and the distinguished gentlemen departed without a committed candidate. Turning to his son, he said, "There's a man who owns New York, and he says to me, 'Admiral, don't you say nothin'.'"

That was not the end, however. More pleas came from "gold Democrats" and from influential businessmen. Civil War generals with one tenth of Dewey's popularity had been elected easily, and there were hundreds who urged him to run. Nathan Strauss, one of the owners of Macy's, and a power in New York, was among those who promised Dewey sup-

*Sullivan, *op. cit.,* p. 324.

port, and almost everywhere Dewey went, in the course of his triumphal tour of the nation, crowds cheered and begged him to be the first President of the twentieth century. The clamor persisted through the winter of 1899-1900, every day bringing him some added pressure. Nor is there evidence that Mildred disapproved of the movement. Senator Redfield Proctor, his principal political guide, strongly favored his candidacy.

"We're going to run him against you, and he'll be a hard man to beat," he had written President McKinley right after Manila Bay.

For a time a coalition movement seemed possible. John R. McLean, publisher of the Cincinnati *Enquirer* and the Washington *Post,* and one of the leading Democrats of Ohio, was Mrs. Dewey's brother. Senator Foraker of Ohio, another important figure in the Middle West, was a Republican. When Senator Proctor, who was sure that Dewey would run well in New England, asked Foraker how the Admiral would do, Foraker replied:

"Very well, but if you want him, tell him not to say a word on any political question."

It was good advice, which Proctor probably failed to pass on—for Dewey committed the blunder of commenting inconsistently on America's foreign policy. Soon after Manila Bay he informed the President that the Filipinos were far better suited for independence than the Cubans, but in October, 1899, he signed the report of the Philippines Commission advocating control of the archipelago by the United States. This unexplained change in his attitude offended the Democrats, who were violently opposed to Republican imperialism in the Far East.

During the spring of 1900 newspapermen literally hounded the Admiral for a statement, but he consistently refused to talk. Nevertheless, the Deweys discussed the matter frequently at the dinner table, and their secretary, John Crawford, blurted out one day to a newspaperman that the Admiral was not altogether unfavorably disposed to the candidacy. Shortly afterward the story appeared that Dewey would run for President and that his wife would be his principal campaign manager.

The story was embarrassing, but it seemed to tip the scales. On the evening of April 3, 1900, the New York office of the *World,* which had led in supporting Dewey's candidacy, asked its Washington bureau to make a final effort to obtain a statement from him. It seemed a useless assignment, but Horace J. Mock of the Washington staff dutifully went to 1747 Rhode Island Avenue, where he arrived at 6:30 with the New York telegram, which he showed to the Admiral.

"Yes," said Dewey, to the utter amazement of the reporter, "I have decided to become a candidate." Then he invited his dazed guest into his home and gave him an interview.* Mock persuaded the hero to give his paper the exclusive story. Only the most complete novice in political affairs could have consented to such a procedure. By it, Dewey alienated the rest of the press, which, to hide its chagrin over being scooped, immediately treated the announcement in the worst possible light, and the interview itself, as printed in the *World* the next morning, made the innocent Dewey the butt of the nation's humor at its most irreverent level.

On the morning of April 4, 1900, the *World* offered to its readers the following amazing article:

"Yes," said the Admiral, "I realize that the time has arrived when I must define my position. When I arrived in this country last September, I said then that nothing would induce me to be a candidate for the Presidency. Since then, however, I have had the leisure and inclination to study the matter, and have reached a different conclusion, inasmuch as so many assurances have come to me from my countrymen that I would be acceptable as a candidate for this great office.

"If the American people want me for this high office, I shall be only too willing to serve them.

"It is the highest honor in the gift of this nation; what citizen would refuse it?

"Since studying this subject, I am convinced that the office of the President is not such a very difficult one to fill, his duties being mainly to execute the laws of Congress. Should I be chosen for this exalted position I would execute the laws of Congress as faithfully as I have always executed the orders of my superiors."

"On what platform will you stand?" asked the *World* correspondent.

"I think I have said enough at this time, and possibly too much," answered the Admiral.

Political judgment aside, the statement may have been sensible and succinct. Dewey did not say he would run, he merely stated he would be willing to become President. There was nothing of the politician in George Dewey, and at no time in his life did he demonstrate that fact more conclusively than on April 3. His very innocence doomed him to the tragicomedy that followed. On April 5 the New York *Times* wrote:

Washington read with much amusement and incredulity the statement published this morning that Admiral Dewey wishes to be regarded as inviting a nomination for the office of President of the United States. Reports of like tenor had been heard before, but prompt denials by the Admiral had disposed of them.

*Sullivan, *op. cit.*, p. 310.

After quoting the *World* story, the paper added that Republicans and Democrats alike regarded the whole thing as the Admiral's "joke." At the very bottom of the story appeared the reasons given by Dewey for his change of heart:

My health was not as good then as it is now. I did not know as well the feeling of the people toward me. Ever since my return I have been receiving letters urging me to announce my willingness to become President, and I have discovered that the position of Admiral is not the highest in the United States. The highest position is that of President, and if the American people want me to act as President, how can I refuse?

Everywhere I have gone I have been most warmly received, and people in the crowds have exclaimed, "We want you for President." Thirty years ago I would not have thought the South could be so warm in its reception to a Northerner. Everywhere I was met with the greatest warmth and courtesy. The Spanish-American War has brought the country together.

To the politically unaware Admiral, everything seemed as simple as that. Great crowds had swarmed about his carriage cheering him, demanding his leadership in victories of statesmanship as they had received it in victories at sea. If the Spanish War had healed the wounds of the North and South (as he firmly believed), he had been led to think that more than any other man he was responsible for this outcome and he, above all others, therefore, should head the reunited nation.

The days that followed brought new attacks from the press and fresh ridicule of every statement he made. He was willing to take the nomination from either party, the *Times* wrote sardonically when Dewey declared that it was not up to a candidate to announce his platform, that he was trusting to his friends for that, and that, therefore, he would not commit himself to the politicians of either party. The same journal charged that Mrs. Dewey was responsible for the statement because she wished to gratify a desire to be mistress of the White House.

The *Times* also devoted two columns to the comments of politicians on Dewey's interview. Mark Hanna, working for McKinley's renomination, said, "Who will nominate him? Of course he has a perfect right to aspire to be nominated, but he will not be the nominee of the Republican party."

Cordell Hull, then representative from Tennessee, declared, "I don't believe Dewey is responsible for that fool interview. If he is, he does not realize the dignity of the position of President when he says all he has to do as President is carry out the orders of Congress."

Theodore Roosevelt told the paper he had nothing to say for publication, but three days later he admitted his fear that Dewey might be the

Democratic nominee. Bryan, T. R. said, would be preferable to Dewey, whose candidacy would be "merely ridiculous," were it "not for the fact that the unthinking, under the glamour of his naval glory, might support him."*

Truly the hounds were after the Admiral. What party did he belong to? they demanded to know; and although he indicated he would run on either ticket, on April 6, in Philadelphia, he admitted simply, "Yes, I am a Democrat."†

William Jennings Bryan, worried about his sudden rival, commented, "I do not wish to discuss the subject." But he was almost the only man in the country who did not. Boss Croker, in Europe at the time, could not help. Only the barbs of the Hearst press were milder than the others. Even naval officers shied away from supporting Dewey. Captain Sigsbee, asked his opinion, replied, "I have no criticism to make of his action. Its apparent inappropriateness is characteristic of a man whose life has been spent at sea."

At this juncture the Admiral and Mrs. Dewey chose to move to Beauvoir for the summer. Reporters immediately explained it as a means of evading the press. In a New York *Times* story, it was charged that a sentry stood at the door to prevent the ringing of the doorbell, and that callers "are expeditiously repulsed." On April 17, however, the *Times* had to admit that the supposed guard was only a colored servant at the Dewey home who had taken it upon himself to rule out any caller he personally disliked. The man was publicly fired, whereupon the *Times* printed the news and explained that the Admiral was "the most democratic and genial of men."

Among other attacks was that of April 15 in the Chicago *Times Herald*, alleging that the real reason for the Admiral's candidacy was his resentment against President McKinley's payment of $10,000 to the members of the Philippine Commission, while the Admiral, because of his position in the Navy, had been "robbed" of the fee. Dewey had "lost his temper and declared that he would have revenge for his wrongs," the newspaper reported. The false story was immediately denied by Dewey's friends, for it soon developed that both McKinley and Secretary of State John Hay had sent a request to the Senate to waive the rule against double salaries to government employes so that Dewey could be paid.

About the same time an unfortunately timed claim was filed against the government in Dewey's behalf. The men who fought at Manila Bay had been paid a bounty of $100 apiece, while Dewey as commander-in-

---

*Pringle, *Theodore Roosevelt*, p. 224.
†*The New York Times*, April 7, 1900.

chief had received $9,570. Now twice that amount was sought, on the ground that the enemy's force had been superior to the American fleet. Although Dewey was not responsible for the action, political capital was made of it by his opponents.

As days passed, the press began to suspect there was more to the Dewey candidacy than had first been believed. On April 19 the New York *Times* announced that the Dewey boom was managed by "shrewd, prominent public men," a fact which explained the delay in his statement of a platform. Almost at the same moment, the Admiral made front pages with a denial of a scurrilous story which charged that he had said, "Well, I'll tell you what a Democrat is. In time of war a Democrat is a damned traitor. In time of peace he is a damned fool."

The journalistic field day was joined by American magazines. A Washington observer, commenting in the April issue of *The Independent* on Dewey's original interview, wrote:

> Does it hit McKinley or Bryan? Or is it simply a blank cartridge. . . . At any rate, it is too late. . . . He is a candidate without a party. . . . To the officers of the Navy and to their professional sentiment, Dewey's confession that there is a place higher than that of the first officer of the United States Navy, and his admission that he would like to have it, seems like an abandonment of the highest ideals and the highest achievements of his profession for another field in which his naval victories are simply used to bolster his ambitions. . . . Clearly his decision is not taken at the counsel of his brother officers nor of professional politicians. . . . It is ill-advised and the greatest mistake of his life. . . . He is extremely sensitive to criticism. He is happy enough when on a wave of popularity, but when the tide turns and he feels the chill breezes of sarcasm and reproach, he wilts under its first bitter flavor. . . . He is not fitted to be a politician, and I believe he will be the first to regret this move.

The *Review of Reviews* for May, 1900, took the Admiral to task in similar vein:

> Ecstatic hero worship is not a continuing mood. No American in his lifetime, not even Washington or Lincoln, experienced the sensation of being idolatrously worshipped by his fellow citizens with unflagging zest for more than a few days at a time. . . . This is a practical world, and while we do not mean to neglect our heroes, we cannot make it our business to think of them all the time. . . . Last year the whole country was thinking of Dewey with such ardor that if the Presidential election had occurred then and his name was before the people nobody would have cared to run against him, and his election would have been practically unanimous. This year the platform is more important than the candidate, business is more important than glory.

The *Outlook* on April 14, 1900, pointed out that Dewey's candidacy could not be acceptable unless the Democratic party should junk its platform of currency and anti-imperialism. "The President," it argued, "must represent a set of principles and not be a lone wolf. He must be the leader of his own party and must have a policy to be followed. . . . No personal enthusiasm will elect one without it."

But it remained for the *Nation* of April 12 to strike the Admiral most bitterly when it compared his past exhibition of decorum, equipoise, and sterling sense plus the great attributes of a naval hero which captured the imagination of the public as well as the respect of thinking people," with his present "cheapening of a great office" in subordinating it to the dictates of Congress. Praising him for his firmness, modesty, and clarity in his Manila dispatches, the *Nation* attacked him for his shift of stand on acquisition of the Philippines. "Until then he had the destiny of the country in his hands."

These attacks deeply wounded the Admiral, to whom the Presidency seemed not merely the gratification of ambition but the acceptance of responsibility. But where reasoned editorials stung, the biting humor of Finley Peter Dunne ridiculed his Presidential aspirations into oblivion:

I hope to hiven he won't git it. No relative if mine iver held pollytical office, barring meself. So it is with Cousin George. I'm agin him. Of course I don't blame Cousin George. I'm with him f'r annythin' ilse in the gift if th' pipple, fr'm a lovin' cup to a house an' lot. . . .
After he be over here a while an' got so 'twas safe f'r him t' go out withaut bein' torn t' pieces f'r souveneers, or lynched be a mob, he took a look ar-roun' him an' says he, to a polisman, "What's the' governmint iv this countree?"
"Tis a raypublic," says th' polisman.
"What's th' main guy called?" says George.
"He's called a prisidint," says th' polisman.
"Is it a good job," says Cousin George.
"Tis betther than thravelin' beat," says th' bull.
"What's th' lad's name that's holdin' it now?" says George.
"Mac," says the cop. . . .
"Where fr'm?" says George.
"Ohio," says the peeler.
"Where's that?" says George.
"I dinnaw," says the bull, an' they parthed the best iv friends.
"George" then goes up to the White House to see for himself and watches "Mac" dictating his "Porther Ricayan policy." He decides to take the job: "It looks good. I cu'd nail it."
Then, calling in a "rayporther," he says, "I always believed in dealin' frankly with th' press. I haven' seen manny papers since I bin at sea, but

270

whin I was a boy, me father used t' take the Montpelier Palaejum. Twas r-run be a man be th' name if Horse Clamback. He was quite a man whin sober. . . . But what I asked ye here f'r was t' give ye a item ye cu'd write up in ye'er own way, an' hand to th' rresht iv th' boys. I'm goin' t' be President. . . . I wish ye'd make a note iv it, an' give it t' th' ither papers," he says.

"Are ye a Raypublican or a Dimmycrat," the rayporter asks.

"What's that?" says Cousin George.

"Do ye belong to the Raypublican or th' Dimmycrat parthy?"

"What are they like?" says Cousin George.

"Th' Raypublicans ar-re in favor iv expansion."

"Thin I'm a Raypublican."

"Th' Dimmycrats are in favor iv free thrade."

"Thin I'm a Dimmycrat."

"Th' Raypublicans ar-re f'r upholdin' the gould standard."

"So'm I. I'm a Raypublican."

After a few more such quandries developed, Cousin George says, "I tell you, put me down as a Dimmycrat, divil I care a bit. Just say I'm a Dimmycrat with sthrong Raypublican leanings. Put it this way, I'm a Dimmycrat be a point Rayppublican. Anny sailor will understand that."

"Ye'll have t' stand on a platform."

"I do, do I? Well, I don't. I'll stand on no platform, and I'll hang on no sthraps. What d' ye think the President is, a throlley car? . . . Go out now, an' write y'r little item, f'r tis late an' all hands ar-re piped to bed," he says.

An' there ye ar-re. Tis a hard year Cousin George has in store f'r him . . . he'll larn iv several previous convictions in Vermont. Thin he'll discover that they was no union label on th' goods he dilivered at Manila.

An' George'll wake up th' marnin' afther iliction, an' he'll have a sore head an' a sorer heart . . . an' chances ar-re he caught could fr'm goin' withaut his shawl, an' cuddn't vote. He'll find th't a man cin be right an' be prisidint, but he can't be both at th' same time, an' he'll go down t' breakfast an' issue giniral order number wan, "To ALL Superior Officers Commanding Admirals in th' U.S. Navy: If anny man mintion a Admiral f'r Prisidint, hit him in th' eye an' charge same t' me!"*

In the autumn before his political announcement Dewey had accepted an invitation from Chicago to attend celebrations marking the second anniversary of Manila Bay. By the time he was ready to leave in April, the papers immediately saw political implications in the visit.

"There is absolutely no political significance to the trip," Lieutenant Caldwell replied in Dewey's behalf. Nor, as far as his admirers went, was there any. At the Union Station, where a luxurious special train for Chicago awaited him, a crowd of more than one thousand Washingtoni-

*Harper's Weekly, April 21, 1900.

ans saw him and his party leave. At Pittsburgh mobs greeted the train as it passed, and in Chicago at least ten thousand gathered to welcome the great hero to the Middle West.

After being met by Mayor Carter Harrison, the party rode through the Loop, while thousands lined the streets to catch sight of the famous pair. That night a splendid ball was held in the Auditorium, where ornate floats of the American fleet at Manila lined the walls and a group of Manila veterans formed a guard of honor, while the Admiral, in his full-dress uniform, held court beside his beautifully gowned wife.

On May 1 all of Chicago turned out for the Dewey Day celebrations. More than six hundred thousand persons stood in the line of march, waving flags, cheering, and huzzaing as the Admiral passed at the head of the parade. Hundreds tossed flowers into his carriage. On the steps of the Art Institute three hundred girls, whose blue and white dresses formed the letters "Dewey," sang and cheered. Veterans of Manila escorted the Admiral to the reviewing stand on Jackson Boulevard opposite the United States Courthouse, and for two solid hours the Admiral stood, his wife and son beside him, saluting every flag which passed in the parade.

It was two years after Manila Bay, yet the cheers and tumult surpassed any previous demonstration in his experience, and it seemed to Dewey that his popularity was undimmed. After a tour of inspection that included the new $33,000,000 drainage canal, of which an immense photographic portfolio bound in dark, gold-tooled leather was presented to him, the Admiral went to St. Louis. Here grateful citizens presented to him an engraved silver punch bowl, embossed with scenes of the Manila triumph. His tour continued to Memphis, Tennessee; Nashville and Knoxville, where he visited the birthplace of Farragut, and everywhere parades and crowds cheered and yelled in hysteria. At railroad sidings the special train was besieged by hundreds more, who waited in the countryside for a glimpse of their hero.

On May 16, returning to Washington, he was at once confronted with questions about his Presidential aspirations and in the course of his interviews admitted that he had never voted in his life—he had always been at sea or in Washington where citizens did not enjoy the franchise.

In June he visited Detroit and Grand Rapids, Michigan, where more idolatry and wild scenes of enthusiasm met him, and where Democrats, impressed by the great outpourings of people, now proposed to nominate him for Vice-President. The contrast between the great popular outpourings of enthusiasm for Dewey as a naval hero and the scorn heaped upon him as a Presidential candidate will ever remain a mystery in American political life, for as soon as it became apparent that he could not be a successful candidate, attacks on him subsided, and newspapers again considered him exactly what he was, the greatest hero of the Spanish War. But the great enthusiasm shown in the Middle West in the spring of 1900 must leave a lasting question in the minds of historians as to what would have happened if the nominating conventions of 1900 had been in control of the people instead of the politicians. Even though untrained for the Presidency, Admiral Dewey possessed all the glamour and mass appeal the Democratic party needed to beat the Republican organization. His forthrightness in discussing issues, together with his inconsistency in connection with them, however, made it impossible for the Democrats to accept him as a candidate. He would have been a negation of all the principles for which the party had stood during its period of fealty to William Jennings Bryan.

His brief and unhappy flirtation with political life, clearly the least heroic episode in his career, must be blamed more on his friends than on himself, for they at least knew the game of politics and he did not. No experienced candidate would make the mistake of issuing a secret, exclusive release announcing his plans, or of delivering himself of pronouncements on policy, whose inconsistency could be later thrown back at him. Nor is it clear how Mrs. Dewey, who had lived so close to politics and diplomacy all her life, could have failed to understand what mistakes her husband was making.

Some years afterward, Mrs. Dewey, convinced that Dewey had been thrown to the wolves by President McKinley, who, she said, feared the Admiral's competition more than that of any other man, told her closest friends that the President had sent a "spy" to Manila to help George draft his refusal to run. Then, Mildred charged, McKinley and his friends saw to it that the statement was publicized in large, black type all over the land.

Certainly the Admiral understood little of the mechanics of the press or how easily it could make or break a man. At Manila, far from home, and dealing only with a few correspondents whom he knew closely and respected, his press relations were of the best. Indeed, he owed much of his popularity to the journals which had spread his achievements widely throughout the country. Their subsequent treatment of him as a possible candidate for the Presidency was never, therefore, clear to him. He could not reconcile the fickleness of friends and public, who encouraged him so unreservedly in his hopes, with their cruelty in abandoning him to the cold spotlight of ridicule. But then, Admiral Dewey was not alone in his bewilderment.

27

NAVAL STATESMAN

On March 13, 1900, general order number 544, issued by Secretary John D. Long, established the General Board of the United States Navy. Largely the result of repeated recommendation by George Dewey, who for years had urged the need of effective liaison between professional naval bureaus and the civilian administration of the Secretary's office, it was designed to insure the efficient preparation of the fleet in the event of war, to lay plans for the naval defense of the coast, and to knit together all sections of the service. Fleet dispositions, new construction, and all matters connected with the operations of the Navy came within its province. It was to meet once a month to consider all problems laid before it and at least twice a year hold a week-long session.

Admiral George Dewey was chosen president of the General Board on March 29, 1900.* His appointment gave him a specific, if not arduous, job and established him irrevocably as the "elder statesman" of the Navy, who would advise and consult on all matters of policy but remain free from minute administrative duties. The board's members were the Chief of the Bureau of Navigation (now known as the Bureau of Naval Personnel), the Chief Intelligence Officer and his principal assistant, and the president of the United States Naval War College as members ex officio; and Captain Robley D. Evans, Captain Henry C. Taylor, Captain Charles E. Clark, Captain French E. Chadwick, and Colonel George C. Reid of the Marine Corps.

Dewey moved into new offices in the Navy Department with high hopes that his board might become the means of increasing the efficiency of the fleet and of ending the tragic American misconception of its importance to the country's peacetime security. The Revolutionary War, the War of 1812, and the Civil War had all been followed by nearly complete curtailment of the service.

*Dewey was its only "president." After his death the title was changed to "chairman."

Less than a month after he took his new office, the first underwater ship, the submarine *Holland,* was delivered to the Navy.* It was the result of long and frequently discouraging experiments by its inventor, John P. Holland. A miniature of modern submersibles, it was fifty-three feet long and ten and one quarter feet at its largest diameter. Powered by a gasoline motor, it had a range of fifteen hundred miles on the surface and about forty-five under water. Its armament consisted of one eighteen-inch torpedo gun and two eight-inch dynamite guns, similar to those used on the unsuccessful dynamite boat *Vesuvius.* She was finally turned over to the fleet in April, 1900, under the command of Lieutenant Harry Caldwell, Dewey's aide at Manila Bay, and, possibly inspired by that officer's enthusiasm, Dewey appeared before the House Naval Affairs Committee to urge an appropriation under which America's first class of seven submarines was built.

The advent of the submarine opened a new era in naval war. Although the *Holland* was in itself a slight menace to capital ships, Dewey, particularly alert to new inventions and their possibilities for future development, realized what perfected underwater vessels would mean. In later years he revealed the same foresight with respect to aircraft, even though airplanes were in an embryonic stage at the time of his death.

"All I can say is, Harry, I'm thankful the Spaniards did not have submarines at Manila Bay," the Admiral remarked to his former aide when Caldwell assumed command of the *Holland.*

Dewey, the product of an earlier age, was nearly sixty-three when the new century dawned, yet he remained remarkably youthful in outlook during his later years, and kept abreast of the naval developments science offered. At the same time his life in the early years of the decade was essentially one of ease and society. Received everywhere as befitted the Admiral's fame and his wife's wealth and position, the couple kept occupied attending balls, diplomatic dinners, teas, and all the other kinds of entertainment which made up the social activities of the capital. Mrs. Dewey, whose furs, gowns, and jewels were famous, was in her element at these occasions, while her husband, who loved honor and adulation, was never happier than when sitting at his hostess' right as the lion of the evening.

The accession of Roosevelt to the Presidency following McKinley's assassination in September, 1901, meant additional prestige for the Admiral, a favorite of the new President, who called upon him for advice in all matters of naval policy and naval diplomacy. At one of the first

*Frank T. Cable, "The Submarine Torpedo Boat Holland," *Naval Institute Proceedings,* Feb., 1943.

dinners he gave in the White House, the President praised Dewey and recalled his own part in arranging the appointment to the Asiatic command.

"I did a good day's work when I got McKinley to appoint you, Dewey," said Roosevelt. "Between you and me, if Howell had got it, he'd be blockading Manila yet."

Roosevelt's tenure in the White House, reviving interest in the strategy of the Spanish-American War and in the Sampson-Schley controversy, led to the court of inquiry, presided over by Dewey, which delivered a verdict criticizing Schley's retrograde movement but upholding his conduct in the battle. However, it evaded any reference to the point at issue— the question of whether Schley or Sampson was entitled to the credit for the victory at Santiago. The opinion read:

Commodore Schley, in command of the Flying Squadron, should have proceeded with the utmost dispatch off Cienfuegos, and should have maintained a close blockade of the port.

He should have endeavored on May 23 at Cienfuegos, to obtain information regarding the Spanish squadron by communicating with the insurgents at the place designated in the memorandum delivered to him at 8:15 A.M. of that date.

He should have proceeded from Cienfuegos to Santiago de Cuba with all dispatch, and should have disposed his vessels with a view of intercepting the enemy in any attempt to pass the Flying Squadron. . . .

He should not have made the retrogade turn westward with his squadron.

He should have promptly obeyed the Navy Department's order of May 25.

He should have endeavored to capture or destroy the Spanish vessels at anchor near the entrance of Santiago Harbor on May 29 and 30.

He did not do his utmost with the force under his command to capture or destroy the *Colon* and other vessels of the enemy which he attacked on May 31.

By commencing the engagement on July 3 with the port battery, and turning the *Brooklyn* around with port helm, Commander Schley caused her to lose distance and position with the Spanish vessels, especially with the *Vizcaya* and *Colon*.

The turn of the *Brooklyn* to starboard was made to avoid getting her into dangerous proximity to the Spanish vessels. The turn was made toward the *Texas,* and caused that vessel to stop and to back her engines to avoid possible collision. . . .

Schley's conduct in connection with the events of the Santiago campaign prior to June 1, 1898, was characterized by vacillation, dilatoriness, and lack of enterprise.

His official reports regarding the coal supply and the coaling facilities of the Flying Squadron were inaccurate and misleading.

His conduct during the battle of July 3 was self-possessed, and he encouraged in his own person his subordinate officers and men to fight courageously.

Dewey added a personal memorandum which read:

In the opinion of the undersigned the passage from Key West to Cienfuegos was made by the Flying Squadron with all possible dispatch, Commodore Schley having in view the importance of arriving off Cienfuegos with as much coal as possible in the ship's bunkers. The blockade of Cienfuegos was effective. . . . The passage from Cienfuegos to a point about twenty-two miles south of Santiago was made with as much dispatch as was possible while keeping the squadron a unit. The blockade of Santiago was effective.

Commodore Schley was the senior officer of our squadron off Santiago when the Spanish Squadron attempted to escape on the morning of July 3, 1898. He was in absolute command, and is entitled to the credit due to such commanding officer for the glorious victory which resulted in the total destruction of the Spanish ships.

Dewey's gratuitous support of Schley greatly angered Secretary Long, who believed that Schley's conduct in turning back from Santiago had been "shameful." "I ought then to have detached and court-martialed him," Long wrote. "If so, all this trouble would have been saved, and my duty would have been done."*

Long castigated Dewey's good judgment in adding his personal verdict, asserting that it "has been a subject of surprise and criticism as it left him in the position of agreeing with his associates on all the more important matters which were considered by him and them, and of then expressing an opinion, while his associates properly expressed none, on a matter vital to a brother officer on which the full court had refused to hear any evidence on either side."

More serious events were occupying the attention of the American people. In 1899 the Republic of Venezuela, by the "traditional South American revolution," had acquired a new President, Cipriano Castro, characterized as "an unspeakably villainous little monkey,"† under whose regime the country piled up debts to European powers which it could not pay.

As principal creditors (although citizens of numerous other nations, including the United States, had also invested), England and Germany took the initiative in collecting the debts by dispatching ships to the Caribbean, where they menaced Venezuelan shores and shipping. In

*Entry in Long's *Journal* for Dec. 22, 1901.
†Pringle, *Theodore Roosevelt*, p. 282.

277

1902 they instituted a blockade to enforce collection, whereupon Venezuela appealed to Roosevelt to arbitrate the difficulties. This the President refused to do, as American debts were also involved. The presence of German and British squadrons off Venezuela could have been interpreted as a threat to the Monroe Doctrine, but since Germany had previously informed the State Department of her proposed blockade, no protest was made.

None the less, a sizable American fleet of fifty ships was dispatched to the Caribbean area in November, 1902, commanded by Admiral Dewey as flag officer aboard the converted yacht *Mayflower,** which had been owned by Ogden Goelet and was purchased by the Navy in 1898. In the Spanish War it had achieved the distinction of hitting one Spanish warship with a five-inch shell.

The winter maneuvers of 1902-03 were held off Cuba, within easy steaming distance of Venezuela, although at the time President Roosevelt indicated that no threat to any other power was intended. In 1915, however, he asserted that Germany had planned to seize a port in South America, a clear violation of the Monroe Doctrine. When he made this allegation, the first World War was being fought, and Roosevelt was bitter against Germany.†

The crisis was ended in 1903 when Germany broke away from the other European powers and agreed to negotiate her claims.‡ What actually happened, according to Pringle, "will probably never be known," although he admits that Roosevelt, by acting as his own State Department and talking boldly to the German Ambassador, von Holleben, may have "hastened" negotiation. Whatever the facts, to George Dewey, at least, the maneuvers were an indication of a keenly played diplomatic game by Roosevelt, for in March, 1903, the Admiral told a Newark *Evening News* correspondent that they were an "object lesson to the Kaiser more than to any other person.§ The statement was typical both of Dewey's distrust of Germany and of his tendency to give somewhat blunt statements to the press.

The indiscreet remark embarrassed the President, who promptly wrote the Admiral on March 30, 1903.¶

*Time, July 12, 1943. The *Mayflower* became the Presidential yacht in 1906, continuing in that capacity until 1929, when Herbert Hoover decommissioned her because she was too costly. But in 1943 the ship was repurchased by the Coast Guard and fitted out as a convoy escort vessel to help fight World War II.

†Noted historians, including John Bassett Moore, quickly refuted the statement, while Henry F. Pringle, Roosevelt's most eminent biographer, questions its veracity.

‡Morison and Commager, *The Growth of the American Republic*, p. 831.

§*Newark Evening News*, March 26, 1903.

¶This letter is now at the Chicago Historical Society. Earlier biographies have stated that Roosevelt gave this message to Dewey verbally.

278

My Dear Admiral:

Good-bye and good luck to you while I am gone.

Now, my dear Admiral, do let me beg of you to remember how great your reputation is—how widely whatever you say goes over the whole world. I know that you did not expect the interview you had to be printed, but do let me entreat you to say nothing which can be taken hold of by those anxious to foment trouble between ourselves and any foreign power, or who delight in giving the impression that [as a nation] we are walking about with a chip on our shoulder. We are too big a people to be able to be careless as to what we say.

With warm regards to Mrs. Dewey and assuring you again of my affection and admiration, I am your friend,

T. R.

Yet within a few days Roosevelt expressed his fears of German aggression in a letter to John Hay. The President, convinced that Germany was "tempted" by the Dutch and Danish West Indies, wrote to Hay on April 22, 1903, that the best way to deliver Germany from that temptation was to keep on with the upbuilding of the American Navy.* In 1915, however, he amplified the episode and tried to show that bluntness, supported by a large fleet, had blocked a potential German invasion of the Western Hemisphere.

Dewey went to sea again aboard the *Mayflower* in April, 1903, to inspect the North Atlantic squadron, enjoying a pleasant two-week cruise.

One item of naval procedure which he noticed daily on that voyage bothered the Admiral. This was the lack of uniformity in the music played at morning and evening colors, when the national flag was raised and lowered. No Navy regulation had yet been issued, but the Admiral had always regarded "The Star-Spangled Banner" as the appropriate tune. Remembering his own experience in Hong Kong when the German Prince had offended him, he desired to end the confusion both among American officers and foreigners. He appealed personally to President Roosevelt, and the President instructed Acting Secretary of the Navy Charles H. Darling to issue a general order, dated April 22, 1904, which established "The Star-Spangled Banner" as the official anthem of the Army and Navy. In 1931 it was made the national anthem for civilians as well by Act of Congress.

The Admiral was called upon to deliver many public speeches, an art which he had never mastered. Once at the Naval Academy, while making a formal inspection, he was called upon to speak. Momentarily at a loss for words, he asked:

*Dennett, *John Hay*, p. 388.
†George Dewey, *Autobiography*, p. 184.

"Is there anyone here who can tell me what three ships won the Battle of Manila?" The Admiral looked about the room.

At the rear of the hall a young midshipman rose to attention and said, "I can, sir."

"Indeed," said the Admiral. "Go ahead, please."

"Leadership, fellowship, and seamanship," answered the midshipman.* Dewey liked this, coming from a standard-bearer of the Navy's honor. He enjoyed, too, reading about himself in his favorite books, works on the Spanish-American War, most of them lauding his own exploits to the extreme. All the lives of Dewey were in his library, most of them bound in gold-tooled leather with suitable inscriptions written by the authors on the flyleaves. Almost every naval book written was given to him by its author, and his library became a treasure of first editions and presentation copies of works on naval history, the Philippines, and reminiscences of Annapolis men and heroes of the Civil and Spanish Wars.†

Among his closest friends in these years was, of course, Senator Redfield Proctor, who, until his death in 1908, almost always ate Christmas dinner at the Dewey home. There in the house that the people had presented to the Admiral, with all its trophies, including the gigantic loving cup given by seventy thousand schoolchildren, the old friends from the Green Mountains enjoyed a typical New England holiday dinner: turkey, onions, all the fixings, and hot mince pie.

Proctor always asked Mrs. Dewey for a second piece of pie.

"There's a man," she would exclaim, filling his plate.

"Pshaw, Mildred," said the Admiral laughing. "He's from Vermont. He takes it for the taste of brandy he gets."

"That's right," said Proctor. "My old father on his deathbed cried out, 'Water, water.' Then he told everyone but me to go out of the room. 'Are they all gone?' he whispered faintly. 'Good. Under the bed—the whisky bottle.' I got it out. He took a drink, and died happy."

Every December 26 after Manila the Secretary of the Navy and the General Board of admirals and captains called at the Dewey home in formal uniform to pay their respects to the Admiral. There were no invitations. It was just a custom to wish the white-haired hero happy birthday. And every year Dewey put out large goblets of champagne, and as the leaders of the American Navy stood at attention, one of them proposed the only toast:

"Happy returns, Admiral."

*Miss Elizabeth Ellicott Poe is the authority for the account of this episode.
†Most of Dewey's library is now in possession of the Chicago Historical Society. Some of the volumes have been retained by his son.

Young George Dewey was a participant at one of these gatherings. He had wanted something a little more effective than champagne that day so had filled his glass with bourbon. The Admiral noticed this.

"Great God," he thundered. "Look at the size of George's drink." His son turned red, but the Admiral went on.

"Oh, that's all right, son. It never hurt me. Go ahead and drink it."

Before the war Dewey had ridden horseback every afternoon. So regular had been his route through Rock Creek Park that he became known as "the Commodore ahorseback." One day, while posting down Pennsylvania Avenue, his horse went lame. A young man named David E. Tyler came up, introduced himself, and told Dewey how to fix the horse's foot.

"Put a bit of cork under his front shoes, Commodore," he said. "It will raise the heels and fix him up." Dewey and Tyler walked up the street to a horseshoer on D Street, near 9th Street. Corks were inserted and the horse's lameness disappeared.

After Dewey's return from Asia he remembered Tyler and engaged him as his coachman. "My man Tyler," as the Admiral called him, drove the Admiral to church when he was married in 1899, and took President McKinley and Dewey through the crowd-lined streets to attend services in Arlington Cemetery for the victims of the *Maine*.

Tyler's best story about the Admiral concerns General Corbin, a former suitor of Mrs. Dewey, who was a frequent caller at the Dewey home even after their marriage. Dewey was none too friendly toward the general. One afternoon, as Dewey and Tyler returned home, Corbin preceded them into the house. Just inside, a little throw rug slipped, and Corbin's feet went out from under him. Mrs. Dewey was most sympathetic, but the Admiral took Tyler to his study upstairs, closed the door, and laughed out loud!

"Hah! Hah! Quite funny, eh, Tyler? A United States general down on his behind."

In the summer of 1905, after the ceremonies for the reinterment of John Paul Jones at Annapolis, the Admiral, evidently thinking of a time when similar services might take place for him, turned his attention to a suitable burial site at the Arlington National Cemetery. He selected a plot on a wooded hill, but Mildred, inspecting it on a rainy day, was displeased. It was too far from the main gates, she thought, preferring a more prominent location which every visitor would see. For a few days the matter troubled both of them, but selection of a new location acceptable to both pacified their minds and drew their thoughts from death.

281

They vacationed at Hot Springs in June, and spent August at Richfield Springs, New York. In the autumn the house at 1747 Rhode Island Avenue grew less and less attractive to them, chiefly because many of the public who had contributed to the gift felt free to call at all hours and ask to be escorted through the rooms.* "On several occasions," one account records, "when Mrs. Dewey remonstrated by telling them that the Admiral was not at home or that he was asleep, many would demand the right to go through the house, saying that they had paid twenty-five cents and therefore had a right to go and come whenever they pleased, to which Mrs. Dewey replied: 'I have contributed much more than that, and I don't have that right to wander through the house when the Admiral is asleep or is resting.'"†

However magnificent it may have seemed to average Americans, the house was less well suited to the Dewey's style of living than the one at 1601 K Street, which Mildred's father had owned and given her at the time of her first marriage. During the winter of 1907, therefore, when the K Street house became unoccupied, the Deweys decided to move. The Admiral knew this would be resented by the people, who would think him ungrateful, but they moved in on March 10, 1907, with a minimum of unfavorable comment by the country.

At this time the administration was confronted with domestic Japanese-American tension. About 75,000 Japanese citizens in the United States, most of them living in California, demanded the right to attend public primary schools. Californians objected, and in 1906 the San Francisco school board ordered all Japanese to attend separate schools opened for them. The exclusion order, highly irritating to the Japanese government, immediately brought a protest to Roosevelt.

An alarming report reached the White House through a retired United States Army officer then living in St. Petersburg, Russia, who wrote Major General J. F. Bell, chief of staff of the Army, of an amazing and frank declaration by a Japanese at a dinner party. "Gentlemen, you hear it said that Japan will take the Philippine Islands when she desires it and is ready," the Japanese, somewhat affected by the champagne, is supposed to have said. "She is ready now. . . . But do you imagine that will satisfy us? We never forget and we never forgive a personal injury. Our religion is the worship of our forefathers. They would disown us if we bowed our heads before the enemy who has insulted us and our children merely because we are Japanese. No! San Francisco will see the day when she

*Mrs. Dewey's explanation to Elizabeth Ellicott Poe.
†Related by Elizabeth Ellicott Poe.

will wish that she had perished bodily in the great earthquake. . . . I tell you that we will make a Japanese colony of California and of the Pacific Coast, Alaska included. . . . The United States are our natural enemies in trade and constitute the only nation in the world that has refused to recognize us as equals."*

Similar stories reached the President's ear from English and German sources, even alleging that Japan had hidden ten thousand soldiers in Mexico ready to take the Panama Canal and California. No less a personage than Kaiser Wilhelm was quoted as the source. In 1907 such rumors seemed incredible, yet there was evidence that Japan was looking toward some future time of conquest. Three battleships building on English ways, supposedly for Brazil, were reportedly destined for Tokyo. Certainly Japan's defeat of Russia encouraged her in her dreams of overcoming the Western World.

In Washington the issue became immediate and pressing. Roosevelt was plagued by the complaints of both California and Japan. On February 9, 1907, the President received a delegation of San Franciscans demanding an end of his attempts to force repeal of the exclusion laws.† Warning them that war might result from their program, he proposed a compromise providing for the prohibition of Japanese immigration by way of Hawaii, Mexico, Canada, or the Panama Canal Zone, in return for which the educational restrictions were to be removed. This was worked out as the "Gentlemen's Agreement," in the form of memoranda between Secretary of State Elihu Root and Foreign Minister Takahira of Japan, but it was not a success. Riots against Japanese restaurant owners broke out in San Francisco in June, and resentment in Japan reached new heights.

Then, according to a story Dewey told his nephew, Captain William Winder, the Japanese Ambassador called upon the President at the White House to demand that the agitation against Japanese be stopped. Roosevelt concealed his anger under a mask of serious concern. He went to the door and ordered a secretary to call for Admiral Dewey immediately.

Dewey rushed to the White House as fast as possible, to find the President and the Ambassador sitting sullenly at opposite ends of a table in Roosevelt's office. The Admiral shook hands and sat down.

"Your Excellency," said the President to the Japanese, "please repeat, for the benefit of the Admiral, what you have just said to me." Roosevelt's face was imperturbable.

The visitor turned to the Admiral and declared, "My Emperor has

*Pringle, *Theodore Roosevelt*, pp. 400–404.
†*Ibid.*

instructed me to say to your President that the demonstrations and agitations against the Japanese in California must cease at once."

Dewey sat upright in his chair.

"Sir," he said. "Did I understand you to use the word 'must'?"

"That is the message as I was instructed to deliver it," replied the Japanese.

Dewey stood up and pounded the desk with his fist.

"Mr. Ambassador," he said, "you tell your Emperor that neither he nor you nor anyone else can use the word 'must' to my President in my presence. There is the door, sir. Good morning."

Roosevelt stood up, controlling himself with difficulty.

"You have heard the Admiral," he said. "That will do for my reply as well." The Japanese walked out without a word. Roosevelt slumped into his chair with a sigh.

"My God, Dewey," he said. "Do you realize this means war?"

"No, sir. I don't think so," the Admiral answered. "Our fleet can start for the Pacific in two weeks and get there before the Japs are ready. They won't dare to make a move."

Actually, however, it was five months before the fleet began its famous cruise around the world.

Japan protested again. On July 12, 1907, Count Acki and Admiral Yamamoto (father of the Japanese admiral who launched war in 1941) called upon Roosevelt at Oyster Bay, where they were told that he planned to send the American fleet through the Pacific.* Soon afterward Japan issued a formal invitation to the United States fleet to visit Tokyo Bay. The Emperor was not yet ready for war. Japan's fleet of battleships totaled fourteen, while the United States had twenty-four. Japan's shipbuilding industry was nil, the bulk of her fleet up to that time having been built in the shipyards of England and Scotland.

On December 16, 1907, when sixteen mighty American battleships left Hampton Roads, the President, accompanied by George Dewey, stood on the bridge of the *Mayflower,* and as the signal flag from the yacht's halyards ordered "Proceed to Duty Assigned," the fleet put out to sea. When the American fleet reached Tokyo the next October it was feted for three days amid an atmosphere of great cordiality and mutual respect.

The round-the-world cruise did more than discourage Japan from thoughts of immediate war. It helped make America more conscious of its Navy. Congress had earlier refused to provide funds for the long voyage, but when Roosevelt pointed out that the Navy had enough money

*Pringle, *op. cit.*, p. 410.

to send the fleet to California, where it could stay, the trip was promptly authorized. Thinking of war in terms of European powers, Congress could not tolerate the idea of the fleet's resting in Pacific waters. The country remained for the most part unaware of a Japanese threat, for the rise of German ambitions pushed the Eastern power into the background, where it remained, all too greatly ignored, until a December day in 1941.

But if the layman remained ignorant of that threat, the Navy's General Board did not. In its report for July, 1907, to the Secretary of the Navy, it urged the concentration of the battle fleet and warned that the United States could not hold the Philippines a month unless a fleet in full force was instantly available for action. Signed by Dewey, it further urged immediate adoption of practice in battle tactics and the construction of two new naval bases, one at Guatanamo, Cuba, and the other at Olongapo in Subic Bay, the importance of which, ever since 1898, Dewey had realized. Cavité, he argued, was on the opposite side of Luzon from Japan, the only power Dewey regarded as a threat to the Philippines, whereas a Subic Bay base would permit reinforcements to a fleet fighting in the China Sea. In Dewey's opinion Spain's failure to erect a base at Subic lay in its remoteness from the society of Manila, which her naval officers wished to enjoy, and although this was scarcely the cause of America's failure to fortify Olongapo, the wisdom of Dewey's advice was proved in 1941.

Ten days after the fleet left Hampton Roads, the Admiral of the Navy observed his seventieth birthday. His marriage and his Presidential ambitions, so cruelly assaulted by the press, were forgotten. He was "Mr. Navy," a kind of patriarch revered by all, no longer a cause for jealousy, still cherished by the people and still the recipient of their gifts—paper cutters, eyeglass cases, cigar boxes, and photographs. Letters by the hundreds came to the house on K Street or to his country home, Beauvoir. Children still stopped and saluted him in the streets, and this pleased him most. He would live longer in their memories. The letters he cast away, but the gifts he retained. They piled up in the great house to such an extent that when he moved it was suggested that he needed not so much a larger dining room for entertaining as a larger attic for storing his souvenirs.* One memento above all others he kept close. It was an 1837 penny, minted in the year of his birth,† which always remained in his

---

*In 1900 a more or less apocryphal tale was circulated to the effect that Dewey had told the committee selecting his gift house that he wanted one with "a small dining room—to seat sixteen guests."

†This penny, so jealously guarded by the Admiral, is now among his effects at the Chicago Historical Society.

trouser pocket, his good-luck charm through the Civil War and at Manila.

On May Day, 1908, as he sat on the porch of his house on K Street, looking at the tall flagpole on the front lawn that bore his old broad blue pennant of a commodore, a messenger from the White House arrived with an envelope. It contained a letter* which made him very happy. Type-written in the blue ink the President used for personal messages, it read:

MY DEAR ADMIRAL DEWEY:

On this 10th anniversary of one of the great feats in American history—one of those feats which mark the beginnings of new epochs—I must write a word to you to tell you, not only on my own account, but on behalf of all the people of the United States, with what affectionate regard we look upon you. Surely no man in any country could hope for a higher reward than is yours, for no other man living stands to his countrymen in quite the same position that you do.

With all good wishes for you and yours, believe me,

Faithfully yours,
THEODORE ROOSEVELT.

*In the collection of the Chicago Historical Society.

28

THE ADMIRAL'S LADY

$\mathcal{M}$ildred McLean Dewey had captured the social lion of the hour and reveled in her achievement. Yet she was deeply and completely in love with the Admiral, keenly interested in his professional concerns, in diplomacy, and in the struggle for power and prestige of the leading figures in American national politics. The Deweys dined at the White House with regularity. Their intimates included the Jules Jusserands—the French Ambassador in Washington—Senator Henry Cabot Lodge, the William Howard Tafts, the Elihu Roots, the Theodore Roosevelts, and all the leaders of Washington society. Their world was the world of uniformed butlers, diplomatic dinners, high politics, and petty jealousies.

As "custodian" of the outstanding hero of the day, Mrs. Dewey was proud and jealous. She swelled with pride when the Admiral received the recognition accorded his prestige; her anger boiled when he was slighted. When the newspapers referred to her husband as "Our Peerless Admiral," Mrs. Dewey was happy; when the Roosevelts invited the Deweys to the wedding of the President's daughter, Alice, to Nicholas Longworth, and neglected to enclose a card for the private entrance, her back arched in indignation.

Mildred Dewey was five feet two inches tall, dark-haired, and never weighed more than one hundred pounds, but gowned in long, black silk dresses, as was her wont, and covered with diamonds, she walked through the salons of Washington like a queen, proud, imperious, and assured, yet withal, lonely and afraid. For Mrs. Dewey was growing deaf, and the social empire which was hers was slipping fast away. She could easily hear the Admiral, whose low, baritone tones were always clear and spoken with perfect enunciation, but her hearing after 1905 began to grow too weak for large gatherings. For many years Mrs. Dewey tried various experiments to improve her hearing, such as alcohol-impregnated cotton pads in her ears, yet her deafness increased. With a speaking trumpet she could hear perfectly, but she would not embarrass the Admiral by using that in public. As a result, the Deweys went into society less and less. Demanding as she was, it was not comfortable for the Admiral to go out too often and leave her home alone, so he, too, retired more and more from the plaudits and esteem, missing the "recognition which he so admirably deserved."

In June of 1900 Mrs. Dewey was described as the most prominent woman in America outside of the White House,* a woman whose "innate modesty is coupled with an intense ambition to shine at the topmost heights of social success." She impressed contemporary writers because of her decided fondness for dress and jewels and her devotion to her husband. He gave her the social position in the country which her "heart craves," said one writer.

Mrs. Dewey, a hostess of notable accomplishment, managed her home with perfection and skill, and with her large fortune entertained in a lavish style. Nevertheless, she possessed a New England frugality, and the Admiral and his lady were most scrupulous to keep their household accounts minutely correct. Whenever one borrowed even a small amount from the other, books were kept and the "debt" was promptly repaid. Dinner parties at the Dewey home were models of fine imported dinner tablecloths, the right wines, perfectly cooked food, and meticulous observance of the niceties of social form and conversation. As a hostess Mrs. Dewey saw that all her guests received just the exact amount of attention and respect that their social stations merited. Her residence at the Austrian court stood her in good stead for her position as wife of the Admiral of the Navy. In Washington, where rank was one of the most important aspects of social life, Mrs. Dewey was final arbiter. She knew "gun usage," the table showing the number of guns to be fired in salute of all officials, from beginning to end, and frequently was consulted to decide in what relative rank dinner guests should be seated, and if this was ever ignored with respect to the Admiral, she took ready offense.

Mrs. Dewey was described as the "most dazzlingly ornamented woman who bowed to the President"† at the New Year's Day reception at the White House in 1900. Jewels covered her corsage, and her hair was dressed in "bewildering splendor though in exquisite taste."

That reception, her first as the Admiral's wife, was marked by a major social victory over the wives of other military men. "Mrs. Admiral Dewey," Secretary Long wrote in his journal, "came to me with many pleasant

*"Mrs. Dewey," *Current Literature*, June, 1900.
†*Ibid.*

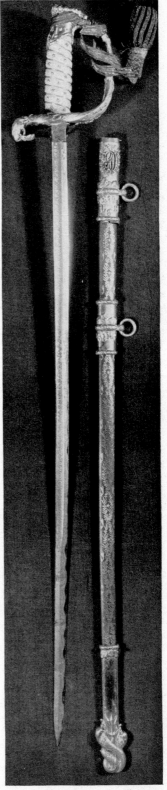

Left. The great silver loving cup made of 70,000 dimes presented by the schoolchildren of America to Admiral Dewey.

Right. The gold and silver sword, studded with diamonds, presented to Admiral Dewey by Congress.

words and asked as a special favor that I take her past the reviewing group, as she was obliged to go home early with the Admiral."* The Secretary did so immediately after the diplomatic corps, and before the Senators and Representatives. Then came the Army, led by General Miles, followed by the Navy, led by Admiral Dewey. As the older service, the Army was entitled to pass the receiving line first.

Secretary Long left the White House in a few minutes and went to another home, where he met Secretary of State John Hay, who said, "with a twinkle in his eye, that all the ladies were in a great state of mind. Mrs. Dewey had stolen a march. The wife of the major general commanding and the other military ladies were quite aggrieved, and intimated that it was a shrewd movement of Mrs. Dewey to go ahead of the Army, since Miles did before Dewey." Mr. Long dismissed the incident in his journal by saying, "Doesn't all this come very pat with . . . *Vanity Fair*." But the other ladies, who had not read Thackeray, nursed the defeat in their hearts.

As a sentimentalist Mrs. Dewey became the custodian of the Manila Bay trophies and gifts from the American people, cherishing them as much as did the Admiral. Through the years new gifts poured in from unknown admirers, and each thrilled her, no matter how much junk it seemed to be, for she reveled in the sentiment it evidenced.

Mildred was perhaps happiest at Beauvoir, her father's palatial estate outside Washington. There in the square old-fashioned house on top of a hill, approached by a fir-lined driveway, looking over Washington and the Potomac, Mildred enjoyed all the attributes of country life combined with the luxury and comforts of a suburban manor. A spacious screened porch encircled the Victorian residence, and on the sloping lawn two wicker armchairs from the *Olympia* flanked a hooded armchair reserved for her.† There Mrs. Dewey kept the *Olympia's* parrot, which had learned to say "Hello, George" and never relapsed into the sailor language it had learned in the fleet. Another prized pet was the dog Bob, named after Dewey's Bob on the *Olympia* which had died on the way home. The second Bob was given the Admiral by Long's successor, William H. Moody, who had taken him for a cruise with the Admiral on the *Dolphin*. Bob was unbearably seasick on the trip and Dewey was the only man who could comfort him. Mrs. Dewey kept her own butterfly collection at Beauvoir, along with such items as a wooden map of the Philippines made by a Filipino woman, a section of the Manila cable cut by the

*Long's *Journal*.
†Abby G. Baker, "At Home with Admiral and Mrs. Dewey," *Woman's Home Companion*, May, 1904.

Zafiro, and hundreds of other mementos which the Admiral planned to give his son, because he felt their value would be "enhanced by the passing years."

Mildred was an avid reader. In 1906, when the Deweys went to Hot Springs, Virginia, for two weeks in July and August, she read the *Recollections of General Robert E. Lee,* written by his son, and nineteen novels, mostly "trash," she wrote, not to mention "all the magazines," as well as embroidering the skirt of a dress, finishing its jacket, and starting a second embroidered linen skirt.

As the Admiral grew older, it became harder for him to sleep. Many nights he was a victim of insomnia. An early riser because of his long naval routine, he was awakened at six o'clock by Ah Mah bringing in a cup of hot tea. Then Dewey would bathe and dress and take a brief walk in the brisk morning air. Returning home, he read until breakfast time. The Admiral always took a nap after lunch, and after dinner he often fell asleep in his easy chair until about ten o'clock, while his wife read.

The Deweys did not entertain as frequently as she would have liked, and their health in the declining years forced them to refuse many invitations. The Admiral was often ill during his later years, and Mrs. Dewey, too, was a frequent victim of colds and influenza. One day she commented to her husband:

"God is good to me."

"He'd be a lot kinder if he did not give you so many colds," answered the Admiral, and the sentiment touched her, even if it did seem a trifle sacrilegious.

The Admiral's prestige was restored in the years after his attempt for the Presidency. Friends still insisted that he run, but both Mrs. Dewey and the Admiral never considered the question again, although such encouragement gave her a thrill of pride second only to the occasions when the Admiral publicly praised her. Once, when Alice Roosevelt was engaged to Nicholas Longworth, Dewey took both her hands in his and said:

"I hope you will be as happily married as I am."

That was the apotheosis for his wife.

The Roosevelts sent flowers on numerous occasions when either the Admiral or Mrs. Dewey were ill. Once Mrs. Roosevelt sent cineraria, which to Mildred represented ashes and flowers of death. When Lord Grey of Fallodon was in Washington, the President entertained formally and Dewey was the lion of the evening, describing the German troubles at Manila to a select group of Roosevelt, Grey, and Secretary Hay.

Prince Louis' visit to Washington in November, 1905, was the occasion for one of Mrs. Dewey's greatest social successes. On Saturday afternoon,

November 3, the Roosevelts held a reception for the British admiral and his staff in the Blue Room. Everyone who mattered in official circles was there. Mrs. Dewey arrived at a quarter to three, in her own words, "exquisitely dressed—gray or rather pastel blue velvet, shading to pale blue—curious lace flounces and lace coat over a liberty satin, which had a liberty velvet blouse of blue shading to pink—lace yoke and sleeves of Mechlin and gold belt." Her hat was of blue cloth of silver, with pastel blue and pink feathers, and her coat and skirt were trimmed with "love knots of mink fur." Around her throat was a string of black pearls with a sapphire clasp. There were a great many compliments, she recalled. Admiral Dewey entered at three, in full-dress uniform, the heavy Congressional sword, worn only on such occasions, hanging at his side. The President and Mrs. Roosevelt entered soon afterward, and Mrs. Roosevelt kissed her hand to Mrs. Dewey as she entered, a signal honor.

It was the Navy's day, and George Dewey was the first through the receiving line. The President greeted him with both arms outstretched as "My best beloved!"

The Admiral told the President what a fine Thanksgiving proclamation he had written, and Roosevelt, in the tone of a small schoolboy receiving praise, said:

"You like it?"

Mrs. Dewey echoed the compliment, saying, "We are all so proud of you."

The President took her hand and interrupted, "But we are all so proud of him," and looking at George, he went on, "He has done—and is doing—great things."

At this point Mrs. Roosevelt entered the conversation:

"Dear Mrs. Dewey, dear Mrs. Dewey, how sweet was the note you wrote me, and how we delighted in it." She referred to a letter praising the President's handling of the Portsmouth peace conference which ended the Russo-Japanese war. Mrs. Roosevelt might have gone on, but the Admiral interrupted with a word to his wife:

"You are blocking the line, deary," and Mrs. Dewey had to end her moment of triumph.

They were introduced to the Prince Admiral by Alice Roosevelt, and there was "a lot of talk and a great many compliments." When Rear Admiral Robley Evans and his wife entered, Mrs. Evans curtsied low to Mrs. Dewey and said in a loud voice, "I salute my chief," while Admiral Evans kissed her hand.

Later that afternoon the Prince Admiral and his staff paid a call on the Deweys at 1747 Rhode Island Avenue, and an official dinner for thirty-six followed at the British Embassy. "Splendidly dressed and be-jewelled," Mildred sat opposite the Prince, who looked at her jewels "many times, and I was correct even to emeralds and diamonds and rings. George was very proud, and Admiral Brownson said to him that I was dressed like a queen, and the most beautifully and exquisitely dressed woman at both places."

There was praise for the Admiral, too, when Prince Louis expansively told him after dinner: "Your entering Manila Bay at night was precisely like Nelson at the Nile."

Dewey was invited to the White House the next day to consult with the President about the next chief of the Bureau of Navigation. ("Set your own time," Roosevelt said. It always pleased Mrs. Dewey that the President asked her husband to choose his own hour for interviews.)

On Christmas Eve the next year, Mrs. Dewey entertained the Roosevelts in the Rhode Island Avenue house. There were twenty-eight at dinner, and the President and Mrs. Roosevelt were flattering guests. Mrs. Roosevelt stopped in the hall and admired the portraits of the Admiral and Mrs. Dewey which had been done by the French painter, Chartran, for $5,000 each, and were the gifts of Charles M. Schwab. Roosevelt "made himself delightful," Mildred told her friends. "Everybody was brilliant and gay, and the women splendidly dressed. The eight men out of fourteen in full-dress uniforms. The mandolin music pretty, the dinner splendid." And there was "nothing but compliments for the dinner" on Christmas Day when friends and naval officers made their calls.

In a way, Mildred was the hero's reward for his battle. Wealthy, stylish, and a leader of society, she complemented the niche he had carved for himself. She was the goal that Susie Goodwin, the governor's daughter, had represented in 1867. Mildred was the leader in a world of international society on a richer plane, as befitted the difference between Dewey's triumph at Fort Fisher and at Manila Bay. Mildred's interests in social prestige became to a large extent his own, and her love of fine surroundings, elegant furnishings, and perfection of service were his as well. Born to wealth and social position, Mildred Dewey almost seemed foredestined to become the Admiral's lady. By education and experience she was so fitted. The tragedy of her life was that the American people never understood her love of aristocracy.*

*For most of the account of Mrs. Mildred Dewey the authors are indebted to Miss Elizabeth Ellicott Poe, one of her close friends. Mrs. Dewey wished her husband to be remembered throughout history. In Miss Poe she found the person to whom she might entrust many stories and much information which would otherwise have died with her. Unexplained quotation marks denote Mrs. Dewey's own words to Miss Poe.

29

THE LOVING CUP

*I*n a corner of the brocaded drawing room on K Street, resting on a high mahogany stand, stood the great loving cup. It was the first object to catch the eye of a visitor, and its spirit pervaded the entire room. Pictures and mementos of the May Day victory crowded the tapestried walls. Indeed, the whole house had become a national museum, filled with smaller loving cups, each the gift of an American municipality, and with gold plates, swords, and trophies. Surrounded by these relics of his greatness, the Admiral grew old and passed from active life into legend. Yet he was not ready to give up his active pursuits altogether. Almost every day he left the house for his office in the Mills Building. Sometimes younger officers passed by on fine mornings in the hope of being able to accompany him on his walk to the General Board headquarters. They enjoyed seeing him swing the gold-headed cane his son had given him one Christmas, just as he had given one to his own father many years before.

The lives of the aging pair were enriched by the advent of the Tafts to the White House. Mrs. Dewey considered Nellie Taft the only "civilized" lady of Theodore Roosevelt's cabinet family, while the Admiral and the new President, who had served as high commissioner of the Philippines, had much in common. Taft's penchant for golf, however, he did not share. "There is a new game here, now," he wrote his son. "It is spelled 'golf' but it is pronounced 'goff.' I shall not try to take it up." The old sports and the old ways he enjoyed best. He disdained a motorcar for his horses and phaeton, despite the fact that Mildred bought her own and took a drive nearly every afternoon. Old friends were best, too, although they were gradually leaving him. Commander Nathan Sargent, his former aide and historian of the Philippines campaign, died in 1906. Sampson had gone in 1902, and every year, when the Society of Manila

Bay, composed of the officers of Dewey's fleet in 1898, met to toast the victory and their "Commodore," there were a few less.

When he wanted music, it was not the new, but the old, favorites he asked his wife, an accomplished pianist, to play for him. She always ended with his favorite march of Manila days, "Under the Double Eagle." Then she closed the music, picked up her long skirts, reached into an inner pocket in her petticoat where she kept her glasses, opened her book and read while the Admiral dozed off. That petticoat pocket was the one eccentricity which caused her husband embarrassment, for whether at dinner, at a ball, or at a White House reception, if she needed anything in that petticoat pocket, she calmly and unself-consciously picked up her outer skirts and reached into it for what she wanted.

With the passing of the years the Admiral grew more mellow. He always had a smile for workers at the General Board, and every year at Thanksgiving time he went to the Navy commissary store to select personally a turkey for every employee. The commissary was his favorite shopping place. Despite Mrs. Dewey's wealth and the Admiral's ample means, the Deweys bought all their foodstuffs there, and every day the Admiral, with a market basket on his arm, marched through the store, rubbing elbows with petty officers, junior lieutenants, and their wives, as he made his purchases.

His only charity was the Navy Relief Society, organized to provide funds for the needy families or widows of Navy men. As president, he sent a handsome check for its support every year.

The Navy, itself, continued to occupy his time. Regular inspections of naval establishments and of the fleet he considered most important, and in these he was the disciplinarian of yore. One apocryphal story of such a review tells of a green cook, who was stirring a huge pot with a long-handled ladle when the Admiral passed. At the sounding of attention, the nervous young chef raised his right hand in salute, while hot, thick stew dripped down his arms. Dewey, noticing his discomfiture, made no comment at the time, but told a friend later that the rank and dignity of naval officers must never be neglected, regardless of any discomfort it might involve.

Nonetheless, the Admiral was keenly interested in the welfare of enlisted men. He ardently believed that American sailors were the finest and best trained in the world, and when, as population moved westward, the number of naval enlistments from the Middle West grew, it was Dewey's foresight which gave recognition to the fact. In his earlier days the fleet was manned largely by foreign seamen, and he was thankful when mercenaries were ruled out of the Navy. In 1909 a Naval Training

Station was founded at Great Lakes, Illinois, and though destined to become the greatest training camp in the entire world, it was none too popular when President Taft presided at its opening on October 28. Dewey, however, quick to see its advantages, stanchly defended it. Three years later, when Congress was considering abolition of the station, he appeared before the Naval Affairs Committee of the House of Representatives to argue against the step. Recounting the history of enlistments, he told the congressmen that whereas in the old days the best seamen came from the seaboard states, the healthiest and best men were now from the Middle West. "We must make this another Annapolis for enlisted men," he argued. "The Navy needs mechanics to man our new ships, and we must have as fine training for the men as for the officers."

If the Admiral's energies dwindled slightly, his interests in the growth of the Navy and the necessity of a definite naval policy did not. They were immensely stimulated in 1909 by the publication of an amazing book, a book largely ignored by the American public, yet one which was to be recalled strikingly after 1941. Its author, Homer Lea,* a crippled hunchback who was a student at Leland Stanford University when George Dewey won the battle of Manila Bay, wished to enlist in the Army and fight in the Spanish-American War. Rejected because of his deformity, he determined to fight for China instead. In 1899 the "crippled dwarf," as President David Starr Jordan of Stanford called him, sailed across the Pacific. Passing Guam and the Philippines on the way, he charted strategic maps for their defense in a coming world conflict which he already foresaw. When he arrived in China, he offered his services to Free China movements then directed against the Dowager Empress Tzu-Hsi. At the age of twenty-four Lea became chief of staff to Sun Yat-sen. After fighting in the Boxer Rebellion, in 1901, he returned to California, where his home became headquarters for the Chinese forces opposing the Manchu dynasty, and where, dressed in Oriental army uniforms, he and Sun Yat-sen spent three years raising funds and gaining converts. In 1904 the eighty-eight pound military genius returned to China and briefly led an army division. After a year he returned to Santa Monica. China was not ready for freedom, and Lea's health was too poor to stand the rigors of military life.

His studies of military science and of the submerged forces in the Orient had convinced him of America's danger. In the Russo-Japanese War of 1904-1905, he discovered a trend unnoticed by his contemporaries. Japan's attack on Russia, he believed, was not only a local attack but the beginning of Japan's move against the entire white race. America seemed to

*Clare Boothe, "Ever Hear of Homer Lea?" *Saturday Evening Post*, March 7, 1942.

him in mortal peril. His one stanch supporter, a hardy ex-sergeant of the American Army named Ansel O'Banion, carried him on his back, while Lea charted the entire Pacific Coast and analyzed its potential defensive arrangements. What he found frightened him, for he realized that it was indefensible from Japanese attack.

Thwarted as he was because of his physical deformity, Lea took a gloomy view of the future, and perhaps because of his own bodily weakness thought of world politics exclusively in terms of force. His book, *The Valor of Ignorance,* traced military movements, principally in Germany and Japan, and foresaw with startling perspicacity the coming of two world wars. He outlined in maps and words a potential attack by Japan on the United States. He told exactly how Japan would take the Philippines, and predicted that England would lose her Oriental empire to Japan, and warned a pacifist America that Japan, despite her weak financial position, was strong enough to wage war almost interminably. Upon completion of his analysis in 1906, he showed it to a few American Army officers, among them Lieutenant General Adna R. Chaffee, chief of staff of the Army, who understood its implications, and who warned of the danger of dismissing as "tommyrot" a possible invasion of this continent.* Major General J. P. Story also praised the importance of the book, admonishing his countrymen that America was "confronted by conditions which may imperil our national security, peace and welfare."†

Lea did not publish his book until 1909, but when it appeared it aroused immediate anger and controversy in many quarters. Dr. Jordan assailed its author as a "loud mouth," who was excessively warlike. Pointing out that Japan was staggering under approaching bankruptcy, Jordan declared that the United States could determine for herself whether she wished to live in peace, and that there was no likelihood that Japan would ever consider war with the United States unless America should "flaunt the red flag for years."‡ This interpretation was generally accepted in America. Lea was forgotten and died in 1912 at the age of thirty-six, but, in Japan, his book was read and pondered. Like Captain Mahan, he analyzed trends and stressed strategic principles designed to teach America, but his work was studied by America's enemies instead.

*Dewey also was aware of the danger from Japan. As years passed, numerous tales of his prophecies appeared. E. V. Durling, Hearst newspaper columnist, wrote on August 26, 1943: "As for prophets, how about Admiral Dewey, who, in 1898, on the deck of his flagship in Manila Bay said: 'I look forward some forty or fifty years and foresee a Japanese naval squadron entering this harbor as I have done and demanding the surrender of Manila and the Philippines, with a plan of making these islands part of a great Japanese empire of the future." No further authority for this statement has, however, been found.
†Homer Lea, *The Valor of Ignorance* (New York: G. P. Putnam's Sons, 1936), p. 6.
‡Clare Boothe, *op. cit.*

Dewey read *The Valor of Ignorance* avidly, seeing in its forthright discussion his own forebodings expressed with crystal clarity. Lea's emphasis on the strategic necessity of fortifying a string of island bases from Hawaii to the Philippines proclaimed Dewey's own tenets for essential naval policy. Repeatedly he had argued for such measures at meetings of the General Board, repeatedly he had urged fortification of Guam before Congressional committees. They remained unconvinced. His interest in the Orient and the Pacific was naturally greater than that of many other naval strategists, for he had helped open the Pacific to American naval power, and while others viewed naval policy almost entirely in relation to the powers of Europe, Dewey looked beyond Hawaii with personal feelings. Had not the Philippines almost been called the Dewey Islands?

He had pressed for an American merchant marine as well, for he wanted to see the islands developed into an essential part of American commercial prestige. "It is a crime," he told his son, "that this great nation's flag does not fly on the seven seas of the world." No nation, as Mahan had shown, could become a great sea power without a mighty merchant marine.* The General Board, advisory only, could not force its opinions into action—a weakness which its members frequently lamented in their reports. "The Navy Department is not required to follow its suggestions," the Admiral stated in a letter to the Secretary of the Navy, adding that the Navy Department was only ten per cent as efficient as "the most inefficient ship in the fleet," that it had no plan of action whatsoever in the event of war, and that it must immediately adopt one.† Attached to the letter was a memorandum containing an outline for complete mobilization of the Navy. It was filed with the report.

*Dewey's championship of a potent merchant marine was never realized during his lifetime. During World War I the United States built Liberty ships feverishly, only to see them rust in dock after 1919. It was not until 1936 that a Merchant Marine Act was passed by Congress. From this stemmed the unequaled fleet of merchant ships which have carried the arms of World War II. The Merchant Marine Act of 1936, which went so far as to justify the earlier demands of George Dewey, stated: "It is necessary for the national defense and development of its foreign and domestic commerce that the United States shall have a merchant marine (a) sufficient to carry its domestic waterborne commerce and a substantial portion of the waterborne export and import foreign commerce of the United States, and to provide shipping service on all routes essential for maintaining the flow of such domestic and foreign waterborne commerce at all times; (b) capable of serving as a naval and military auxiliary in time of war or national emergency; (c) owned and operated under the United States flag by citizens of the United States insofar as may be practicable; and (d) composed of the best-equipped, safest, and most suitable types of vessels, constructed in the United States and manned with a trained and efficient citizen personnel. It is hereby declared to be the policy of the United States to foster the development and encourage the maintenance of such a merchant marine."

†Navy Department files; letter dated October 27, 1914.

Reluctant as Congress was to build new bases toward the Orient, it was more generous than ever before in providing for the Navy. Between 1905 and 1914 it appropriated $170,000,000 for the construction of seventeen first-line battleships. The first four of these were the *Michigan* and the *South Carolina* (16,000 tons each), and the *Delaware* and the *North Dakota* (20,000 tons), completed in 1910. Carrying eight and ten twelve-inch guns, respectively, they were twice as big as the ships of the line of 1898, although their fire power was approximately the same. The first fourteen-inch battleship guns were installed on the *Texas* and the *New York,* completed in 1914, while six more ships of this approximate class, with tonnages ranging from 27,000 to 32,000 tons, were completed before the Armistice of 1918.

In 1915 and 1916 hundreds of millions more for twelve additional battlewagons were appropriated, though none of these were completed until after the First World War. The *Maryland* and the *West Virginia,* the *Colorado* and the *Washington* were the first provided with sixteen-inch cannon. The first three were commissioned between 1921 and 1923, but the *Washington,* under terms of the Washington Naval Conference of 1922, was used as a target ship. The Act of 1916 provided funds for six other 43,000-ton ships, which included the *South Dakota,* the *Montana,* and the *North Carolina,* but they were killed by the conference of 1922, and not until another Roosevelt came into the White House, when war clouds gathered over Europe once again, was work on them begun. Then, greatly changed from their original specifications, they were completed in time to distinguish themselves in the fight against Japan and Germany.

The 1916 appropriation also provided for six battle cruisers, faster, if less powerfully armed, than battleships, listed originally as 43,500-ton giants with a proposed speed of thirty-three knots, but two of these became the *Lexington* and the *Saratoga,* the nation's first aircraft carriers, and now as famous in American history as the Revolutionary battles for which they were named.*

Admiral George Dewey actively participated in this building program. He studied the plans and discussed the construction of the ships. As titular head of the Navy during the years of intensive naval expansion, he may be considered in a very real sense the father of the nation's second new Navy. At Manila Bay, in 1898, he had taken America's first steel fleet into action with the foe. As Admiral of the Navy from 1899 to 1917 he helped sponsor the creation of new mechanical leviathans which became the spearheads of two wars for freedom.

*Harold and Margaret Sprout, *Toward a New Order of Sea Power* (Princeton: Princeton University Press, 1940).

The program was largely adapted from a report of the General Board, signed by Dewey on October 12, 1915, in which Dewey advocated a five-year program with annual expenditures of $100,000,000 on new construction only, to be "so expended that at the end of the quinquennial period a well balanced fleet will have been authorized in which the ships of the several types will exist in the proportions suited to the geographic and strategic situation of the United States."

To accomplish that end the board urged construction of ten dreadnoughts costing $18,810,000 each; six battle cruisers, ten scouts, fifty destroyers, nine fleet submarines, fifty-eight coastal submarines, and thirteen auxiliary vessels.

Nor was naval construction the only aspect of the development of our military power which concerned him. It was on the wintry morning of December 17, 1903, that Orville and Wilbur Wright wheeled an odd-looking machine of cloth and wood onto the beach at Kittyhawk, North Carolina. Orville Wright climbed into the contraption, and lying between a pair of patchwork wings, he started a gasoline engine. A large propellor cut into the wind, as the strange vehicle moved slowly across the sands, gathered speed, and finally, with a last bounce, took to the air. It remained aloft for twelve seconds; then, after a flight of 120 feet,* landed on the beach. Man could fly.

Five years later, after ceaseless experimentation, refinement, and practice, the Wright brothers finally demonstrated their airplane to government officials. The Navy sent observers to Fort Myer, near Washington, to watch the test. The observers were impressed, the Navy was not. Two years later, however, Captain W. I. Chambers, U.S.N., persuaded the Navy Department to arrange the demonstration of an airplane used in connection with a ship. Glenn Curtiss, who had been developing the aircraft simultaneously with the Wrights, provided a plane, and one of his pilots, Eugene Ely, volunteered to take off from a ship. A wooden platform sixty feet long was constructed on the bow of the cruiser *Birmingham.* The plane was loaded on the ship at Hampton Roads, Virginia, and on November 14, 1910, Ely climbed into the cockpit, gunned the engine, and flew his plane off the ship.† Curtiss arranged another, more spectacular test a year later. This time he constructed a 120-foot platform on the battleship *Pennsylvania,* anchored in San Francisco harbor. A crude series of lines, weighted at each end by sandbags, was laid across the deck. Ely's plane took off from the Presidio ashore, circled over the *Pennsyl-*

*The entire flight could have been made within the wingspan of a 1944 Liberator bomber.
†*The Navy Reader*, William Harrison Fetridge, editor (Indianapolis: Bobbs-Merrill Co., 1943), pp. 109–11.

vania, and came in for a landing. As its wheels touched the deck a hook on the plane's tail caught the ropes, and the weight of the sandbags slowed the craft to a stop.*

Despite this highly successful demonstration, the Navy failed to grasp the conception of the aircraft carrier, a ship built exclusively for planes, with a great flight deck.† It was then thought that only seaplanes were feasible. Curtiss made a successful shipside landing in the water in 1911, lifted his plane on deck, lowered it, and took off again, and this demonstration proved to the Navy the possibilities of aviation in association with the fleet. That same year Congress awarded the Navy the sum of $25,000 for further experiments, and Captain Chambers was assigned to establish a naval aviation service. The Navy bought three planes and arranged to train ten officers as pilots under tutelage of the Wrights and Curtiss.

When the fleet went south for its winter maneuvers in January, 1913, Lieutenant John H. Towers accompanied it as the first commander of an aviation unit and showed the success of the co-operation. That spring the General Board undertook the study of a naval aviation service. Although George Dewey was seventy-five years old, his age did not blind him to the enormous significance of the revolution under way. On August 30, 1913, he signed the Board's report to the Secretary of the Navy, recommending "the organization of a Naval Air Service suited to the needs of the Navy in War,"‡ and on October 9, 1913, a board was appointed to draw up plans and specifications for the Naval Air Corps. The order was signed by Assistant Secretary of the Navy Franklin Delano Roosevelt.

The board was headed by Captain Chambers, who recommended the establishment of the country's first Naval Air Station near Pensacola, Florida, which was opened as a training field the next year. During the war with Mexico in 1914, planes accompanied the *Mississippi* and the *Birmingham* to Vera Cruz and engaged in scouting operations with the fleet. The declaration of war against Germany in 1917 found the Naval Air Corps with a total of 38 aviators, 163 enlisted men for ground crews, and 54 airplanes, with one air station to train more fliers. In August the Naval Air Factory was started near Philadelphia, and before the Armistice it had built 183 twin-engined flying boats to be used as reconnaissance planes. By 1941, on the twenty-eighth anniversary of the creation of the

* *The Navy Reader*, pp. 70–71.
† It was not until 1922 that a flight deck was built on the fleet collier *Langley*. Two years later the battle cruisers *Lexington* and *Saratoga* were converted into true aircraft carriers.
‡ *Saturday Evening Post*, August 27, 1943.

Air Corps by orders signed by George Dewey, the Navy possessed 1,100 planes, 7 aircraft carriers, and several seaplane tenders.

Amazing as the rapid expansion was, it was accomplished at the cost of considerable opposition to its adherents. Billy Mitchell of the Army was a case in point; but among those early air advocates who made Admiral Dewey appreciate air power as an essential arm of the fleet was one of his closest friends, Bradley Fiske.

Fiske was the son of a western New York Episcopalian minister. Born in 1854, the year George Dewey entered the Naval Academy, he was graduated from Annapolis in 1874 and served as lieutenant aboard the gunboat *Petrel* on May 1, 1898, when his coolness and alertness in the mopping-up operations against Spanish ships won him a citation from Commodore Dewey for "heroic conduct." Impressed by his younger colleague, Dewey became friendly with him during the weeks between May 1 and August 13, when Manila fell.

During the next years, however, the two men lost contact with one another. Fiske rose through the rank of captain to rear admiral, commanding cruisers and battleships, then divisions of the Atlantic fleet. A dozen years after Manila he returned to Washington as secretary of the General Board. He later served as "aide for naval operations," the post now designated as chief of naval operations.*

A noted inventor, he was responsible for the abandonment of open sights. All told, he perfected more than 130 other inventions, including the electric range finder, the present system of turning battleship turrets, and the electric ammunition hoist. He had watched the experiments of the Wright brothers and of Glenn Curtiss with intelligent respect and had argued with fellow officers about a future of vertical warfare launched by submarines, surface ships, and aircraft. Unable to conceive of war in three dimensions, they laughed at his predictions, but he won the ear of Admiral Dewey, who became his strongest advocate. Sometime in 1910 Fiske entered into a heated debate with other officers on the feasibility of using airplanes to defend islands from sea attack. Like all members of the Manila Bay Society, he was thinking in terms of the Philippines.

"Why you could even make a plane carry a torpedo, and the torpedo, instead of being shot from a destroyer, could be dropped from a plane," he declared.†

"Whoops of laughter greeted his assertion," Fiske said, remembering how fantastic this statement then seemed.

"That is a fool idea," said one of his antagonists, "because if you drop

*The Navy Reader, pp. 137–41.
†Ibid., p. 139.

it from an airplane on the water it will stay there. You have got to start it."

Nettled by the challenge, Fiske went to work to prove himself correct. A year later he had designed a plane and torpedo combination which was theoretically correct, but it was not completely perfected, and his critics called the invention "Fiske's Folly." The butt of ridicule and criticism, in spite of his proved brilliance in developing telescopic sights and electric range finders, he was accused by his critics of having "slipped into senility." Yet Fiske was not downhearted. He had a champion in the Admiral of the Navy.

Dewey was "distracted" because Fiske was not believed, but with him preached the doctrine that airships would become a tremendous menace to surface vessels. After Fiske's retirement from active duty in 1916, he continued his experimentation, refusing to return to active duty during World War I because to him "the perfection of the torpedo weapon would do more for the country than all the paper work a man of his age could do behind a desk."* His critics were incredulous, but Fiske outlived them all and spent his last years in contented retirement until his death on April 10, 1942, by which time Japanese torpedo planes had destroyed the British battleships *Repulse* and *Prince of Wales*. During the next two months of 1942 versions of "Fiske's Folly" sank four Japanese aircraft carriers off Midway Island.

Every country in every age has had its Cassandras whose ominous predictions are met with scornful ridicule. Yet George Dewey accepted these clairvoyant warnings, saw through the irrationality of public disdain, and championed the men whose brilliance and foresight pointed out perils which their countrymen chose to ignore.

The defeat of William Howard Taft by Woodrow Wilson in 1912 scarcely affected the Admiral's position, which was secure from ordinary changes in political life, but he was pleased to receive a testimonial from the retiring President, dated February 10, 1913, eulogizing him for his splendid work and co-operation during the past four years and for his "brilliant leadership" of the General Board.

Wilson's new Secretary of the Navy, Josephus Daniels, who proved himself an able executive, alert to the needs of the Navy, one day brought his Assistant Secretary to the house on K Street to visit the Deweys. The Admiral was not home, but Mrs. Dewey entertained the pair. That evening she wrote a letter to her stepson, George Dewey, describing the visit:

The Secretary this morning brought his new assistant to call on me and see your father's treasures, a very handsome man named Franklin D.

* *The Navy Reader*, p. 139.

Roosevelt, and a relative of Theodore Roosevelt. The Secretary only stayed a short time, but Mr. Roosevelt, most charming and enthusiastic, stayed for some two hours, talking much of plans which in due course he hopes to accomplish for our country as well as Navy. And George, such plans! I suggest you keep this letter, for I predict that if this young man lives, he is going far.

In 1912, on his seventy-fifth birthday, Dewey was still active and alert, although frequently kept in bed by colds and by the liver ailment which had brought him close to death in Malta thirty years before. His house was in order, his burial plot at Arlington was selected, he saw his contemporaries preceding him in death, and his friends urged him, while there was still time, to continue his memoirs, started in 1898. Frederick A. Palmer, "a friend of Manila days," was particularly insistent. A writer himself, he convinced the Admiral that he should leave behind him a written record of his career, and the Admiral sat down with Palmer and told his story. The completed *Autobiography* appeared in September, 1913.

My memory stretches from an apprenticeship under the veterans of the War of 1812, those heroes of the old sailing-frigates and ships of the line, from the earlier days of the steam-frigates through the Civil War; from the period of inertia in the seventies, when our obsolete ships were the byword of the navies of the world, to the building of our new navy, which I was to give its first baptism of fire; and finally, to my service as head of the General Board of the Navy since the Spanish War.

I have been through many administrations and many political changes, and have known many famous men both at home and abroad. . . . I am writing in the hope of giving some pleasure to my countrymen, from whom I have received such exceptional honors, and in the hope that my narrative may be of some value and inspiration to the young men of the Navy of today, who are serving with the same purpose that animated the men of Decatur's, Macdonough's, and Farragut's day, and later, the men of our squadrons which fought at Manila and Santiago.*

When copies of Dewey's *Autobiography* reached the notice of the German Navy in February, 1914, his references to the von Diedrichs troubles were more than annoying to a nation which in less than six months would plunge the world into war. On February 17 the Admiral was answered in a publicized letter by Count Reventlow, who denied every charge that the German officer had attempted to goad the American Admiral into a premature move toward war or a general retreat from the

*Preface to the *Autobiography*.

303

Philippines. Next day, however, the German Admiralty decided to take no official notice of the account, saying that a "rejoinder will come from other quarters."* Nevertheless, Dewey was assailed in the German Reichstag on February 18 by no less a personage than the Kaiser's Grand Admiral von Tirpitz, who had sponsored the German's first big navy bill in 1897, and who now accused Dewey of writing pure fabrications designed to alienate America and Germany. Charging Dewey not only with coloring facts but with attempting to rouse Americans against a "peace-minded" Germany, von Tirpitz told Reichstag members that Germany was threatened by a malicious campaign in the United States to spread anti-German feeling.

Dewey, however, stood firm and announced that he would not modify his version of the von Diedrichs episode as printed in the *Autobiography*. Admiral von Diedrichs himself, emerged from retirement to answer the charges in a German publication, *Marine Rundschau,* alleging that Dewey had threatened him with war and that only the German's forebearance had kept the two nations from open conflict.

Four days later, Bradley Fiske's memoirs, *Wartime in Manila,* were published, and completely confirmed Dewey's interpretation of the Manila conflict, whereupon the Germans, evidently realizing they could not win the argument, decided to let it be forgotten as quickly as possible. A German naval expert, Captain Kurwetter, wrote on March 1 that "Germany is satisfied that von Diedrichs has vindicated our national honor," but two days later Sir Edward Chichester, the son of Dewey's English friend at Manila Bay, announced that his father's account substantiated Dewey's.†

The *Autobiography* offers an interesting insight into Dewey's evaluation of the important events in his life. The battle of Manila Bay, of course, led in emphasis. He skipped entirely such controversial subjects as his relations with the Filipino insurgents, and the period of the native insurrection was dismissed in a few words. The reception in New York and the presentation of the sword by Congress were fully described, but his life after the war was covered in only a few pages. He scarcely discussed his activities on the General Board, and no mention at all was made of his abortive Presidential boom.

During the spring of 1914, when elaborate plans were being prepared for the opening of the Panama Canal, Dewey was invited to assume command of the *Olympia* again, which was to be the first ship to go through the new channel from the Atlantic to the Pacific. The invitation was

*The New York Times, Feb. 19, 1914.
†The New York Times, March 3, 1914.

declined, however, and the canal was opened on August 14, 1914, without the presence of the Admiral of the Navy.

Before it was opened, Europe was aflame. The United States observed strict neutrality, and even George Dewey, who had warned at Trieste, in 1899, that the Kaiser would bring war to the world, was unsure of what to do. In 1915 he participated in a New York pageant, the "Battle Cry for Peace," but in a few months he was certain of the real enemy and lent his efforts and prestige to building up the fleet. His program, enunciated early in 1916, was to make the American Navy the second largest within a period of three years.

Rear Admiral Charles J. Badger, U.S.N., became the Admiral's "staff and principal support" in these years. Badger was a source of constant encouragement and assistance. In later years he advised Mrs. Dewey frequently and remained one of her stanchest aids.

The nearness of war in 1916 led to renewed activity by both the Admiral and his wife. Mrs. Dewey, long an ardent suffragette, had been one of the founders of the National Women's Party, and in 1916, with Miss Elizabeth Ellicott Poe, helped establish the Woman's Naval Service. Although a private organization, it was in many respects the forerunner of the Navy's Yeomanettes in World War I and of such organizations as the WAVES, WACS, SPARS, and Women's Marine Corps in the second World War.

Admiral Dewey became an advisor of the Woman's Naval Service, which was formally opened with the establishment of the National Service School, a camp designed to train women for war activities, at Chevy Chase, Maryland, on May 1, 1916, a date fortuitously chosen to fall upon the eighteenth anniversary of the Battle of Manila Bay. A large drill hall, donated by Mrs. Dewey and christened Dewey Hall, was turned over to the camp at ceremonies at which she presided and the President of the United States and the Admiral of the Navy made speeches. On an inspection tour which followed, the Admiral passed a young sentry who had just arrived at the camp, and who, not yet knowing the requisites of military courtesies, failed to salute. Stopping short, he fixed his eyes sternly on the young woman, and demanded:

"Young woman, show me my honors."

The sentry, not recognizing the Admiral in his civilian clothes, was too confused to know what to do.

Miss Poe finally said, "Private, this is Admiral Dewey."

The sentry almost broke into tears as she saluted. The Admiral walked on and said to Miss Poe:

"Dignity can only be preserved in the Navy by the proper display of honor due senior officers."

As the days passed the Admiral became more and more a legendary figure. As he rode through Washington, a younger generation, which viewed the Battle of Manila as past history, watched him as English boys and girls watched Wellington long after Waterloo.

The Deweys spent the summer of 1916 at Atlantic City, as they had for several summers past. That fall Dewey continued going to his General Board offices almost daily, although his hours were shorter than before, and younger, more vigorous men were assigned the heavy duties. America was drifting into war, and the fleet was being expanded as rapidly as was possible. In Europe, Russia was fighting desperately as the power of Czar Nicholas tottered from the pressure within the country. Rumania fell to the Central Powers before the year's end, but in the west Marshal Pétain's French armies checked the German advance at Verdun, and French and English cadres launched an offensive near the Somme. President Woodrow Wilson, who had been re-elected in November because "he kept us out of war," urged preparedness. The calendar moved relentlessly toward February 22, when unrestricted U-boat war began.

The Deweys celebrated Christmas quietly that year in the mansion on K Street. The next day, after the customary birthday toasts, officers walked about the museum-house to gaze once again at the loving cup and the Congressional sword, and at the many pictures on the walls. They recalled old times, talked about faraway Manila Bay, and looked through the Admiral's bulging scrapbooks of newspaper clippings that told of his glory.

The world of his seventy-ninth birthday was far different from the one into which he had been born. Planes and zeppelins flew through the skies, the telegraph and cable connected the continents, and a battlefield in France was helping determine the destiny of the United States. The sailing ships of Dewey's boyhood were now hobbies of pleasure seekers, while the clippers which had taken weeks from Liverpool to Boston had given way to the Cunarders which took five days.

The Admiral moved slowly about his treasures, pointing them out again to his subordinates, who knew them all but who listened with the greatest deference. The wide gold stripes on his sleeves seemed a little heavier at the end of that day, although he gave no sign of it as he stood straight in his uniform and saluted his departing guests with smart precision.

And as the new year of 1917 dawned, the Admiral put aside holiday festivities and resumed his daily work. He studied the problems of his fleet and watched the war news from Europe with an experienced eye. He who had seen the storm clouds gather in 1860 and 1897 realized that those of 1917 were darker and more threatening, and he knew they would blow away less easily. With all the energy left to him, he stepped into the job ahead, to give of his effort and of his wisdom in making his country ready for the storm.

30

TAPS SOUND

The Admiral rose slowly from his leather chair on the afternoon of January 10, 1917, and was handed his gray hat and cane by an orderly standing near the door. After a final glance to make sure that his desk was cleared, he left his office in the Mills Building to call upon the Secretary in the Navy Department. Mr. Daniels was seated at his desk. Dewey walked in hesitantly, his old bones hurting a little as he stepped. Quickly the Secretary stood up and welcomed him.

"You look splendidly, Admiral," said Josephus Daniels, "Won't you sit down a minute?"*

For a few minutes the two men chatted. Admiral Dewey was like a father to Woodrow Wilson's Secretary of the Navy.

"You know," Dewey told the Secretary that day, "I knew what Germany was up to all along. When Mr. Roosevelt was President he sent me down to the Caribbean on our winter maneuvers, as an object lesson to the Kaiser. Oh, but that is old history now—" and the Admiral broke off. He left a minute or two later.

"Good night, Mr. Daniels, I'll see you in the morning."

Outside his carriage was waiting for him, and the coachman helped the Admiral into his seat, spread a robe over the thin knees, mounted the cab, and flicked the team into a trot. The old man closed his eyes, and dozed, his thin, bony hands lying idly on his lap.

A few minutes later he was home. Millie was sitting in the parlor, her ear trumpet on her black silk dress and her hands supporting an unread book.

"Good evening, Millie," the Admiral called in a deep, resonant voice, the only one she could really hear.

*Chicago Daily News, Jan. 18, 1917.

"Oh, George, my dear. I was wondering when you would come."

In the stately dining room the old couple ate their usual dinner,* then moved into the living room. The Admiral smoked the last of the three cigars his doctors allowed him each day, and remembered wryly how indignant he had been when he had first been cut down from his customary eight. In a few minutes he was sound asleep. Mildred sighed. Much younger than her husband, she found herself left in loneliness when his drowsiness overcame him these long evenings. If only there were not old age, she thought. Soon Mildred herself dozed. A little later the Admiral roused himself, read a bit, then put his spectacles back into the gold case which an admiring citizen had given him long ago, and went up to bed.

The next morning he was dressed and ready to leave the house for his office when he felt a twinge in his side. Such attacks, caused by hardening arteries, had been recurrent for almost two years, sometimes severe enough to keep him in bed for days, sometimes needing only a few minutes of rest. That morning the twinge was not too acute, and he said good-by to Mildred and walked out the front door. When he reached the steps, however, he was overcome by a searing pain. He put his hand to his side and swayed dizzily. The coachman caught him just as he began to fall.

Dr. Fauntleroy arrived a few minutes later. He stayed with the Admiral for an hour and then, when a nurse arrived, returned to the Navy Department. There was nothing serious, he told Mrs. Dewey. Admiral Dewey just needed rest. A few days in bed would make him as well as ever. When newspaper reporters inquired about the illness, the servants told them the Admiral had a slight cold and would soon be up again.

By Sunday, when he was no better, the public was informed of his condition, and his son was summoned from Chicago.

He rallied slightly the next morning although his temperature was 102°, and reached his hand out to Mildred, who was sitting beside the bed.

"Millie, I have to get up and get back to work," he protested. "I'm shirking my duty, Millie. This nation is faced with a perilous period, my dear. This war could be the forerunner of other wars. I must finish my work for my country. It must be victorious."†

His words came spasmodically between coughs and labored breathing. He passed a fitful night on Monday, and the next morning his doctors issued a bulletin to the press, saying he had "declined."

*According to Miss Elizabeth Poe, it never varied from a menu of rare roast beef, mashed potatoes, stewed tomatoes, green salad, and apple pie, with a glass of claret for the Admiral.
†Miss Elizabeth Ellicott Poe, third cousin of Edgar Allan Poe and in her own right a distinguished Washington newspaperwoman and author, was for many years Mildred Dewey's closest friend. To her the authors are indebted for this description of Dewey's final illness.

At noon another report was given out: "The Admiral is slightly worse than at the time the first statement was issued today. Mrs. Dewey and his son, George Goodwin Dewey, are with him and have been told the end is near."

At 1:40 the doctors gave out a third report: "The Admiral is slowly sinking. The end may come at any time."

Through the long afternoon of January 16 Admiral Dewey tossed in his bed, crying out in delirium, fighting his life all over again. Now he was a boy, calling out, "I hope, father, you think I have done well. I hope you are proud of me, father." Then he lapsed into a coma.

Later he was living through the Civil War once more, sailing through heavy fire up the Mississippi, ministering to Admiral Farragut. "I hope this will make you more comfortable, Admiral," he called. "Your nation cannot spare you." *Was* this Admiral Farragut he was calling to or were the words Dr. Fauntleroy's, trying to comfort the Admiral of Manila Bay?

Now he was quelling a mutiny, "Answer the roll, sir. Answer the roll when your name is called."

"The United States shall never know the humiliation of defeat," he called out in broken gasps. "Our nation shall grow great only by victories on the high seas."

His strength was ebbing, and he fought for breath, but in a moment he called again through his delirium, "The Navy shall always be indebted to you, sir, for your courage, and this nation . . . shall . . . always . . . do . . . you honor." Was this Theodore Roosevelt he addressed? Or was this Roosevelt praising the conqueror of Manila?

"Gentlemen," he whispered. "The battle . . . is . . . done. The victory . . . is . . . ours."

The Admiral's heart stopped beating at 5:56 o'clock on Tuesday afternoon, January 16, 1917.

The next morning President Woodrow Wilson issued executive order 2516:

> As a token of respect to the memory of Admiral George Dewey, who died at his residence in this city on yesterday, January sixteenth, at 5:56 o'clock, it is hereby ordered that the national flag be displayed at half-mast upon all public buildings at all forts and military posts and naval stations, and on all vessels of the United States in commission until after the funeral shall have taken place, and that on the day of the funeral the executive offices in the city of Washington be closed.
>
> WOODROW WILSON
>
> THE WHITE HOUSE
> 17 JANUARY, 1917.

310

The United States, which had forgotten John Paul Jones for almost 112 years, more than compensated for that neglect in honoring at his death the only Admiral *of* the Navy in American history. In his message to Congress the same day, Wilson said:

It was as a commodore that he rendered the service in the action of Manila Bay which has given him a place forever memorable in the naval annals of the country. At the time of his death he held the exceptional rank of Admiral of the Navy by special act of Congress. During the later years of his life he was the honored president of the General Board of the Navy, to whose duties he gave the most assiduous attention, and in which office he rendered a service to the Navy quite invaluable in its sincerity and quality of practical sagacity.

It is pleasant to recall what qualities gave him his well-deserved fame; his practical directness; his courage without self-consciousness; his efficient capacity in matters of administration; the readiness to fight without asking any questions or hesitancy about any details. It was by such qualities that he continued and added lustre to the best traditions of our Navy. He had the stuff in him which all true men admire, and upon which all statesmen must depend in hour of peril.

The whole nation will mourn the loss of its most distinguished naval officer, a man who has been as faithful, as intelligent and as successful in the performances of his responsible duties in time of peace as he was gallant and successful in time of war. It is just such men that give the service distinction, and the nation a just pride in those who serve it.

The people and the government of the United States will always rejoice to perpetuate his name in all honor and affection.

On the high seas and in all the ports of the world, United States ships sailed with their flags at half-mast. In the Philippines, buildings were draped in mourning crepe, and along Dewey Boulevard the Stars and Stripes were lowered in grief.

On Thursday, January 18, a repeated manifestation of the earlier hero worship was seen in Congress when Representative Allen of Ohio introduced a joint resolution to change the name of the Danish West Indies, acquired by the United States that year, to the "Dewey Islands." The resolution, however, was never voted upon.

The funeral was set for eleven o'clock Saturday morning.

At ten o'clock Saturday a few mourners gathered in the house on K Street for private services, attended by Woodrow Wilson, Josephus Daniels, and the members of the General Board, led by Admiral William S. Benson, now senior ranking officer in the Navy. Chaplain J. B. Frazier, who had served aboard the *Olympia* at Manila, read a brief service, after which a group of Navy men carried the coffin, flag draped and covered with oak leaves as Dewey had requested, out the door and placed it on a gun caisson. Around the driveway were assembled the Midshipmen's Junior Defense Guard and a branch of the Women's Naval Service. The uniformed boys walked past the metal casket in a stately column, each depositing a white carnation on the top. Then the funeral procession followed the caisson to the Capitol. Every midshipman from Annapolis was in the march.

The casket was carried reverently to a great catafalque under the round dome and placed in the spot where the bodies of many Presidents had lain. The national flag was draped upon the bier. On top of it lay the wondrous sword presented by a grateful Congress almost eighteen years before.

A flood of funeral wreaths send by all classes of people surrounded the catafalque. Below the Admiral's feet on the marble floor was a cannon of white roses. Its muzzle pointed upward to a glistening crescent of gold, wreathed in orchids, the gift and testimonial of the men of the Atlantic fleet.

Just before eleven o'clock the gowned justices of the United States Supreme Court entered the great hall and took their places. Members of the cabinet and committees of the House and Senate, all in black suits, walked in. Diplomats, headed by M. Jules Jusserand, with whom the Deweys had been so friendly, marched in their morning suits before the bier. President Wilson was the last to enter. Chaplain Frazier stood beside the catafalque and read the Episcopal funeral service in a low voice touched with emotion and sorrow.

There were no funeral orations and no eulogies. The service was chaste and simple, as the Admiral had desired. A naval choir sang the hymns he had requested long before—"Lead Kindly Light" and "Abide with Me." Then a company of Annapolis midshipmen marched to the bier, lifted the metal casket, and carried it to the gun caisson outside on the Capitol steps. The long burial procession followed the coffin to the gates of Arlington National Cemetery.

Behind the bier marched twelve body bearers,* men of the U.S.S. *Dolphin* and of the *Mayflower,* who had served aboard those ships when the four-starred flag of the Admiral waved at the masts. Behind them

---

*In naval funerals the order of rank is customarily reversed in keeping with the humble biblical precept that the first shall be the last and the last first. In Dewey's funeral this was not followed.

312

came a color bearer, carrying the blue admiral's flag at half-mast. George Goodwin Dewey, garbed in black, and the members of the General Board in full-dress uniform followed, and after them one hundred veterans of Manila Bay. Next in the procession walked companies of sailors from the *Dolphin,* the *Mayflower,* the *Arkansas,* and the Washington Navy Yard, while the entire student body of the Naval Academy marched ahead of a company of Marines and a troop of soldiers.

Secretary of the Navy Daniels, accompanied by Assistant Secretary Roosevelt, led members of the cabinet, and then in order came the President, the diplomatic corps, congressional committees, and groups of citizens representing all the major patriotic societies of the land.

For more than one hour the mile-long procession followed the flag-draped casket through the avenues of Washington, following in reverse the route of the triumphal parade of October, 1899, across the Potomac to the National Cemetery. There the motor vehicles halted. Uniformed troops followed the gun caisson past the Robert E. Lee mansion, beyond the memorial to the men killed aboard the battleship *Maine,* and stopped under the stately elms around the mausoleum erected for General Nelson A. Miles. Mrs. Dewey and the Admiral's son had purchased a magnificent marble mausoleum for the naval hero, but since it would not be finished until the next summer, the casket would remain in a crypt in the Miles memorial.

There, near the graves of Lamberton of the *Olympia* and Coghlan of the *Raleigh,* not far from the wooded slopes where lay Sampson and Schley, Chaplain Frazier read the committal service, while the President and statesmen stood with bowed, bare heads. Below, the Potomac stretched for miles in either direction, a ribbon of bright silver on the winter day. Flurries of snow fell through the frosty air as the remains of George Dewey were laid to rest.

Mildred, unable to attend the services in the Capitol, sat with her friend, Elizabeth Poe, in a room overlooking the route of the procession. She did not wish to look, to see with her own eyes, her beloved being carried away. At Miss Poe's insistence that she come to the window to watch the demonstration, Mildred, with great effort, raised herself from her chair and with slow, difficult steps walked to the window. She saw the sailors and the midshipmen, and in the lead she saw a patch of red and white and blue covering the casket. Dry-eyed, she watched the horses carry away her husband. Then, in a hoarse whisper, she murmured:

"Good-by George . . . Brave George . . . Wonderful George . . ."

As the long line passed into the distance across the Potomac bridge, Mildred turned back into the room.

"There goes my life," she said.

EPILOGUE

That might have been the end, but it was not. Like the body of John Paul Jones, the body of the Admiral of the Navy was to find little peace for many years. The mighty battle fleet which Dewey had helped create soon was called to its biggest test, to guard a convoy line three thousand miles long from Germany's underseas boats. The end of the World War found America with its biggest navy in all history, although not for long. Faced with the prospect of entering a costly naval race with Britain and Japan, the isolationist Republican administration of President Harding chose the alternative of naval parity, and in the Washington Conference of 1922 agreed to scrap a goodly portion of the fleet. In a world of imperialistic rivalry the United States pulled in its horns.

The Admiral was not forgotten although the global strategy to which he subscribed was. In 1936 a destroyer named after him was launched to perpetuate his name. "I, the officers and crew," wrote its commanding officer, "take great personal pride in the privilege of serving in the ship named for Admiral Dewey. We pray we may so emulate him in the performance of our duties and conduct in battle as to bring credit to the ship which bears his name."*

The house on K Street never changed. A purple sash was stretched across the arm of his favorite chair, and the trophies of his fame grew dust-covered as his widow sank into old age. During the World War she bestirred herself to do much war work, leading the National Service Schools for Women, and equipping naval hospitals with dressings, but more and more she retired from society. For a time she wrote editorials for the Washington *Post,* and thrilled in 1921 when the gallant *Olympia* was selected to bring home the body of an American soldier who died in

*This letter was written in 1943 to Congressman Charles S. Dewey, a relative of the Admiral, who sent the destroyer *Dewey* a set of phonograph records for the recreation of the crew members.

France "known but to God"; but after 1923 her deafness and infirmities increased. Through the years she wore a widow's black and became a noticed figure in Washington and New York, wearing old-fashioned skirts which touched her toes. Through the stimulus of Bishop Freeman, Mrs. Dewey became keenly interested in the project to build the Washington Cathedral of Saints Peter and Paul, conceived to become the "Westminster Abbey" of America. Woodrow Wilson was buried in its crypt, and Mrs. Dewey was prevailed upon to move the Admiral's body there. After lengthy arrangements, this was done. On the morning of March 30, 1925, a Navy honor guard and band proceeded to Arlington and Dewey's casket was placed on a gun caisson for the transfer to the Bethlehem Chapel, where, after the briefest of ceremonies, it was laid away until the cathedral was sufficiently completed to permit formal interment beneath the nave.

Five years later the tiny widow appeared at the War Department to ask permission to return her husband's body to Arlington, because she feared she could not be buried beside him in the cathedral. A codicil to her will was later found ordering the transfer, and lengthy litigation ensued, but inasmuch as she was buried next to him his body was not again disturbed. The lonely widow had experienced sadness and trouble during her final years. She had drawn five different wills, first giving her estate to George Goodwin Dewey, then to her grandnephew, Frederick McLean Bugher, and to her nephew, Edward B. McLean. Months of unraveling evidence in court preceded the final distribution of her $750,000 estate.

Too deaf and weak to go out any more, the widow lived with her lonely memories in the K Street mansion until February 21, 1931. That afternoon she struggled from her bed and walked across the hall into the Admiral's room, where everything was still the same. The four-starred flag of the Admiral of the Navy was on the wall above the bed, and at its foot was the heavy Congressional sword. His trophies lined the walls, and his blue uniforms, with broad stripes of gold upon the sleeves, gathered dust in the closet. Mildred crawled onto his bed and held her side to stop a sharp pain. When the servants came she was dead.

And the years passed by, until——

It was December 7 again—a different day entirely from the one of forty-four years before. Between those days had come many inventions: radios, motion pictures, automobiles, and dive bombers.

The world was at war again. France had fallen, and although America was an island of peace, the midshipmen who had marched behind the casket of George Dewey were in command of cruisers, battleships, and aircraft carriers all over the world. Some were in the Philippines, and their crews, enjoying liberty ashore, strolled along Dewey Boulevard in Manila. Some were in Pearl Harbor.

In Washington the Japanese peace ambassadors, Kurusu and Nomura, smilingly posed for photographs as they waited to call upon the Secretary of State. But in Hawaii the Japanese planes suddenly hurtled over the American fleet and killed peace with their bombs.

The American fleet at Pearl Harbor that day was in many respects the fleet of George Dewey. The battleships *Arizona, Oklahoma, Nevada,* and *Pennsylvania,* and the target ship *Utah,* had all been launched while he was still alive. And the other great ships, the *California, Tennessee, West Virginia,* and *Maryland,* had all been planned or laid down while he was president of the General Board. In Tokyo Admiral Yamamoto waited to hear the results of his infamous attack, and he was in a way a product of George Dewey too, for as a boy he had resented the American conquest of the Philippines and became a naval officer to win them for his "God-Emperor."

The Jap had plotted well, achieving complete surprise and damaging 19 American ships, destroying 117 aircraft, and killing 2,117 of the best trained men in the American Navy during those two hours of treachery. Yet the Jap had not reckoned with America. His spies, like Dewey's serving man, had studied American factories and fleets, industries and inventions. His armies fought with metal sold to Japan by Americans in the false years of peace. Yet the Jap had forgotten something of the history of the American Navy, its traditions, and its men: John Paul Jones, David Farragut, and George Dewey. He had forgotten "I have just begun to fight," and "Damn the torpedoes." The American fleet rose from its Pearl Harbor grave to range the wide Pacific.

Under the brilliant leadership of the Navy's wartime secretary, Frank Knox, the fleet grew to unheard of size, to more than ten times its strength before Pearl Harbor. As the Secretary flew to every war theater, he inspired the fighting men and personified for them the unity of a civilian populace working to provide the tools of war and victory.

Captain "Mike" Moran stood on the bridge of the cruiser *Boise* one dark night and ordered: "Pick out the biggest one and fire." Commander Howard Gilmore, wounded on the conning tower of his submarine, cried "Take her down." A flier in the Coral Sea radioed his carrier: "Scratch one flattop," and Donald Mason in the Atlantic said laconically, "Sighted sub; sank same."

"We will hit them hard and hit them often," said Admiral William

316

Halsey, and the Marines did just that on Guadalcanal, Tarawa, and in the Marshalls. On every sea Navy ships, built from American steel, throwing American shells, and manned by American fighting men, battled the foes of liberty. Their names were the same foreign names of nineteenth century sailors who served a foreign government, but now they were Americans all, in the same fight.

The Navy had been sadly neglected after 1922, and an isolationist America had almost invited the attack against liberty, but from the carnage of Pearl Harbor rose the greatest fleet in man's history—50,000-ton battleships, aircraft carriers by the score, cruisers, submarines, destroyers, planes, and invasion craft by the thousands—to avenge the wrong. The ships were mightier than any known to George Dewey, but their men were in the same mold he had known and revered, men of the United States Navy.

It was another December 7, a day of infamy, yet a day which called courage to the test and proved that another generation of free men could be as unbeatable as they had been since 1775. In their minds was the tradition he had loved, and in their hearts was the Admiral's favorite verse:

> Then conquer we must, when our cause it is just,
> And this be our motto: "In God is our trust";
> And the Star-Spangled Banner in triumph shall wave
> O'er the land of the free and the home of the brave.

BIBLIOGRAPHY

BIBLIOGRAPHY

"A Navy Flier's Creed," *Saturday Evening Post,* Aug. 27, 1943.

ADAMS, HENRY. *The Education of Henry Adams.* Boston: Houghton Mifflin Co., 1930.

ADAMS, JAMES TRUSLOW. *The March of Democracy.* New York: Charles Scribner's Sons, 1933.

"Admiral Dewey's Candidacy," *The Outlook,* April 14, 1900.

BAKER, ABBY G. "At Home With Admiral and Mrs. Dewey," *Woman's Home Companion,* May, 1904.

BARRETT, JOHN. *Admiral George Dewey: A Sketch of the Man.* New York: Harper & Bros. 1899.

BARTLETT, JOHN RUSSELL. "Watching for the Enemy in the Spanish War," *Century Magazine,* Oct., 1898.

BEARD, CHARLES A. and MARY R. *History of the United States.* New York: The Macmillan Co., 1921, 1925.

———.*The Rise of American Civilization.* New York: The Macmillan Co., 1927.

BELL, FREDERICK J. *Condition Red; Destroyer Action in the South Pacific.* New York: Longmans, Green & Co., 1943.

BENNETT, FRANK M. *The Steam Navy of the United States.* Pittsburgh: Warren & Co., 1897.

BENNS, F. LEE. *Europe Since 1914.* New York: F. S. Crofts & Co., 1930.

Bluejackets' Manual. Annapolis: United States Naval Institute, 1940.

BOOTHE, CLARE. "Ever Hear of Homer Lea?" *Saturday Evening Post,* March 7, 14, 1942.

Bowers, Claude G. *Beveridge and the Progressive Era*. Boston: Houghton Mifflin Co., 1932.

Brown, George Rothwell, "Political Parade," *Chicago Herald-American*, Dec. 30, 1941.

Cable, Frank T. "The Submarine Torpedo Boat Holland," *United States Naval Institute Proceedings*, Feb., 1943.

"Casualties, Thank You, Mr. Yamamoto," *Time*, May 31, 1943.

Chicago Daily News, Jan. 14-22, 1917.

"Chicago Vets Recall Dewey Victory," *Chicago Herald-American*, Aug. 13, 1943.

Coolidge, Archibald Cary. *The United States as a World Power*. New York: The Macmillan Co., 1921.

Damon, Charles Ripley. *American Dictionary of Dates*. Boston: Richard G. Badger, 1921.

Dennett, Tyler. *John Hay: From Poetry to Politics*. New York: Dodd, Mead & Co., 1933.

Dewey, Adelbert M. *The Life and Letters of Admiral Dewey*. New York: The Woolfall Co., 1899.

Dewey, George. *Autobiography of George Dewey, The Admiral of the Navy*. New York: Charles Scribner's Sons, 1916.

"Dewey Presidential Candidacy," *New York World*, April 4, 1900.

Dewey, William S. "Commemorative Store Cards of Admiral Dewey," *Numismatist Magazine*, March, 1939.

Dibble, Roy F. *Strenuous Americans*. New York: Boni & Liveright, 1923.

Dunne, Finley Peter. *Mr. Dooley's Philosophy*. New York: Harper & Bros., 1900.

Durling, E. V. "On the Side," *Chicago Herald-American*, Aug. 26, 1943.

Encyclopaedia Americana

Encyclopaedia Britannica

Evans, Robley D. *A Sailor's Log*. New York: D. Appleton-Century Co.

Fairbarn, William. *A Treatise on Iron Shipbuilding*. London: Longmans, Green & Co., 1865.

FAY, SIDNEY B. *The Origins of the World War.* New York: The Macmillan Co., 1928.

FETRIDGE, WILLIAM H. (ed.) *The Navy Reader.* Indianapolis: Bobbs-Merrill Co., 1943.

FISKE, BRADLEY A. *War Time in Manila.* Boston: Richard G. Badger, 1913.

———*From Midshipman to Rear Admiral.* New York: Century Co., 1913.

GOOCH, G. P. *History of Modern Europe, 1878-1919.* New York: Henry Holt & Co., 1923.

GRAMLING, OLIVER. *AP: The Story of News.* New York: Farrar & Rhinehart, 1940.

HALSTEAD, MURAT. *Life and Achievements of Admiral Dewey from Montpelier to Manila.* Chicago: The Dominion Co., 1899.

HAMM, MARGHERITA ARLINA. *Dewey the Defender.* New York: F. Tennyson Neely Co., 1899.

"Hardy Perennial," *Time,* July 12, 1943.

Harper's Weekly, Oct. 28, 1899.

Jane's Fighting Ships (edited by Francis E. McMurtrie) . New York: The Macmillan Co., 1943.

KING, MOSES. *The Dewey Reception and Committee of New York City.* New York: Chasmar-Winchell Press, 1899.

KNOX, DUDLEY W. *A History of the United States Navy.* New York: G. P. Putnam's Sons, 1936.

Ladies' Home Journal, Oct. 1899.

LANGER, WILLIAM L. *Encyclopedia of World History.* Boston: Houghton Mifflin Co., 1940.

LEA, HOMER. *The Valor of Ignorance.* New York: Harper & Bros., 1909.

LEWIS, WILLIAM D. *The Life of Theodore Roosevelt.* Philadelphia: John C. Winston Co., 1919.

LIPPMANN, WALTER. *United States Foreign Policy: Shield of the Republic.* Boston: Little, Brown & Co., 1943.

LODGE, HENRY CABOT. *The War with Spain.* New York: Harper & Bros., 1899.

LONG, JOHN D. *The New American Navy*. New York: Outlook Co., 1903.

LORENZ, LINCOLN. *John Paul Jones: Fighter for Freedom and Glory*. Annapolis: United States Naval Institute, 1943.

LOVETTE, LELAND P. *Naval Customs, Traditions and Usage*. Annapolis: United States Naval Institute, 1939.

MACLAY, EDGAR STANTON. *A History of the United States Navy from 1775 to 1901*. New York: D. Appleton & Co., 1901.

MAHAN, ALFRED THAYER. *The Interest of America in Seapower*. Boston: Little, Brown & Co., 1897.

_____.*Great Commanders—Admiral Farragut*. New York: D. Appleton & Co., 1892.

_____.*The Influence of Seapower upon History*. Boston: Little, Brown & Co., 1897.

_____.*Lessons of the War with Spain*. Boston: Little, Brown & Co., 1899.

Mahan on Naval Warfare (edited by Allan Westcott). Boston: Little, Brown & Co., 1918, 1941.

MASON, GREGORY. *Remember the Maine*. New York: Henry Holt & Co., 1939.

MAYO, LAWRENCE SHAW. *America of Yesterday as Reflected in the Journals of John D. Long*. Boston: Atlantic Monthly Press, 1923.

MILTON, GEORGE FORT. *Eve of Conflict*. Boston: Houghton Mifflin Co., 1934.

_____.*Conflict, The American Civil War*. New York: Coward-McCann, 1941.

MORISON, SAMUEL ELIOT and COMMAGER, HENRY STEELE. *The Growth of the American Republic*. New York: Oxford University Press, 1930.

"Mrs. Dewey," *Current Literature*, June, 1900.

MUZZEY, DAVID SAVILLE. *The United States of America*. New York: Ginn & Co., 1933.

NEVINS, ALLAN and COMMAGER, HENRY STEELE. *America, The Story of a Free People*. Boston: Little, Brown & Co., 1942.

New York Times (The), covering 1898-1932.

Notes on the Spanish-American War. Washington: United States Government Printing Office, 1900.

"Our Washington Letter," *The Independent,* April 5, 1900.

PECK, HARRY THURSTON. *Twenty Years of the Republic, 1885-1905.* New York: Dodd, Mead & Co., 1905, 1906.

PRATT, FLETCHER. *The Navy: A History.* Garden City: Doubleday, Doran & Co., 1938.

PRINGLE, HENRY F. *Theodore Roosevelt, A Biography.* New York: Harcourt, Brace & Co., 1931.

PULESTON, W. D. *Life and Work of Captain Alfred Thayer Mahan.* New Haven: Yale University Press: 1939.

RHODES, JAMES FORD. *The McKinley and Roosevelt Administrations, 1897-1909.* New York: The Macmillan Co., 1922.

RODMAN, HUGH. *Yarns of a Kentucky Admiral.* Indianapolis: Bobbs-Merrill Co., 1928.

ROOSEVELT, THEODORE. *Theodore Roosevelt, An Autobiography.* New York: Charles Scribner's Sons, 1920.

_____*The Rough Riders.* New York: Charles Scribner's Sons, 1899.

RUSSELL, PHILLIPS. *John Paul Jones, Man of Action.* New York: Brentano's, 1927.

SEIDLE, THOMAS C. *Thomas S. Seidle's Photographs of the Most Eminent Modern Statesmen and Politicians of the United States of America.* Reading: Thomas C. Seidle Co., 1894.

SMITH, THEODORE CLARK. *James Abram Garfield, Life and Letters.* New Haven: Yale University Press, 1925.

SOLAY, JAMES RUSSELL. *The Navy in the Civil War.* New York: Charles Scribner's Sons, 1883.

SPROUT, HAROLD and MARGARET. *Toward a New Order of Sea Power.* Princeton: Princeton University Press, 1940.

STEFFENS, LINCOLN. *The Autobiography of Lincoln Steffens.* New York: Harcourt, Brace & Co., 1931.

STICKNEY, JOSEPH L. *Life and Glorious Deeds of Admiral Dewey.* Chicago: C. B. Ayer Co., 1898.

SULLIVAN, MARK. *Our Times, 1900-1925.* New York: Charles Scribner's Sons, 1936.

SWAIN, JOSEPH WARD. *Beginning the Twentieth Century.* New York: W. W. Norton & Co., 1933.

THAYER, WILLIAM ROSCOE. *Theodore Roosevelt, An Intimate Biography.* Boston: Houghton Mifflin Co., 1919.

"The Dewey Candidacy," *The Nation,* April 12, 1900.

"The Progress of the World—Admiral Dewey's Candidacy," *American Monthly Review of Reviews,* May, 1900.

TREVELYAN, GEORGE MACAULAY. *History of England.* London: Longmans, Green & Co., 1933.

VAN METRE, THURMAN W. *Economic History of the United States.* New York: Henry Holt & Co., 1921.

Washington Post, period of Feb., 1931.

WELLES, GIDEON. *Diary of Gideon Welles.* Boston: Houghton Mifflin Co., 1925.

WEST, RICHARD S. *Gideon Welles.* Indianapolis: Bobbs-Merrill Co., 1943.

WILDMAN, EDWIN. *Aguinaldo.* Boston: Lothrop, Lee & Shepard Co., 1901.

WINDAS, CEDRIC W. *Traditions of the Navy.* Brooklyn: Our Navy, Inc., 1943.

WINKLER, JOHN K. *W. R. Hearst: An American Phenomenon.* New York: Simon & Schuster, 1928.

WISTER, OWEN. *Roosevelt: The Story of a Friendship.* New York: The Macmillan Co., 1930.

YOUNG, LOUIS STANLEY. *Life and Heroic Deeds of Admiral Dewey, and Battles in the Philippines.* Philadelphia: National Publishing Co., 1899.

INDEX

INDEX

330

336

Date Due